Also by Ronald Johnson:

Aficionado's Southwestern Cooking
Southwestern Cooking New and Old
Simple Fare
Company Fare

THE
AMERICAN
TABLE

More Than 400 Recipes That
Make Accessible for the First Time the Full
Richness of American Regional Cooking

by Ronald Johnson

Drawings by James McGarrell

A Fireside Book
Published by Simon & Schuster
New York   London   Toronto   Sidney   Tokyo   Singapore

to the meals
my mother served me

Fireside
Simon & Schuster Building
Rockefeller Center
1230 Avenue of the Americas
New York, New York 10020

First Fireside Edition 1991
Published by arrangement with the author.

FIRESIDE and colophon are registered trademarks
of Simon & Schuster Inc.

Manufactured in the United States of America

10 9 8 7 6 5 4 3 2 1 Pbk.

Library of Congress Cataloging in Publication Data

Johnson, Ronald, date.
     The American table :   more than 400 recipes that make accessible
for the first time the full richness of American regional cooking   /
by Ronald Johnson   ;   drawings by James McGarrell. — 1st Fireside ed.
         p.   cm.
     Reprint. Originally published: New York   :   Morrow, 1984.
     "A Fireside book."
     Includes Index.
     1. Cookery, American.   I. Title.
     [TX715.J714   1991]
     641.5973—dc20   91-11397
                                                                                                          CIP

ISBN 0-671-73238-2 Pbk.

ACKNOWLEDGMENTS

A lot of the recipes in this book are worn smooth as river pebbles, and I can no longer say for certain where I first clipped them, who cooked them for me, even what part of the country they come from. The list of friends who have traded recipes over decades is too long to record, but they know who they are and how much thanked—most of their names have been embedded in the text.

In addition I would like to thank Anne Mendelson for her advice on textual matters, Molly Finn for cooking through the book, Herb Leibowitz and Judith Jones for their help in getting it published, but most of all Maria Guarnaschelli for her tenacious editing, and James McGarrell for his sprightly drawings.

Contents

Introduction

*T*homas Jefferson was our first noted gourmet, to the point Patrick Henry complained the President "abjured his native victuals." In truth, Illinois pecans and Vermont maple syrup shared a shelf with Parmesan cheese, in his pantry, for he was intent on widening the common table with anything fine he could lay a hand on. He took pride in his macaroni maker, and a new gadget called a waffle iron. These had been brought back from Europe, along with a pocketful of rice he could have been executed for smuggling out of Italy. This packet started an industry which now exports back to Europe. He wrote back for new strains of vegetables for his garden at Monticello. Among the profusion grown there, he promoted both potatoes and tomatoes, then commonly believed poisonous. His back porch sported a bright spanking new machine to turn out ice cream, as did George Washington's, a few miles down the road.

"Native victuals" those days tended to be a sorry hodge-podge of salted pork, corn in all forms, beans, any stray game, with a daily molasses pudding to round it out. Not till a hundred years later, with the advent of the brothers Delmonico, did dining in the wide Jeffersonian style start to take on character and breed invention. The Delmonicos took a plot of ground outside New York City, where they grew endive, broccoli, and eggplant. They unveiled the avocado, and introduced salads made from native plants. There had always been pockets of fine food: some Yankee hostelries, many a Southern plantation, and in the quiet of the Shaker communities. With Delmonico's it became a fashion. Oscar of the Waldorf soon followed, and we were off and running.

Variety for everyman came about only with refrigerated shipping. By then, variety was no longer as individual as Jefferson had imagined, for large growers quickly standardized produce, and Prohibition had begun leveling vineyards (and as a by-product, excellent dining). The results were clear enough, though, even to a Kansas boyhood. My grandfather, who had settled in a covered wagon, was now able to order barrels of oysters still in the shell, packed in ice and sawdust, from "back East." Wheels of cheese came along the rails, along with canned goods of all kinds, and then, with swiftness—packaged mixes, puffed cereals, condensed milk, denatured breads.

As a consequence home canning from the garden fell off, and bread making became rare. There were few trustworthy cookbooks, magazines touted canned soups to substitute for sauces, and casseroles came to be born. Fruited gelatin salads rose in tribes. Abroad, Gertrude Stein and Alice Toklas were considering an American tour after decades away. They had been advised by a friend who had recently traveled there strange vegetable cocktails, and tinned fruit salads, might be pressed on one. "Surely" Alice wrote in her cookbook "you weren't required to eat them. You could have substituted other dishes. Not, said he, when you were a guest."

If Brillat-Savarin was correct in his remark that "The destiny of nations depends on how they nourish themselves," we were indeed in more trouble than Gertrude and Alice could have expected. Consider this dish, that very year the rage of Los Angeles:

CANDLE SALAD

4	slices canned pineapple	1	Brazil nut
2	bananas	¼	cup mayonnaise dressing
4	pieces of citron or green pepper		

*P*eel bananas. Cut them in two crosswise. Place a slice of pineapple on a salad plate; insert one half banana in center of each pineapple. Place a thin strip of Brazil nut in the top of the banana to represent a wick. The oil in the nut will burn if the nut is lighted. Let mayonnaise drip down the side of each candle. Make a handle to the candlestick of citron or of pepper. A piece of cherry may be used for a flame instead of the lighted nut.

As it turned out, they enjoyed their trip immensely. In hotels, Gertrude stuck to melon and oysters, while Alice investigated any unknown item, with the nose of a true cook. But home cooking really turned them round. They tasted turtle soup, home brewed orange wine they uncorked to find "ambrosia," abalone, sand dabs, soft shelled crab, passion fruit, and a confection called Tarte Chambord which had since been lost to France. They ate wild rice for the first time, and sampled Oysters Rockefeller, both of which they served back in Paris.

They were lucky to be so fêted, and to travel when they did, for most of those Hotels have not survived, at least any to order oysters and melon in. Not only Hotels, the legendary truck stop, Pullman's ideas of fine railroad dining, the corner bakery, soda fountain—all vanished. Even when a good spot to eat does exist, there is no trusty way to find it, no one to point out one of the two cafés which still serve "mountain oysters in cream gravy" in Lexington, Kentucky, the best Basque table set in Elko, Nevada, the most gracious Georgia fish camp, the little *brasserie*-deli a couple of nice boys down the way run, an annual "ramp" festival over the next hill, a Greek Church Supper around the block, or ultimate Burrito Palace right next door. They are all hidden as home cooking to any passing traveler.

The only answer to this I learned from fellow poet Jonathan Williams, whose migrations the birds might envy. His advice was to make far friends, and dine there (he also wrote about twenty letters a day). This encouraged me early on to learn the art of turning conversations to food and recipes—an art of some stealth, tact, and persistence, as this letter from Emily Dickinson to a neighbor shows:

> Sometime when our dear Mrs Hills has an unoccupied moment tho aware that her innumerable company of Angels leave her very few of what are called so, will she, please, tell Vinnie's sister how to make a little loaf of Cake like one she sent in April which is still a remembrance of nectar.
> It was what Austin calls Loaf Cake and the Almanac calls raised Cake— Then Vinnie spied a Loaf of Bread at our lost neighbors, which enthralled her—steamed Bran Brown Bread she thought it, from the same hand—and lovelier the same Heart—could I know the secret of that Though I desire crumbs for but a few Robins.

Timing is all, here, and one learns never to be discouraged by the overworked, as Alice discovered, seeking out a surprised and "inspired negress cook and the enormous kitchen over which she presided" who had no time for chitchat.

I've gathered recipes for twenty years in this manner, here and about, looked through every tiny spiral-bound cookbook put out by local church ladies that came my way, and it's surprising how many fine recipes turn up from our amateur cooks. Sometimes a trick is turned, or an ingredient used, which would never occur to the tradition-bound chef who already knows what's right and what's not. This can be as simple as substituting a handy ingredient, as cooks have done with French recipes for years in New Orleans. Of course I stumble now and then on fine dishes from restaurants, but the large part of those collected here, to stand on my table, are simple "home cooking" at its everyday best.

Looking over this spread, as it is piled, is to make out distinct mountains through the jumble. The highest of these, perhaps, a toppling heap of recipes from the South. I've lived in the four corners, and was brought up in the middle of this country, but my admiration is unbounded and continual for the pluck and inventiveness of cooks there. You can examine any local cookbook to find how far tradition, in the large old sense, is alive in many a kitchen still today. New England folk seem to share the British reservation about food talk of any kind, but in the South it is mannerly to comment the victuals, low and high, and sing the praises of the cook. Recipes are shared across the fence, church suppers look like groaning boards of lost plantations. If they had only New Orleans to show, they would have cause for pride.

And, leafing through, how often the sturdy hills of the Shakers crop up, fit for use after 200 years. But then they made almost every article they needed, and thought that form follows function from barn to chair, or a dish of "Alabaster" or "Yellow Velvet" for dinner. Sheer necessities of catering for a whole community, and duly recording it for daily revolving help, gave them an edge the single housewife seldom need sharpen. They left a trove of handsome recipes.

The Southwest seems to also carve a mesa, culinarily speaking, out from the rest. It was literally my first exotic food. My aunt, who had gone to live in New Mexico, brought tortillas and chiles back, on a visit, and it was like a trip to India for us all. Everybody crowded into the kitchen, and my mother there and then decided to import tortillas, and learn enough tricks to supply us with this strange delight forever. Though it rises alone, out of what the most of us eat, to me it's always worth climbing, at least once a month—I lust for it as some do for a Chinese dinner, dill pickles, popcorn, or ice cream late at night.

But from Vichyssoise through Ambrosia, I've gone on the notion that if Provence has more recipes than Oklahoma, it has had a long head start, and Oklahoma might have a few bright dishes yet for Provence. From what I've unearthed, I suspect our new chefs have a culinary El Dorado all around them, just waiting to be mined, from sea to shining sea.

San Francisco, 1983

SOUPS

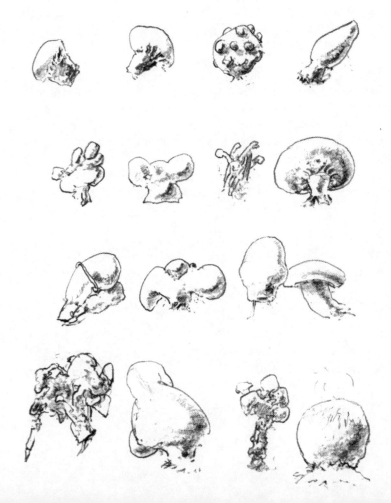

After a velvety oyster soup came shad and cucumbers, then a young broiled turkey with corn fritters, followed by a canvas-back with currant jelly and a celery mayonnaise.

—Edith Wharton, The Age of Innocence

Soups
from Cold to Hot

*E*xtremes of climate—scorching summers to snowdrifts piling the eaves—have left their mark on New World foods. Doughty settlers could skirt winters by the fireside, but it took more than a breezy verandah to keep the cream and butter cool and fresh when the temperature hovered in the hundreds. Most farms had an ice house where winter ice could be stored, laid down in sawdust, though it took advances in cutting and hauling to make the ice wagon a common sight in towns. In 1815, Brillat-Savarin noted a fellow exile from the French Revolution, a certain Captain Collet, who survived by introducing, to New York City, ices and sherbets: "It was especially difficult for them to understand how anything could stay so cold in the summer heat of ninety degrees." Louis Diat and others followed the admirable captain, to put the verandah breeze into the soup, to chill and lift the palate August nights.

LOUIS DIAT'S VICHYSSOISE

1½	cups chopped white part of leek	4	cups hot water
½	cup chopped onion	2	teaspoons salt
1	tablespoon butter	3	cups hot milk
3	cups peeled diced potatoes	2	cups heavy cream
			Minced chives

*I*n a kettle set over medium heat, sauté the leek and onion in the butter until they are soft. Add potatoes, water, and salt, then simmer, uncovered, over low heat 30 to 40 minutes, or until the potatoes are soft.

Either sieve the soup or purée it in a blender (a food processor will not smooth it enough, I find). Return purée to the kettle; add the milk and 1 cup of the cream. Bring to a boil. Set to cool in the refrigerator.

When cool, either sieve the soup again, or whirl in the blender. Finally, stir in the other cup of cream and taste for seasoning. Chill for several hours, and serve in soup cups sprinkled with chives.

Serves 8 to 10.

Louis Diat's creation for the old Ritz-Carlton is probably the most famed American soup, and justly so. Its origin is one of France's simplest staples, chilled, thoroughly puréed, enriched with extra cream, and with a sprinkle of chives for bounce.

"VICHYSSOISE" OF BEET GREENS

4	young beets with tops	1	cup milk
2	tablespoons butter	½	cup heavy cream
1	cup chopped onion	2	tablespoons lemon juice
2	cups peeled and diced potatoes		Salt
3	cups chicken stock		Lemon slices

*C*ut off the beet greens and wash thoroughly. Melt the butter in a kettle set over medium heat, and sauté the onion in it until limp. Add the potatoes and chicken stock and cook, uncovered, over medium heat 10 minutes.

Strip the greens from the beet stems and chop coarsely—there should be

1¾ to 2 cups of greens packed down. Add them to the soup, and cook 20 minutes more.

Place in a blender and—going from a slow speed to a fast one—purée thoroughly. Return to the pot, then add the milk, cream, lemon juice, and salt to taste (remember a cold soup will have less flavor than a hot one). Chill thoroughly.

The beets themselves can be cooked in salted water at any time during this process. They will take about 20 minutes, depending on size and age. When they are tender, drain them and run cold water over. Slip off their skins and chop into ¼-inch dice. To serve, place the chilled soup in chilled cups and garnish with slices of lemon and diced beets.

Serves 4 to 6.

This is adapted from a little 1962 book titled The Art of Creole Cookery, *by William I. Kaufman and Sister Mary Ursula Cooper, O.P., which promises on its cover "a delicious composite of familiar and not-so-familiar Creole recipes." A soup definitely and delightfully not-so-familiar, indeed it is a small triumph of regional invention. Beet greens are full flavored, suavest of all the leafy tops—but are unfortunately seldom used by anyone. Here they compose a subtle cold soup the color of celadon, which, sprinkled with dice of red beet root, and floating a yellow slice of lemon, makes a dish as easy on the eye as on the tongue. Serve it with a white wine, and The Duchess of Windsor's Cornpones (page 316).*

CHILLED PUMPKIN CREAM

1 can (1 pound) pumpkin (or 1½ cups fresh purée)	1 bay leaf Salt and freshly ground
½ cup chopped onion	pepper
2½ cups chicken stock	1 cup heavy cream
⅛ teaspoon ground mace	1 lime (or lemon), sliced
Pinch of curry powder	

Combine the pumpkin, onion, stock, spices, bay leaf, and salt and pepper to taste in a kettle. Bring to a rolling boil, then lower the heat and simmer 30 minutes with the pot uncovered.

Remove the bay leaf, place in a blender or food processor, and purée till almost—not quite—smooth. Chill in the refrigerator an hour or more.

When quite cold, stir in the cream and taste for seasoning. Chill several more hours, or overnight. (The soup acquires further taste with some sitting.) To serve, place in chilled soup plates, and garnish with thin slices of lime. Serves 6.

This is about the best use for a can of anything I've ever come across, but of course pumpkin seems to can with little loss of flavor. A surprising soup cold, there is no reason to limit this to summer—in fact it strikes rather a fine note to a Thanksgiving or Christmas dinner. At any time, serve it with white wine rather than red, and a basket of hot yeast rolls, Charleston Benne Wafers (page 327), or crisp Beaten Biscuits (page 327).

COLD CUCUMBER AND POTATO SOUP

1 cup chopped onion	2 cups chicken stock
¼ cup olive oil	Salt
4 cucumbers, peeled	1 cup buttermilk
1 pound potatoes (about 3 medium), peeled and sliced	Tabasco
	2 tablespoons minced chives

Sauté the onion in olive oil, in a large kettle set over medium heat, until it is limp. Slice the cucumbers in quarters lengthwise and cut the seeds out with a small sharp knife. Chop the cucumbers in small dice and reserve ½ cup.

Add all but the reserved cucumbers to the onion, stir, and cook a few more minutes. Add the potatoes and stock and bring to a boil, then turn down the heat and simmer 30 minutes with the pot uncovered.

Salt the reserved cucumbers and let stand while the soup cooks, then wash them with cold water and drain.

When the soup is cooked, purée in a blender, going from slow to fast speed, and pour into a bowl. Add salt to taste and cool in the refrigerator. When it has cooled, stir in reserved cucumber, the buttermilk, a few drops Tabasco, and taste again for salt.

Lastly, stir in the chives and chill, covered, in the refrigerator 3 hours or more. Serves 4 to 6.

How fine this Iowa farm recipe is on a hot day. The buttermilk is its secret— tart and creamy, but still light. Though to be summoned from any larder (except for the chives—paprika will do) you will find it sits proud on any table set for company. Complement it with crusty bread and light dry wine.

AVOCADO CREAM

1 large ripe avocado	Pinch of curry powder
1 cup heavy cream	Salt
2 cups chicken stock	Tabasco
Juice of 1 lime	Minced chives
1 tablespoon light rum	

Whirl avocado, cream, stock, lime juice, and rum in a blender until smooth—going from a slow speed to a high one. Place in a bowl and add curry powder, salt to taste, and Tabasco (please, only a drop or two).

Cover and refrigerate several hours. To serve, put in cold cups or soup plates and sprinkle with chives.

Serves 4.

What could be simpler? It is also a kind of test dish for any would-be chef's palate—the final product suavely depending exactly on the balance of rum and curry, and both only faintly suggested, whispered rather than hollered. In Texas, it would be served with home-fried tortilla chips, and chilled light beer or white wine.

EPHRAIM DONER'S
POOR MAN'S CHILLED SALMON BISQUE

	Head, tail, and trimmings from 1 medium salmon	2	tablespoons rice
2	cups water	2	cups milk, scalded
½	cup chopped onion	1	tablespoon tomato paste
1	bay leaf	1	teaspoon anchovy paste
1	clove garlic, flattened and peeled	1	cup heavy cream
3	sprigs parsley		Salt and freshly ground pepper
	Pinch of ground cloves	1	teaspoon lemon juice
	Pinch of ground mace	2	tablespoons dry sherry
			Paprika

*P*lace salmon trimmings in a kettle with water, onion, bay leaf, garlic, parsley, spices, and rice. Bring to a boil, then lower the heat and simmer, covered, 20 minutes.

Lift out salmon and bay leaf, and boil the liquid, uncovered, till it is reduced by half and the rice is very soft—about 15 minutes. Meanwhile, pick all the pieces of meat off the salmon (don't forget the cheeks—they aren't as lovely a pink, but they are some of the best-tasting flesh on the fish).

Purée rice mixture, salmon, and scalded milk in a blender or food processor. Put in a large saucepan set over a low flame. Whisk in the tomato and anchovy pastes, then the cream. Heat gently, but don't let boil.

Taste for seasoning, then chill, covered, in the refrigerator for several hours. To serve, add the lemon juice and sherry, and again taste for seasoning. Place in chilled soup plates and dust paprika on top.

Serves 4.

Those lucky enough to find trimmings in their market will admire this silky soup. For very little, a cook may expect a singular lunch (with forethought always to good bread, green salad, chilled wine). Artist, and friend of artists, Ephraim Doner was the first person to teach me that even economy could be an art. May he still be waving his hands in joy over a box of castoff artichokes, promising a feast.

COLD CRAB GUMBO MARYLAND

1	tablespoon butter	¾	cup drained canned tomatoes
¼	cup chopped onion	¼	cup rice
¼	cup chopped celery	¾	cup crabmeat
2	tablespoons chopped green pepper		Salt and freshly ground pepper
¾	cup thinly sliced okra		Tabasco
4	cups chicken stock		Lemon juice

Melt butter in a soup pot over medium heat. Sauté onion, celery, and green pepper until they are soft. Add okra, stock, tomatoes, and rice. Bring to a boil, then lower the heat and simmer 1½ hours.

Remove from the heat and purée in batches in a food processor or blender. Put in a bowl, cover, and chill thoroughly. To serve, stir in the crab and season to taste with salt, pepper, Tabasco, and lemon juice. Serves 6 to 8.

The only first-course gumbo, brought to an exquisite pitch, and unexpectedly cold. Treat it well with the finest Pinot Chardonnay your wine merchant points out, and either Zephyrs (page 317), The Duchess of Windsor's Cornpones (page 316), or homemade yeasty rolls.

GOLDEN GATE SOUP (HOT OR COLD)

6	carrots, scraped and sliced	1	bay leaf
1	medium onion, chopped		Pinch of ground mace
1	clove garlic, flattened and peeled	1	cup heavy cream (or half cream, half milk)
3	cups chicken stock	1	carrot, scraped and cut in very fine matchstick lengths
2	tablespoons rice		Curry powder (optional)
	Salt and freshly ground pepper		

Add all but the cream, matchstick carrots, and optional curry to a large kettle and cook over medium heat 30 minutes. Remove the bay leaf and purée the soup till quite smooth in a blender.

Return to the kettle, add the cream, and taste for seasoning. Add the matchstick carrots, and simmer 5 to 10 minutes more, or until the carrots are just tender.

Serve hot or cold. If cold, add a touch of curry during the cooking, and garnish the soup with a dollop of chutney.

Serves 4 to 6.

In catering I learned two things—first, that the rich like their elegance also inexpensive, and second, this soup, to prove the point. Draper Morrow, who taught me the business, trotted this out to social "dos" for years with nothing but praise, and little out of his pocket. Not only that, but he transformed its basic use of rice for thickening, and balance of mace and bay leaf, to any vegetable at hand—onions, turnips, cauliflower (with a little sherry), cucumbers, green beans, or peas. It is a gem, again and again.

SUMMER SQUASH BISQUE (HOT OR COLD)

1 cup chopped onion	Pinch of sugar
2 tablespoons butter	Salt
2 pounds summer squash	Freshly grated nutmeg
(yellow, zucchini, or	2 cups heavy cream
pattypan)	Minced parsley
2½ cups chicken stock	

*I*n a large kettle set over medium heat, sauté the onion in the butter until it is limp. Trim and slice the squash. Add, with the stock, and cook over medium heat 15 to 20 minutes, or until the squash is tender.

Place in a blender and purée, going from slow speed to fast. Return to the kettle. Season with sugar, salt, and nutmeg to taste. Stir in the cream and taste again for seasoning.

To serve hot, heat the soup without bringing to a boil. To serve cold, chill, covered, for 3 hours or more in the refrigerator. Place in soup plates and sprinkle with minced parsley.

Serves 4.

When you are able to obtain small farm-fresh squash this is a noble but inexpensive dish. Even with somewhat tired produce it holds up—with homemade bread of some kind and a friendly white wine. Chilled, it is worthy of the shiniest table.

GILDED LILY SOUP (HOT OR COLD)

2	cups chopped onion	4	cups chicken stock
2	bunches green onions,		Tabasco
	chopped with part of tops		Salt
½	cup minced shallots	2	tablespoons flour
2	large cloves garlic, minced	1	cup heavy cream
5	tablespoons butter		Minced chives

*I*n a soup pot, sauté onions, shallots, and garlic in 3 tablespoons butter over medium heat. When they are limp, pour the chicken stock over and add a few drops of Tabasco, and salt to taste. Cover and cook gently 30 minutes.

Strain the stock into a bowl and place the onion mixture in a blender. Add some of the stock and purée to a smooth pale green.

Melt the remaining 2 tablespoons butter in a large saucepan, stir in the flour, and cook, while stirring, 4 to 5 minutes. Add the hot stock all at once, and cook, stirring, until it thickens. Add the onion purée and cook gently 15 more minutes.

To serve hot, taste for seasoning and ladle into soup plates with a sprinkle of chives. To serve cold, refrigerate in a covered bowl for 3 or more hours before garnishing.

Serves 4.

This is a "what if?" kind of soup, put together one evening I'd a gift of shallots, and chives blooming at the windowsill. What if there were a dish built around some harmony of all the culinary lilies: regular yellow onions, green onions, shallots, garlic, snipped chives?

WINTER TARRAGON TOMATO SOUP

1½	cups chopped onion	½	cup dry white wine (or
½	cup butter		vermouth)
1	quart canned tomatoes (or a	1	tablespoon sugar
	large can of Italian plum	1	teaspoon dried tarragon
	tomatoes)		Salt
			Sour Cream

*I*n a large saucepan or kettle set over medium heat, sauté the onion in butter till it starts to turn gold. This will take about 15 minutes, and the onions should be stirred so they take color evenly. Add the tomatoes, juice and all, and mash down with a potato masher.

Add wine, sugar, and tarragon and stir. Cover, turn the heat down, and simmer 45 minutes. Turn the heat off and let sit until you prepare the rest of the dinner.

When you are ready to get the meal started, purée the soup in a blender and push it through a sieve into a saucepan. Heat it, tasting for salt, and keep warm without boiling till serving time. Serve ladled into warm soup plates, and add a dollop of cold sour cream to each.

Serves 4.

Frankly, most tomato soups are boring, but not this one, which has been elaborated from one my mother used to prepare from home-canned tomatoes. Even with store-canned tomatoes it can be served to gourmets, and with garden fresh, if you raise your own, it's a downright wonder. Try it with The Duchess of Windsor's Cornpones (page 316), and a full-bodied white wine, for the best of all possible worlds.

GREEN CORN SOUP

4 to 5	ears corn		Pinch of sugar (optional)
3	cups milk	½	cup heavy cream
	Salt	2	tablespoons butter
	Tabasco		Minced parsley or chives
4	sprigs parsley		

*C*ut the corn kernels off the cob with the sharp blade of a knife, holding the ears over a bowl. Then use the backside of the knife to scrape the cobs and release all their "milk." Place the corn (you should have 2 cups) in a large saucepan with milk, salt to taste, and a drop or two of Tabasco.

Bring to a boil and add the parsley (and some sugar if the corn is not fresh from a field). Lower the heat and simmer gently 30 minutes. Remove the parsley sprigs and purée the soup in a blender. Rub through a sieve to make sure any hard parts of the kernels are removed.

Return the soup to the pan and cook gently till the consistency is slightly thick. Add the cream and butter and let heat through without boiling. To serve, ladle into soup plates or bowls, and sprinkle with parsley or chives. Serves 4.

"Green corn" in early recipes implies young corn rushed from the field, barely ripe. Nowadays we most must make do with market corn—so be on the lookout for a lively crop as fresh as possible. This is a perfect summer soup, sparing of flavors, to let the delicate kernels themselves permeate and thicken. Try Summer Cloud or Happy Valley Biscuits (page 322) with it.

SHAKER HERB SOUP

2	tablespoons butter	4	cups chicken stock
1	cup minced inner celery stalks with leaves		Salt and freshly ground pepper
2	tablespoons minced chives		Pinch of sugar
2	tablespoons minced fresh chervil		A few drops of lemon juice
2	tablespoons minced fresh sorrel	4	slices trimmed white bread, toasted
½	teaspoon minced fresh tarragon		Freshly grated nutmeg
		¾	cup grated aged cheddar

Melt the butter in a kettle, and when it has stopped sizzling add the celery and chives. Cook over a low flame 5 minutes, or until the celery is soft. Add herbs, stock, salt and pepper to taste, and a pinch of sugar.

Cover the pan and let simmer 20 minutes. Taste for seasoning and add a few drops of lemon juice—it should be faintly tart. To serve, place a slice of toast in the bottom of each soup plate, ladle the soup over, grate a wisp of nutmeg over, then sprinkle the cheese on top. Serves 4.

The Shakers were purveyors of seeds and herbs, to the great benefit of their kitchens as well as their pocketbooks. You will probably need a garden too (or at least a windowbox of fresh herbs) for dried chervil has little flavor to it. A respectful substitute for sorrel would be ¼ cup minced watercress leaves— the full effect is worth a little subterfuge.

NEW ORLEANS SUMMER FAST DAY SOUP

1	head Boston or butter lettuce	3 cups water
1	onion	Pinch of sugar
½	cucumber, peeled and seeded	Salt and freshly ground
½	cup parsley leaves	pepper
2	tablespoons butter	Mint sprigs
2	cups shelled fresh green peas	

Chop lettuce, onion, cucumber, and parsley very fine (this is a perfect job for a food processor). Put in a saucepan with the butter, and stew gently with the pan covered for 15 minutes.

Cook the peas in another saucepan, with a handful of their pods for flavor, in the 3 cups water, along with some sugar and a little salt and pepper. When soft, remove the pods, and purée the peas with their cooking liquid in a food processor or blender.

Pour into the stewed vegetables, taste for seasoning, and simmer gently 15 to 20 minutes more, or until the flavors are melded. To serve, ladle into bowls or soup plates and garnish each serving with mint.

Serves 4 to 6.

Such a lively tasting soup could, I suppose, be well adapted to use frozen peas, though it is perfect for the somewhat overlarge peas shipped to market in spring and summer. The original recipe, culled from The Picayune Creole Cookbook (a wonderful compendium of New Orleans cuisine, though often fuzzy as to process and desired effect), calls for a total of 2½ hours cooking; I suspect this would only tend to dissipate the flavor of its delicate vegetables. It should be partnered with a chilled fine dry white wine, and a French loaf or homemade rolls.

PECAN SOUP

2	tablespoons butter	Tabasco
2	tablespoons flour	1 teaspoon Worcestershire
1	cup chicken stock, heated	sauce
3	cups milk, scalded	2 egg yolks
1	cup pecans	1 cup heavy cream
	Salt	Sour cream

*M*elt the butter in a large saucepan, stir in the flour, and cook over medium heat for several minutes as you stir. Add the hot stock and milk all at once, and stir the mixture until it thickens and is smooth. Place half this mixture in a blender or food processor, add the pecans, and go at a clip until the pecans are finely granular (not a purée). Return to the pan, stir, and simmer 30 minutes, uncovered. Add salt, a drop or two of Tabasco, and the Worcestershire—the soup should not be hot from the Tabasco, only slightly perked up as to flavor. Simmer 10 more minutes. Beat the egg yolks with the cream, and whisk them into the soup off the fire. This can sit, covered, for an hour or so to gather flavor, if you have time. To serve, heat without letting the soup come to a boil. Ladle into soup plates and garnish each with a dollop of sour cream. Serves 4 to 6.

You'll want to attempt this exquisite, delicately flavored Southern soup when you are able to find new-crop pecans in bulk. The small packets of nuts available year round in the market are not only sometimes stale, but too expensive to bother with here. It's good to nose around every year and buy pound bags of shelled new-crop nuts, and keep them frozen. Rather than with wine, I like to serve this as I first had it from a candlelit Virginia table—with a small glass of the fine dry sherry known as Tio Pepe.

CHESTNUT SOUP

3 tablespoons butter	8 cups chicken stock
1 small onion, chopped	2 cups cooked chestnuts (see
1 carrot, scraped and sliced	Chestnut Purée, page 229)
1 stalk celery with its leaves,	¼ cup dry Madeira
chopped	¼ cup heavy cream
3 sprigs parsley	Salt and freshly ground
2 whole cloves	pepper
1 bay leaf	

*M*elt the butter in a kettle set over medium heat. Add onion, carrot, and celery. Cover and steam over low heat 15 to 20 minutes.

Tie the parsley, cloves, and bay leaf in a cheesecloth bag and drop them in, along with the stock. Simmer another 30 minutes. Remove the cheesecloth bag and add the chestnuts and Madeira. Simmer only 3 minutes, then purée in a blender or food processor.

Return the purée to the kettle and add the cream and salt and pepper to taste. Heat to desired hotness, but do not let it ever boil. Serve in warm soup plates. Serves 6.

Don't limit this gracious soup to holidays, though it does introduce a goose or turkey admirably. It is a dish in the fine old New England tradition, and it dates from before the chestnut blight, when native trees grew everywhere in abundance. Nowadays we get shipments from Italy—but always buy more than you need, for often many of them are moldy or withered inside. Offer it with a small glass of Madeira, and Parker House Rolls (page 331).

DELAWARE CLAM SOUP

½	cup shucked clams with their juice		Pinch of dried thyme
			Salt and freshly ground
¾	cup minced green onions with tops		pepper
			Cayenne
3	tablespoons butter	1	egg
2	tablespoons flour	2	tablespoons dry Madeira
2	cups milk, scalded		Minced parsley
1	cup heavy cream		

Drain and reserve the clam juice, and chop the clams coarsely. Sauté the onions in the butter in a kettle set over medium heat. When they are soft, add the flour and cook, stirring, several minutes.

Add the hot milk and cream all at once. Let boil up, then lower the heat. Add clam juice, thyme, salt and pepper to taste, and a bit of cayenne. Simmer 10 to 15 minutes.

Beat the egg together with the Madeira. Add some of the hot soup, bit by bit, while whisking, then beat it into the soup pot. Add the chopped clams and let the mixture heat through without boiling. (Actually, it is best to turn off the heat at this time and let the soup rest for some time—it brings out flavor.)

To serve, warm without boiling, and ladle into warm soup plates with a pinch of parsley. Serves 4 to 6.

*There are versions upon versions of clam soup, but this from Delaware is best
of all, I think. I've even been tempted to try it with canned clams (whole
clams, not the chopped, which are too full of tough bits). It is not as fine,
but it holds up tolerably for those with no access to fresh sweet clams. Serve
it with a white wine or the Madeira you have used in cooking, and perhaps
Charleston Benne Wafers (page 327).*

CHARLESTON SHE-CRAB SOUP

1	tablespoon butter		Pinch of ground mace
1	teaspoon flour		Salt and freshly ground
3	cups milk, scalded		pepper
1½	cups heavy cream	½	teaspoon Worcestershire
2	cups crabmeat, with their		sauce
	eggs	¼	cup dry sherry
¼	teaspoon onion juice		Paprika

*M*elt butter in the top of a double boiler over simmering water. Stir in the
flour and cook 3 to 4 minutes, then add the milk slowly, whisking constantly. When smooth and thickened, add 1 cup of the cream, the crab, and
all the seasonings except the sherry.

Turn the fire very low, cover the pot, and let it heat 20 minutes. Meanwhile, whip the remaining ½ cup cream until stiff. To serve, place a spoon
of sherry in each soup plate and add the soup. Top with whipped cream and
a dust of paprika.

Serves 4 to 6.

*Legend is right. I have prepared this many times with fresh-caught crab, but
it is not as good as eating it on a Carolina table made only from "she crabs."
A subterfuge, I'm told, is to crumble a bit of hard-boiled egg yolk in the
bottom of each soup plate. Whatever crab you can muster, however, this soup
should be spooned as if you were serving caviar. It is adapted here from a
Junior League sampler called Charleston Receipts (for further information on
this splendid cookbook, see Maum Nancy's Scalloped Oysters on page 62). To
be authentic, accompany it with Charleston Benne Wafers (page 327), and
either a fine white wine or a respectable dry sherry.*

Meals in a Bowl

*W*hat a rich heritage we have in hearty soups to warm the bones. Our stews, chowders, gumbos, and native *bouillabaisses* range from simple thrifty feasts, through lobster stew (our ancestors gave humble names to often elegant dishes) into the complex dark gumbos and court-bouillons of the Gulf States. Turtle soup, prepared with lacings of cream and Madeira, and a crumble of eggs, was considered one of the grandest dishes of all, but turtles were so easily caught they almost became extinct, and it is now rare to see this delicacy on any menu. A soup or stew could be made in one pot hung over the fire, and as such they were the first meals of the pilgrims, a staple of chuckwagon cooks, the constant companion of homesteaders.

SENATE BEAN SOUP

1 cup dried lima or navy beans	1 bay leaf
1½ cups chopped onion	¼ cup sliced carrot
1 clove garlic, minced	2 slices lemon
1 tablespoon butter	1 small ham hock
2 sprigs parsley	Salt and freshly ground pepper
¼ teaspoon dried thyme	Minced parsley

Wash the beans and cover them by several inches of water in a large kettle. Let sit overnight, then drain them and add 1 quart water. Place the kettle on a high fire, and while it comes to a boil sauté the onion and garlic in butter in a skillet, then add them to the kettle.

Tie parsley sprigs, thyme, bay leaf, carrot, and lemon in a cheesecloth bag. Add them with the ham hock to the bubbling beans. Lower the heat and cook 3 hours, or until the liquid is reduced and the beans are starting to fall apart.

Discard the cheesecloth bag, then remove the ham and let it cool. Scoop out 1 cup of the beans and purée them through a sieve, blender, or food processor, then return the purée back to the kettle.

Strip the meat from the hock and cut into small dice. Add to the kettle, with salt and pepper to taste, then reheat the soup slowly. Serve garnished with minced parsley.

Serves 4.

Anyone who dines in the restaurant in the United States Senate is well advised to try this specialty—really a meal in itself. There is some confusion as to exactly how this soup is made. One version even has mashed potatoes rather than puréed beans, but this seems closest in my memory to the soup as it is actually served. During the depression in Kansas, my mother used to make a similar dish she called "stewed butterbeans," which she would ladle over a slice of whole-wheat bread as a succulent budget stretcher. I still like it that way, so I usually double this recipe, and freeze batches of it to have as a simple dinner with a glass of beer and a salad.

KENTUCKY BLACK BEAN SOUP

½	pound dried black beans	¼	teaspoon sugar
1	onion, chopped	1	ham bone, 1 small ham
2	carrots, scraped and grated		hock, or ¼ cup diced salt
2	stalks celery, chopped		pork
2	cloves garlic, minced	3	cups chicken stock
2	tablespoons olive oil	¼	cup brandy
¾	cup peeled and chopped	⅛	teaspoon dried thyme
	(fresh or canned) tomatoes	2	strips orange peel
	Salt and freshly ground		
	pepper		

Soak the beans overnight in a large kettle of water. The next day drain them and rinse in cold water. Cook onion, carrots, celery, and garlic in olive oil in the bottom of a kettle until they are limp.

Add the beans, along with all the other ingredients. Bring to a boil, then reduce the heat and simmer, uncovered, 4 hours, or until the beans are tender. If necessary, cook down liquid the last half hour of cooking, to bring the beans to a creamy consistency.

Before serving, remove the hambone or hock and the orange peel. Chop any meat and return to the pot.

Serves 4.

One of our finest soups, often repeated in books on American cookery (none quite so fine, however, as this Kentucky version with a hint of orange peel). Black beans are not easily found these days, but they are usually available in Hispanic markets. The soup may be served as is, or puréed with slices of orange for garnish. For a hearty meal, serve fat squares of cornbread alongside, and a tossed salad.

ANCESTRAL TURKEY RICE SOUP

1	turkey carcass, broken up	¼	teaspoon dried thyme
6	cups water	4	sprigs parsley
3	stalks celery with leaves, sliced	4	peppercorns
			Salt
1	large onion, sliced	1	cup (more or less) turkey
2	carrots, scraped and sliced		meat
1	bay leaf	¼	cup uncooked rice

*P*lace the turkey bones in a kettle with the water, vegetables, herbs, pepper, and salt. Bring to a boil, then lower the heat and simmer, partially covered, for about 1½ hours. Strain, and if it is very greasy, chill the stock and remove the fat on top when it has hardened.

To complete the cooking, add the turkey meat and rice to the stock and simmer 20 to 30 minutes. Taste for seasoning and serve.

Serves 4 to 6.

Except for turkey sandwiches, this final rest of the holiday carcass has always been my favorite part of an overused and overbred bird. It was cooked by my mother and her mother before, and it is I'm sure one of the staples around the country in one form or another. It is conceived essentially as a supper, with perhaps the last of the cranberry relish and buttery toasted day-old rolls.

OXTAIL SOUP

3	pounds oxtails, cut in sections	6	peppercorns
		2	whole cloves
	Flour	2	bay leaves
2	tablespoons vegetable oil	⅛	teaspoon dried thyme
1	large onion, chopped		Salt
2	carrots, scraped and sliced	2	tablespoons tomato paste
2	stalks celery, sliced	1	cup diced carrot
¼	cup parsley stems	1	cup diced turnip
4	cups beef stock (or as needed)	2	tablespoons dry sherry

Shake the oxtail sections in flour. Brown them in oil either in a Dutch oven or, preferably, a pressure cooker, if you have one. They should get quite brown on all sides, so cook them at a high heat for 15 to 20 minutes, turning now and again to make sure they brown evenly.

Turn the heat down to medium, then add the onion and brown it as well, tossing with the tails. Add sliced carrots, celery, parsley stems, and stock to cover. Add spices, herbs, and salt to taste, then stir in the tomato paste.

Cover, turn the heat down low, and cook up to 6 hours, or until the meat falls off the bones. (I cook this 3 to 4 hours in a pressure cooker, for they can't really cook too much.)

When done, strain the broth (reserving the oxtails) and put it in the refrigerator to let the fat congeal on top. Remove the fat, put the soup in a kettle, and bring to a boil. Add the diced carrots and turnips and cook swiftly 15 minutes, or until the vegetables are done, and the soup has reduced slightly.

Carefully shred the meat from the oxtails, discarding the fat. Add to the soup, along with the sherry. Heat and serve in warm soup plates or bowls. Serves 4 to 6.

Those curious people finicky about oxtails will find this old time New England rib-sticking soup the surest way to conversion. Strange that one of the sweetest, most savory parts of the whole beef should be its tail—but there it is. Though it used to be a grand first-course soup, I like its rich beefy essence as the center of a meal. You might begin with a first course vegetable or salad— an artichoke, say, or Celery Victor (page 278), then serve the soup with a red wine and homemade bread, and end with some substantial dessert.

BLACKEYED PEA SOUP

2	cups dried blackeyed peas		Freshly ground pepper
4	cups water	1	cup chopped canned or fresh
2	small ham hocks (or 1		tomatoes
	large)	6	green onions with part of the
2	stalks celery with leaves,		tops, minced
	chopped	¼	cup minced parsley
1½	cups chopped onion	1	tablespoon olive oil
1	clove garlic, minced	1	teaspoon wine vinegar
1	bay leaf		Salt and freshly ground
	Pinch of ground cloves		pepper

Wash and pick over the peas, then place them in a large kettle with 4 cups water. Bring to a boil, turn the heat off, cover, and let sit while the ham hocks cook.

Place the hocks in another kettle, cover them with water, and simmer 1½ hours, or until the meat is falling off the bones. Take the hocks out, let cool, then strip the meat from them and chop it coarsely.

Add the ham stock to the peas, along with the meat, celery, onion, garlic, bay leaf, cloves, and pepper to taste. Simmer, partially covered, for 1½ hours, or until the peas are soft. Add more hot water if it boils too low.

While the soup cooks, combine tomatoes, green onions, parsley, oil, vinegar, and salt and pepper to taste. Let this sit at room temperature.

During the final cooking of the peas, add salt to taste. Let the soup sit till you are ready to serve it, then heat it up, and ladle into a bowl or soup plates. Pass the tomato–green onion "relish" for diners to garnish their own soup.

Serves 6.

Black-eyed peas are about the most flavorful dried bean (and they are a bean, whatever their name) in the native cupboard, but though they are used constantly in the South, both fresh and dried, they get short shrift in other parts of the country. If they're not part of your repertoire, try this Tennessee soup— it makes a fine inexpensive family meal, which could become a favorite. Serve it with a frosty glass of beer, and Bacon Buttermilk Cornbread (page 318), then, later, pie and coffee.

POSOLE

1	pork loin or shoulder (3 pounds), trimmed of fat
3	cups chicken stock
1	onion, sliced
1	whole clove garlic, peeled
½	teaspoon dried oregano
	Salt
1	chicken (about 2½ pounds)
1	tablespoon bacon fat (or butter)
2	onions, chopped
2	cloves garlic, minced

1 to 2	tablespoons chili powder
2	large cans (1 pound 13 ounces each) white hominy, drained
1	cup chopped canned tomatoes
1	can mild green chiles (4 ounces), chopped
¼	cup chopped fresh coriander (or parsley)
	Garnishes as listed below

*E*arly in the day, or the day before, simmer the pork in a large kettle with the stock and enough water to cover the meat, sliced onion and whole garlic clove, and oregano and salt to taste. Cook 45 minutes, then add the chicken and cook 30 minutes more—always at a simmer. Strain the stock and refrigerate, along with the meats.

To cook the posole, lift fat off the cold stock and cut both the pork and meat of the chicken into ½-inch cubes. In the same large kettle, sauté the onion and garlic in the bacon fat until the onion is limp. Add the pork cubes and chili powder and cook several more minutes, stirring well. Add the stock—there should be about 8 cups of it. Then add hominy, tomatoes, green chilies, and coriander.

Simmer 20 minutes, then add the chicken cubes and cook another 15 minutes. Serve ladled into bowls, with small bowls of the following garnishes for guests to help themselves: Small strips of crisply fried tortillas, diced avocados, chopped green onions, tiny dice of cream cheese, lime wedges, sliced radishes, shredded lettuce tossed with a little salt and vinegar.

Serves 6 to 8.

Posole is an overlooked dish from the Southwest that makes a superb dish for entertaining. It is worthwhile making a large batch of it, even if you feed a small family, as it freezes admirably. Everyone likes the zesty taste of this combination soup and stew, and the table looks pretty spread with its array of garnishes. Serve it as well with a stack of fresh tortillas that have been sprinkled with a bit of water and put to steam in a warm oven, wrapped in foil. A plate of butter for these, and a pitcher of fine beer, then finally some such dessert as a flan with good coffee.

BEVERLY HILLS RANGOON
RACQUET CLUB CHAMPIONSHIP CHILI

1	large can Italian plum tomatoes (or 3½ cups chopped fresh)	2½	cups chicken stock
		½	cup beer
2	cups chopped onion	2½	tablespoons chili powder
1	stalk celery, chopped	1½	teaspoons dried oregano
1	teaspoon sugar	1	teaspoon ground cumin
2	pounds pork loin	½	teaspoon dried thyme
2	pounds flank steak	1	tablespoon minced fresh coriander leaves

2	cloves garlic, minced		chopped
1	can (4 ounces) mild green	¼	cup oil
	chilies, chopped	½	pound natural Monterey Jack
2	pickled jalapeño peppers,		cheese, grated
	seeded and minced		Wedges of lime
1	small sweet green pepper,		Coriander sprigs (optional)

This recipe takes nearly all day, but it can be speeded up considerably with a food processor and a pressure cooker.

To begin, mash the tomatoes in the bottom of a kettle. Add onion, celery, and sugar and cook an hour or more, gently. As they cook, cut the meat and prepare the other ingredients.

Trim the pork of fat, and cut into tiny cubes. Cut the flank steak in slightly larger cubes—not more than ¼ inch, however. When the tomatoes look (and taste) good, add all the ingredients listed from the chicken stock through all the peppers. Let this cook while you fry the meat.

Fry each meat separately in small batches over a hot fire, adding a little oil as you need it. As each batch is seared brown, lift it out into the chili pot. When all are done, pour a cup of hot water into the pan and whisk to scrape up all the brown pieces. Pour this into the pot, taste for salt and pepper, and simmer slowly until the meats start to disintegrate and it makes a composite mass. (This takes about 3 hours.)

Stir the chili now and again while it cooks, skim any fat off the top, and taste. (It tastes good all the way through the process of cooking—in fact, that is one of the rewards of spending the day making it.) When it is to your satisfaction, eat a bowl for yourself and refrigerate the rest.

The next day, heat it before serving, taste again, and stir in the Monterey Jack. If it is a good natural Monterey Jack it will dissolve in a creamy sauce as you stir. Serve immediately the cheese is dissolved and garnish with wedges of lime for guests to squeeze over the chili to taste. A sprig of coriander is nice, too.

Serves 6 to 8.

Chili is perhaps more American even than apple pie, but this particular dish (derived from C. V. Woods' champion winner) is brought to a certain pitch where it could favorably be compared to any fine curry. It takes at least 4 hours of cooking, though with a pressure cooker you can get by with less. (Try the tomatoes for 30 minutes, and the meat mixture should take an hour and a half or so.)

It is also very very rich—a good-sized bowl of it is almost more than any-

one could consume. So the rest of the meal should be made quite light. You could serve it with Avocado Slices Marinated in Rum (page 191) for a first course, then the chili with beer and home-fried tortilla chips, and finally some such dessert as Pink Grapefruit Ice (page 388). Since it takes all that work, I never make it in batches less than this. If you have only yourself to feed, however, it freezes well (except for the cheese, which should be added fresh) and assures you with a long string of superb suppers.

LONG ISLAND OYSTER STEW

4 tablespoons butter	Salt and freshly ground
2 cups milk	pepper
1 cup heavy cream	Paprika
3 cups fresh-shucked oysters with liquor	

*P*lace 4 soup bowls in a warm oven with a tablespoon of butter in each. Bring the milk and cream to a simmer in one saucepan, and in another pour the oysters with their liquor and poach them just till they plump and curl at the edges.

Immediately pour the hot milk and cream over the oysters. Add salt and pepper to taste, and ladle the stew into the warm buttered bowls. Sprinkle with a dust of paprika and serve immediately with any cracker you fancy, or good bread.

Serves 4.

Oyster stew is one of the best simple meals ever devised. Many recipes complicate the dish needlessly—even to the point of adding Worcestershire—but these are to be avoided. In the East the stew is always served with crackers, but some prefer a fresh loaf of crusty French Bread—I know I do.

LOBSTER STEW

1 lobster (2½ pounds), cooked	Cayenne
4 tablespoons butter	Salt
2 cups milk	2 tablespoons dry sherry (or
2 cups heavy cream	Madeira) (optional)

*P*ick out all meat from the lobster, reserving the coral. Discard the intestinal veins and the sacs near the base of the head. Crack the shell and bones from which the meat has been extracted, and put them in a large kettle.

Cut the larger pieces of lobster meat in small slices, and toss in the butter in a pan set over low heat, then turn off the heat.

Add the milk to the lobster shells (adding all juices that have escaped while shelling the lobster). Simmer 5 minutes, then strain into the pan with buttered lobster.

Mash the reserved coral with some of the cream, and add it to the pan with all the cream. Bring just to the boiling point, and season with a dash of cayenne and salt to taste. Swirl in sherry or Madeira just before serving in warm soup plates.

Serves 4 to 6.

Lobster Stew is flat out one of the glories of our cuisine. Unlike most of the "stews" it should be served as the first course to a banquet (preferably in the White House, to all visiting foreign dignitaries). In principle I don't like to fiddle much with any lobster, but this seems to concentrate flavor rather than to mask it as many elaborate lobster concoctions do.

SWEET SCALLOP STEW

1	pound scallops, cut in quarters if they are large	1	teaspoon flour
2	tablespoons butter	1	cup milk, scalded
½	cup minced green onions with part of tops	1	cup heavy cream
			Salt
			Butter

*I*n a large saucepan set over medium-low heat, sauté the scallops in butter for 3 to 4 minutes—or until they just stiffen slightly. Remove with a slotted spoon and reserve.

Add the green onions and sauté them till limp. Sprinkle the flour over and cook, stirring, another 3 to 4 minutes. Add the hot milk all at once, stirring until the soup thickens and is smooth.

Add about a quarter of the scallops, turn the heat down low, and cook gently a few more minutes. Place in a blender and whirl until smooth. Return to the pan and add the cream and salt to taste.

Add the remaining scallops and let the stew heat gently without boiling. Serve with a lump of butter on top.

Serves 4 to 6.

Another classic. There should never be anything to interfere with the sweet flavor and delicate texture of scallops, and this shows them at their simple, sensuous best.

NEW ENGLAND CLAM CHOWDER

¼ pound salt pork, cut in ¼-inch dice
1 onion, chopped
3 medium potatoes, peeled and cubed
1½ cups water

¼ teaspoon dried thyme
2 cups shucked clams
2 cups milk, scalded
Salt and freshly ground pepper

*S*auté the salt pork in the bottom of a soup kettle set over medium heat. When it is crisp and golden, remove with a slotted spoon and reserve.

Sauté the onion in the pork fat released in the kettle, over low heat till pale gold. Add the potatoes, water, and thyme and cook gently for 10 minutes.

Drain the clams, strain the juices, and heat in another pan. Chop the clams coarsely as the juice heats. Add both the clams and hot clam juice to the onion, then the scalded milk. Add salt and pepper to taste and simmer, uncovered, 30 minutes.

To serve, ladle into soup plates and sprinkle the crisp salt pork over the top of the stew. Serve with crackers.

Serves 4.

This is a misunderstood soup, often gussied up in restaurants by thickening or by adding unnecessary ingredients to make up for the lack of fresh-dug clams. It is so pure, in fact, that there is probably no use cooking it without same—and washed beach, woodsmoke, salt breeze, good friends.

HYANNIS FISH CHOWDER

½ cup diced (¼ inch) salt pork (or bacon)	Salt and freshly ground pepper
2 cups chopped onion	3 pounds fish fillets, cut in pieces
4 cups fish stock	2 cups milk, scalded
3 cups peeled and cubed potatoes	2 cups heavy cream
Pinch of dried thyme	6 tablespoons butter
	Paprika

In a soup kettle set over medium heat, sauté the salt pork until it releases its fat and is crisp and golden. Lift it out with a slotted spoon and reserve.

In the fat left at the bottom of the kettle, sauté the onion until limp. Add fish stock, potatoes, thyme, and salt and pepper to taste. Simmer, uncovered, 20 minutes, or until the potatoes are done.

Add the fish and simmer 5 minutes. Add the scalded milk, then the cream, and taste for seasoning. Turn off the heat and let the chowder stand for an hour to gather flavor.

To serve, gently heat the chowder without letting it come to a boil, add the butter, and ladle into warm bowls. Garnish with the crisp salt pork and a dusting of paprika.

Serves 6.

This was one of the favorites of Jack Kennedy, and was supplied to the press as such during his presidency. (All Presidents, for some reason, are required to have at least one recipe in their pocket.) In a chowder freshness is all—the daily catch of haddock or cod are treated to this bath of hot milk nightly throughout New England. Inland, it's perhaps not worthwhile using frozen fish, but there's no reason why a Southerner, say, couldn't take his local cat-fish to the uses of this Yankee dish.

IDEAL GUMBO

1	chicken (about 2½ pounds)	1	pound okra, tipped and sliced (or 1 package frozen)
	A meaty ham bone (or a meaty ham hock)		
1	small onion, sliced	2	cups chopped tomatoes (canned or fresh), with their juices
2	stalks celery, chopped		
2	sprigs parsley		
1	whole clove garlic	3	bay leaves
1	bay leaf	1	teaspoon dried thyme
6	peppercorns		Tabasco
	Salt		Freshly ground pepper
3	tablespoons fat (vegetable oil, bacon fat, or ham fat)	1½	pounds fresh shrimp, cooked and shelled
2	tablespoons flour	2	cups fresh crabmeat plus cracked claws
2	cups chopped onion		
3	cloves garlic, minced	2	dozen oysters, shucked
½	cup minced green pepper		Filé powder
			Hot steamed rice

*P*ut chicken to cook in a large soup kettle with the ham bone, onion, celery, parsley, whole clove garlic, bay leaf, peppercorns, salt to taste, and water to cover. Simmer, covered, an hour, or until the chicken is tender. Lift out both chicken and ham bone, and strain and reserve the stock.

(Much to-do is made over the New Orleans, or Creole dark roux, but it is really very simple, if a trifle time-consuming to prepare. A gumbo is worth anyone's time. French cooking recognizes only a simple mixture of butter and flour that is stirred until the particles of flour fully absorb the butter, the butter bubbling lightly all the while over low heat. That, and another roux with the butter let get golden for a "darker"-tasting sauce. Creole cooks went farther toward prizing this dark taste and developed an even browned roux made often with other fats that burn less easily than butter. It can take anywhere from 20 to 30 minutes of stirring to achieve flour granules so goldenly browned they no longer actually thicken the sauce to which they are the base.)

So make a dark roux with any tasty fat and the flour. Add onion, minced garlic, and green pepper. Stir them in the kettle till limp. Stir in the okra a few minutes, then add the tomatoes, herbs, and spices. Add the reserved stock and cook gently, uncovered, for 30 minutes, or until the okra has thickened the whole and it starts to look glutinous.

Add the cut-up meat from the chicken, the meat from the ham bone, the shrimp, and crab and crab claws. Simmer the gumbo gently for 2 or more hours, stirring now and again to make sure it doesn't stick to the bottom. (This long cooking of shrimp and crab will seem curious outside the South, but that's how it is usually done for the deepest flavor.)

Taste for seasoning near the end—it should be hot slightly with Tabasco, not too salty, and of a deep, rich flavor.

When you are ready to serve the gumbo, add enough filé powder (about a tablespoon) to thicken the gumbo to about the texture of a good stew. At the last add the oysters, and let the gumbo heat without boiling. (After adding filé powder the gumbo should never boil, or it will become stringy and much flavor is somehow lost.) To serve, ladle onto steamed rice on warm plates, and pass filé powder to sprinkle over.

Serves 6 to 8.

In practice no two gumbos are alike, and here are only approximations of what might go into yours. They may have many balances, and ham and chicken can be used alone—though a gumbo is usually conceived as a shellfish-based dish. The chicken is often, in the South, a game carcass—I have even found one recipe for home-smoked wild duck gumbo with fresh oysters. If you have fresh cheap seafood, there is no reason to use chicken at all.

Crab may be used alone, as in this recipe from Gourmet's Guide to New Orleans, a splendid cookbook published in 1933, for Shadows of the Teche Gumbo, said to make the late painter Weeks Hall "desert his easel":

> *Wash (1 doz.) crabs thoroughly, then boil them in just enough water to cover, and cook until done, saving water the crabs were boiled in. Remove the shells, picking out all the meat of the crab. Now put (2 lbs.) okra cut up in round slices and add it to the hot lard (1 kitchen spoon), to fry until dry. Add (4) cloves minced garlic. Fry all this together, then add the water in which the crabs were boiled. Add salt to taste, and set it all to boil about two hours.*

The recipe goes on to add a tablespoon of flour to three ears of scraped corn, and this is added half an hour before serving, along with the crabmeat. Some vinegar is added to cut the okra toward the end. It can almost be sniffed through the Spanish moss of the Teche, almost tasted.

Probably the only way to cook a gumbo is to have eaten some and know where you're heading—plain sailing through fellow gourmet–traveled waters. You will find that either okra or filé powder can be used to thicken, though both are nice, and you will come to the darker the roux the better point and back, and above quite all you will find how a fine gumbo ages till (like a cassoulet) it is almost better at last dense taste.

Gumbos, though always listed as a soup, are definitely a main-dish stew served with dry fluffy rice. I serve them as one would a curry, on plates. Since they are so rich, I usually start the meal with a fine plain salad and The Duchess of Windsor's Cornpones (page 316), follow that with a gumbo and a fine white wine from California, then some such dessert as Roanoke Rum Cream (page 382).

TURKEY OYSTER GUMBO

	The remains of a turkey	¼	teaspoon dried thyme
½	pound ham	3	dozen small oysters, shucked
2	tablespoons butter		Salt and freshly ground
1	large chopped onion		pepper
2	quarts boiling water		Cayenne
1	bay leaf	2	tablespoons filé powder
3	tablespoons minced parsley		Hot cooked rice

*R*emove any meat from the turkey (there should be 1 to 2 cups), and cut it with the ham into ½-inch dice. Melt the butter in a soup kettle and sauté the meats and onion till the onion is limp.

Add boiling water, bay leaf, parsley, and thyme, and break up the turkey carcass and add it as well. Let this simmer, covered, over low heat for an hour or more, then remove the bones.

Add the oysters, salt and pepper to taste, and enough cayenne to make it slightly hot. Cook till the oysters begin to curl, then stir in the filé powder and cook without boiling until the gumbo thickens. Serve over fluffy hot cooked rice.

Serves 6.

What better and unusual way to serve the last of a turkey? An example of how the Creole cook constructs a gumbo from food at hand, in just proportions.

GUMBO Z'HERBES

4	pounds any combination of greens—turnip, mustard, beet, collards, spinach, watercress, lettuce, onion tops, radish tops, etc.	1	heaping tablespoon flour
		1½	cups chopped onion
		2	cloves garlic, minced
		1	green pepper, minced
			Salt and freshly ground pepper
2	cups water	¼	teaspoon dried thyme
1 to 2	meaty ham hocks (or 1 pound salt pork, or duck carcass or any game, or a veal knuckle, etc.)	1	bay leaf
		1	small pod of dried red pepper (or cayenne, or Tabasco)
			Filé powder
2	tablespoons bacon fat (or goose fat)		Hot cooked rice

Wash thoroughly whatever your garden, or market, can claim for fresh greens and place them in a large kettle. Add the water and bring the greens to a boil over a medium flame. If the kettle won't hold all of them, start with the first batch of greens and let it wilt, then add another batch, etc.

Place the meat over the greens, cover, and cook slowly an hour. Remove the meat, drain the greens, and save the "pot liquor." Place the bacon fat in another pot and thoroughly brown the flour in it over a low flame, stirring for 20 to 30 minutes.

Remove all meat from the bones and cut into ½-inch dice. Add the onion to the browned flour and cook till golden, then add garlic, green pepper, and the meat. Chop the greens and return them to the pot along with the "pot liquor," and let this boil up. Add salt and pepper to taste, then add thyme, bay leaf, and red pepper.

Simmer, uncovered, gently for 2 hours, and at the very end add enough filé powder to thicken it—about a tablespoon. (It should not boil after you add the filé.) Serve on hot cooked rice.

Serves 6.

This tonic apotheosis of southern "greens" is as wild as its name—from the French des herbes. Obviously no two versions are alike, even from the same cook, for it is possible to go from a full-scale production to a rather suave dish using the leftovers from a duck, cooked with lettuce and spinach. I like it. Of course it would never be served in a restaurant, but how pleasant to come upon it on a menu—a dish the like of which gourmets have scoured the homes of many a French peasant to find. If I were able to order it up, I would have oysters on the half shell, to begin, with good bread and white wine, then on to the gumbo with a robust red wine, with fruit and cheese or a light dessert to follow.

CREOLE COURT-BOUILLON

1 cup chopped onion	Salt and freshly ground
½ cup chopped celery	pepper
1 cup chopped green (or red)	Cayenne
pepper	1 tablespoon paprika
½ cup chopped green onions	2 cups fish stock
with part of tops	2 pounds redfish (or red
2 cloves garlic, minced	snapper or other fresh
¼ cup olive oil	firm fish)
Flour	Vegetable oil
2 bay leaves	1½ tablespoons lemon juice
¼ teaspoon dried thyme	⅓ cup dry red wine
2 cups (fresh or canned	½ lemon, sliced
preferably Italian Plum)	Hot cooked rice
tomatoes	

*I*n a soup kettle set over medium-low heat, sauté the chopped vegetables in oil till they start to turn gold, then add 2 tablespoons flour and stir until the flour starts also to turn golden.

Add bay leaves, thyme, and then tomatoes—mashing them down with a slotted spoon or potato masher to break them up. Add seasonings, then stock, and simmer, uncovered, 30 minutes.

While this cooks, cut the fish into 1-inch strips, shake them in flour, and place on a plate. Heat some vegetable oil in a frying pan and sauté the fish for several minutes on each side over rather high heat, or until they start to brown.

Add the fish to the pot along with the lemon juice and wine, and simmer 10 to 12 minutes more. Add lemon slices, then taste for seasoning—it should be quite spicy and rather hot with cayenne—and serve in bowls over hot cooked rice.

Serves 4.

Though the Creole cook makes this dish from the tasty redfish from the Gulf, not available generally anywhere else, this rather primitive bouillabaisse, *highly spiced and slightly dark from the roux of vegetables, is a fine way to treat any fresh firm-fleshed fish. It certainly has more gumption than any chowder. It might be preceeded by a salad or first-course vegetable, served with a fine red wine rather than a white, and followed by a rich dessert and coffee.*

(The knowledgeable cook will wonder as to the title of this dish, for he knows a court-bouillon in French cookery is a simple bath of water, vinegar, vegetables, and herbs used to poach fish. The Creole cook throws all that to the winds, and puts everything in the pot.)

CIOPPINO

½ cup olive oil	Salt
1 cup chopped onion	Cayenne
2 cloves garlic, minced	3 pounds crabs, cleaned and cooked
3 tablespoons minced parsley	
1 cup dry white wine	1½ pounds sea bass (or other firm fish)
1 cup chopped fresh or canned (preferably Italian Plum) tomatoes	1 pound shrimp, shelled
	2 dozen clams in their shells
1 bay leaf	3 dozen mussels in their shells (optional)
2 whole cloves	
¼ teaspoon saffron threads	

*H*eat the oil in a heavy kettle and sauté the onion, garlic, and parsley until limp. Add the wine and let it cook for a few minutes, then add tomatoes, bay leaf, cloves, and saffron. Let simmer, covered, for an hour, or until the sauce has a well-balanced flavor. Season to taste with salt and cayenne.

Crack the crabs, remove the flesh from all but the large claws, and reserve. Cut the fish in bite-sized portions. Add the crabmeat, claws, and fish with the shrimp to the kettle and cook, uncovered, 15 minutes over low heat. Add the clams and mussels and steam them, covered, until they open.

Serve in warm soup plates or bowls, accompanied by either San Francisco sour dough bread, or any crusty French bread.

Serves 6 to 8.

Cioppino is a native California dish that has not yet been boosted as one of our great native bouillabaisses. *At its best I have had it only at Italian festivals in San Francisco, but it is far from impossible in any seacoast kitchen.*

FISH & SHELLFISH

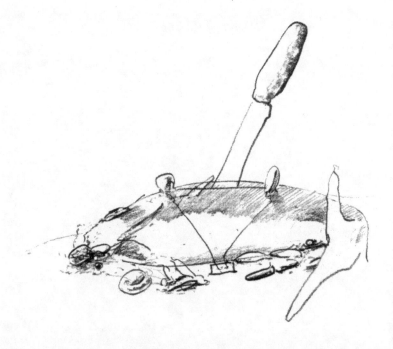

There, *having reduced some damp driftwood, which I had picked up on the shore, to shavings with my knife, I kindled a fire with a match and some paper, and cooked my clam on the embers for my dinner; for breakfast was commonly the only meal which I took in a house on this excursion. When the clam was done, one valve held the meat, and the other the liquor. Though it was very tough, I found it sweet and savory, and ate the whole with a relish.*

—Henry David Thoreau, Cape Cod

Fish

*E*arly on, I always skipped the fish chapter of a foreign cookbook, with their eels and *loups* and faraway *fruits-de-mer*. Until I lived a long time in a seashore city, with equally unidentifiable Chinese finny things, I didn't figure out any catch should be cooked simply and lightly as possible. As a trout fisherman once advised me, on asking over the campfire: "It's how the critter takes to heat—he should skip just like he's still in the stream."

TARRAGON FILLETS
WITH CUCUMBER BUTTER

4   serving portions sole (or   ½   cucumber
    flounder or other tender   ½   cup plus 2 tablespoons butter
    fillet)   1   teaspoon lemon juice
    White wine tarragon vinegar   Lemon slices
    Salt

Place the fish fillets on a plate and sprinkle them lightly with vinegar. (If you don't have a good tarragon vinegar, bring 2 tablespoons white wine vinegar to a boil, add some fresh or dried tarragon, let it cook briefly, and sprinkle over the fish.) Salt lightly and place the fish to marinate in your refrigerator.

Have the ½ cup butter at room temperature. Peel the cucumber, slice it lengthwise, and cut out the seeds. Mince finely in a blender or food processor. Drain the cucumber as well as possible—squeezing the juice out in your hands. Whip it bit by bit into the room-temperature butter until creamy. Add the lemon juice and incorporate it thoroughly. (All this can be done with a fork, or in any manner that incorporates the cucumber, but a food processor is best.)

Smooth the cucumber butter on a plate and place it in the refrigerator to harden. When it comes time to cook the fish, drain off any juice that has accumulated and pat dry with paper towels.

To prepare the dish, heat the 2 tablespoons butter in a frying pan large enough to hold the fish at once. When it begins to sizzle, add the fish to the pan and sauté over a medium flame 1 to 2 minutes a side. Place the fillets on a warm plate, salt again to taste, and top with pieces of cucumber butter. Garnish with lemon slices. If you have it, it's pretty to tuck in a sprig of fresh tarragon.

Serves 4.

A recipe assembled from two hints in Irma Rombauer's Joy of Cooking, *the one indispensable tool of any American cook. Everything can be found there, and can be depended on for style, economy, brevity—even wit. Her marinade of tarragon vinegar makes a surprise of supermarket fillets. The cucumber butter is subtler than it sounds, and should exactly balance the faint tarragon. The dish could either be a first course, with chilled white wine and hot rolls, or constitute a main course with some such starch as Farmhouse Skillet Creamed Potatoes (page 256), or Thomas Jefferson's Pilau (page 266).*

CRISP SOLE WITH ANCHOVY CREAM

4	serving portions sole (or flounder or other tender fillets)	½	teaspoon salt
		2	egg whites, beaten stiff
			Vegetable oil
½	cup flour	1	cup heavy cream
2	tablespoons olive oil	2	teaspoons (or to taste) anchovy paste
6	tablespoons water		

Wash and dry the fillets with paper towels. Mix flour, oil, water, and salt into a paste, then fold in the beaten egg whites just before ready to cook the fish.

To do so, heat about an inch of oil in a frying pan (this can be a small pan, and they can be done in batches). Dip the fillets in the batter, and fry them until gold on each side—this should take no more than 2 minutes a side. Remove to drain on paper towels, and keep warm while you prepare the anchovy cream.

Beat the cream stiff, adding the anchovy paste toward the end. Taste the sauce—it should not be too salt or fishy. To serve, slide the fillets onto warm plates and place a dollop of the cream on top of each.

Serves 4.

This is a recipe from Theodora Fitzgibbon's Country House Cooking *I picked up once, thinking it would be about American food, and promptly became enchanted by this British writer. So here I cheat, with only the flimsy excuse that I like the recipe, and that if so much of our food has stemmed from England at its dullest, there is no reason not to choose again from the best. Theodora Fitzgibbon, though not so well known as Elizabeth David, is surely one of the best writers on food we have. Perhaps only rivaled by France's Edouard de Pomiane for brevity and shine and sheer usefulness, the book above is a revelation of best family receipts and stout cooks long dead, obliged to hustle a sudden tea for Queen Victoria on a swoop, or edify a whole weekend of city guests such as Henry James. But any of her books, though difficult to find, are worth the price. As a first course, the recipe here needs nothing but the finest white wine. As a main dish, it could be accompanied by a simple green vegetable such as asparagus or green beans carefully turned out, and perhaps with a crisp pile of Saratoga Chips (page 254) cooked in the same fat.*

PAN-FRIED FILLETS
WITH FRENCH QUARTER SAUCE

4 serving portions sole (or flounder or other tender fillet) Milk Flour (or cornmeal)	Salt and freshly ground pepper 2 tablespoons butter 2 tablespoons vegetable oil French Quarter Sauce (page 293)

*D*ip the fillets in milk, then into flour or cornmeal seasoned with salt and pepper to taste. Lay on waxed paper until ready to cook. This is done in the butter and oil sputtering in a frying pan set over medium hot heat. Sauté until the fillets are gold on either side—a good guide is James Beard's 10 minutes per inch thickness for any preparation of fish.

Lift out the fish on paper toweling to drain. Serve warm, coated with French Quarter Sauce.

Serves 4.

It is the piquant New Orleans sauce that makes this dish stand out among simple preparations of fish—a little-known sauce with in fact many fine applications, and simplicity itself prepared with either blender or food processor. If you've never tried, do not hesitate to use cornmeal rather than flour, for it results in a fine crispiness flour cannot touch. Serve it with French bread and dry white wine.

CHILLED HYANNIS COD FILLETS

4 cod fillets (or other thick fish fillets or steaks) ¼ cup prepared horseradish, drained 2 cups sour cream ½ cup minced green onions with part of tops 1 teaspoon white wine vinegar	3 tablespoons minced fresh dill (or 2 tablespoons dried) Salt and freshly ground pepper 4 lettuce leaves 2 hard-boiled eggs, quartered 2 ripe tomatoes, peeled and quartered (or 8 radish roses)

*S*team the fish, covered, in a little water for 8 to 10 minutes, or until it flakes easily. Lift out to a plate and let cool.

While the fish cooks, mix horseradish with sour cream, green onions, vinegar, dill, and salt and pepper to taste. Place half the mixture in a shallow dish large enough to hold all the fish in a single layer. Place the fillets on top of the sauce, spread the rest over, cover the dish, and refrigerate for at least an hour.

To serve, place a lettuce leaf on each plate, place a fillet in the middle, and garnish with eggs and tomato. Spoon any leftover sauce on top of the fish.

Serves 4.

Another recipe from the Kennedy Compound. Such an easy tangy horseradish sauce is the perfect foil for any strong-tasting, sturdy-fleshed fish such as cod, but it works with any cold fish. With a good crusty bread and chilled white wine, it makes an exceptional summer lunch or supper—and is easily assembled the day before.

FLORIDA ORANGE SNAPPER

4 red snapper fillets (or other fillets or steaks)	Salt
	Tabasco
½ cup minced green onions with part of tops	Freshly grated nutmeg
	4 orange slices
Grated peel and juice of 1 orange	

Marinate the fillets with green onions, orange peel and juice, salt to taste, and a few drops Tabasco for at least 30 minutes.

Preheat oven to 400 °F.

Place fish with its marinade in a shallow casserole large enough to hold all the fillets in one layer. Sprinkle with a little grated nutmeg and bake basting once or twice, 10 minutes, or until the fish flakes easily with a fork.

Serve hot or cold, garnished with orange slices.

Serves 4.

Discovered in one of those ladies' church cookbooks, which promise so much and deliver so little, this is an excellent recipe from the Orange State. It is also a dieter's delight. As it's even better the next day cold—make too much and have enough for lunch. Either way, it should be served with a fragrant, not too dry white wine.

FRIED FISH WITH HUSH PUPPIES

4	serving portions any fish at all	1	recipe Hush Puppies (page
	Milk		320)
	Salt and freshly ground		Lemon wedges
	pepper		Parsley sprigs
	Cornmeal		Tartar Sauce (page 292)
	Fat for deep frying		

*D*ip fish, whole or in fillets, into milk, then roll in salted and peppered cornmeal. Lay on waxed paper and refrigerate 30 minutes or more, to set the cornmeal.

To cook, fry in deep fat (heated about 370°F, or sizzling up when a bit of cornmeal is dropped in) until they are golden on all sides. Drain on paper towels, and keep warm in an oven while you prepare the hush puppies in the same fat.

Serve each with a heap of hush puppies, lemon wedges, a sprig of parsley, and the tartar sauce.

Serves 4.

Seldom seen in cookbooks, this is the way Southerners cook fish—and they are to my mind right. The method is a joy on just-caught fish over a campfire, and it is an enhancement even to frozen fish fillets. It's easy, but the trick is to have the fat just the right temperature for it. If not hot enough, both the fish and the hush puppies will be greasy. Serve with cole slaw and cold beer.

MARYLAND BAKED FISH WITH CREAM

1	whole fish (4 to 5 pounds)	3	slices bacon
	(any catch of the day)		Cayenne
1	lemon, halved		Flour
	Salt	4	whole cloves
¼	teaspoon ground allspice	¾	cup heavy cream
2	tablespoons butter		Parsley sprigs
1	tablespoon Dijon mustard	1	pimento-stuffed olive slice

Preheat the oven to 375°F.

Take a fish that has been cleaned but left whole, and rub inside and out with some of the juice from the lemon. Sprinkle inside and out with salt and allspice. Mix the butter and mustard together with a fork, and place in the inner cavity.

Take a casserole large enough to hold the fish, and line it with aluminum foil so it comes up the sides of the casserole (this is for easy removal later to a platter. If you have a nice dish and wish to serve the fish at table, this will be unnecessary.) Grease the foil, and lay the bacon in the bottom. Rest the fish on the bacon. Dust with some cayenne and salt, and squeeze the rest of the lemon juice over. Dust the fish with a bit of flour—preferably through a sifter. Stick the cloves in the flesh, and pour cream around the edges.

Bake 35 to 40 minutes, or until the flesh flakes easily with a fork. Baste occasionally while it cooks, and when done remove to a serving platter and pour the cooking cream around and over it.

Serve garnished with a pride of parsley, and a sliced olive for eye.

Serves 4 to 6.

Ordinary baked fish, with a simple bread stuffing—perhaps with some grated cucumber tossed in—and strips of bacon cresting the top, is always welcome, but this antique Maryland recipe in a slightly spiced cream is superior in every way. I've tried it on all sorts of fish, and it worked in every case, though you'll want to stay away from very thin and thus very long fish, or you won't have a dish large enough to hold it. Since it is so simple it can be preceded with an interesting soup (with no cream of course) or a vegetable first course such as Celery Victor (page 278). To accompany it, try Zucchini-stuffed Baked Potatoes (page 258) or Portland Potatoes (page 259). That, and a toasting good white vintage.

POMPANO EN PAPILLOTE, ANTOINE

3 medium pompano (or trout)	2 tablespoons flour
3 cups water	4 green onions with part of
1 teaspoon salt	tops, chopped
1 stalk celery, sliced	1 cup cooked shrimp
1 small onion, sliced	1 cup cooked crabmeat
1 bay leaf	1 clove garlic, minced
Pinch of dried thyme	Tabasco (optional)
2 cups dry white wine	2 egg yolks, beaten
6 tablespoons butter	Parchment baking paper

*H*ave the fish filleted and ask for the trimmings. Place the heads and bones in a kettle with water, salt, celery, onion, bay leaf, and thyme and simmer, uncovered, 30 minutes. Strain and reserve 1 cup of the stock. Pour the rest of the stock in a saucepan and add ½ cup of the white wine.

Poach the fillets in this 5 minutes. Remove from the heat, and let cool in the stock.

To make the sauce, melt 2 tablespoons of the butter in a saucepan. Stir in the flour and cook several minutes. Add the reserved cup of stock and let the sauce bubble up. Whisk smooth and turn the fire down very low.

In another pan, sauté the green onions in the remaining butter (4 table-spoons). When they are limp, add the shrimp, crab, garlic, and a drop or two of Tabasco if you like. Toss until the garlic starts to cook, then add the rest of the wine (1½ cups) and let cook, uncovered, 15 minutes over a low flame. Add the thickened sauce, and beat in the egg yolks. Stir until heated, but do not let it boil. This can sit until you are ready to assemble the dish.

Preheat the oven to 425°F. Make papillotes by cutting six 12 x 8-inch hearts from the parchment baking paper (which is usually found in food specialty shops). Brush each heart with oil, and dollop a little sauce on. Lay a fillet on the sauce, and top with the rest of the sauce. Fold the paper hearts over in half so they form an ice cream cone, or balloon, shape, and seal their edges by folding over and pinching together all around.

Lay the sealed hearts on an oiled baking sheet and bake for 15 minutes, or until the paper begins to brown. Serve at once, cutting open the paper at table.

Serves 6.

An elegant exuberance created in 1901 for the French balloonist Alberto Santos-Dumont. Antoine's honored him with a dish in the shape of his vehicle in what is by now famed as a culinary coup. Pompano is undeniably one of our best native fish, though it is not widely found outside the Gulf. Thus most of us must content ourselves with trout en papillote—itself a dish worthy the time and effort. But it takes not only time and effort, like most restaurant extravaganzas it also takes a lot of hard-earned cash, and culinary knowhow.

If you take this recipe in hand, look out for the new brands of parchment paper being offered in gourmet shops: they say clearly on the package that they are meant for lining cake pans (as if plain waxed paper weren't enough!). These brands are too light for papillotes—regular cooking parchment is about the weight of a good shopping bag, and that is exactly what to use if you haven't a source for parchment.

SALMON GEORGE WASHINGTON

1	piece (2½ to 3 pounds) fresh salmon	4	thin slices onion
	Salt and freshly ground pepper	1	clove garlic, peeled
	Pinch of dried thyme		Parsley sprigs
3	tablespoons butter	2	cucumbers
1½	cups heavy cream	2	teaspoons Dijon mustard
1	bay leaf		Lemon juice (optional)
			Lemon slices

*P*reheat the oven to 350°F.

Rub the salmon with salt, pepper, and a little thyme. Choose a baking dish large enough to hold the fish that also has a cover. Melt the butter in it, add the salmon, and turn to coat it thoroughly in the butter. Pour the cream around the fish and strew around bay leaf, onion slices, garlic, and 3 parsley sprigs.

Peel the cucumbers, slice lengthwise in quarters, remove the seeds, and cut each slice in half at the middle. Place them around the fish, cover, and bake about 40 minutes—or until the salmon flakes easily and the center bone can be pulled away.

Carefully remove the fish from the baking dish and lay on a baking sheet or some such surface. Slip off the skin, bone the fish, and reassemble on a hot serving platter. Place the cucumber around it and keep warm.

To make the sauce, strain the cream into a saucepan, turn the heat high, whisk the Dijon into it, and add a few drops of lemon juice if the sauce seems to need it. Boil down until slightly thickened, pour over the salmon, and serve with additional parsley sprigs and lemon slices.

Serves 4 to 6.

By far my favorite American fish dish, this is not complicated to prepare. It is also of incomparable subtlety and is a pleasure both to see and eat. If you don't find a good piece of salmon for it, salmon steaks do nicely—but as they take less time to cook, the cucumber must be simmered awhile in the cream on top of the stove, to complete the cooking. Since it has both sauce and vegetable the dish should probably not be served with anything else but a fragrant rounded white wine. I have been unable to trace the origin of this recipe. I've seen it written as "Martha Washington's Salmon," as well, but it doesn't appear in her family cookbook. At any rate, whoever named it, it is a proud dish for our first President.

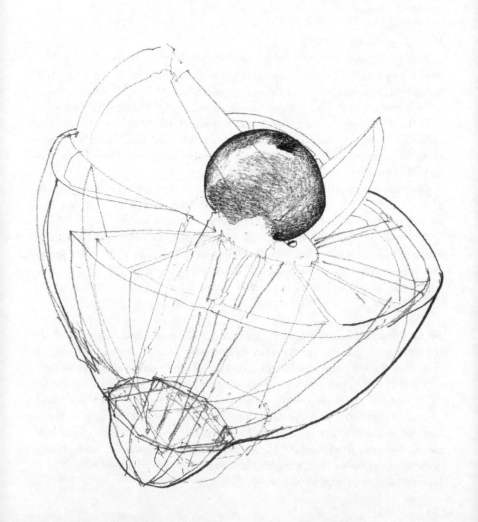

NORTHWESTERN SCALLOPED POTATOES AND SMOKED SALMON

4	tablespoons butter, melted	1 cup heavy cream
4	medium potatoes, peeled and	Freshly ground pepper
	thinly sliced	Ground allspice
1	onion, minced	Minced parsley
¾	pound smoked salmon,	
	thinly sliced	

*P*reheat the oven to 325°F.

Grease a shallow casserole or gratin dish with some of the butter. Place a layer of potatoes on the bottom, sprinkle with half the onion, lay half the salmon on, then put another layer of potatoes over. Repeat the process, ending with a layer of potatoes.

Pour the cream over, sprinkle lightly with pepper and allspice, and dribble the rest of the butter on top. Bake for an hour, or until most of the cream is absorbed and the top is golden.

To serve, sprinkle parsley on top and bring to the table to be scooped directly out of the casserole.

Serves 4.

When you find relatively inexpensive scraps and trimmings from sliced smoked salmon, run to this dish! It's every bit as good as it sounds. Pair it with a simple fresh green vegetable, and you have a fine family dinner indeed.

SHAD ROE POACHED IN BUTTER

½	cup butter	¼ cup minced parsley
4	shad roe	2 tablespoons minced chives
	Salt and freshly ground	8 slices bacon, cooked
	pepper	2 lemons, quartered
	Lemon juice	

*I*f you have a skillet large enough to hold all the roes, that's fine, but if not, either use two pans or fry the roes in stages—holding the first batch warm in the oven. Either way, melt butter over a low flame. Add the roes, sprinkle with salt and pepper to taste, and cook them about 6 minutes a side—making sure the heat is low enough never to discolor the butter. (Each roe should be golden on each side, but not crusty.)

Remove with a spatula to warm serving plates, squeeze a few drips of lemon juice into the skillet, and add the parsley and chives. Heat, stirring, and pour over the roes. Place crisp bacon beside them, along with lemon quarters, and serve immediately.

Serves 4.

Roe of shad, which used to be given along with the fish, are now so expensive I only allow myself this delicacy once a year, in season. They are our native caviar indeed.

TROUT WITH
LE RUTH'S SAUCE À LA NEIGE

4 trout	A few drops Tabasco (or
Items at hand (see list below)	cayenne)
1 egg white	¾ cup bubbling hot butter
1 tablespoon lemon juice	2 pimiento-stuffed olives,
1 teaspoon white wine tarragon	sliced
vinegar	

Steam the trout in a stock made up of some of the following: water, white wine, dry vermouth, a good white vinegar, lemon juice, vegetables such as onion, celery tops, parsley stems or a stray carrot, and any such herbs and spices as bay leaf, thyme, tarragon, cloves, or a strip of orange peel—perhaps, even, a couple of whole allspice.

The trout should steam with a lid on for 10 minutes. Lift them out onto a platter and let cool enough to slip their skins off, leaving neatly both head and tail intact. You can keep them warm, or chill them, covered.

In either case, to serve them, place egg white, lemon juice, and vinegar in a blender. Whirl at low speed and add the Tabasco. Dribble the hot butter in drop by drop as you whirl it. As it starts to thicken, you can increase the flow of the butter to a fine, very thin stream.

Frost the trout up to their heads and tails with the sauce, and place an olive slice for an eye on each.

Serves 4.

A dish constructed around a sauce invented, for a now forgotten Vice-President, by Warren Le Ruth—one of New Orleans' best restauranteurs. It is an inspired switch on a hollandaise by use of the then-new electric blender. In his restaurant, Mr. Le Ruth serves it on a fillet of trout encircling a lobster tail, but that is both elaborate and expensive for home cooking. It is a virtually unexplored sauce, simple to prepare and with a host of possibilities. It makes, for instance, a fine foil for artichokes or asparagus.

Shellfish

*U*ntil lately, native coasts have been blessed with an abundance of shellfish, so past largesse has left us a host of durable recipes—oysters being the best example. In Europe they are a delicacy presented hardly anywhere off the half-shell, whereas here we stew and stuff, and fry and roast with abandon. These recipes are a boon, particularly for those able to buy the rather coarse (and still inexpensive) Western oysters, or the fine Gulf oysters, packed fresh in bottles. Many of our shrimp dishes, too, can be prepared from the inexpensive little cooked shrimp available rather than elegant prawns. The rest is up to the tide, and purse.

CLAMS PHILLY

Salt

Cornmeal

4 dozen littleneck clams (or
    razor clams in the West)

6 green onions with part of
    tops, chopped

4 tablespoons butter

4 tablespoons dry sherry

4 tablespoons brandy

4 egg yolks

1 cup heavy cream

  Cayenne

  Toast points

*C*lams are sandy and need care in cleaning. They should be scrubbed with a brush and washed in several waters. Then soak them in salt water (⅓ cup salt to 1 gallon water), with cornmeal sprinkled over. Leave 3 or more hours—the meal helps rid them of sand, and makes them better tasting. After soaking, wash again under cold running water. Open clams over a bowl to catch their juices; use a sharp small knife, running it along the shell edge, to pry open. Cut the clams from the shell and reserve.

To cook the dish, strain the clam juices into a saucepan and bring to a boil. Lower the heat, and steam the clams, covered, in the juices 3 minutes. Drain the clams and reserve—the juices may be discarded or saved for fish stock.

Put the butter in a medium saucepan set over medium heat. Add the green onions and sauté until they are limp. Add both sherry and brandy, and boil down, uncovered, over high heat until reduced by half.

Beat the egg yolks with cream till light and frothy. Stir into the onion mixture. Cook stirring, over low heat, until the sauce is smooth and thickened—be careful not to let it boil. When the sauce is ready, add the clams and let them heat for 2 minutes.

Season to taste with salt and cayenne, and pour over toast points on warm plates.

Serves 4 (or 6 as a first course).

Years ago I had my first taste of raw clams when the late poet Walter Lowenfells took us out to a New Jersey fishermen's shack to buy just-caught clams from a bucket. He ordered two dozen for each of us, and though the first several were delightful, I found it increasingly difficult to get them down with no lemon, no bread, no wine, no nothing. Ever since I have shied away from this tonic delicacy, though I delight in most any cooked clam dish. After having tried many fancy stuffed clams of one kind and another, though, I find I settle on this classic clam dish to show fresh clams at their succulent best.

CLAM FRITTERS

1½ cups bread crumbs	Tabasco
1 cup minced clams	Clam juice (or milk)
2 eggs, separated	Butter (or hot fat)
1 tablespoon minced parsley	Lemon wedges
Salt	Tartar Sauce (page 292)

*P*ut the bread crumbs in a heavy frying pan over medium heat and toast them until golden, shaking now and again. Turn off the heat and set aside.

Drain the clams of their juice (reserving for later) and place them in a bowl with the egg yolks. Toss briskly, then stir in crumbs, parsley, salt to taste, and a few drops of Tabasco. Add enough clam juice or milk to make a heavy batter that will drop off a large spoon in a plop.

Beat the egg whites stiff and fold into the batter. I like these best cooked in butter—dropped from a spoon and then browned on either side over medium-high heat. They can also be cooked dropped from a spoon into hot fat (370°F) and fried till crisp and golden.

Serve on warm plates with lemon wedges and homemade tartar sauce.

Serves 4 as a first course.

Hands down, these win the classic fritter race. They are an old-time Eastern fritter, and it's the bread crumbs that seem to make the difference. The batter is so good, in fact, that you can use canned clams if need be (the whole ones, not the chopped), and they are delightful with bits of cooked fish, or mushrooms. The recipe is easily doubled or tripled for larger portions, and they do make a fine light supper with a glass of beer, a salad, and dessert.

DELTA CRAB PIE

4 cups ½-inch cubes from homemade-type bread	1 lemon, sliced paper thin and seeded
2 tablespoons dry sherry	Salt and freshly ground pepper
1 cup heavy cream	Milk
1 pound crabmeat	Watercress (optional)
½ cup butter, melted	

*T*oss the bread cubes with a good sprinkling of sherry, then soak in cream for at least 30 minutes—or until ready to assemble the dish.
Preheat the oven to 375°F.
Grease a soufflé dish, or a shallow gratin dish, with a little of the butter. Then layer the bread cubes, some crab, a douse of butter, a thin layer of lemon slices, salt and pepper to taste, then more butter. End with a layer of bread and the last of the butter.
Pour milk in to within ¼ inch of the top and pop into the oven. Bake 30 to 40 minutes, or until the top puffs up and is golden. Serve immediately, perhaps with a mound of watercress.
Serves 4 as a first course.

This is one of those marvelous, simple recipes handed down family to friend in the South. Its only exactions of the cook are fresh crab and thinnest lemon slices. If you are unsure of your knife, it may be prepared with grated lemon peel and squeezed juice.

GREEN CRACKER CRAB

½ cup celery	1½ cups crushed soda crackers
½ cup green onions, with part of tops	1 teaspoon Dijon mustard
	Tabasco
½ cup green pepper	¼ cup heavy cream
¼ cup parsley	⅔ cup butter, melted
1 pound crabmeat	

*P*reheat the oven to 350°F.
Carefully mince the vegetables fine with a knife (or place them in a food processor and chop with the steel blade. If using a processor, blot the vegetables with paper towels before proceeding). In a bowl, toss vegetables lightly with the crab and 1 cup of the crackers.
In another bowl, beat the mustard and Tabasco to taste into the cream. (This dish should be slightly hot, so use about ¼ teaspoon Tabasco, at least.) Toss this, with ½ cup of the melted butter, with the crab. Taste for seasoning at this point—the crackers may or may not have added enough salt.
To cook, grease a soufflé dish, or individual ramekins, with some of the rest of the butter. Place the crab mixture in the dish and sprinkle with the rest of the crackers, then dribble all the remaining butter over the top. Bake for 30 minutes, or until golden brown on top. Serve immediately.
Serves 4 as a first course.

This crisp dish is an example of how dishes freely travel. I found it in a women's club cookbook, then later found it again looking through James Beard's superb memoir-cookbook Delights and Prejudices—*certainly where the lady or one of her friends had found it. It was remarkably unchanged, and she had resisted putting Worcestershire or whatnot in it. It is simple sounding as to ingredients, but it is better than any so-called deviled crab dishes you'll ever have a chance to eat. Serve it with an equally crisp dry white wine, and cloverleaf rolls.*

GALATOIRE'S EGGPLANT
STUFFED WITH CRAB (OR SHRIMP)

2	medium eggplants	1	pound cooked crabmeat (or small shrimp, or half and half)
⅔	cup minced green onions with part of tops		
⅓	cup chopped onion	2	eggs
1	clove garlic, minced	¼	cup minced parsley
1	teaspoon dried thyme		Salt and freshly ground pepper
1	bay leaf		Bread crumbs
2	tablespoons butter		Paprika
1½	cups bread, soaked in water and squeezed dry		Melted butter

*P*reheat the oven to 350°F.

Trim the tops off the eggplants and split each in half lengthwise. Make crosswise slashes in the flesh of each, being careful not to pierce the skin. Parboil in boiling salted water 5 minutes, or until the flesh can be scooped out with the skins left firm and intact. Scoop them so, squeezing out as much liquid as possible from the flesh, and chop or mash it fine.

In a frying pan, sauté green onion, onion, garlic, thyme, and bay leaf in 2 tablespoons butter gently for 5 minutes, or until the onion is limp.

Mash the soaked bread into the eggplant—the best way to do this is with your hands or through a ricer. It should all come to a light pulp. Add this to the onions. Beat in crab, eggs, parsley, and salt and pepper to taste—it should be a mite peppery. Cook gently 5 more minutes, then remove the bay leaf and stuff the mixture into the eggplant shells.

Place them in a greased baking dish, sprinkle each with bread crumbs, a dusting of paprika, and dribbles of melted butter. Bake 10 minutes, or until the tops are slightly crisp and the eggplant halves are warmed through.

Serves 4.

I was served this dish at Galatoire's on my first trip to New Orleans—my eye as usual scanning a menu for something I'd never heard of before. Useless years were spent thereafter attempting to reproduce its singular flavor and texture, both vying in subtleties. When research for this book turned it up, I was delighted to find no whit of remembrance was better than what I had before me. It needs little accompaniment but white wine and fine bread.

FAIRMONT HOTEL CRAB MUSTARD RING

1	envelope unflavored gelatin		Salt and freshly ground
¼	cup cold water		pepper
1	cup boiling water		Paprika
1	cup white wine vinegar	1	cup heavy cream, whipped
¼	cup sugar	1	pound cooked crabmeat
2½	tablespoons dry mustard		Cracked crab claws
1	teaspoon butter		Inner leafy celery stalks
4	eggs, whipped to a froth		

Sprinkle the gelatin over the cold water, stir in, and let sit till it softens. Add the boiling water and stir till dissolved.

In the top of a double boiler, mix the vinegar, sugar, mustard, butter, eggs, salt and pepper to taste, and a pinch of good paprika. Cook over simmering water, stirring with a whisk, until the mixture begins to coat the whisk. Remove from the heat, stir in the gelatin, and put in a bowl. Set in refrigerator until thick and syrupy (about an hour).

Whip the cream and fold it into the gelatin mixture, then ladle into a greased ring mold. Chill in the refrigerator till set.

To serve, unmold on a good platter, place the crabmeat inside the ring, and decorate the outer rim with crab claws and celery stalks.

Serves 6 to 8 as a first course.

The native habit of drowning delicate crab or shrimp in a "cocktail sauce" made of catsup, horseradish, Tabasco, and lemon makes me think we are not after all too far from barbarism at the table. The delicacy of fresh shellfish needs—if indeed anything at all beyond a squeeze of lemon—similarly delicate support. In the best tradition of San Francisco dining, this light sweet-sour gelatin with an aftertang of mustard makes the best of a very fine thing, in an admirable presentation for company. For a first course, it should be proudly brought to table and served on plates there, or, pretty as it is, it may form the center of a party buffet.

CAPITOL HILL
SOFT-SHELLED CRAB SANDWICH

1	soft-shelled crab, cleaned	2	slices good white bread
2	tablespoons butter		Tartar Sauce (page 292)
2	tablespoons vegetable oil		Lemon wedges
	Salt and freshly ground pepper		

*W*herever you buy soft shelled crabs will most likely also clean them for you, but if not, this is the way to do it. First you freeze the crab 5 minutes or so, to numb it, and proceed more or less as you clean cooked hard-shelled crab. You peel back the triangular "apron" on the underside, then scrape out the stomach and intestines that lie beneath it. Then you scrape out the spongy lungs under the points of the shell, snip off the head of the crab behind the eyes, and finally squeeze the body so the sand sac pops out of the head opening. Wash it well with water, and pat dry with a towel.

Sauté the crab in butter and oil over medium heat until it is golden on both sides—about 3 to 4 minutes. Salt and pepper it in the pan as it cooks, and lift out onto paper towels.

Serve between two slices of bread that have been spread with tartar sauce, with lemon wedges to squeeze on as you eat.

Serves 1 (may be adapted to any number).

There used to be a restaurant in Washington, D.C., that not only had the advantage of a deck looking out over the water but served these sandwiches— surely one of the best meals in the world, served with frosty ale and crisp slab fries. Soft-shelled crab is only available on our Eastern shores, and that seasonally (when the crab molts its shell). They should make it a national monument.

SOFT-SHELLED CRABS WITH ALMONDS

2   cloves garlic, flattened and
    peeled
½   cup butter
4   slices white bread, trimmed
    to rounds
4   medium cleaned soft-shelled
    crabs (or 8 small ones)

Salt and freshly ground
    pepper
½   cup slivered blanched
    almonds, toasted
Watercress

*I*n a large skillet, sauté the garlic in half the butter until it starts to get crisp and golden. Remove the garlic and sauté the bread rounds in the butter. The heat should be an even medium-high. When the bread rounds are crisp on both sides, place them on paper towels and keep warm.

Sprinkle the crabs with salt and pepper, add the rest of the butter to a skillet (if you use the same one, wipe it out first), and cook them 3 minutes a side, or till golden. Add the almonds during the last minutes and toss with the crabs.

Lift out onto the croutons placed on a warm plate, sprinkle the almonds over, and garnish with watercress sprigs.

Serves 4 as a first course.

Simple and superb. Everything is crunchy in a different way.

LOBSTER NEWBERG

3   tablespoons sweet butter
2   cups cooked lobster meat,
    cut in thick slices
2   tablespoons flour
1½ cups heavy cream
4   egg yolks

2   tablespoons dry sherry (or
    Madeira)
1   tablespoon Cognac
    Salt
    Cayenne (optional)
    Toast points

*M*elt 2 tablespoons of the butter in a saucepan and toss the lobster in it, heating gently but thoroughly. Keep warm in a chafing dish or heated serving dish.

In the same saucepan, melt the remaining tablespoon of butter, stir in flour, and cook several minutes. Add the cream, beaten with the egg yolks, and cook until thickened and smooth, stirring the while. Do not let it boil.

Add the sherry or Madeira, the Cognac, cayenne if you wish, and taste for salt. Let it all heat several minutes, then pour over lobster with a sprinkle perhaps more sherry or Madeira. (In a chafing dish carefully regulate the heat or the mixture will curdle). Serve hot over toast points.

Serves 4.

So seldom do I get lobster I always want it red and plain with drawn sweet butter, but this justly famous dish (which originated at Delmonico's via one Ben Wenberg, a sea captain with fastidious tastes in food) is both suave and rich, in a sauce that seems, rather than mask the lobster, to extend and gently amplify. The story goes that the Delmonico brothers had a falling out with Wenberg, but liked his sauce so much they retained it as "Newberg."

MAUM NANCY'S SCALLOPED OYSTERS

1	cup fresh bread crumbs		Salt and freshly ground
6	tablespoons butter, melted		pepper
¼	teaspoon freshly grated		Pinch of cayenne
	nutmeg	1	quart shucked oysters with
	Pinch of ground mace		½ cup liquor
¼	teaspoon ground cloves	¼	cup Madeira

*P*reheat the oven to 350°F.

Take a small frying pan and sauté the crumbs with 2 tablespoons of the butter. Toss over medium heat until they are golden. Remove from the fire and mix in all the spices.

Grease the bottom and sides of a smallish casserole or soufflé dish with some of the butter, and sprinkle the bottom and sides with some of the sautéed crumbs.

Make 2 layers of oysters, some oyster juice, some buttered crumbs, some butter, and Madeira, ending with crumbs and a good dribble of butter on the top. Bake for 45 minutes, or until it is starting to bubble. Serve immediately.

Serves 4.

Every cookbook has its oyster scallop, but this is one apart. It has been adapted from Charleston Receipts, *a Junior League cookbook (as so many of our best native ones are) to be obtained by inquiry to P.O. Box 177, Charleston, SC, 29402. It was first pointed out to me by a friend who had lived there, insisting it was quite simply one of the best cookbooks ever written or compiled on the culinary arts of the Southern black cook. At the same time it holds the pick of specialties from Charleston's considerably shiny and gracious tables, food that has been served to admiring guests unchanged since antebellum days.*

OYSTER PAN ROAST WITH COLE SLAW

1	quart shucked oysters	¼	cup milk
	Flour	½	cup butter (or deep hot fat)
	Ground mace		Lemon wedges
	Fresh bread crumbs		Cole slaw
2	eggs		

*D*rain the oysters. Put flour mixed with mace and the bread crumbs on separate pieces of waxed paper, and beat the eggs with milk in a bowl. Dip each oyster in flour, then egg, then into the bread crumbs to coat. Put them on waxed paper.

Fry either in butter or deep hot fat, only a minute or two each side, or till golden. Drain on paper towels and serve with lemon wedges and a crisp mound of cole slaw.

Serves 4.

Superior to the familiar Grand Central Pan Roast nostalgic to New Yorkers, this simple, traditional dish makes one of the best meals ever devised—and that includes ones of great restaurant hoopla. Serve with thin brown bread to be authentic. And not with wine, but good beer. (The slaw should be Grison's Steak House Slaw, page 275.)

WILLIAMSBURG OYSTERS UNDER GLASS

1½	cups stone-ground cornmeal	12	thin slices Canadian bacon
2	tablespoons flour		(or Virginia ham)
½	teaspoon baking soda	2	tablespoons vegetable oil (or
1	teaspoon salt		bacon fat)
2	eggs	1	pint shucked oysters with
1½	cups buttermilk		liquor
½	cup plus 2 tablespoons		Freshly ground pepper
	butter, melted		

Sift the dry ingredients together into a mixing bowl. Beat the eggs with buttermilk in another bowl, and add, with the 2 tablespoons melted butter, to the dry ingredients. Stir the batter until smooth.

Drop by spoonfuls onto a greased griddle to make twelve 3-inch pancakes. They should be cooked over medium heat, and turned when they begin to make bubbles on top. They need only a minute or so on each side to cook. Keep them warm on a plate in the oven while you prepare the ham and oysters.

Sauté Canadian bacon—or better yet good Virginia ham—in a little oil or bacon fat, until just lightly browned. Keep these warm with the pancakes.

Heat the oysters in a small saucepan with their own juices, until their edges just curl—don't try to overcook, they just need warming.

To assemble the dish, place the pancakes on a warm plate, lay a slice of Canadian bacon over each pancake, then arrange the oysters over the top. Sprinkle pepper over the top, and pour the ½ cup melted butter over. Serve immediately.

Serves 6 as a first course, 4 as a main dish.

A simple but indescribably sumptuous dish, deemed worthy of being served under a glass bell in Williamsburg. What doesn't show from the recipe is how delicate a foil these buttermilk cornmeal pancakes make to the thin cooked ham and plump oysters. No salt is needed, but I sometimes garnish the dish with lemon slices for those who might like a drop or so. Regular cornmeal is no substitute for stone-ground meal, here, but Canadian bacon is fine instead of the original expensive Virginia ham because a slice of it is exactly the size of the pancakes. Even without glass bells this dish makes an impressive beginning to an important meal—perhaps even for Christmas or Thanksgiving.

But I like it so well I don't wait for important dinners, for, with some crisp cole slaw, it makes a splendid quick supper or brunch for family.

OYSTER LOAF

1 loaf French bread (sweet or sourdough, preferably round)	Salt and freshly ground pepper
½ cup butter	Lemon juice
2 dozen shucked oysters	Minced parsley
	Tabasco (optional)

*P*reheat the oven to 375°F.

Slice the top third off your loaf and scoop out the center of both top and bottom, leaving a 1-inch crust all round. Slice the scooped-out portions thin, put on a baking sheet, and let dry out as the oven heats—enough to make bread crumbs.

Melt the butter and use half of it to coat the inside and top of the loaf generously. Put it in the oven and cook 10 minutes, or until the loaf is lightly toasted.

Meanwhile, make bread crumbs with a rolling pin, or in a blender or food processor. Drain the oysters and roll in the crumbs. Fry the oysters in the remaining butter (adding more if necessary) 4 to 5 minutes.

Layer the oysters in the toasted loaf, sprinkling with salt and pepper to taste, and with a few squeezes of lemon and sprinklings of parsley (and Tabasco if you like it). Put the top of the loaf back on, paint the outside of the loaf with a little more butter, put on a baking sheet, and cook 8 to 10 minutes. Bring to the table on a cutting board and slice in serving portions.

Serves 4 to 6.

In Consider the Oyster, M.F.K. Fisher tells of a memory of a memory of an oyster loaf—her mother's tale of "midnight feasts" at her 1890s boarding school, where a loaf was smuggled into the dormitory by a chambermaid: "I can see it, and smell it, and I even know which parts to bite and which to let melt against the roof of my mouth, exquisitely hot and comforting, although my mother surely never told me," she writes. It was such a one as this recipe, surely, for oyster loaves used to be served extensively around San Francisco, but the dish is only common now in New Orleans, where it is called La Médiatrice (or "the mediator"), since it was usually purchased, in small French rolls, to soothe a waiting wife after a carousal through the late saloons of the French Quarter.

It makes a good picnic dish still, if it is well wrapped so it keeps a modicum of warmth. And it really only wants a side dish of crisp cole slaw, with a flagon of beer or wine, to make a meal better almost than any memory of a memory. . . .

TONY'S HIGHWAY BARBECUE OYSTERS

Fresh oysters on the half shell	Lemon juice
Barbecue sauce	Minced parsley

*T*his recipe takes a charcoal smoker. Lay the number of oysters you please over coals, drop a small spoon of sauce over each, and top with a squeeze of lemon and some minced parsley. Cover the smoker and let cook 6 to 8 minutes, or until the oyster's edges begin to curl in the shell. Serve on paper plates.

Can be adapted to any number.

A wonder captured by observation from Tony's in Marshall, California, Highway 1. The rest of Tony's food is good but pedestrian, but on weekends he throws open his barbecue and they come from all around, through the oysters being opened on the front porch, some with picnic baskets of slaw and sandwiches of black bread and sweet butter, some just to sit out on the dock and eat a plate of Tony's inspired invention.

OYSTERS ROCKEFELLER

*N*o other American dish, it now comes to seem, has received so much praise and attention as this one invented in the 1850s by Jules Alciatore of Antoine's to replace snails Bourgignon. The original recipe (said to contain eighteen ingredients) has never left the restaurant, but has been so adapted and evolved in a host of ways that it has been called by Louis De Gouy a dish of "composite genius." M. De Gouy recounts that Alciatore exacted a promise on his deathbed that the exact proportions be kept forever a secret. He then goes on to relate as much as Alciatore told him: The sauce was compounded of green onions, celery, chervil, tarragon leaves and crumbs of stale bread pounded in a mortar with butter and Tabasco, with finally a dash of absinthe—no spinach (which is used in most versions), no proportions certainly, and definitely not eighteen ingredients.

One of the most elegant variations is reported by Alice B. Toklas, who served hers on silver sand rather than rock salt. She minced fourths of parsley and raw spinach with eighths of tarragon, chervil, basil, and chives. Topped with salt, pepper, bread crumbs and melted butter, this makes an extremely delicate version, though it omits the anise flavor usually associated with the dish. This is supplied by a Louisiana liquor called Herbsainte, or by Pernod, ground anise, or chopped fresh fennel.

Given so much leeway, I find it advisable to proceed as for snail butter and see what the garden and market provide. (Snail butter for about two dozen oysters is a mixture of ½ cup room-temperature butter, 2 tablespoons minced shallots or green onions, 2 to 3 minced cloves garlic, and 2 tablespoons minced parsley—and salt and pepper to taste.)

If fresh herbs are not available, then dried may do in combination with spinach, watercress leaves, parsley, green onion tops, and celery leaves. Tasting as you go, flavor with drops of lemon and Tabasco, then as much Pernod, etc., as it will take without tasting overtly of licorice. These can all be compounded easily in a blender or food processor, either with the bread crumbs, or with bread crumbs sprinkled later over the top. Serve 6 oysters per person laid on pans of rock salt, with sauce over their tops, and baked 4 to 5 minutes in a 450°F oven until hot and bubbly.

OYSTERS BIENVILLE

3	dozen oysters	1	cup minced mushrooms
2	cups minced green onions	3	egg yolks
	with part of tops	½	cup heavy cream
½	cup butter	½	cup dry vermouth
2½	tablespoons flour		Salt and freshly ground
2	cups chicken or fish stock,		pepper
	heated		Tabasco
1½	pounds cooked shrimp,	¼	cup bread crumbs
	shelled, deveined, and	¼	cup grated Parmesan cheese
	minced	⅛	teaspoon paprika

Shuck the oysters and reserve half the shells and all the liquor. Sauté green onions in butter until limp, then add flour and stir over a low flame until the mixture is golden brown. Add hot stock, shrimp, and mushrooms and simmer until the mixture begins to thicken. Set aside and allow to cool.

Beat the egg yolks with the cream and vermouth, then slowly pour the warm sauce into the egg mixture, stirring constantly to keep smooth. Add all the liquor from the oysters and season to taste with salt, pepper, and Tabasco. Preheat the oven to 375°F.

Return the sauce to a low fire and let simmer 10 to 15 minutes, stirring to keep smooth. When it has thickened, remove from the fire.

To cook the oysters, place a good layer of rock salt (ice cream salt) over 6 pie plates. Place 6 oysters, each on the half shell, in each pan, and bake for 10 minutes, or just until they curl around the edges. Remove from the oven, turning the temperature to 400°F; spoon the sauce over the oysters and sprinkle with combined bread crumbs, cheese, and paprika. Bake 7 to 8 minutes, or until bubbly.

Serves 6.

This is another specialty at Antoine's, and one for which the recipe is blessedly available—and I think even better than Rockefeller. One of the best places to test them, in New Orleans, is at Brennan's, which features a plate of two oysters Rockefeller, two oysters Bienville, and two oysters Roffignac: such are the delights of that mild city! Like all restaurant food, it requires a lot of advance footwork, but is easily got to table, and there should be served with fine bread and even finer white wine.

DELMONICO SCALLOPS

2 pounds scallops (preferably small bay scallops)	¼ cup bread crumbs
3 tablespoons lemon juice	2 tablespoons Parmesan cheese
1 tablespoon olive oil	3 tablespoons finely minced ham
1 teaspoon minced parsley	1 tablespoon minced chives
Salt and freshly ground pepper	Vegetable oil for deep frying
Cayenne	Tartar Sauce (page 292)
1 egg, slightly beaten	Lemon wedges

*M*arinate the scallops in lemon juice, olive oil, parsley, salt and pepper to taste, and a hint of cayenne for 30 minutes or more.

To cook, beat the egg in one bowl and combine the bread crumbs, cheese, ham, and chives in another. Drain the scallops, and dip first in egg and then into the bread crumb mixture. Fry in deep hot oil (at 385°F) till golden, then drain on absorbent paper.

Sprinkle with salt, and serve with tartar sauce and lemon wedges.

Serves 4 (or 6 as a first course).

The Delmonico family established the first luxurious restaurant in the country, and they set a standard that was to make New York a culinary center on a par with Paris. They popularized unknown vegetables such as endive and eggplant, they helped a heavily meat-eating populace discover salads (many of them invented for New World plants) and ices. Many of their dishes were simple in execution, as these scallops prove, with all the fanciness in the presentation. This dish, for instance, was garnished with hard-boiled egg quarters and slices of sautéed green tomato topped with a mushroom cap browned in butter. It all sounds fresh and lively (and even likely) for a dish a hundred years old.

TIDEWATER SCALLOPED SHRIMP

4	tablespoons butter	1	tablespoon Worcestershire sauce
1	medium onion, finely chopped	2	pounds cooked shrimp, shelled and deveined
½	pound mushrooms, sliced		Salt and freshly ground pepper
2	tablespoons flour		
½	cup heavy cream	1	teaspoon sweet paprika
¼	cup dry sherry	½	cup bread crumbs
1	tablespoon lemon juice		

*P*reheat the oven to 350°F.

Sauté the onion in 2 tablespoons of butter till it is limp, then add the mushrooms and cook until they begin to release their juices.

Sprinkle the flour over and cook over medium heat, stirring, for several minutes. Pour the cream in and stir until the sauce thickens. Add sherry, lemon juice, and Worcestershire, then cover the pan and let cook gently 10 minutes.

Add the shrimp and seasonings, and taste (I find this dish might use a bit more sherry or lemon depending on the quality of the shrimp).

To serve, divide the mixture into 6 individual shells or ramekins, sprinkle

with bread crumbs, and dot the other 2 tablespoons butter over the tops. Bake 20 minutes, or until browned and bubbly.
    Serves 4 (or 6 as a first course).

Shrimp is so plentiful and cheap along the Southern coast still that it is served from breakfast through lunch and dinner. Needless to say this makes a visitor's mind (and tastebuds) boggle, and the restless recipe-hunter's pen get poised for action. My tactic is to invade the kitchen and help shell the daily catch, for there you uncover the best-kept secrets. Either as a first course, or main dish accompanied by a green vegetable and hot rolls, this recipe is in the finest tradition of home cookery. It's even tasty enough, for those stuck inland, to survive the frozenest shrimp.

SHRIMP AND CORN PIE

5 to 6	ears corn	1½	teaspoons Worcestershire sauce
3	eggs, slightly beaten		Salt and freshly ground pepper
¾	cup heavy cream (or milk)		Pinch of ground mace
1½	cups cooked small shrimp, peeled and deveined	6	tablespoons butter, melted

*P*reheat oven to 325°F.
    Cut the corn from cobs with a sharp knife, then use the back of the knife blade to extract the "milk." You should have 3 cups kernels. Combine all the ingredients except 4 tablespoons of the butter.
    Use part of the reserved butter to grease a gratin dish or casserole large enough to hold the shrimp-corn mixture in about a 1½-inch layer. Pour the mixture into it, then dribble the rest of the butter over.
    Bake 30 to 40 minutes, or until the custard is set and the top has begun to take color.
    Serves 4.

What a lovely, easy, delectable casserole this dish from the Carolinas is—it's a recipe that has been passed down from colonial times, and when fresh corn is available it remains one of my favorite seafood dishes for family dinners. Serve it forth with Cream Dilly Bean Salad (page 270) and either Summer Cloud or Happy Valley Biscuits (page 322).

FRANCES PARKINSON KEYES'
CUCUMBER ASPIC WITH SHRIMP

1 medium cucumber, peeled, seeded, and cut in ¼-inch dice	1 teaspoon white wine tarragon vinegar
Salt	1 cup heavy cream
Juice of ½ lemon	1 pound cooked shrimp, peeled and deveined
2 teaspoons unflavored gelatin	½ cup oil and vinegar dressing
2 tablespoons cold water	Minced parsley
¼ cup milk, heated	Parsley sprigs
¼ cup chopped pimiento	

*P*ut the cucumber in a bowl of salted ice water for 10 minutes. Drain and add the lemon juice. Soak the gelatin in cold water, and when soft dissolve in the hot milk. Add this to the cucumber, along with the pimiento and vinegar.

Whip the cream and fold it in. Place it in a lightly oiled 4-cup decorative mold, or a ring mold, and chill for 12 hours.

An hour before serving, toss the shrimp in the oil and vinegar dressing with plenty of minced parsley. To serve, unmold the aspic on a good platter, place the shrimp around it, pour shrimp marinade over the top, and garnish with parsley sprigs.

Serve with black bread and butter.

Serves 6 to 8.

My mother donates this favorite dish. It is an easily prepared, but sumptuous, first course for a summer dinner. The whipped cream gives it a particularly light texture for a gelatin preparation—so much so that guests usually request the recipe. One warning—don't be tempted to save time by grating the cucumber, for that texture is not quite right for the dish. For less festive occasions, the shrimp may be omitted and the mixture put in individual molds and served on lettuce leaves as a simple salad.

PRAWNS MARIN

2	pounds good-sized shrimp	2 to 3	tablespoons cream sherry
4	tablespoons butter		A few drops Angostura
⅛	teaspoon curry powder		bitters (optional)
	Salt and freshly ground		
	pepper		

Cook the shrimp in water and whatever good things you have on hand (see Fish Stock in Methods & Ingredients Section). They will take 5 minutes. Drain, and peel and devein them when they are cool enough. Set aside till just before serving.

The dish may be prepared in a few minutes away from guests or in a chafing dish at table. Bring the butter to a sizzle over high flame and add the shrimp. Toss till they are coated with butter, then add the curry powder and salt and pepper to taste.

Add the sherry and let it bubble down to almost a syrup while still tossing—a matter of only a few minutes. Add a few drops of bitters if you like. Serve immediately on warm plates, with a full-bodied white wine and crusty fresh bread.

Serves 6 as a first course.

The unexpected sweetness of cream sherry is decisive for this invention of California chef Draper Morrow. It is a fine dish to serve as a first course when your main offering is a rich, complex one.

VIRGINIA SHRIMP PASTE

1½	pounds medium shrimp	1	teaspoon finely grated onion
½	cup butter at room	1	tablespoon dry sherry (or
	temperature		Madeira)
	Dash of ground mace		Salt and freshly ground
1	teaspoon Dijon mustard		pepper

Cook the shrimp in salted water 5 minutes. Let cool, then peel and devein them. Pound in a mortar, run through a grinder, or whirl in a food processor

until a paste. Mix thoroughly with the other ingredients and place in a bowl covered with plastic wrap—or in a pot with melted butter poured over the top to seal it. Refrigerate overnight.
Serves 4.

In most cookbooks—even M. F. K. Fisher includes in her With Bold Knife and Fork *an example or so—this would be given as a spread served with cocktails. In parts of the South, however, it is served in a pot alongside a chafing dish of cooked grits, as part of a buffet hunt club breakfast, along with many another collation. As the shrimp paste melts in tiny granules through the only slightly larger granules of the soft grits, you will resolve slowly to go out next day and purchase a package so this dish will always be available. I serve it with scrambled eggs, and crisp bacon, for breakfast, or with an exemplary white vintage, for itself alone, at supper.*

SHRIMP AND CHICKEN ETOUFFÉE

6	tablespoons butter		Salt and freshly ground
¼	cup flour		pepper
1	cup minced onion	¼	teaspoon cayenne
½	cup minced celery	1	teaspoon lemon juice
½	cup minced green pepper	1	cup chicken stock
⅓	cup minced green onion tops	1	pound shrimp, shelled and
3	cloves garlic, minced		deveined
2	tablespoons minced parsley		Hot cooked rice
3	half breasts of chicken		

*I*n a large heavy saucepan, melt the butter over low heat, then add the flour and, stirring the mixture, cook over very low heat for 15 to 20 minutes, or until the roux is golden brown. Add all the vegetables (a food processor is a quick and efficient tool to mince all the vegetables finely and evenly) and cook another 20 minutes gently, stirring now and again to make sure they are all glazed and tender.

During this process, bone and skin the chicken breasts and cut each half in three or four pieces. When the vegetables look done, add the chicken and toss for several minutes. Season with salt and pepper to taste, then add the cayenne and lemon juice.

Stir in the stock and let the mixture cook, uncovered, until thickened and smooth, then cover the pan and cook gently 15 minutes. Add the shrimp and cook another 5 minutes. Taste for seasoning, and if necessary add water to make the sauce the consistency of a thick soup.

It is best to make the etouffée well ahead and let it sit at least an hour before serving, to gather flavor. To serve, reheat gently and spoon over hot cooked rice.

Serves 4.

The bliss of an etouffée in situ, made from Louisiana crawfish, is one of our finest culinary triumphs. Unfortunately the rest of us are unable to get crawfish, so I have poked around and found this fine example from a Biloxi, Mississippi kitchen. Etouffée means "stuffed" in French—here it refers to the blanket of vegetables cooked with the meats. It is very easily made (for an explanation of the Louisiana roux see under Ideal Gumbo, page 32), and is a splendid dish to double or treble for larger groups. Serve it with white wine and good French bread, with perhaps a salad course, then a handsome dessert.

MEATS &
FOWL

I lost the head of my first bull because I forgot to tell Mrs. Culbertson that I wished to save it, and the princess had its skull broken open to enjoy its brains. Handsome, and really courteous and refined in many ways, I cannot reconcile to myself the fact that she partakes of raw animal food with such evident relish.

—John James Audubon, Journals

Beef

When tender, hung grain-fed beef is available, it should be served simply as possible, without fuss of sauce or truffle. My family lived for a time in a small town in Missouri that had a plant known locally as "the a-bay-tor" (a Plains derivation from the French *abattoir,* a place to slaughter cattle). They had locally aged meats very few restaurants ever even get a whiff of, and restaurants get the cream of the finest Midwest crop. Most of the rest of us must make do with our friendly butcher for advice—if we have one at all—and even from him, more often lower grades and cuts that need long slow processes to gather flavor and ensure tenderness.

ROAST RIB OF BEEF WITH YORKSHIRE
PUDDING AND HORSERADISH ICE CREAM

Early in the day prepare Horseradish Ice Cream:

¼ cup grated fresh horseradish	Salt
½ cup orange juice	1 cup heavy cream

*S*tir the orange juice and a pinch of salt into the grated horseradish in a bowl. Whip the cream stiff, and fold into the horseradish. Freeze in a refrigerator ice tray. Meanwhile, prepare the roast:

1 standing 4- to 5-rib beef roast	1 cup water (or beef stock)
Freshly ground pepper	Salt
	Cold butter

Remove the roast from the refrigerator 1 to 2 hours before cooking. When it has reached room temperature, preheat the oven to 325°F.

Dry the meat with a paper towel and rub freshly ground pepper all over. Do not salt, as this has a tendency to toughen meat and draw out juices (anyway, good beef is tasty enough to need little salt).

Insert a meat thermometer in the thickest part of the roast—it should not touch the bone. Place the meat, fat side up, on a rack in a roasting pan. Cook without basting till the thermometer registers 130°F for rare, 140°F for medium-rare, 150°F for medium, or 160°F for well done. At this oven temperature you can caculate on timing your roast at about 20 minutes per pound. (Anyone who can afford rib roast these days can also afford a meat thermometer. It is the only way to ensure perfect meats, since oven temperatures vary more widely than one would think.)

Remove the meat from the oven, and immediately turn up the heat to 450°F. Let the meat stand while you cook your pudding—it will be a better texture for it. Pour off fat from the roasting pan, rescuing 3 tablespoons of it for Yorkshire Pudding:

2 eggs	½ teaspoon salt
1 cup milk	3 tablespoons beef drippings
1 cup flour	

Beat the eggs with the milk. Sift the flour with the salt, then combine with the egg-milk mixture. Beat until well blended. Add the beef drippings to a rather high-sided 8- or 9-inch baking pan, and put the pan in the oven to heat. When the temperature reaches 450°F, remove the pan and pour the pudding mixture in. Bake 10 minutes at 450°F, then reduce the heat to 350°F and bake another 15 to 20 minutes, or until the pudding is puffed way up and browned.

While the pudding cooks, add a cup of water—or stock—to the roasting pan, and over direct heat stir and scrape all its crustinesses together. Add salt to taste, and at the end add a nut of cold butter. Stir this in to smooth and slightly thicken the sauce.

To serve, slice the beef onto warm plates. Scoop the horseradish ice cream into individual small cups and place beside each serving of beef. From a side plate serve wedges of Yorkshire pudding. Put the sauce in a sauceboat to pass at table.

Servings: The cream and the pudding are for 4, and they may be easily doubled. For the roast, count on 1 rib per serving.

As beef grows more and more expensive, this kind of recipe is something most of us need only for special feasts—New Year's Day, or even Christmas when a turkey is too large for a small family. So when it is done at all, it should be with all the trimmings. Yorkshire pudding is traditional, and always welcome, and the horseradish ice cream makes an unusual condiment to perk up the whole affair. Needless to say, it should be accompanied with a splendid red wine.

LADYBIRD'S FILLET OF BEEF

1   whole fillet of beef   Fresh kumquats
    Bacon (about ¾ pound)   Parsley sprigs
    Broiled or sautéed mushroom
      caps

*P*reheat the oven to 400°F.

Remove the fat from the fillet and wrap it entirely in bacon strips. Place in a roasting pan and cook for 20 minutes at 400°F, or until a meat thermometer reads 120°F (for rare meat) in the thickest part of the meat—that way some pieces will be rarer than others to the taste of the guests. Remove from the oven and place under a broiler until the bacon is crisp on both sides.

Cut carefully into 1-inch slices and reassemble as if whole. Garnish the platter

with hot mushrooms and cold kumquats in equal proportions, then lay parsley sprigs down the center of the meat.
Serves 10 to 12.

The former first lady's recipe is a kind of paradigm of American cookery: no fancy sauces, no marinade of wine, no blazing of brandy, just best-quality ingredients combined in an attractive and contrasting manner. The kumquats are an unexpected relish to the meat, while mushrooms give it substance and added flavor. It is also graceful for company, for, as Mrs. Johnson assures us, it may be kept warm wrapped in a heavy towel, and put under a broiler to warm just before serving.

SIRLOIN CLEMENCEAU

4	medium potatoes, peeled and cut in ½" dice	8	mushrooms, sliced
	Vegetable oil	2	cloves garlic, minced
2	sirloin steaks, cut at least 1" thick	1	cup tiny peas, cooked
½	cup butter		Salt and freshly ground pepper
			Minced parsley

Cook potatoes in hot vegetable oil as in American Fries (page 253). Remove with a slotted spoon to paper toweling and keep warm.

Start the steak to grill in your favorite manner, while in a saucepan you sauté mushrooms with garlic in butter for 5 minutes. Add the peas and heat another minute.

To assemble the dish, cut each steak into two equal portions and place on warm plates. Toss the potatoes with mushrooms and peas, then with salt and pepper to taste; toss again with parsley. Bring to a quick heat and pour equally over the steaks.
Serves 4.

A hearty way to prepare an epicurean steak and potatoes, in not more than 20 minutes. Clemenceau is a staple New Orleans restaurant dish, equally adapted to serving over sautéed chicken rather than steak, and for that matter I see no reason not to treat hamburger with this unusual saucing. It is constructed around Brabant potatoes, with the addition of peas (in New Orleans they used canned petits pois, but certainly frozen or fresh peas may accomplish the thing as well). They also use an incredible amount of butter, which I have halved here.
Most restaurant dishes are assembled from ingredients prepared in advance,

and this is no exception, for the potatoes may be prepared ahead and kept warm in an oven, then assembled while the steak is prepared. A fine dinner would be to prepare some such soup as *Winter Tarragon Tomato* (page 12), and then serve the sirloin accompanied only by a bottle of red wine, a green salad to follow, and finally a simple easily prepared dessert, like *Roanoke Rum Cream* (page 384) or *Strawberries in Strawberry Sauce* (page 392).

MARYLAND POT ROAST MADEIRA

3	tablespoons olive oil	2	whole cloves
3	pounds rump roast (or other boneless cut)	2	bay leaves
		1½	teaspoons good wine vinegar
1	large onion, chopped		Salt
2	cloves garlic, minced	1	tablespoon (¼ square) grated bitter chocolate
1	tablespoon flour		
½	cup white wine	1	tablespoon dry Madeira
2	cups water		Parsley sprigs
6	peppercorns		Orange slices

*H*eat the oil in a casserole the meat fits well into, and brown the roast thoroughly on all sides. Remove the meat, add the onion and garlic, and stir them until limp over low heat. Sprinkle the flour over the onion and cook, stirring, until the flour begins to stick to the bottom of the pan—a matter of about 5 minutes.

Add the wine and water, stir till the whole has begun to thicken, then place the meat back in the casserole. Tie the spices in a small bag and add with the vinegar. Cover tightly (with foil as well as a lid) and simmer very gently over lowest flame for 3 hours.

Halfway though cooking, remove the lid, turn the roast, and add salt to taste (remember, the sauce will be reduced later, so salt sparingly). When the meat is quite soft, wrap in foil and keep in a warm oven until ready to serve. It can be left in the oven, in this manner, for several hours if need be.

To make the sauce, skim off the fat from the top of the juices, remove the spice bag, and boil down over high heat until reduced by half. Place in a blender, and going from low to high speed, smooth out the sauce. The onions should thicken it slightly.

Return the sauce to the pan and stir in the chocolate over a low flame until it is dissolved. Add the Madeira and stir until silky. The chocolate will thicken the sauce—it should have the consistency of cream. Taste for seasoning and let heat several minutes before serving over slices of the pot roast. It looks very nice indeed served with a sprig of parsley and a bright slice of orange. Serves 6.

This old-time Maryland dish is one of our great regional specialties. It does only good to marinate the meat overnight in a slosh of wine if you have some on hand. The chocolate in its sauce yields a subtly dark savor usually associated with complex French reductions, and if you leave the meat in the oven as suggested, in foil, it assumes unheard-of tenderness. For the best of all possible worlds, serve it with Georgia Spoonbread (page 319) and a sound California red vintage.

SAVOY PLAZA POT ROAST

2 pounds boneless chuck, round, etc.	1 cup dry red wine
Flour	½ cup beef stock
2 tablespoons vegetable oil	4 medium potatoes, peeled and quartered
2 medium onions, sliced	Juice of ½ lemon
1 clove garlic, minced	Minced parsley
Salt and freshly ground pepper	

*C*ut the meat into 2-inch chunks and shake with enough flour to coat. Put a heavy casserole or Dutch oven over a high flame and put the oil in. When it is near smoking, sear the meat until all sides are brown and crusty—this should be done in batches, or the meat won't brown properly.

Turn the heat down to medium and add the onions and garlic. Stir them into the meat, and cook until the onion softens. Add wine, stock, and salt and pepper to taste. Cover, and simmer very gently for 2 hours. Add the potatoes, and cook another 15 to 20 minutes, till they are done.

Stir in the lemon juice just before serving, and taste for seasoning. Sprinkle well with minced parsley. Serves 4.

Savoy Plaza's is one of the nicest variations on the theme of pot roast I know— although it really is more a sort of stew—its secret being perhaps the final squeeze of lemon. It would certainly make the reputation of any lesser restaurant, it is easily adjustable to any size family, and will be a family favorite to be cooked again and again. All in all, I would walk across town to eat it.

HOME BEEF BARBECUE

3 pounds rump roast (or other boneless cut)	1 clove garlic, minced
2 tablespoons vegetable oil	1 cup beer
1 onion, chopped	2 bay leaves
	1 cup Barbecue Sauce (page 294)

*D*ry the meat thoroughly. Place the oil in a Dutch oven and brown the meat well over a high flame. Turn the heat down, add the onion and garlic, and cook till they are limp. Then add the beer and bay leaves. Cover the Dutch oven with foil, as well as the lid, and place over very low heat. Cook gently for 3 hours, turning in the liquid several times as it cooks.

Preheat the oven to 375°F.

When done, remove the roast to another pan and glaze it with half the barbecue sauce in the oven for 15 to 20 minutes.

While it glazes, reduce the cooking liquid in the Dutch oven till it begins to thicken, then add the rest of the barbecue sauce. To serve, slice the meat and spoon some of the sauce over each portion.

Serves 6.

If not the authentic hickory-smoked barbecue, which takes all night over a glowing pit, this yet makes a very decent home substitute. It can be served with any of the traditional accompaniments, such as slaw and cornbread, but I like it best as my mother used to serve a similar dish: hot between slices of rye bread, with crisp sweet onion rings, and cold beer.

NEW ENGLAND
BOILED DINNER THREE WAYS

5 pounds corned beef (brisket)	8 carrots, trimmed and scraped
1 bay leaf	4 medium onions
6 peppercorns	4 parsnips, trimmed and scraped (optional)
1 clove garlic	
4 medium potatoes, peeled	1 small head cabbage, cut in quarters
4 turnips, peeled	

*P*lace the meat in a large kettle. Cover with water, then add the bay leaf and peppercorns. Bring to a boil and skim. When the liquid is clear, turn down the heat very low, cover the kettle, and barely simmer for 3 hours.

Add the vegetables, except for the cabbage, to the kettle; simmer 20 minutes. Remove the corned beef and keep warm. Add the cabbage to the kettle and cook about 10 minutes longer. Drain (saving the broth) and serve the sliced meat and vegetables decoratively on a warm platter. (Sometimes beets cooked separately are served as well for added color.) Accompany with horseradish and mustard pickle, along with a pitcher of the broth. Serve with a good dark beer.

Serves 4 (with enough left to make hash).

This is the American pot au feu. Although it is to be found in almost any cookbook—indeed it hardly needs a recipe—I have included it here because it may be used to concoct two more excellent thrifty meals for four people, and nothing wasted. One of these is Corned Beef Hash with Eggs, and the other a hearty soup (recipes for both follow). Although it is thought that the stock from corned beef is too salty for soup stock, and is always thus discarded after, here it comes into its own.

CORNED BEEF HASH WITH EGGS

2 to 3	medium potatoes	2	tablespoons melted butter
2	cups minced corned beef		Salt and freshly ground
½	cup minced green onions with part of tops		pepper
			Paprika
1	tablespoon butter	4	eggs
2	tablespoons minced parsley		Parsley or watercress sprigs
			Broth to cover
⅓	cup heavy cream		

*B*oil the potatoes (with skins on) in the corned beef broth until they are tender. Remove, let dry till you can handle them, then skin and crumble into the minced corned beef. (A richer hash may be made by adding any of the vegetables left over from a boiled dinner—about 1½ cups will be sufficient.)

Preheat the oven to 450°F.

Melt 1 tablespoon butter in a skillet and sauté the green onions and parsley until the onions are softened. Add potato-meat mixture, cream, salt and pepper to taste, and a dash of paprika. Toss all together.

Pour half the melted butter in a pie plate, pack in the corned beef mixture, and dribble the rest of the butter on top. Bake at 450°F for 15 minutes, then remove from the oven, turning the oven down to 350°F. Make 4 indentations in the top of the hash with a large spoon or custard cup, and break an egg into each. Salt and pepper, then bake 15 to 20 minutes, or until the eggs are set. Remove from the oven, slice in 4 wedges, and serve garnished with parsley or watercress.

Serves 4.

WINTER SOUP

4 cups stock from a New England Boiled Dinner (see preceding recipe)
2 cups peeled and cubed (¼ inch) potatoes
½ small cabbage, cored and chopped
½ cup minced green onions with part of tops

1 tablespoon butter
1 tablespoon flour
½ cup cream
Tabasco
Salt and freshly ground pepper
½ cup sour cream
Caraway seeds

*T*aste the stock—some corned beef is more salty than others, and if the stock seems excessively salty cut it with some water or chicken stock. Put it in a kettle and bring to a boil. Add the potatoes and cabbage, then lower the heat and let simmer.

Sauté the green onions in butter till limp, then add the flour and cook slowly for 5 minutes. Add some of the hot stock and cook, stirring, until the mixture thickens. Pour this into the soup, stir until smooth, and let simmer 30 minutes, or until the potatoes are beginning to crumble and the cabbage is very tender.

Add cream, a few drops of Tabasco, and taste for seasoning—you may need a very little salt, or wish some pepper. Place in soup plates and float a dollop of sour cream mixed with caraway seeds on each. Serve with rye bread, beer, and a good salad.

Serves 4.

THOMAS JEFFERSON'S RAGOÛT OF BEEF

2	pounds boneless beef round, cut in 1-inch cubes	8	peppercorns
	Vegetable oil	3	whole cloves
½	pound ham, cut in ¼-inch dice	4	stalks celery, cut slantwise in ½-inch pieces
2	tablespoons butter	1	teaspoon butter
2	cups dry white wine	1	teaspoon flour
¼	teaspoon freshly grated nutmeg		Minced parsley

Dry the beef with paper towels. Film the bottom of a dutch oven with oil and put it over high heat. Brown the meat in batches, lifting the cubes out with a slotted spoon when brown on all sides. When all are done, tip out any fat in the pot and put in the ham and butter. Lower the heat to medium and toss several minutes, then add the beef, wine, and all the spices.

Cover the pot, lower the heat, and let simmer 1½ hours—or until the beef is tender. Add the celery and cook, uncovered, 10 to 12 minutes—the celery should still be a mite crunchy. Rub about a teaspoon of butter and a teaspoon of flour together until all the flour is absorbed. Thicken the sauce with little pieces of this—stirring after each addition. Use only enough to make a lightly thickened sauce.

Serve sprinkled with parsley, with buttered noodles, mashed potatoes, or even spoonbread.

Serves 4.

One of Thomas Jefferson's favorite dishes, this is a distinguished stew flavored with ham and spices rather than the usual garlic-onion-bay leaf, etc. It is a little heavy on the nutmeg, so I've cut it down, and you might want to even a little more. It has no salt because of the ham—Jefferson had the best Virginia hams at hand at Monticello—so you will want to taste it if you use ordinary market ham.

COLONIAL BEEF STEAK PUDDING

2 tablespoons vegetable oil
1 pound boneless beef, cut into
   bite-sized pieces
1 onion, chopped
1 cup plus 1 tablespoon flour
1 cup beef stock, heated
2 tablespoons tomato paste
½ teaspoon Worcestershire sauce

Salt and freshly ground
   pepper
⅔ cup sliced mushrooms
2 tablespoons mixed butter and
   vegetable oil (or beef
   drippings)
2 eggs
1 cup milk

*P*ut the oil in a medium saucepan set over high heat. Brown the steak in batches, then return all the pieces to the pan. Add the onion and cook over medium heat until limp. Add 1 tablespoon flour and cook a few minutes longer, stirring well. Add hot stock, tomato paste, Worcestershire, salt and pepper to taste, and the mushrooms. Cook gently, uncovered, 1½ hours, or until the steak is tender. When it is done, all of the liquid should be absorbed—if it tends to dry out either add some more stock or cover the pan.

To prepare the pudding, preheat the oven to 450°F. Put the butter and oil (or, better, beef drippings if you have any) in a 1½-quart casserole (with at least 2-inch sides so the pudding can puff up) and put the casserole in to heat.

In a bowl, whisk the eggs with milk, then sift the 1 cup flour and ½ teaspoon salt over, and beat the batter until smooth and bubbly. When the fat in the casserole starts sizzling, pour in the batter. Drop the steak mixture by spoonfuls on the top, and place immediately in the hot oven. Bake 15 to 20 minutes, or until the pudding is puffed and brown.

Serves 4.

Another variation on Yorkshire pudding invented by our ancestors. (The British to this day make a similar dish by dropping sausages in the batter and calling it Toad-in-the-Hole.) It seems a trusty dish to bring back for family suppers—it's easily prepared, fairly economical, and best of all, crusty and savory. It doesn't need much but a vegetable or salad to accompany it, and perhaps a sturdy red wine.

MASSACHUSETTS
BRAISED SHORT RIBS AND CELERY

2	pounds beef short ribs, cut in 3-inch lengths	2	carrots, trimmed and sliced
	Flour	¼	cup minced parsley
	Vegetable oil		Salt and freshly ground pepper
1	small bunch celery	1	cup red wine
1	cup chopped onion	¼	cup tomato paste
2	cloves garlic, minced		Beef stock

Shake the ribs with flour. Film the bottom of a stew pot with oil and brown the ribs thoroughly on all sides over medium-high heat. While they brown, prepare the vegetables.

Separate the celery stalks, remove tops and leaves, and pare away the tough ribbing on the outer stalks. Cut in 3-inch lengths, and mince enough celery leaves and tops to measure 1 cup—save the rest for soups or salads, etc. Prepare all the other vegetables.

When meat is well browned, remove from the pot and tip out most of the accumulated fat. Sauté celery tops, onion, garlic, carrots, and parsley till soft over low heat, then return the meat to the pot. Season with salt and pepper to taste, then add the wine. Let it boil up and cook 5 minutes or so, then add the tomato paste and enough stock to cover the meat.

Cover the pan and cook at a bare simmer on top of the stove for 3 hours— or until meat is nearly falling off the bones. Add the celery stalks and cook another 30 minutes. Skim off most of the fat, arrange the ribs and celery on warm plates and pour some of the strained braising liquid over them.

Serves 4.

A melting pot recipe, I suppose, as I got it from the kitchen of a great Greek lady in Lowell, Massachusetts, as I stood and watched. It didn't seem particularly Greek until she served it later with a huge dish of large macaroni moistened with the sauce and sprinkled with grated Parmesan. It could be made with any cut of beef, really, that is economical—the real secret I learned that day was how good all that celery was in a stew.

BRAISED OXTAILS WITH MUSHROOMS

3	pounds oxtails, cut up at joints	3	tablespoons finely chopped parsley
3	tablespoons vegetable oil	3	tablespoons tomato paste
1	cup finely chopped onion	1	cup red wine
2	cloves garlic, minced	2	cups beef or chicken stock
1	cup finely chopped carrots		Salt and freshly ground
1	cup finely chopped celery		pepper
16	mushrooms, caps separated from stems and stems finely chopped	2	tablespoons butter
		3	tablespoons Madeira

*I*n a Dutch oven or heavy casserole, sear the oxtails in 2 tablespoons of the oil till brown all over. Turn the heat down to medium, add the onion and garlic, and toss till the onion softens. Add the carrots, celery, mushroom stems, and parsley. Cook a few more minutes, tossing.

Stir in the tomato paste and the wine, and let the wine cook, uncovered, at a full boil down to half. Add stock and salt and pepper to taste, then cover the Dutch oven and let simmer 4 hours or more—the meat should be near to falling off the bones. (A pressure cooker is a great help in cooking oxtails, as it's almost impossible to overcook them. If you do so, it will take about 2½ hours.)

If possible, cook the meat early in the day, then refrigerate to harden the fat so it can all be lifted out. If not, soak up as much of the fat as possible and lift the oxtails out onto a plate.

Put the pan juices and vegetables in a blender or food processor and whirl until smooth. Put this, with the oxtails, back in the Dutch oven and bring to a rolling boil. Cook down till it is slightly thickened.

Meanwhile, sauté the mushroom caps in the butter and remaining 1 tablespoon oil in a roomy skillet. Cook these only 4 to 5 minutes, or until they start to exude juices, then add them to the oxtails. Add the Madeira and cook 10 minutes longer.

This dish seems to only gain on reheating, so it may be completely prepared ahead and simply reheated when dinner is to be got together. Serves 4.

Mushrooms seem a particularly good partner for the rich glutinous meat of the oxtail. The recipe also makes lots of dark sauce, so you will need some-

thing to put it on. Try Georgia Spoonbread (page 319) or just plain fluffy mashed potatoes.

JOE'S SPECIAL

1 cup chopped onion	1 teaspoon dried basil
1 clove garlic, minced	Salt and freshly ground
3 tablespoons olive oil	pepper
1 pound fresh spinach (or 1	Freshly grated nutmeg
package frozen)	1 pound ground beef
1 zucchini, grated (optional)	4 eggs, beaten
2 tablespoons chopped parsley	Grated Parmesan cheese

*I*n a saucepan, sauté the onion and garlic in olive oil until the onion is transparent. Put the spinach to boil in a little water. Cook only a few minutes, then run cold water over it and drain well.

When the onion is done, add zucchini, parsley, and basil and cook a few minutes longer—the zucchini should still be slightly crisp. Remove this from the fire.

Squeeze all the water you can from spinach with your hands, then mince it fine. Add the spinach to the onion-zucchini mixture and season to taste with salt, pepper, and nutmeg.

In a large frying pan, cook the ground beef over medium heat until it begins to brown. If it is of high fat content, drain it on paper toweling, then return it to the frying pan, add the onion-zucchini mixture, and toss over medium heat until thoroughly mixed.

Add about three fourths of the beaten eggs, and turn and lift until the eggs are cooked. Add the rest of the eggs, and toss for a few minutes longer. Serve on warm plates with Parmesan cheese sprinkled over, and, if possible, with plenty of crusty sourdough bread.

Serves 4 to 6.

Joe's Special, with all its Italian overtones, has long been a favorite of San Franciscans, particularly as a late supper after theater, where one could sit at the counter of Original Joe's and watch it being made to order. Children particularly seem to like it (even with all that spinach), and it makes a quick, easy, satisfying family supper dish any time. It's best made with fresh spinach, but frozen does almost as well, and if San Francisco sourdough is not on hand you'll have to make do with whatever French bread you can get.

ALFRED LUNT'S MEAT LOAF

1	pound lean ground chuck	1	tablespoon butter
	Salt and freshly ground	1	cup coarsely grated zucchini
	pepper	⅔	cup sour cream
⅓	cup rice	¼	cup chicken stock
1	cup boiling salted water		Paprika
½	cup chopped onion		Minced parsley

*L*ine bottom and sides of a pie plate with the meat, salt and pepper it, and leave aside while you prepare the filling.

Preheat the oven to 375°F.

To do this, heat 1 cup water to boiling, add salt, and cook the rice in it 20 minutes. Drain the rice and place in a bowl. Sauté the onion in the butter till limp and add to the rice. Stir in the zucchini and sour cream, and season lightly with salt and pepper.

Pour into the meat shell, pour the stock over the pie—loosening its sides to let the stock run down around the meat—and carefully place in the oven. Bake 40 to 45 minutes, or until the meat is done and the center is puffed and starting to turn straw colored.

To serve, sprinkle with paprika and parsley and cut into pie-shaped wedges. Serves 4.

This recipe is a tour de force of humble ingredients invented by the late actor Alfred Lunt, who seems to have been as creative in the kitchen as he was on stage. It is said that, when he and his wife Lynn Fontanne were on tour, they grew so tired of restaurant cooking Lunt would go shopping early in the day, then drop in on friends after the performance to use the kitchen.

SMOKED OYSTER BURGERS

1½	pounds best-quality ground		Freshly ground pepper
	beef	16	smoked cocktail oysters
1	tablespoon grated onion		Grated peel of 1 lemon
1	tablespoon heavy cream	4	slices bacon

*M*ix the beef with the onion, cream, and pepper to taste. Divide into 8 equal balls and flatten them to about 3-inch rounds. Place 4 oysters on 4 of the rounds, sprinkle grated lemon equally over them, then top with the remaining 4 rounds.

Pinch the edges together and ring each patty with a slice of bacon, securing with a toothpick. Broil over hot coals or under the oven broiler until they are to your taste. Remove the toothpicks and serve, with or without buns.

Serves 4.

The only true way to construct a hamburger is with the best possible local breads and condiments, but this little fantasia on the theme is good as it sounds, just as is. The first time I had one I couldn't quite believe my tongue. They are good served with My Mashed Potato Salad (page 281), or with New Potato Salad (page 280) and probably fine local beer rather than wine.

Veal

"Veal", Elizabeth David writes in her *French Provincial Cooking*, "is a meat which makes a good background for quite a variety of flavorings and sauces." That background, these days, both elusive and expensive, though we still have an unexpected foreground of recipes from former homestead slaughter. These range from sauces of Midwestern green tomatoes or Northeastern sand plums, to the Southern method of throwing in a handful of chestnuts and the Pennsylvania Dutch remembering Old World paprika and sour cream. The Shakers and the Creoles also chime in with their distinctive notes.

VEAL STEAKS
WITH GREEN TOMATO SAUCE

4	veal steaks, cut ¾ inch thick (or 8 veal chops)		6 to 8	green tomatoes
	Flour			Freshly grated nutmeg
	Salt and freshly ground pepper			Pinch of ground ginger
				Pinch of dried thyme
4	tablespoons butter		½	cup beef or chicken stock
2	slices onion, punched in rings		⅔	cup heavy cream

Shake the veal in lightly salted and peppered flour. Bring the butter to a sizzle in a frying pan large enough to hold all the meat in one layer, then put the meat in and sauté over medium heat for 5 minutes a side—or until golden. Remove the meat to a plate and add the onion to the pan. Sauté several minutes until the onion is limp, then place the meat over the onion.

Drop the tomatoes in a pot of boiling water for a couple of minutes, or until they can be peeled easily. Slip off the skins, and cut them in slices over the meat. Sprinkle with more salt and pepper, nutmeg, ginger, and thyme. Pour the stock over and let it come to a bubble, then cover the pan closely and simmer gently over lowest heat for 1 hour—or until meat is very tender.

At this point lift the meat out onto a warm platter, and keep warm in the oven. To make the sauce, mash down the tomatoes and onions with a large fork or potato masher. Stir in the cream, taste for seasoning, and bring the heat up to high. Stir till the mixture becomes a green tomato–studded gravy, partly silky smooth, part not. Pour this over the warm veal and serve.

Serves 4.

With green tomatoes often to be found among the underripe shipped to market these days, this gem of farmhouse cookery is one still to be emulated in apartments. The slight tartness of green tomatoes beautifully perks up bland veal, and there is plenty of sauce for mashed potatoes or Georgia Spoonbread (page 319). The wine should be white, and very dry.

GRILLADES AND GRITS

2	pounds veal, sliced ¼ inch thick (or beef Swiss steaks)	½	cup drained and chopped canned tomatoes
	Salt		Minced parsley
	Cayenne	½	teaspoon dried thyme
2	cloves garlic, minced	1	bay leaf
	Flour	1	tablespoon red wine vinegar
¼	cup lard	2	teaspoons Worcestershire
1	cup chopped onion		sauce
½	cup chopped green pepper	3	cups cooked hominy grits
2	cups beef or chicken stock		

Cut the meat into 2-inch squares and flatten with a mallet or studded meat tenderizer. Rub salt, cayenne, and garlic well into the meat, then rub in flour. Melt the lard in a heavy skillet and fry the veal in batches over high heat until golden on each side. Reserve the meat on a plate.

Add onion and green pepper to the pan and stir till the onions are a straw color. Add 1 tablespoon flour and stir for several minutes, then add stock, tomatoes, ¼ cup minced parsley, thyme, and bay leaf. Cover and simmer 15 minutes.

Put the veal back in the pan, with the vinegar and Worcestershire and simmer, covered, for 1 hour, turning the meat now and again and checking to see it doesn't stick to the bottom of the pan. There should be plenty of rich brown sauce.

To serve the grillades, place on a warm plate inside a ring of cooked grits, and sprinkle additional parsley over.

Serves 4 to 6.

In New Orleans, home of this spicy concoction, beef is used often as veal. I find round steak perfect for this—one only has to cut the steak in 2-inch squares then carefully slice through the middle with a sharp knife to make thin pieces. With either beef or veal it rivals any so-called Swiss steak you've ever eaten. Before President Carter came into office you could probably count the Yankees on one hand who had even heard of grits, but now they are even available and used all over the country. Unfortunately, these are usually "instant grits" and not the kind the Southerners simmer for an hour or more. The best thing to do with these is to ignore the package directions, add more water, and cook them in a double boiler for 20 to 30 minutes—they have time that way to gather more flavor.

PENNSYLVANIA DUTCH PAPRIKA VEAL

4	slices bacon, cut in ¼-inch strips		Salt
1½	pounds veal steak, or any thin slices	1	cup sour cream
		1	tablespoon tomato paste
¼	cup chopped onion	½	cup water
1	teaspoon paprika		Cooked egg noodles

*I*n a medium skillet, fry the bacon until it has rendered its fat but is not yet crisp. Remove it with a slotted spoon onto paper toweling. Cut the veal into serving portions and brown it quickly in the bacon fat, over a medium-high flame.

Toss in the onion and cook a few minutes more, until it is soft, then add the paprika and salt. Stir in the sour cream, tomato paste, the reserved bacon, and water.

Simmer, covered, for 20 to 30 minutes, or until the veal is tender. Check occasionally to see if it needs more water. Serve the veal with its sauce on cooked egg noodles.

Serves 4.

This is a definite addition to our repertoire of fine veal recipes. It does not differ substantially from many European paprika dishes, except perhaps in the delicacy of the paprika sauce itself, and of course all that bacon to savor the veal.

SHAKER VEAL FRICASSEE

4	pounds boneless veal shoulder	6	peppercorns
2	onions, quartered	4	tablespoons butter
2	stalks celery, cut in 2-inch pieces	⅓	cup finely chopped onion
1	teaspoon dried thyme	¼	cup flour
	Salt		Heavy cream
6	whole cloves	4	egg yolks
			Juice of 1 lemon

| ½ teaspoon freshly grated nutmeg
1 cauliflower, cut in florets (optional) | 12 mushrooms, quartered and sautéed in butter (optional) |

*C*ut the veal into 2-inch pieces, making sure to discard any connective tissue. Put the quartered onions and the veal in a Dutch oven. Turn the heat to medium and add celery, thyme, salt to taste, cloves, and peppercorns. Add water to cover and simmer gently for 1 hour, with the cover on the pot.

When tender, remove the veal and keep warm. Strain the broth and reserve. Melt the butter in a medium saucepan and cook the onion and flour for 5 minutes or more, stirring. Measure the veal broth, and if there are not 2 cups, add enough cream to make up the balance.

Add this to the onions and bring to a boil, whisking till smooth and thickened. Remove from heat immediately. Beat the egg yolks with the lemon juice and the nutmeg. Beat some of the hot sauce into the yolks, then whisk the whole into the sauce.

Add the veal, and when ready to serve, allow to heat without boiling. To construct a more complex dish, add the cauliflower 30 minutes before the veal is done, and all the mushrooms when you add the veal to its sauce. Both should be slightly underdone.

Serves 8 to 10 (may be easily halved).

Visitors came from all over to eat the Shakers' veal and chicken fricassees at Hancock Village. The trolley ended a mile short of the village, in West Pittsfield, and they gladly walked all the way, braving summer dust and winter drifts. The veal fricassee—simply, slowly executed—especially combines great suavity with richness. It needs some absorbing foil, and for this I like to serve a side bowl of My Grandmother's Drop Noodles (page 263), stirred with some butter and minced parsley, but either creamy mashed potatoes or regular egg noodles will do.

CHARLESTON SMOTHERED VEAL
WITH CHESTNUTS

1	slice (2 inches) of veal from the leg (about 3 pounds) Salt and freshly ground pepper	12 ½	small white onions, peeled teaspoon dried thyme Minced parsley
1	pound chestnuts, peeled (see directions in Chestnut Purée, page 229)	1	cup diced (¼ inch) carrots
		1	cup diced (¼ inch) celery
		1	cup diced (¼ inch) turnips
3	cups chicken stock	1	tablespoon butter
6	slices bacon	1	tablespoon flour

Preheat the oven to 325°F.

Choose a casserole about 2 inches larger around than the veal slice. Lightly salt and pepper the meat. Boil the chestnuts for 5 minutes in the chicken stock, then drain them and reserve the stock.

To assemble the dish, lay 3 strips of bacon on the bottom of the casserole, lay the veal on, then lay the other slices of bacon over. Put the chestnuts over the top, and place onions in a ring around the meat. Sprinkle with the thyme and ¼ cup parsley. Scatter the diced vegetables evenly over the dish—to be fine these should be cut by hand.

Pour the reserved stock over, cover the casserole tightly—if necessary, with both foil and a lid—put in the oven and cook 2 hours. Baste with juices every 20 minutes, and when the meat is tender remove to a hot platter.

With a slotted spoon, arrange the vegetables and chestnuts over and around the meat, discarding the bacon strips. Rub the butter and flour together and whisk it bit by bit into the pan juices over high heat. This will make a slightly thickened sauce. Nap the meat with some of the sauce and serve the rest in a sauceboat. Sprinkle with additional minced parsley and serve.

Serves 6.

This is a superbly contrived company dish, needing only a basket of home-made rolls and a fine chilled white wine for accompaniment—that, and candlelight.

ROAST VEAL WITH WILD PLUMS

6	slices bacon		Juice of ½ lemon
1	leg of veal (4 pounds), boned and tied (the butcher will do this)	1	bay leaf
		6	whole allspice
		¾	cup water (or stock)
	Butter	1	cup preserved wild plums (or tart plum jam)
	Salt and freshly ground pepper		Brown sugar (or dry mustard)
1	cup chopped celery tops		

*P*reheat the oven to 300°F.

Cut the bacon in small strips. Take a small knife and cut into the roast, then insert the bacon strips with the tip of the knife—space these evenly over the whole roast. Rub the meat well with butter, and salt and pepper generously.

Lay the meat in a roasting pan, place the celery tops over, sprinkle with lemon juice, then add bay leaf, allspice, and water or stock. Insert a meat thermometer in the thickest part of the roast, put it in the oven, and roast until the thermometer registers 170°F—about two hours. Baste the meat frequently as it cooks, and half an hour before it's done add the plums.

When done, remove celery tops, bay leaf, and allspice and place the meat on a cutting board. Skim the fat from the surface of the pan juice, then stir the juices and plums till smooth over medium-high heat.

Taste for seasoning, and depending on the tartness of the plums you use, add brown sugar or dry mustard to taste (wild plums are quite sharp and tart and need a bit of sugar, while commercial plum jam requires the bit of dry mustard).

Serves 6.

If you live in an area that grows any of the varieties of wild plum—from beach plums to prairie sand plums—this will be a dish to savor often. If not, there are some plum jams that are tart enough to serve, and I've even used canned greengage plums for this that answered pretty well to the general effect. When growing up in Kansas, we used to make great expeditions for sand plums in season, and my mother would put them up both in jelly and jam. As a child I thought them rather too tart for comfort, but I long for them now.

Pork and Ham

My grandparents crossed Kentucky to Kansas in that "Prairie schooner," the covered wagon, no doubt hurrying along a school of pigs. The porker came along for the ride, as it were, from Old World to New, and made settlement a good gamble. They multiplied on the run, cost nothing to keep, and slaughtered they kept long months brined in a barrel. Salt pork kept most of the wilder margins of our country alive and kicking early on. Homesteads put every bit of the pig to use—from snout bristle into brush, down to dessert gelatin extracted out of trotter.

PORK ROAST WITH STUFFED ONIONS

1	rolled boneless pork roast (shoulder or butt) (4 pounds)	6	large flat onions (preferably Bermuda)
1	teaspoon dried thyme	2	tablespoons butter
	Salt and freshly ground pepper	¾	cup bread crumbs
½	cup beef stock	½	cup chopped walnuts
½	cup dry white wine	¼	teaspoon dried thyme
			Salt and freshly ground pepper
		1	cup heavy cream

*P*reheat the oven to 350°F.

Rub the meat with thyme and salt and pepper. Place in a roasting pan, pour the stock and wine around it, and roast 30 to 35 minutes per pound (or to an internal temperature of from 175°–185°F, depending on whether you like your pork just done or quite tender). Make sure the juices don't all cook away, and if they do so add a little water from time to time.

While the roast is cooking, begin to prepare the onions. Peel them, but leave the root ends on so they will remain whole. Slice the tops off each onion, and drop them in boiling salted water to cover. Cook until just tender—about 30 minutes. Drain and cool. Scoop out the centers to form cups with walls about ½ inch thick. Take the centers and chop fine.

Heat the butter in a pan and add chopped onion, bread crumbs, walnuts, thyme, and salt and pepper to taste. Mix well, then stuff the onions with the mixture.

30 minutes before the roast is done, place the stuffed onions around it, basting them several times with the pan juices.

To serve, remove the roast and onions from the roasting pan and keep warm. Skim the pan juices of most of the fat. Add the cream to the pan and cook over medium-high heat, stirring until the sauce is smooth and begins to thicken as it bubbles away. Slice the roast, place on warm plates with an onion, and pour some sauce over both.

Serves 6.

My mother used to serve pork roast in this manner, and I remain to this day fond of nut stuffed onions—though it has been years since I encountered them anywhere but my own kitchen. For some reason, many of our best things seem to have become rare as buffaloes. To my mind, one doesn't need much else on a plate here, but it could use a little color, such as a pile of slightly cooked and buttered green beans, or just a sprig of watercress. I like it, too, with white wine rather than red—but that may be an aberration on my part.

PLANTATION STUFFED LOIN OF PORK WITH RUM PRUNES

1	pork loin (4 pounds, or 3 pounds boned)	½	teaspoon dried thyme
		½	teaspoon dried sage leaves, crumbled (not powdered)
12	dried prunes		
¾	cup dark rum	2	cloves garlic, minced
1½	cups croutons		Cayenne
	Chicken stock		Salt and freshly ground pepper
1	tablespoon minced parsley		
¼	cup minced green onions with part of tops		

*E*ither buy a boned pork loin, or bone it yourself—it takes only a long sharp knife or boning knife, no special knowledge, and about 5 minutes time to bone a pork loin. (It is also much cheaper than having a butcher do it. And don't worry about the neatness of the thing because it will be tied up later.)

Place the boned pork and prunes in a bowl and let them marinate in ½ cup of the rum for several hours.

Preheat the oven to 325°F.

Put the croutons in a bowl and moisten with some chicken stock. Add parsley, green onions, herbs and spices, and the rum marinade from the pork and prunes. Toss well.

Lay the pork flat out with the fat side down and lay a line of prunes the length of it. Pat the stuffing on top of the prunes. Wrap the meat back into its original shape, and tie it well with cotton string at 2-inch intervals. Bake for 2½ hours.

When done, remove the pork, pour off the fat from the pan, add the remaining ¼ cup rum and 2 cups chicken stock, and reduce, uncovered, over high heat to about half. Stir as it cooks, until a slightly thickened sauce is obtained.

Remove the string from the loin and slice it in ¼-inch slices. Pour some of the sauce over and serve on warm plates, accompanied by the remaining sauce.

Serves 6.

This Southern specialty from one of the great plantations makes an interesting company presentation—one both good to look at and to taste. Spoonbread is good (see Georgia Spoonbread on page 319) with it (I have two ovens, but if you don't, simply turn up the oven to the temperature for spoon bread when you take the pork out, and have the batter ready to pop in, for the pork will actually benefit by sitting, if kept warm). Otherwise, something like Cottage Roasted Jerusalem Artichokes (page 235) which can be basted with some of the pork juices, and a simple green vegetable will complement the roast nicely. It should be served either with a full-bodied white wine, or a sprightly red.

SHAKER APPLE CIDER PORK CHOPS

4	loin pork chops	1	tablespoon Dijon mustard
2	tablespoons butter	½	cup heavy cream
½	cup hard cider (or unsweetened apple juice)	2	tablespoons minced chives (or parsley)
	Salt and freshly ground pepper		

Choose a medium frying pan just large enough for the chops. Put it over medium-high heat, add the butter, and when it stops sizzling add the chops, cover, and turn the heat down.

Turn the chops occasionally as they cook—in about 30 minutes they should begin to take on a good golden brown color on both sides. At that time add the cider, cover again, and let cook for 15 to 20 minutes more, turning once.

By this time the chops should be tender and most of the liquid evaporated. Pour off all the fat from the pan, then salt and pepper the chops and add mustard, cream and chives. Raise heat and whisk the sauce till smooth. It is probably easier to remove the chops and then put them back during this process.

Cook another few minutes, turning the chops in the sauce, until the cream is reduced and thickened slightly. To serve, place the chops on warm plates and pour the sauce over.

Serves 4.

Ah the wonderful Shakers! If you are able to find hard cider these days, this is an extraordinary way to prepare pork chops—if not, the best substitute would be unsweetened apple juice with a tablespoon or so of Calvados to give some boost. I know people don't drink much hard cider these days, but it would *be nice to have more of it around to resurrect all the old dishes where it played such an important part. The best garnish for these chops is, of course, Fried Apple Rings (page 220).*

PORK CHOPS BRAISED WITH QUINCES

	Salt	¾	cup peeled and grated quince
4	loin pork chops, cut ¾ inch	4	tablespoons honey
	thick	½	cup water (or chicken stock)
1	tablespoon butter	2	teaspoons white wine vinegar
1	tablespoon vegetable oil		

*P*reheat the oven to 350°F.

Lightly salt the chops, then sauté in hot butter and oil until golden on both sides. Remove and put in a buttered casserole wide enough to hold the chops in one layer—and one that has a lid if possible. Sprinkle grated quince over each chop, dribble on the honey, and bring the sauté juices to a bubble. Add water or stock to the juices, along with the vinegar. Allow to bubble up and pour over the chops.

Cut a round of waxed paper to fit the casserole, butter it, and lay buttered side down over the chops. Cover with a lid as well, or foil if need be, and bake in the oven without peeking, for 1 hour. This can sit for some time before being served, with its juices poured over.

Serves 4.

On being handed a quince or two—not enough certainly for their legendary jelly or preserves—I dropped back on my files to uncover this recipe still waiting the advent of a quince crop. It is unearthly, and even more so if you use raspberry vinegar. Serve with halved baked yams slashed with curls of butter, and a white wine that is not too dry.

PORK CHOPS WITH
SCALLIONS AND SOUR CREAM

4	loin pork chops, cut about ¾	Salt and freshly ground
	inch thick	pepper
	Flour	Paprika

2 tablespoons vegetable oil
⅔ cup chopped green onions
with part of tops
2 tablespoons minced parsley

½ cup beef or chicken stock
½ cup sour cream
Parsley sprigs

Shake the chops with flour, salt, pepper, and some paprika. Put the oil in a skillet large enough to hold all the chops and sauté them over a medium-high flame until they are golden on both sides.

Pour out the fat from the pan, sprinkle the green onions and parsley over the meat, then pour in the stock. Cover and cook over low heat 45 minutes, or until the pork is tender but not dry. Check occasionally to see that the liquid hasn't boiled away—if so, add some extra water.

When done, lift the onion-covered chops out onto warm plates. Add the sour cream to the pan and cook, stirring, until the sauce is smooth and thickened. Pour over the chops, garnish with sprigs of parsley, and serve.

Serves 4.

This recipe is adapted from the Wisconsin novelist Edward Harris Heth's The Country Kitchen Cook Book. *It was first published in the late 1950s and has since been reissued, so is commonly available. I recommend it highly as one of the few cookbooks on native food that is jammed full with really usable and interesting recipes. Mr. Heth was a fine writer as well, and he arranges the book for seasonal cooking—from spring garden delights to the "blizzard cupboard"—with beautifully evoked scenes of country living, food gathering, and neighboring cooks.*

MISS DOROTHY'S STUFFED PORK CHOPS

4 loin pork chops, cut 1 inch
thick
6 ounces cream cheese
¼ pound Smithfield or country
ham, thinly sliced
1 cup dry white wine
¼ cup olive oil

¼ cup minced green onions
with part of tops
2 tablespoons minced parsley
1 cup bread crumbs
2 tablespoons butter
Salt
Lemon juice
¼ cup heavy cream

Slice the chops with a small sharp knife held parallel to the surface, so that a pocket is formed through the flesh clear to the bone. Spread some of the cheese in each pocket, lay in slices of ham, and secure with toothpicks. Marinate in wine, oil, green onions, and parsley for a few hours—or even overnight.

When ready to cook, preheat the oven to 350°F.

Take a frying pan large enough to hold all the chops, put in the bread crumbs, and shake them over medium heat until they are evenly and lightly browned. Drain the chops (reserving the marinade for later) and turn them in the crumbs off the fire. When they are evenly coated, put them onto a plate and clean out any remaining crumbs in the pan.

Melt the butter in the pan and sauté the chops over medium heat until they are crisp and golden on each side. Add about ¼ cup of the marinade, then cover the pan and bake about 1 hour—or until quite tender.

When done, remove to warm plates, swirl a few drops of lemon juice and the cream into the pan juices, and when the sauce amalgamates as you stir it, pour over the chops and serve at once.

Serves 4.

A rich, sumptuous dish, and a specialty of Mrs. Dorothy Neal of Demorest, Georgia. Any good cured ham may be used if you can't locate the real Smithfield, or have no access to country hams. Westphalian Ham is to be found in many specialty shops, and is particularly fine here. Serve it with Miss Dorothy's Mashed Potatoes (page 250) and pickled crabapples.

NANTUCKET FIREMEN'S SUPPER

4 pork chops, about 1-inch thick
Salt and freshly ground pepper
1 bay leaf
4 medium onions, sliced
4 medium potatoes, peeled and sliced
2 cups milk

*P*reheat the oven to 350°F.

Trim the chops of excess fat. Try the fat out in a frying pan set over medium heat. When the pieces are golden brown, remove them with a slotted spoon and fry the chops in the released fat 5 minutes a side.

Put chops then in a casserole of a size to hold them all in one layer. Add salt and pepper to taste and lay the bay leaf on top, then put a layer of onions then one of potatoes, over. Salt and pepper again.

Pour the milk over, cover the casserole closely with foil and a lid, and bake

2 hours. When the dish is done, all the liquid will be absorbed and the whole will be golden.

Serves 4.

The hearty simplicity of this one-dish meal makes it a family favorite any time. And like the firemen, the busy cook may put it in the oven and forget it for 2 hours—longer, if you turn the oven off and let it sit warm.

OLD-FASHIONED PORK CASSEROLE

1 pound boneless pork, cut in 1 inch cubes and trimmed of fat	1 onion, chopped
½ teaspoon powdered sage	1 large apple, peeled, cored, and sliced
3 medium potatoes, peeled and sliced	2 tablespoons minced parsley
2 teaspoons paprika	Juice of ½ lemon
	Salt and freshly ground pepper
	1 cup chicken stock

*P*reheat the oven to 350°F.

On a large strip of waxed paper, rub the sage into the pork cubes, coat the potatoes with a blush of paprika, make a pile of the onion, and sprinkle the apples with parsley and lemon juice.

You will need about a 1½-quart casserole for this. Make first a layer of half the potatoes in it, then a layer each of pork, apple, onion, etc., ending with potatoes on top. Salt and pepper as you go, to taste.

Finally add the chicken stock, cover the casserole tightly, and bake 2 hours, uncovering the last 30 minutes and pressing down gently into the juices.

Serves 4.

As casseroles go, this is a fine example, though you should be careful to trim as much fat off the meat as possible or it will be greasy. It needs little accompaniment except perhaps a pickled peach or crab apples—or even a nice homemade chutney.

GEORGIA BARBECUE SPARERIBS

1 cup chopped onion	1 teaspoon dry mustard
1 cup peach preserves	¼ teaspoon Tabasco
1 tablespoon catsup	4 pounds spareribs, left whole
¼ cup brown sugar, packed	Salt and freshly ground
1 teaspoon paprika	pepper
¼ cup white vinegar	2 lemons, thinly sliced
¼ cup Worcestershire sauce	

*P*reheat the oven to 400°F.

In a saucepan, combine the onion, preserves, catsup, sugar, and all the seasonings and simmer 10 to 15 minutes.

Rub salt and pepper into the ribs and place them in a shallow roasting pan, meaty side down. Brush them with some of the sauce and bake 30 minutes.

Turn the ribs, brush with some more sauce, and put the lemon slices on top. Bake another hour, brushing with sauce as the ribs cook several times more, removing the lemon slices before the last time.

To serve, slice into serving portions.

Serves 4.

Frankly, I will eat spareribs cooked almost any way, but this hot, tangy, sweet-sour sauce made with peach preserves is absolutely irresistible (Georgia grows the best peaches on earth!). Accompany them with any kind of good corn-bread, or simple mashed potatoes, crisp cole slaw, and cold beer.

GOURMET SPARERIBS

4 pounds spareribs, cut in 2-rib sections	1 cup catsup
2½ teaspoons salt	¾ cup beer
½ teaspoon freshly ground pepper	½ cup minced onion
1 teaspoon granulated sugar	1 clove garlic, minced
¼ teaspoon paprika	½ cup minced green pepper
¼ teaspoon ground turmeric	⅓ cup vinegar
¼ teaspoon celery salt	¼ cup brown sugar, packed
	1 tablespoon Worcestershire sauce

1   teaspoon dry mustard   ½   teaspoon dried basil
½   teaspoon Tabasco

*P*reheat the oven to 325°F.

Cut up the ribs. Mix 2 teaspoons salt, ¼ teaspoon pepper, granulated sugar, paprika, turmeric, and celery salt and rub the mixture into the ribs. Mix all the rest of the ingredients, including the remaining salt and pepper, into a sauce—the best way to do this is either in a blender or food processor. Just put everything and whirl in pulses until there are no large lumps.

Place the ribs, meaty side down, in a baking pan large enough to hold them all in one layer and spoon some of the sauce over them. Bake 2 hours, basting with sauce every 30 minutes and turning the ribs once. After 2 hours, turn the heat off, and let the ribs sit in the oven another 30 minutes, or until ready to serve.

Serves 4.

I grew up, culinarily speaking, on Gourmet *magazine and the* Gourmet *cookbooks. Always one of the best ways to get the tone and temper of current American cooking is in the "Sugar and Spice" column, where readers send in their favorite recipes. Sometimes lovely old treasures turn up, and often an amateur cook turns a trick on a standard, making it new again. This recipe has been slightly adapted from that column to my own uses, but in essence it has remained the same—certainly one of the best ways to cook spareribs in the world. The ingredients are all the things one would ordinarily use in a barbecue sauce, but they are arranged differently. And what a difference! Wait till you smell them cooking—you'll hardly ever need another recipe.*

SPARERIBS AND SAUERKRAUT

12 to 16   ribs   1⅓   cups stock
     4   cups sauerkraut   (beef, chicken, or either
     1   cup chopped onion   with some white wine)
     2   cups grated apple   Salt and freshly ground
                                      pepper
                                4   bay leaves

*P*reheat the oven to 350°F.

Put the kraut in a large bowl of water and soak several minutes, changing the water, until some of the sharp flavor is left, but not too much. (This is all a matter of taste.) Drain in a colander and squeeze out all of the water by hand. Put the kraut in a casserole, toss with onion, apple, and stock, and cook, covered, in the oven 1 hour.

While the kraut is cooking, boil the ribs in a large pan of water for 15 minutes to remove some of their fat. Remove from the water and sprinkle all over with salt and pepper.

Place the sauerkraut mixture in the bottom of a shallow roasting pan big enough to hold the ribs in one piece. Put the bay leaves over, then the ribs. Put in the oven and cook 1½ hours, basting with the kraut juices every 15 to 20 minutes.

When done, the ribs should have browned on top and the kraut absorbed most of the juices. To aid this process, during the last half hour of cooking, lift the ribs, remove the bay leaves, and stir the kraut into the juices in the pan. Then place the ribs back over and baste.

To serve, place the kraut on warm plates, cut the ribs between bones, and spread 3 or 4 in a fan over the kraut for each serving. Garnish with parsley sprigs and flank with plain boiled potatoes. Dijon mustard makes a welcome side to the crisp ribs.

Serves 4.

Though it appears in some version in every one of our usual cookbooks, one seldom meets this fine native choucroute braisée at table. It is not a dish for the faint hearted, nor (since the ribs are eaten by hand) the fastidious, but, served with a fine dry white wine or good cold dark beer, it is a feast for the rest.

HOMEMADE COUNTRY SAUSAGE

2½	pounds boneless pork shoulder	½	teaspoon freshly ground pepper
½	pound pork fat	½	teaspoon dried thyme
2	teaspoons salt	½	teaspoon dried summer savory
½	teaspoon cayenne	¼	teaspoon powdered bay leaf
1	teaspoon powdered sage		Pinch of allspice

*C*ut the meat into dice and grind with all the other ingredients. Cook a bit to taste for seasoning—some prefer much more sage, and others like it hot with cayenne. Other ingredients are also sometimes added—coriander, nutmeg, cloves, etc. To cook, form into sausage patties and fry until crisp on both sides.

Store-bought sausage is usually rather crudely overflavored with sage or hot pepper, so those who want a better balanced product (with no preservatives) might wish to experiment at achieving their own variety. The easiest way to get the meat ground is to buy a pork shoulder and ask your butcher to grind it with some extra pork fat. The sausage will keep for a few days in the refrigerator, and it freezes well shaped into patties and placed between sheets of waxed paper. The patties make a fine breakfast dish topped with some sour cream and accompanied by scrambled eggs.

CHAURICE

5	pounds boneless lean pork	2	cups finely chopped onion
1	pound pork fat	1	clove garlic, minced
3	teaspoons salt	¼	teaspoon dried thyme
2	teaspoons freshly ground black pepper	½	cup minced parsley
½	teaspoon cayenne	1	teaspoon powdered bay leaf
½	teaspoon chili powder	½	teaspoon ground allspice
1	teaspoon paprika		Sausage casings (optional)

*E*ither have the butcher grind all the pork and fat together, or cut in dice and grind it twice through a food grinder. (A food processor has difficulty with pork.) Mix all the ingredients—except the sausage casings, of course—in a bowl with your hands until everything is well combined.

These can be used as sausage patties, or they can be made into sausage lengths. To do this, scald the casings, wash again thoroughly, and let dry. Fill with the sausage mixture, and tie in even lengths.

This highly seasoned Creole sausage is splendid to use in any way you like sausages. In the South it is most often served cooked in a sauce Creole (a good example of this can be found in Almond Chicken Creole, page 153). And it is then accompanied by mashed potatoes or grits for a supper or brunch dish.

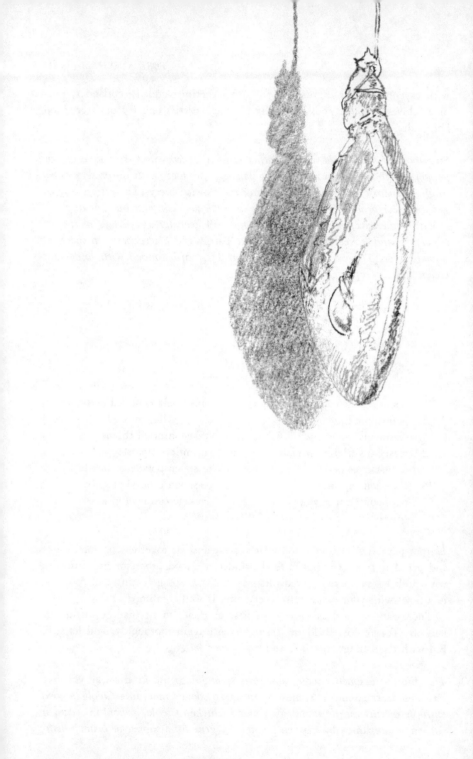

STUFFED BAKED HAM PONTALBA

1 (12 to 16 pounds) country-cured ham
4 cups pecans, ground
1 tablespoon plus 2 teaspoons dried sage
1 teaspoon dried thyme
1 teaspoon ground cloves
½ teaspoon cayenne
2 small cans truffles (optional), drained and truffles cut in quarters

½ cup Madeira
4 bay leaves
1 onion, chopped
1 apple, peeled, cored, and chopped
1 cup light molasses
Freshly ground pepper
Cornmeal
Brown sugar

*E*ven if you buy the ham by mail, ask your butcher to bone it for you—he'll charge you, but it's an impossible task at home. Soak the ham in water to cover 12 to 24 hours, changing the water 2 or 3 times (the larger the ham, the longer soaking it needs). Remove the ham and scrub with a brush under cold running water.

Remove about ½ pound of the ham from around the boned cavity. Grind this through a food grinder, and combine with the pecans, 2 teaspoons sage, ½ teaspoon thyme, cloves, cayenne, truffles, Madeira, and 2 of the bay leaves, crumbled. Stuff the ham with this, and sew the opening tight. Sew a cloth securely around the ham.

Place in a large deep pan and cover with water. Add the onion, remaining 2 bay leaves, the 1 tablespoon sage, remaining ½ teaspoon thyme, the apple, and molasses. Bring to a simmer on top of the stove, then reduce the heat to low and let simmer partially covered for 6 hours—or until tender. Turn off the heat and let the ham get cold in its broth.

Preheat the oven to 400°F.

Finally, remove the ham and dust it with a mixture of pepper, cornmeal, and brown sugar. Bake 20 minutes, or until the glaze is richly browned. Serve at room temperature, cut into very thin slices. It will keep for several weeks.

Even in the South, of course, fine country-cured hams are a specialty item not found on just any grocery shelf. They are, however, available shipped from quite a few different firms as advertised in fine food magazines. They make an especially good holiday treat, as one ham will stretch over both Thanksgiving and Christmas—with all your visitors on and in between. The thinly sliced pieces make a focal point of a buffet, perhaps with some such dish as Maum Nancy's Scalloped Oysters (page 62) along with various vegetables, starches, hot rolls, pickles, and relishes, etc. You cook an unstuffed ham much as this one is cooked—with the necessary soaking, of course—but this fantasy preparation from New Orleans makes a fine thing even nicer. It makes a splendid hors d'oeuvre with Beaten Biscuits (page 327), and slices from the unstuffed portions make a special breakfast of Country Ham with Red-Eye Gravy (below). The extra bits and pieces not suitable for this kind of presentation may be used as an addition to biscuits, or in such dishes as Miss Dorothy's Stuffed Pork Chops (page 107) and Smithfield Chicken (page 148). Be sure to use every scrap!

COUNTRY HAM WITH RED-EYE GRAVY

4 slices cooked country-cured	½ cup heavy cream
ham, cut ¼-inch thick	Freshly ground pepper
1 cup brewed coffee	

*T*rim the extra fat from the ham slices. Try the fat out in a large skillet until the pieces are golden and have released their fat. Remove the pieces with a slotted spoon and fry the ham slices in the released fat over medium heat for several minutes on each side. Remove and keep warm.

Add the coffee to the skillet and turn the heat up to high. Scrape all the brown bits clinging to the pan with a spoon, and stir until the gravy turns reddish. Add the cream and pepper to taste, and cook slowly 10 minutes.

To serve, pour the gravy over the ham slices.

Serves 4.

One of the best of simple regional dishes for those lucky enough to obtain country ham. It may be prepared from ordinary smoked ham slices, but of course it won't be nearly so good. I had it at its best once while hiking the Appalachian Trail. A farmer found us in sleeping bags near dusk in his orchard, and after asking us if we'd seen any snakes (a formal conversational gambit in the Southern mountains), politely asked us for breakfast next morning. On a scrubbed, bleached kitchen table we were spread a feast of ham with plenty of red-eye gravy, fresh high biscuits, hot grits, new-laid eggs, good steaming coffee, and homemade wild strawberry preserves. After living for more than a month on dehydrated goods, it tasted like a banquet out of the Arabian Nights rather than fairly humble victuals.

TO GLAZE A HAM

*T*here are about as many ways to glaze a ham as there are people who cook them. It can be as simple as a dusting of sugar over the fat, or it may involve much spicing and fruiting and dousings in liquids—from beer to champagne. First the ham is cooked, then the rind is removed, the fat trimmed to about ½ inch and slashed in a diamond pattern, each diamond stuck with a clove, and then you have a choice of the glaze itself. In principle this is usually brown sugar, some liquid such as vinegar or fruit juice, and a little dry mustard for nip. Then the ham is put back in a hot oven till the whole mess melts and glisters.

In the South the liquid of choice is bourbon, and then orange slices are pinned on with toothpicks, whereas in New England the choice for the sweet is maple syrup. In California this can all get rather out of hand, with one recipe calling for Dijon mustard, cloves, cinnamon, ginger, nutmeg, pepper, pomegranate jelly, both scotch *and* brandy, and brown sugar as well! There are also variations using bread crumbs—one interesting recipe from Williamsburg calling for crumbs, a little water from boiling the ham, butter, and homemade chowchow, and another, a favorite of President Hoover, which uses simply currant jelly and bread crumbs.

A favorite in my kitchen comes from a friend who uses a 16-ounce can of whole-berry cranberry sauce, with enough port wine to thin it. This is then put in a 400°F oven and watched closely, as it can quickly burn. But oh what a pretty berry-studded glow it makes! Perhaps the best of all, though, would be Mammy Pleasant's Bar-le-Duc Sauce for "a New Year's ham." She crushed 2 pounds of fresh currants with 1 pound raspberries, and added ¾ pound sugar for every pound of pulp. It was them simmered 40 minutes, or till the syrup thickened and jelled. It was then sealed in crocks for use as both a glaze and a sauce for the ham.

A freed slave, with one blue eye and one brown, Mary Ellen Pleasant is one of the most amazing characters in our culinary history. She cooked her way through Boston, Charleston, New Orleans (where she cooked for "The Voodoo Queen"), finally to bonanza San Francisco—starting at the age of nine. She amassed what could be called an up-and-down fortune. When rich she went from plantation to plantation, smuggled in dressed as a jockey, to arouse the slave revolt, and met John Brown to present him with a purse of gold collected from California Negroes. When poor she played hostess for rich playboy patrons who could throw money about on their palates.

In San Francisco she was the first to find new cheeses, Tahiti oranges, Ceylon cinnamon, Chinese tumeric, Puget Sound oysters, and citron from the Indies. She also quickly established a country place she turned into a truck farm for special vegetables, made raspberry vinegar, cheese with cowslip petals, strewed her butter with rose geranium leaves for cakes, adapted Chinese recipes for catering, served fried chicken with a shallot sauce, and came up with a greengage plum sorbet. "Mammy" Pleasant, as she termed herself in those Victorian times, may have been the first truly modern chef.

ALMOND HAM SLICES

1 center slice precooked ham,	1 egg, beaten
cut ½ to ¾ inch thick	⅔ cup blanched almonds
1 clove garlic, mashed	4 tablespoons butter
Flour	

*R*ub the ham with the garlic, and discard any bits that cling. Dip the ham first in flour, then in beaten egg, and lay aside on waxed paper.

Grind ½ cup of the almonds in a food processor or chop them very fine by hand (a blender will make a paste of them). Dust the ham slice in the almonds, pressing them in on both sides, wrap in waxed paper, and refrigerate till needed.

To cook, sliver the remaining almonds and toast them golden in 1 tablespoon of the butter. In the remaining butter sauté the ham till the coating is golden brown on each side—over medium heat, this will take about 5 minutes a side. Cut the ham in serving pieces and sprinkle with the toasted slivered almonds.

Serves 4.

A superb way to serve a slice of good ham, or for that matter smoked pork chops. It needs tart currant jelly alongside, or perhaps chutney, and mounds of creamy mashed potatoes.

MY MOTHER'S HAM PLATTER WITH HOMINY AND PEACHES

4 serving slices precooked ham,	3 tablespoons butter
cut ½ to ¾ inch thick (or	4 ripe peaches (or 8 drained
4 smoked pork chops)	halves canned freestones)

Bourbon (optional)	Salt and freshly ground
4 cups canned yellow hominy,	pepper
drained	

*T*rim any fat off the ham. Try the fat out in a frying pan until the pieces brown and release their fat. Lift them out with a slotted spoon, add the butter to the pan, and fry the ham slices slowly on each side until slightly golden. This done, remove to a warming platter in the oven.

Place the peaches cut side down in the fat and brown them also on both sides. At this time you can blaze them with a good capful of bourbon, if you like.

In either case, lift the peaches out onto the ham platter and add the drained hominy to the pan. Add more butter if there is little fat, and toss the hominy until it too starts to become crusty and golden.

To serve the dish, rearrange the hominy, ham, and peaches attractively on the warm platter and bring it to table.

Serves 4.

A long-time favorite in our family. That it can be put together easily is not the least of its charms. I have used it for years as a rush meal got together with a slice of ham and two cans—accompanied by cole slaw or lettuce tossed with a simple creamy salad dressing. It deserves even a good white wine of its own—one rather more full bodied and mellow than dry and crisp.

HAM, YAMS, AND CHESTNUTS, BAKED WITH PIPPINS

6 yams, baked, peeled, and sliced	Salt and freshly ground pepper
1 pound cooked ham, sliced	½ cup apple cider
1 pound chestnuts, peeled, cooked, and crumbled	¼ cup brown sugar, packed
4 green apples, peeled, cored, and sliced	⅛ teaspoon ground mace
	¼ cup butter, melted

*P*reheat the oven to 350°F.

In a 2-quart casserole, alternate slices of yams, ham, chestnuts, and apples—beginning and ending with the yams. Sprinkle with salt and pepper over each layer of yams and chestnuts. (Not too much salt if the ham is salty.)

Pour the apple cider over. Mix the brown sugar with the mace and sprinkle over next, then dribble the melted butter on top. Bake, uncovered, for 45 minutes, or until bubbly. Serve warm.

Serves 6.

A superb New England way to offer up part of a baked ham—everything in it compliments everything else, and there is a host of flavors and textures all melded together. It makes a fine company dish if served with your best rolls and a glass of full-bodied white wine.

HAM LOAF WITH
RED CURRANT–HORSERADISH GLAZE

1	pound cooked ham, ground			Freshly ground pepper
½	pound pork, ground	½	cup bread crumbs (or crushed crackers)
1	onion, finely chopped			
1	apple, pared, cored, and finely chopped	½	cup sour cream
		2	eggs
1	teaspoon dry mustard	3	tablespoons red currant jelly
¼	teaspoon ground allspice	2	tablespoons prepared horseradish
	Pinch of ground mace			
	Freshly grated nutmeg			

*P*reheat the oven to 350°F.

Mix all the ingredients (except the jelly and horseradish) thoroughly by hand. Place in a standard loaf pan and bake for 2 hours. The last half hour, baste with warmed currant jelly mixed with horseradish.

Serves 4 to 6.

This is a family standard, finely honed. It makes a good end to the last of a ham, served with a simple green vegetable, and perhaps Deep-fried Sweet Potatoes (page 260). If there is any left for the next day, it makes a splendid cold sandwich spread with plenty of Dijon mustard. All the chopping is a perfect job for a food processor—even the pork can be ground if cut in small pieces with most of the connective tissue cut out.

FARMHOUSE HAM HOCK BOILED DINNER

2	large meaty ham hocks (or 4 small ones)	8	medium potatoes, peeled and quartered
1½	pounds green beans, washed and trimmed		Salt and freshly ground pepper

*P*ut the hocks to boil in water to cover in a large kettle. Simmer gently 1½ hours, then add the beans, raise heat to medium, and cook for 10 minutes. Add the potatoes and cook another 20 minutes, or until the potatoes are tender.

To serve, remove the hocks, cut off the meat, and chop coarsely. Place the potatoes and beans on warm plates, ladle some broth over them, then sprinkle with ham and salt and pepper to taste. Serve with a cruet of vinegar and a small pitcher of the cooking broth.

Serves 4.

This is one of those humble dishes all cooks secretly like to cook for themselves when no one is looking. I know I do, and would even if I could afford lobster and truffles every day. To speed up the process, the hocks can be cooked in a pressure cooker 30 minutes or so.

Lamb

When America became beef country, after the far-feeding buffalo, no sheep could share its range, for they crop closer than cattle. I grew up in the heart of cattle lands without tasting any of this good woolly beast, and still my mother on travel treats it as an exotic to be approached on a menu with care. Even in these days of wide shipping, more veal is consumed in the country than lamb, which is hard to understand, since mutton was a British staple and *gigot* part of any Frenchman's larder. For one, I frankly dote on its distinctive taste, to the point of upstaging even pork and beef, so it was a pleasure to find some singular recipes from the native trove, delicious right down to the lowly shank and rib.

LEG OF LAMB
WITH PARMESAN POTATOES

1 leg of lamb (5 to 6 pounds)	8 large potatoes, peeled and
3 cloves garlic, peeled and	sliced
slivered	4 tablespoons butter
1 teaspoon dried rosemary	1 cup chicken stock
Salt and freshly ground	Freshly grated Parmesan
pepper	cheese

*P*reheat the oven to 325°F.

Remove most of the fat from the lamb and lard it with garlic slivers all over. (The fell may be removed or left on, as you wish—some folks like the quality it takes on during roasting.) Rub the rosemary and salt and pepper into the roast.

Rub the bottom of a roasting pan the size of the leg of lamb with part of the butter, and layer the potatoes in it, salting and peppering and buttering each layer. Cover the potatoes with stock—it should come up almost to their tops—and place the lamb on top of them.

Roast about 15 minutes to the pound, or until a meat thermometer inserted in the thickest part of the flesh registers 140°F for rare, 160°F for medium, or 175°F for well done.

Remove the roast lamb to a carving board and look at the potatoes—the stock should almost all have cooked away and they should be gold and crusty. Sprinkle them with Parmesan cheese, and return to the oven for the cheese to melt while you carve the lamb.

Serves 8.

The potatoes in this sheepherder preparation sop up all the lamb drippings and become almost as tasty as the roast itself. If you are not afraid of a little oven cleaning, an even better way to roast it is to place the leg on an oven rack with the potatoes set fairly closely on the rack beneath. No other accompaniment is really needed except perhaps a simple green vegetable or watercress sprig, and a glass of good red wine.

BARBECUED BUTTERFLIED LEG OF LAMB

1   leg of lamb (5 to 6 pounds),   1   clove garlic, minced
    boned and butterflied by   1   teaspoon dried rosemary (or 1
    the butcher   tablespoon fresh)
¾   cup olive oil   1   bay leaf, crumbled
¼   cup red wine vinegar   Freshly ground pepper
½   cup chopped green onions
    with part of tops

*C*hoose a pan large enough to hold the meat flattened out, and marinate it for 3 to 5 hours in the rest of the ingredients.

Start a charcoal fire, and when it has come to medium embers, grill the lamb set about 3 inches over the coals. Brush it from time to time with some of the marinade. It should be brown and crusty on the outside and still pink within in 35 to 45 minutes. To serve, let cool for 5 minutes, then slice on the diagonal.

If you don't have a grill, the lamb can also be cooked in an oven. Preheat it to 450°F and cook the lamb for 20 minutes—or until it has browned. Then reduce the heat to 325°F and cook 10 to 15 minutes per pound, according to whether you wish it rare or medium.

Serves 6 to 8.

This makes, I think, a much nicer party centerpiece than grilled steaks—which are often too thinly cut to cook properly outdoors. It is a quite common treat in California (where everything seems to be done outdoors), and the first time I had it the host brushed on the marinade with a sprig of fresh mint. New Potato Salad (page 280) makes a nice partner to the lamb, as does either fine beer or red wine.

CREOLE STUFFED SHOULDER OF LAMB

1   shoulder of lamb (3 to 4   1   green pepper, seeded and
    pounds), boned   chopped
    Salt and freshly ground   4   tablespoons vegetable oil
    pepper   1   cup drained and
1   cup chopped onion   chopped tomatoes

3 tablespoons olive oil	¼ cup minced parsley
1 clove garlic, minced	¼ teaspoon dried thyme
2 bay leaves	8 to 12 small turnips, peeled
	½ cup Madeira

*P*reheat the oven to 325°F.

Cut a large pocket through the center of the large muscle of the lamb, and salt and pepper it inside and out. Sauté the onion and green pepper in 1 tablespoon of the oil for several minutes, until the onion is limp. Combine this with the tomatoes, off the fire, and stuff the lamb with the mixture. Firmly skewer the pocket.

In a large Dutch oven, sauté the lamb in the remaining 3 tablespoons oil until browned on all sides. Turn off the heat and add the garlic, herbs, turnips, and Madeira. Bake, covered, 1 to 1½ hours, or until a meat thermometer inserted registers 150°F. Every 20 minutes or so, turn the meat and turnips. The turnips should be glazed brown all over by the time the roast is done.

To serve, remove the meat from the pan and let sit 15 minutes while you cook down the juices with the turnips, turning occasionally to glaze them more. Slice the meat and serve in a pool of the juices with the turnips alongside. Serves 6.

All the definite flavors here, each strong in its own right, meld into one lovely succulence. It makes a relatively inexpensive company dish, not difficult to prepare if you find a butcher who will bone a shoulder for you. Serve it with a delicate Grits Soufflé (page 262) and a robust red wine.

ZUÑI LAMB STEW
WITH CORN AND GREEN CHILIES

1 pound boneless lamb shoulder, cut in 1-inch cubes	1 cup chopped, peeled, and seeded fresh or canned tomatoes
Flour	
Salt and freshly ground pepper	3 cups corn kernels
	6 juniper berries, crushed
2 tablespoons butter	1 teaspoon dried oregano
2 tablespoons vegetable oil	Salt
1 clove garlic, minced	2 small dried red chili peppers
1 can (7 ounces) mild green chilies, chopped	

*P*at the lamb cubes dry with paper towels. Shake them in a bag of flour seasoned with salt and pepper, then sauté in batches in a large casserole in hot butter and oil. When the lamb is golden on all sides, lift out onto a warm plate.

Sauté the garlic in the same pot set over medium heat for a minute or two, then add the green chilies, tomatoes (with any juice if you use canned), corn, juniper berries, and oregano. Let this bubble up over high heat, then add the lamb, salt to taste, and the red chilies. Examine the chilies for any breaks in their skin—if they are not perfect, then remove the hot seeds before adding.

Stew slowly, covered, for 1½ hours, or until the lamb is quite tender. Check the pot now and again to make sure there is enough liquid—if not, add a little water, tomato juice, or stock.

When done, remove the red chilies, and serve in a heated dish.
Serves 4.

One place the sheep prospered was the scrublands of the West, where forage was too sparse for cattle. This native Indian dish uses everything the Zuñi have at hand—right down to local desert juniper berries. It's good served with a stack of warm tortillas, butter to slather over them, and a pitcher of cold beer.

RACK OF LAMB ALMONDINE

2 racks (6 to 8 chops each) of lamb	1 cup dry vermouth
Salt and freshly ground pepper	1½ cups toasted blanched slivered almonds

*P*reheat the oven to 400°F.

Trim most of fat off the lamb, and rub with salt and pepper. Place the racks, bone side down, in a shallow roasting pan.

Roast for 25 minutes, or until the lamb is crisped and golden on the outside and pink and juicy inside. When done, remove from the pan and let sit while you prepare the sauce.

To do this, drain all the fat off, add the vermouth to the drippings, and stir over a medium flame till all the brown specks are dissolved and the liquid is reduced by half.

To serve, slice into serving portions, fan them on warm plates, sprinkle with almonds, then pour the vermouth sauce over.
Serves 4.

A rack of lamb is everybody's restaurant favorite, but there is no reason not to serve it at home. This fine recipe is a specialty of Le Ruth's in New Orleans.

It makes an unlikely pair, but I serve it with Shaker Alabaster (page 247) and the best red wine I can afford.

SALEM LAMB CHOPS
WITH CAPER–BREAD CRUMB SAUCE

4	meaty shoulder lamb chops, cut ¾ inch thick	½	cup butter, melted
	Fresh bread crumbs	3	tablespoons minced capers
	Salt and freshly ground pepper	1	tablespoon caper juice
2	tablespoons butter	2	tablespoons white wine vinegar
1	tablespoon vegetable oil	¼	cup bread crumbs

*T*rim the chops of fat, and coat with bread crumbs, salt, and pepper. Melt the butter and oil in a frying pan large enough to hold all the chops, and brown them over medium heat 5 or more minutes a side, depending on the thickness of the chops—they should be golden brown on the outside and still pink on the inside.

While the chops are frying combine the melted butter with capers, caper juice, vinegar, and ¼ cup bread crumbs. Serve the chops on heated plates with some of the sauce at their sides, and the rest in a sauceboat.

Serves 4.

Serve these with Spokane Scalloped Onions (page 238), and you have a meal so delectable you won't notice the lack of fancy expensive loin chops.

NEW ORLEANS EPIGRAM OF LAMB

4	pounds breast of lamb		Melted butter
1	large onion, quartered		Salt and freshly ground pepper
2	carrots, trimmed and sliced		Bread crumbs
2	stalks celery, sliced		
¼	cup parsley stems	1	tablespoon butter
1	clove garlic	2	tablespoons flour
1	bay leaf	2	cups beef stock, heated
¼	teaspoon dried thyme	¼	cup Madeira
6	whole cloves	½	cup sliced mushrooms (optional)
6	peppercorns		

*T*rim the lamb of any fell and outside fat and put in a large kettle. Cover with salted water and bring to a boil with the onion, carrots, celery, parsley stems, garlic, bay leaf, thyme, cloves, and peppercorns. Simmer gently 1 hour, or until quite tender and the small bones will slip out easily.

Drain and let cool enough to be able to pull out all the bones. Press down with a heavy weight and chill till ready to serve dinner. (The stock can be used to make a barley soup.)

To prepare the dish, cut the breast into portions about 3 inches wide and cut these into three triangular pieces. Dip in melted butter, sprinkle with salt and pepper, then roll in bread crumbs.

Make a sauce by melting 1 tablespoon butter in a saucepan and stirring in the flour. Let cook several minutes over medium heat, then add all the hot stock at once. Turn heat low, and simmer 15 to 20 minutes, then add the Madeira and mushrooms and simmer another 5 minutes.

Preheat the broiler. Broil the pieces of lamb till golden on each side and serve with the Madeira sauce.

Serves 4 to 6.

For years I used to look at this unpromising cut of meat and wonder what could be made of it. After finding this recipe in that compendium of New Orleans cooking, The Picayune Original Creole Cookbook *(still in print from the Times-Picayune Publishing Corporation in New Orleans), I prepare lamb breast often. "Epigram" is an apt name for these concentrated nuggets of lambness, and their preparation is really simpler than it sounds.*

BARBECUED LAMB RIBLETS

2 racks lamb breast	1 cup barbecue sauce of your
Salt and freshly ground	choice
pepper	

*P*reheat the oven to 400°F.

Cut off any fell and fat from the top of the ribs—the surface should be mostly a thin layer of meat. Also remove as much fat from the bottom as you can. Rub the ribs all over with salt and pepper, then cut into 3- or 4-rib sections.

Lay the sections, meaty side down, in a large shallow roasting pan. Brush

well with tangy barbecue sauce and bake for 1 hour, turning once, draining any fat off, and brushing the tops with more sauce.
Serves 4.

There is little meat to lamb ribs, but what there is is choice. This, plus the fact you eat them with your fingers, makes them a family rather than a company matter. I like them so much I often prepare them when I'm home alone— with corn on the cob (another finger food) and crisp slaw and beer.

"RAGOO" OF LAMB AND ASPARAGUS

1	pound boneless lamb, cut in 1 inch cubes from a rare-cooked leg (about 2 cups)	1	bay leaf Salt and freshly ground pepper
4	tablespoons butter Freshly grated nutmeg	¼	teaspoon dried rosemary
3	tablespoons flour	1	pound asparagus, cleaned and cut in 1-inch sections (reserving tips)
¾	pound mushrooms, cleaned and quartered		Juice of ½ lemon
2	cups beef stock, heated		

*I*n a frying pan, sauté the lamb cubes in butter for several minutes over a medium-high flame. The butter should not burn. Remove the cubes with a slotted spoon and scrape some nutmeg over them.

Add the flour and mushrooms to the pan and cook for several minutes, stirring. Add the hot stock and seasonings and simmer 10 minutes, stirring occasionally.

Add the asparagus (all but the tips) and cook 5 minutes. Finally add the tips and lamb and cook another 5 minutes, or until the asparagus is tender. Add the lemon juice and taste for seasoning. Serve immediately.
Serves 4.

This remarkably modern-looking dish is adapted from an old colonial receipt. It is an almost Chinese method for use of leftover lamb, though it may also be made from raw pieces if you cook the meat rather more than you would here. A fine way to serve it is with rice tossed with toasted pine nuts.

FOUR SEASONS GROUND LAMB

1 pound lean ground lamb	⅓ cup pine nuts
1 teaspoon curry powder	1 tablespoon butter
¼ teaspoon ground coriander	1 tablespoon vegetable oil
½ teaspoon paprika	⅓ cup ice water
Salt	Chutney

*P*ut the lamb in a bowl and combine with the spices and salt to taste. Sauté the pine nuts in the butter and oil over medium heat until they are golden, then drain them on paper towels. Mix them into the meat, then add the ice water, bit by bit, until the meat absorbs all of it. Shape into oval patties about an inch thick and refrigerate for 2 hours or more.

These are best cooked over a charcoal fire, but they can also be broiled or sautéed 5 to 7 minutes per side—they should be brown on the outside and still a little pink on the inside. Serve with dollops of chutney.

Serves 4.

Knowing my fondness for ground lamb, a friend sent me this recipe from New York's Four Seasons Restaurant. It is a delight served with something like saffron rice and a green vegetable—or perhaps Deep-fried Eggplant (page 233). Ground lamb is not easy to find, for some reason, for it seems to take a thrifty, smart butcher to realize that all the lamb scraps can be used up this way. And such a delicious way.

Variety Meats

*E*veryone has his terror among the innards, and mine seems to be tongue. For some it is as simple as an aversion to liver, this terror—but always it is irrational, having more to do with texture than actual flavor, or even a repugnance to handling in preparation. No matter, everyone has sweepingly silly dislikes, culinary or not, inexplicable to anyone else. This chapter is for that anyone else. Except for tongue (and brains, for which I could find no clearly home-grown recipe) there is a little of everything to go around, from liver to kidney to sweetbreads to heart.

MY LIVER AND ONIONS

2	tablespoons butter		Tabasco
2	cups sliced onions	4	slices bacon
	Freshly grated nutmeg	4	portions calves' liver
2	tablespoons heavy cream		Lemon juice
	Salt and freshly ground		Minced parsley
	pepper		

*M*elt the butter in a saucepan, add the onions, and when they start to cook, toss and turn the heat as far down as possible. Cover the pan with a tight-fitting lid, and simmer until the onions become mushy—about 45 minutes. (Take care, they should not brown or burn. The onions themselves usually release liquid enough, if the heat is not too high, to stew beautifully.) When quite soft, whirl in a blender or food processor, with a pinch of nutmeg, the cream, salt and pepper to taste, and a drop or two of Tabasco. Return to the saucepan to keep warm.

Fry the bacon until it is crisp, drain it on paper toweling, and crumble. Dry the liver and sauté quickly in the bacon fat so that it is golden outside but still pink in the middle—the time will vary depending on the thickness of the liver.

Sprinkle with a bit of lemon juice and salt and pepper to taste. To serve, place the liver on warm plates, coat each slice with some onion purée, and sprinkle the bacon, then some minced parsley, on top.

Serves 4.

This dish exists as a result of twenty years or so refining the already excellent American dish of liver, onions, and bacon. Here, the three tastes and textures are simultaneous rather than side by side, and I am proud to call it mine. As liver is seldom submitted to guests, however, it remains a secret family triumph. There, I accompany it simply with creamy mashed potatoes and butter, and a bottle of mellow red wine.

LIVER MADAME BÉGUÉ
WITH FRENCH-FRIED SWEET POTATOES

1½ to 2	pounds calves' liver (or chicken livers)	¼	cup minced parsley
	Salt and freshly ground pepper	½	cup dry white wine
		1	tablespoon brandy (optional)
	Pinch of ground mace		Vegetable oil
1	cup chopped green onions with part of tops	1	recipe Deep-fried Sweet Potatoes (page 260)
			Lemon quarters
1	clove garlic, minced		Parsley sprigs

*H*ave your butcher cut the liver in 1-inch-thick slices, or buy a whole piece. Remove any outer skin and tough blood vessels, and cut the liver into 1-inch dice. (Or take chicken livers, cut in half through the separating strand, and prick several times with a fork to allow the marinade to permeate.)

Cover with salt, pepper, mace, green onions, garlic, parsley, wine, and brandy if you use it. Let marinate for an hour or more.

When ready to cook, drain, pat dry with paper towels, and fry in deep oil—it should have begun to smoke (375°F)—for about 1 minute, or until still just pink inside. Test a piece to see.

Drain on paper towels, and keep warm while you prepare the sweet potatoes in the same fat (skimmed). To serve, sprinkle with salt, place attractively on warm plates with lemon quarters, parsley sprigs, and a heap of crisp potatoes.

Serves 4.

A recipe with a curious history. I had passed over Madame Bégué's liver non-chalantly: "Secure a fine bit of calf liver, fresh and of good color. Skin well. Have a quantity of lard in frying pan, well heated. Slice liver in thick pieces. Place in lard and let cook slowly after seasoning with pepper and salt. Let lard cover liver. Simmer on slow fire and when cooked drain off grease and serve on hot plate." Then I found in a Prudence Penny cookbook from 1947 a rec-ipe for Liver à la Madame Bégué that marinated the liver in onion and parsley for several hours before cooking in deep fat, with a garnish of lemon and pars-ley. Such is the secret life of recipes, that in the process of trying Prudence Penny's version I came on a marinade from the night before, and thought if it's to have onion and parsley—why not the whole shebang? The result is, if somewhat beyond La Bégué, ineffable. Do also try the French-fried sweet potatoes with it since you have the fat right there—they are every bit as good as the liver itself.

COUNTRY LIVER WITH HERBS

1½	pounds calves' or beef liver, sliced ½ inch thick	½	cup flour
	Milk (optional)	6	tablespoons butter
	Salt and freshly ground pepper	2	tablespoons white wine tarragon vinegar
1	teaspoon paprika	½	cup minced parsley
		2	tablespoons minced chives

*T*rim the liver of its tough outer skin and veins, then cover with milk and let sit an hour or so. The milk is not necessary if you use fine calves' liver, but it mellows beef liver considerably.

When ready to cook, drain the liver and pat dry with paper towels. Shake with salt, pepper, paprika, and flour. Melt the butter in a frying pan and sauté the slices over medium heat just until they are lightly browned—not more than 4 to 5 minutes a side. Remove to a hot plate.

Stir the vinegar into the pan juices, scrape up all the brown bits, and stir over a medium flame. Add the parsley and chives, and turn the liver in the sauce several times. Place immediately on warm plates and serve with buttered noodles.

Serves 4.

A farmhouse dish identical to the French aux fines herbes, *except there white wine is used rather than vinegar. I find, though, that a delicate tarragon wine vinegar is actually more interesting in the finished product—a very fine dish indeed.*

LIVER MARYLAND

2	tablespoons butter		Cayenne
3	slices bacon, cut in ¼-inch	1	cup sliced mushrooms
	strips	½	cup Madeira
1	medium onion, chopped	1	tablespoon catsup
1	clove garlic, minced	1	anchovy fillet, minced (or
	Minced parsley		½ teaspoon anchovy
	Pinch of dried thyme		paste)
	Pinch of dried summer savory	1½	pounds liver (either calf or
	Pinch of ground cloves		beef)
	Salt and freshly ground		Flour
	pepper		Vegetable oil

*M*elt the butter in a saucepan over medium heat. Add the bacon, onion, and garlic and sauté until the onion is transparent. Add ¼ cup minced parsley, the remaining herbs, spices, and mushrooms, then turn the heat down low, cover the pan, and let simmer gently 1 hour. Check occasionally—the mushrooms should give off enough liquid, but if not add a little Madeira from time to time.

To finish the sauce, add ½ cup Madeira, catsup, and anchovy. Turn up the heat and let the sauce bubble, stirring until thick and rich.

To cook the liver, trim well and slice in bite-sized strips. Shake them in flour, then sauté in hot oil for several minutes—or until golden on the outside but still pink inside. Remove the pieces as they cook and put into the sauce. Heat several minutes and serve sprinkled with parsley.

Serves 4.

For liver fanciers this dish reaches new heights, and one suspects even those who are not might find something to savor in this complex balanced preparation. I don't know why Maryland seems to be such a font of fine cooking, but it was and is and will probably continue to be. The liver needs, of course, some such bland foil as potatoes, noodles, or toast points, and certainly a decent red wine.

CHICKEN LIVERS IN MADEIRA CREAM

1½	pounds chicken livers	1	teaspoon Worcestershire
4	tablespoons butter		sauce
1	tablespoon flour		Few drops of lemon juice
¼	cup dry Madeira	¼	cup minced parsley (or
1	cup heavy cream		chives)
	Salt and freshly ground		
	pepper		

Cut the livers in half where the small tendon holds them together, pat dry with paper towels, and sauté in the butter until they are lightly browned but still pink on the inside—about 8 to 10 minutes.

Remove about three fourths of the livers and keep warm. Sprinkle the flour over the livers remaining in the pan and cook a few minutes, stirring. Add the Madeira and cream, stir over low heat till the cream thickens, then purée in a blender or food processor.

Return the purée to the pan, and over low heat add salt, pepper, the Worcestershire, and a few drops of lemon to taste. If the sauce seems too thick, add a little more cream.

Add the reserved livers to the sauce and heat without boiling. To serve, place on warm plates and sprinkle with parsley—or better yet chives if you have them.

Serves 4.

What a suave concoction this is, with the livers making part of the sauce. They can be served with potatoes or noodles, but my favorite is to have them with toast points that have been sautéed in butter till crisp and brown. They are so rich you won't need much else but a vegetable and salad.

HUNTSVILLE DEVILED KIDNEYS

6	lamb kidneys (or 4 veal	1	tablespoon Worcestershire
	kidneys)		sauce
3	tablespoons butter		Cayenne
1	tablespoon Dijon mustard		Toast
2	tablespoons lemon juice		Minced parsley
1	tablespoon finely grated onion		

*I*f the kidneys have a thin filament still covering them, peel it off. Cut them in ¼-inch slices, and cut out any fat or white tissue. Mix the butter, mustard, lemon, onion, Worcestershire, and cayenne to taste in a frying pan set over high heat. When the mixture bubbles, put the kidneys in and toss until all traces of pink are gone—about 5 minutes. Serve immediately on toast, sprinkled with parsley.

Serves 2 (can be easily doubled).

One seldom finds many kidneys at once, but when you do it's easy to freeze them until you've collected enough for a meal. Look them over carefully, and choose only the freshest looking—if they seem even a little darkened or dry, they will have a strong odor and are beyond cooking. This recipe seems to be of British descent (they dote on deviled kidneys of any stripe) and comes from a pretty little ladies' club cookbook with unusually good recipes.

STUFFED LAMB KIDNEYS

6	lamb kidneys	1	egg, beaten
¼	cup finely mined onion		Milk
¼	cup finely minced celery		Salt
1	tablespoon butter		Paprika
1	cup bread crumbs	6	slices bacon
2	tablespoons minced parsley		

*P*reheat the oven to 400°F.

Wash the kidneys, peel off any filament, and slice them in half lengthwise. Cut out the knob of fat at the base of each and set aside.

In a small pan, sauté the onion and celery for several minutes or until limp, in the butter. Combine with the bread crumbs and parsley. Add the egg, and enough milk to make the dressing moist, then season to taste with salt and a pinch of paprika.

Cut the bacon slices in half and spread the dressing evenly over them. Lay each kidney half, uncut side down, on a bacon slice and wrap it up with the stuffing. Secure with a toothpick.

Place on a baking pan and bake 20 minutes. Serve immediately.

Serves 2 (can be easily doubled).

These may be served as a dinner dish, but I prefer them as part of a breakfast or brunch, with eggs and hot buttered toast.

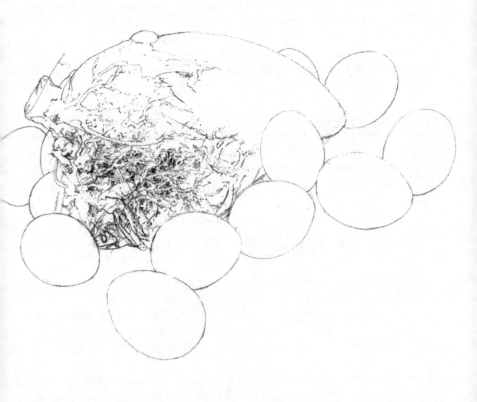

IOWA LEMON-BRAISED LAMB HEARTS

3 lamb hearts	Pinch of dried thyme
3 tablespoons butter	Salt and freshly ground
1 tablespoon flour	pepper
2 thin slices lemon	Pinch of ground mace
1 bay leaf	¼ cup minced parsley

Wash the hearts inside and out, then cut in slices across the grain—removing any of the larger veins, etc. Put the butter in a frying pan over medium heat, and when it sizzles brown the heart slices quickly.

Add the flour and let it become golden, then add the lemon slices, herbs, and spices. Cover with water, stir well, and let it come to a boil. Reduce the heat and simmer gently, covered, for 1½ hours.

When done, most of the liquid should have cooked away, the hearts should be tender and moist, and there should be a rich lemony sauce. To serve, discard the bay leaf and lemon slices, and place on warm plates sprinkled with parsley.

Serves 4.

For those who like the curious texture of heart (beef heart will also do in this recipe), this Midwestern dish will be a welcome one to try with either Purée of Cauliflower (page 228) or Shaker Alabaster (page 247), and of course a full-bodied red wine.

SWEETBREADS COUNTRY STYLE

2 pounds veal sweetbreads	Freshly ground pepper
Juice of 1 lemon (or 2	¼ teaspoon dried thyme
tablespoons vinegar)	4 slices bacon, cut in small
Salt	strips
Flour	3 tablespoons butter, melted

Soak the sweetbreads for several hours in ice water, changing the water twice. Drain, then soak again in ice water, with the juice of ½ lemon (or 1 tablespoon of the vinegar) and a little salt, for another hour.

Drain, and put in a saucepan with water to cover, the rest of the lemon juice or vinegar, and a little salt. Bring to a boil, lower the heat, and simmer 15 minutes. Drain, then put the sweetbreads in ice water for 15 minutes more. Take them out of the water and pat dry.

Separate the lobes of the sweetbreads, discarding any membrane and connective tissue. Refrigerate until ready to assemble the dish.

Preheat the oven to 450°F.

Shake the sweetbreads in a bag of flour, and put them in a casserole large enough to hold them in a single layer. Sprinkle with salt and pepper to taste, then the thyme. Scatter the bacon strips on top, then dribble with melted butter.

Bake 25 minutes, basting with the pan fat twice during the cooking. When they are done, the bacon and the sweetbreads both will have crisped.

Serves 4.

All that lengthy soaking and draining and soaking and draining, then the careful peeling away of membranes, makes most people steer away from preparing sweetbreads at home—though these same people may seek them out on restaurant menus. It's not really all that difficult, but it does take time and a bit of patience. With all this in mind, and the fact that restaurants want to make as much money out of this labor as possible, most preparations of sweetbreads are so sauced and mushroomed and sherried as to obscure their delicate flavor. But not this Midwestern farm recipe, which presents them at their simple sensuous best. They should be accompanied by similarly delicate flavors—perhaps Georgia Summer Squash Soufflé (page 243) and Colonial Green Beans with Mace (page 223).

VIRGINIA SWEETBREADS
WITH HAM AND MUSHROOMS

1½	pounds veal sweetbreads	½	cup heavy cream
	Juice of 1 lemon	1	teaspoon lemon juice
	Salt		Cayenne
½	cup dry sherry	4	slices white bread, trimmed
4	tablespoons butter		of crusts
1	cup sliced mushrooms	4	thin slices ham

Soak the sweetbreads for several hours in ice water, changing the water twice. Drain, then soak again in ice water with the juice of a lemon and 1 teaspoon salt for another hour.

Drain, then cook with water to cover and ¼ cup of the sherry, at a simmer, for 15 minutes. Drain, place again in ice water for 15 minutes, then drain again and pat dry.

With your hands, separate the lobes of the sweetbreads, discarding outer membranes and connective tissue. Refrigerate until ready to assemble the dish.

Sauté the sweetbreads in 2 tablespoons of the butter a few minutes until they start to brown, then add the mushrooms and sauté a few minutes more, until the mushrooms are limp. Add the remaining ¼ cup sherry and the cream, and let the mixture boil over high heat until it thickens slightly. Add 1 teaspoon lemon juice and salt and cayenne to taste. Keep warm.

Preheat the oven to 375°F.

Sauté the bread in the remaining 2 tablespoons butter until lightly browned on both sides, and top each with a slice of ham. Place in four individual ramekins, and top with the sweetbreads and their sauce.

Bake 15 minutes, or until the sweetbreads begin to take color and bubble. Serve immediately.

Serves 4.

This fine old recipe is worth all the time and trouble of sweetbread preparation. In the opulent nineteenth-century tradition of dining, these would constitute one course out of many, but these days they will happily accommodate the main course of a meal, with soup, salad, and dessert. They deserve a fine mellow white wine.

Chicken

From the far-off days of my mother or grandmother chopping heads on the chicken-coop block is a long way to remember a flavor, particularly as there were then no comparisons. But I can yet as an adult recall the taste of a chicken ordered in an English village, brought up "on the ground" as we would say, but there one simply ordered "real." And a real bird it was—succulent from crisp skin to pulled wishbone. True, today's chickens cost little, as they leap off assembly lines into every pot, packaged and plucked of any true savor, but there we have them—and fortunately with a galore of past recipes to make even the most tasteless meat a daily shared delight.

NEW ENGLAND BAKED SPRING CHICKEN

1 chicken 3 to 4 pounds	6 sprigs parsley
Salt and freshly ground	¾ cup dry sherry (or dry
pepper	Madeira, or dry white
Butter	wine)
1 large onion	2 slices bacon

*P*reheat the oven to 325°F.

Rub the chicken inside and out with salt, pepper, and butter. Chop the onion coarsely and stuff the cavity with it and the parsley. Put a lump of butter in, and skewer and truss.

Place in a baking pan and pour sherry over. Lay the slices of bacon crisscross over the breast. Put in the oven and bake 2 hours, basting every 15 minutes or so.

Serves 4.

The slow cooking and basting here produce an extremely succulent, tasty meat. In fact, it is by far the best way to cook chicken for any dish calling for such, as the flesh is so beautifully textured (you can substitute chicken stock for the wine if you so wish, for this). Roast chicken can be served very simply with potatoes and carrots cooked round it, being doused also in the juices—or, if you feel extravagant, with whole cooked artichoke bottoms glazed in the juices toward the end, then filled with sautéed chicken livers.

CHICKEN STUFFED WITH CRAB APPLES

1 chicken (3 to 4 pounds)	1 onion slice
Salt and freshly ground	2 slices bacon
pepper	¼ cup dry sherry (or Madeira)
Butter	Saffron rice
1 jar spiced crab apples (home	Toasted almonds
style, not the bright red	
ones)	

*P*reheat the oven to 325°F.

Rub the chicken inside and out with salt, pepper, and butter. Put a lump of butter inside the cavity, with the giblets, a slice of onion, and as many crab apples as will fit.

Skewer and truss the bird, and crisscross the bacon over its breast. Place in a roaster with ½ cup of the juice from the crab apples, and the sherry or Madeira. Bake for 2 hours, basting every 15 minutes with the juices. During the last 15 minutes place the rest of the crab apples around the chicken to glaze and heat.

To serve, remove the bacon and place the chicken on a bed of saffron rice. Sprinkle with toasted almonds and garnish with the hot crab apples.

Serves 4.

Needless to say, this makes a spectacular company dish—and of course it may be carved in the kitchen, if you wish, before placing on the rice, to save any despair at carving before guests. The process can also be adapted for duckling, though the crab apple juice and sherry should be added to the pan after most of the fat has been rendered from the duck, and the bacon should be omitted.

PENNSYLVANIA CHICKEN STUFFED WITH SAUERKRAUT AND APPLES

1	chicken (3 to 4 pounds)	½	cup chopped celery
	Salt and freshly ground	3	cups sauerkraut
	pepper	2	tart apples, peeled, cored,
4	tablespoons butter		and grated
1	medium onion, chopped	1	tablespoon caraway seeds

*P*reheat the oven to 350°F.

Rub the chicken inside and out with salt and pepper. Melt the butter in a large frying pan. Sauté the onion and celery in it till they are limp.

Place the kraut in a colander and run water over it in order to remove some of its sharpness. Drain thoroughly and add to the onion mixture. Add the apples and caraway seeds, salt and pepper to taste, and toss over medium heat for a few minutes.

Remove from the flame, and when cool enough to handle, stuff the chicken loosely, truss it, and rub with butter. Put the remaining dressing in a casserole or small roasting pan and nestle the chicken into it.

Tuck the giblets into the sauerkraut. Cover and bake for 1¼ hours, then uncover and bake another 45 minutes to brown.

Serves 4.

This hearty dish should be accompanied by a full-bodied, fragrant white wine, and either boiled potatoes sprinkled with parsley or My Grandmother's Drop Noodles (page 263).

MY BUTTERMILK FRIED CHICKEN

1	chicken, cut-up	1	bay leaf
	Buttermilk		Salt and freshly ground
¼	cup minced parsley		pepper
1	small onion		Flour
1	stalk celery, cut up		Vegetable oil
1	carrot, cut up		

*R*emove the wing tips from the chicken and put together with its neck and giblets. Marinate the chicken in buttermilk to cover, and minced parsley, for several hours.

Take the trimmings and giblets and place in a saucepan with water to cover, the vegetables, bay leaf, and salt and pepper to taste. Simmer for 2 hours, then drain and reserve the stock.

To cook the chicken, mix flour with salt and pepper. Without wiping the marinade off the chicken, shake the pieces in seasoned flour and lay aside on waxed paper.

Over medium-high heat, fry the chicken, in batches, in ½ inch hot oil till each piece is golden brown. As they are cooked, lift out into a baking dish that will hold all in one layer.

Preheat the oven to 300°F.

Pour enough buttermilk around the chicken to come up to less than half the depth of the chicken. Bake, uncovered, for 1½ hours, or until quite tender and crisp on top.

When done, remove the chicken and keep warm. To the pan of coddled drippings, add some of the chicken stock, stirring and scraping over high heat. Add this to a blender or food processor and whirl till smooth.

Place back in the pan and cook over medium heat, adding stock and stirring, until the sauce is the consistency of thick cream.

Serve the chicken, in a pool of the sauce, on warm plates. Pass the rest of the sauce in a sauceboat at table, with hot biscuits.

Serves 4.

My fried chicken is the horror of some purists, who insist that it is neither fried nor has the "right" kind of gravy. That there are as many ways of frying chicken as there are cooks is no argument to such people, and I can only say that this is the way I fry chicken. It is particularly savory, with much delicate crust on top and a creamy underside. It also makes a good sauce I think much better than floury milk gravy. If you wish, it may be served with the coddled drippings as they come from the pan, rather than the sauce—it may be less pretty, but this residue is wonderful spread on biscuits.

ALABAMA FRIED CHICKEN WITH MILK GRAVY AND FRIED BISCUITS

1 chicken, cut up	Flour
1 egg	Fat for deep frying
½ cup milk	½ cup chicken stock, heated
Salt and freshly ground	1½ cups milk
pepper	1 recipe biscuit dough

Wash and dry the chicken. Beat the egg with the milk and some salt and pepper. Dip the chicken in this, then shake in flour. Put in refrigerator to "set" for 30 minutes or more.

Preheat the oven to 350°F.

In a frying pan or deep fat cooker, bring 1 inch fat to 350°F. Fry the chicken, first on one side, then the other, till golden brown on both.

Place in the oven for 20 minutes while you make the gravy and fried biscuits.

To prepare the gravy, drain off the fat from the pan, putting 2 tablespoons of it and any fried bits in a saucepan. Add 2 tablespoons flour and cook, stirring, until golden over medium heat. Add the stock, milk, and salt and pepper to taste. Cook, stirring, until the gravy thickens, then turn the fire low and let bubble 10 minutes, or until ready to serve. If it gets too thick, add some more milk.

To prepare the biscuits, heat the deep fat to 375°F. Roll out the biscuit dough ¼ inch thick and cut into strips 1 x ½ inch. Drop these strips, in batches, into the hot fat and fry until golden brown on the bottom. Turn and fry until the other side is brown. Lift out with a slotted spoon onto paper towels, and salt lightly.

To serve, place the pieces of chicken on warm plates with a heap of fried biscuits. Pass the milk gravy separately.

Serves 4.

This one is for purists, not to mention those who fancy fried biscuits.

SMITHFIELD CHICKEN

1	chicken, cut up	2	cups heavy cream, heated
1	medium onion, chopped		Freshly grated nutmeg
1	carrot, sliced	2	cups bread crumbs
1	stalk celery, sliced	½	cup minced green onions
2	sprigs parsley		with part of tops
2	whole cloves	2	tablespoons minced parsley
4	peppercorns	1	teaspoon dried summer
	Salt		savory
2	tablespoons butter		Freshly ground pepper
2	tablespoons flour	8	thin slices Smithfield ham

*S*tew the chicken in water to cover with the onion, carrot, celery, parsley, cloves, peppercorns, and salt to taste for 1 hour, or until the chicken is tender.

Remove from the broth, and when cool remove all the flesh and discard the bones and skin; strain the broth and reserve. Cut the meat into bite-sized pieces and place in a baking dish that can be brought to table.

Melt the butter in a saucepan, stir in the flour, and cook over low heat for several minutes, stirring. Add the hot cream all at once, then cook, stirring, until the sauce thickens and is smooth. Add salt to taste, some nutmeg, and let simmer 15 to 20 minutes over very low heat.

Preheat the oven to 300°F.

Pour the sauce over the chicken and let stand while you make the stuffing. Mix the bread crumbs with the green onions, parsley, savory, and salt and pepper. Add just enough of the reserved broth to make the stuffing hold together. Reserve ¼ cup of the stuffing, and divide the rest into 8 heaps.

Place the stuffing in the center of each slice of ham and roll the slices around in the shape of peaked croquettes. Nestle these down into the chicken in an attractive arrangement.

Sprinkle the reserved stuffing on top and bake at 30 minutes, or until the sauce begins to bubble and brown lightly. Serve immediately.

Serves 4.

When Smithfield Ham is available in your specialty store, seize on it, for this is certainly one of our most distinguished chicken dishes. It is particularly gracious to modern tasteless birds, which are too bland for most roasting and stuffing treatment. The ham gives a savor to the whole that is well worth its expense. Other cured hams can be used, certainly—Westphalian Ham particularly makes a splendid, if not authentic, substitution.

COLONIAL CHICKEN PUDDING

1	chicken, cut up	¼	teaspoon dried thyme
1	medium onion, chopped	1	bay leaf
1	carrot, sliced		Flour
1	stalk celery, sliced	4	tablespoons butter
2	sprigs parsley	3	eggs
	Salt and freshly ground	1	cup milk
	pepper	2	tablespoons butter, melted

Take the back, neck, wing tips, and giblets (except the liver) of the chicken, and cover with water in a kettle to cover. Add the onion, carrot, celery, parsley, and seasonings, then simmer about 1 hour. Strain and reserve the stock.

Shake the pieces of chicken with flour seasoned with salt and pepper. Heat the butter in a frying pan, and sauté the chicken until brown-gold all over. Add enough stock to come up halfway on the chicken, cover the pan tightly, and cook gently 45 minutes, or until the chicken is tender.

Preheat the oven to 450°F.

Transfer the chicken pieces with a slotted spoon to a greased baking dish, 1½ inches deep or more, and large enough to hold all the chicken in a single layer. Reserve the juices in the pan.

Make a batter by sifting 1¼ cups flour with ½ teaspoon salt into a bowl. Beat the eggs until frothy, pour the milk and melted butter into them, and mix well into the flour till the batter is smooth. Pour this over the chicken making sure all the pieces are covered as evenly as possible.

Pop immediately into the hot oven. Bake 15 minutes at 450°F, then lower the heat to 350°F and continue baking for another 20 to 25 minutes, or until the topping puffs up and is browned—like a Yorkshire pudding.

While the pudding bakes, scrape the juices from the chicken pan into a blender or food processor, whirl, and return to the pan. Cook down gently, and if it is necessary, thicken with a bit of soft butter worked with flour.

Serve the sauce separately in a sauceboat, as you bring the pudding to table.

Serves 4.

Considering this pudding seems a common one in colonial days, and is so particularly delicious, it is curious that it is seldom served these days. It is much more interesting than any of the various pot pies, etc., and is quite a simple dish to master. It makes even a quite ample company meal with good white wine, a fresh light soup before, an interesting salad or vegetable after, and any outstanding dessert.

SHAKER CHICKEN IN CIDER CREAM

1	chicken, cut up		Salt and freshly ground
4	tablespoons butter		pepper
½ to ¾	cup hard cider	1	cup heavy cream
	Grated rind of 1 lemon		

*I*n a large frying pan, sauté the chicken in the butter over a medium flame until it is golden on both sides. Add ½ cup cider, then cover the pan and cook over low heat for 30 to 40 minutes, or until tender.

Check while cooking, and if the chicken tends to get dry, add more cider. When done, lift the pieces out with a slotted spoon onto a warm platter and keep warm in the oven. Add enough cider so there is about ¼ cup liquid in the pan, along with the lemon rind and salt and pepper to taste.

Add the cream, turn the heat up high, and cook, stirring with a whisk, until the sauce thickens slightly. Pour over the chicken and serve.

Serves 4.

A delicious dish reminiscent of Normandy in its use of cider. If hard cider is not available, unsweetened apple juice is acceptable—with a squeeze or so of extra lemon juice, or a dash of Calvados, added along with the grated rind. It should be served with Fried Apple Rings (page 220) and a fragrant chilled white wine.

CHICKEN CHARLESTON

1	chicken, cut up	2½	teaspoons curry powder
4	tablespoons butter	1	cup heavy cream
4	cups chopped onion	⅓	cup dark rum (or brandy)
1	clove garlic, minced		Hot cooked rice
	Salt and freshly ground		
	pepper		

Wash and dry the chicken pieces. Melt the butter in a frying pan and sauté the chicken lightly. Lift the pieces onto a plate. Add the onion and garlic to the pan and cook over medium heat until straw colored. Sprinkle with salt and pepper. Place the chicken pieces, skin side down, into the onion, cover, and cook slowly on top of the stove for 15 minutes.

Remove the cover, turn the chicken, and cook slowly, uncovered, 20 minutes more. Add water if it gets too dry. Remove the chicken from the pan when its juices run golden when stuck with a fork, and keep warm.

Sprinkle curry powder over the onion and cook a few minutes, stirring, then add the cream and rum. Boil down, stirring, until the sauce is slightly thickened. Taste for seasoning, pour over the chicken, and serve with fluffy rice.

Serves 4.

This Charleston extravaganza is one of my all time favorites to serve company. It is rich and delicately flavored (neither the curry nor rum should be so evident as to overwhelm either the chicken or onion flavors) as well as both easy and elegant. The original recipe had twice as much butter and cream, but that was perhaps gilding the lily too much! It is at its best served with Thomas Jefferson's Pilau (page 266) rather than plain boiled rice.

CHICKEN IN GREEN CORN

1	chicken, cut up		Salt and freshly ground
2	tablespoons butter		pepper
6 to 8	ears of corn	½	cup heavy cream
		6	slices bacon, cut in half

*P*reheat the oven to 325°F.

Wash and dry the chicken pieces, then sauté until golden in the butter. Place the pieces in a casserole of a size to hold them all nicely in a single layer, then add salt and pepper.

Scrape the corn kernels into a bowl with the sharp side of a knife, then scrape the "milk" out with the dull side; you should have 4 cups. Salt and pepper this to taste, and pour over the chicken..

Add the cream and place the bacon in a pattern over the top. Put in the oven, covered with foil or a lid, for 30 minutes. Then uncover and cook 30 more, or until the bacon crisps and curls.

Serves 4.

Green corn means always fresh young corn rushed from the field, but any fresh market corn is fine here. It is a dish to come to over and over for family, served with cole slaw and hot biscuits. (But one has an idea that secretly company would sometimes prefer such homely fare to more elegant dishes.)

ALMOND CHICKEN CREOLE

1 chicken, cut up	2 cups drained and chopped
Flour	canned tomatoes
Salt and freshly ground	½ cup beer
pepper	¼ cup dried currants (or raisins)
Olive oil	½ cup toasted blanched,
2 cups chopped onion	slivered almonds
1 clove garlic, minced	Saffron rice
½ cup chopped green pepper	

*R*inse and dry the chicken pieces. Shake in flour seasoned with salt and pepper. Heat enough olive oil to cover the bottom of your frying pan and brown the pieces over medium heat until golden on all sides. Remove with a slotted spoon and keep warm.

Add the onion and garlic to the oil, then the green pepper, and cook till soft. Add the tomatoes and bring to a boil. Replace the chicken in the bubbling vegetables, and add beer and salt to taste.

Spoon the sauce over and around the chicken, cover, and simmer 45 minutes, turning the chicken several times. Add currants or raisins the last 10 minutes of cooking. If necessary, this may be kept warm some time before serving.

To serve, place the chicken in a ring of saffron rice and sprinkle with toasted almonds.

Serves 4.

If it had a pinch of curry, this would be called "Country Captain"—I find it simply delicious as is. Frankly this sauce Creole (for that is what it is) seems the best of all tomato sauces, perhaps because of the beer. With the presentation on a bed of yellow rice, and sprinkled with almonds, it makes a fine, inexpensive company dish. For that it is pleasant to begin with some such first course as Watercress Salad à la Germaine (page 285), with perhaps hot rolls or homemade individual loaves of bread, then the chicken itself served with a fine California Chardonnay, and lastly a dessert such as Roanoke Rum Cream (page 382).

CHICKEN FRICASSEE

1 chicken, cut up	⅓ cup minced parsley
Salt and freshly ground	1 medium onion, chopped
pepper	2 cloves garlic
1 bay leaf	4 tablespoons butter
6 peppercorns	¼ cup flour
2 whole cloves	2 egg yolks
1 teaspoon dried summer savory	1 cup heavy cream, heated
1 teaspoon dried tarragon	

*R*emove any fat from the chicken and render it by placing it in a small saucepan with some water and letting it cook down gently 15 minutes, or until the water is cooked away and only liquid fat and golden nuggets are left. Take out the nuggets and measure 3 tablespoons of the fat into a frying pan.

Wash and dry the chicken, sprinkle with salt and pepper, then brown thoroughly in the fat over medium heat. Put in a stew pot, add boiling water to cover, the spices, herbs, and onion.

While the water comes to a boil, put the cloves of garlic in hot water to cover and simmer gently for a few minutes. Drain, slip off their skins, and add them to the pot. Cook gently an hour, adding salt to taste the last 10 minutes.

Remove the chicken pieces with a slotted spoon and keep warm. Strain the stock and measure—there should be 3 cups. If not, add more chicken stock to make it up.

In a saucepan, melt the butter, stir in the flour, and cook several minutes, stirring. Pour 1 cup of the stock in. Simmer a bit, stirring till smooth, then add the rest of the stock, stirring again till free from lumps. Cook, uncovered, over low heat 10 minutes.

Beat the egg yolks in a bowl, then add the hot cream gradually, stirring constantly. Add this to the thickened stock, along with the chicken pieces, and heat slowly without allowing the mixture to boil. Serve with homemade dumplings, or noodles.

Serves 4.

What a lost world the word fricassee calls up! It is still the Sundayest of Sunday dishes, suave, rich, and satisfying to the soul as well as body.

CHICKEN CHILE VERDE TAMALE PIE

1 chicken (2½ to 3 pounds)
1 onion, sliced
1 clove garlic, flattened
  Salt
6 peppercorns
1 bay leaf
½ teaspoon dried oregano
1 cup chopped green onions, with part of tops
1 clove garlic, minced
5 tablespoons minced parsley
2 tablespoons minced fresh coriander (optional)
1 medium green pepper, seeded and grated (discarding the skin)

1 can (4 ounces) mild green chilies, drained and chopped
2 jalapeño peppers (bottled en escabeche), seeded and minced
¼ cup flour
1¼ teaspoons sugar
  Juice of ½ lemon
3 cups milk, scalded
1 cup cornmeal (preferably stone-ground)
1 tablespoon butter
3 eggs, separated
¼ cup pumpkin seeds (or toasted pine nuts)

*E*arly in the day, or the day before, boil the chicken in water to cover with the sliced onion, garlic, salt to taste, peppercorns, bay leaf, and oregano for 45 minutes. Let chill in the stock. When the fat has hardened, remove and save it. Remove the flesh from the chicken, melt the stock down, and strain it into a large pan. Boil the stock down, uncovered, till you have about 4 cups.

In another suacepan, sauté the green onions and minced garlic in 2 table-spoons of the chicken fat for several minutes, then add, one by one, 2 table-spoons of the parsley, coriander, green pepper, green chilies, and jalapeños. Cook 5 minutes, stirring now and again. Stir in the flour and let cook another 5 minutes, then add the stock all at once and stir until smooth over high heat. Add ¼ teaspoon of the sugar and the lemon juice, then taste for season-ing. Let simmer, uncovered, 20 minutes, then remove from the fire, add the chicken meat, and pour into a 12 x 9-inch casserole.

Preheat the oven to 350°F.

Sprinkle the cornmeal over the hot milk in a saucepan and stir 5 minutes over medium heat, or until the mixture is smooth and thick. Stir in 1 tea-spoon salt, remaining 1 teaspoon sugar, and butter, then the remaining 3 ta-blespoons parsley. Stir in the egg yolks, one by one, then whip the whites stiff (but not dry) and fold carefully in.

Spoon the tamale mixture in dollops over the chicken mixture and spread out as far as you can to the edges. Sprinkle pumpkin seeds or pine nuts over the pie and bake 40 to 45 minutes, or until golden, puffed, and bubbly.

Serves 6.

There are as many tamale pies as cooks in the Southwest, most simply a meat-chili mixture, perhaps with beans and some cheese, nestled in a cornmeal mush. As you can see, this both breaks and keeps the rules. It sounds like a lot of work, but it is the most interesting way I've ever found to stretch one chicken over six people. It should be accompanied by a fine beer rather than wine, and a sound green salad.

BREAST OF CHICKEN MAITLAND

2	whole chicken breasts, halved	2	teaspoons flour
1	cup chicken stock	1	teaspoon Worcestershire
	Salt and freshly ground		sauce
	pepper	1	tablespoon dry sherry
¼	cup sausage meat	½	cup pecan halves
4	green onions with part of tops, chopped		

*T*ake the skin off the chicken breasts and lay them, flesh side down, in a saucepan large enough to hold them in one layer. Pour the stock over, and sprinkle with salt and pepper to taste. Bring to a boil, cover, then lower the heat and cook gently 25 to 30 minutes.

Remove the breasts and keep warm; reserve the stock. In a small pan, fry the sausage until it releases its fat. Add the green onions and cook together until the onions start to brown. Add the flour and cook another few minutes, stirring. Scrape into a blender.

Add the stock to the blender and whirl over high speed, then place back in the pan and cook over medium heat until it thickens. Add the Worcestershire and sherry, then taste for seasoning. Just before serving, add the pecan halves to the sauce and pour over the breasts.

Serves 4.

An unusual dish, and an adaptation of a specialty from Dunbar's in New Orleans. It is relatively simple to prepare and has an especially rich flavor from the unexpected (and here almost unidentifiable) bits of sausage. It can be accompanied by a starch if you like, or as a course on its own, garnished with watercress and accompanied by a fine white wine.

NEBRASKA CHICKEN CUTLETS

2	whole chicken breasts, halved, boned, and skinned		Fine dry bread crumbs
	Juice of 1½ lemons		Vegetable oil
6	tablespoons flour	4	tablespoons butter, melted
	Salt and freshly ground pepper	1	teaspoon paprika
1	egg, beaten		Parsley
			Lemon wedges

*P*ound each boned breast thin between waxed paper with a rolling pin. Put on a plate, pour the juice of 1 lemon over, and let marinate an hour, covered, in the refrigerator.

To assemble for cooking, dredge each breast in flour mixed with salt and pepper, dip that in beaten egg, then in bread crumbs. (These can also sit awhile in the refrigerator to "set" the coating if you have time.)

Heat oil in a frying pan to the depth of about ⅛ inch and fry the cutlets 2 to 3 minutes on a side, or until golden. Remove to warm plates and pour over them the 4 tablespoons melted butter mixed with the juice of ½ lemon and paprika. Garnish with parsley and more lemon wedges.

Serves 4.

Now that both price and quality of veal are in question, this is a good compromise for those who like their schnitzel. The cutlets may be sauced, in fact, in any of your favorite ways for veal scallops or schnitzel—anchovies or capers are particularly good additions to the above butter lemon sauce.

BREAST OF CHICKEN, DELTA STYLE

2	whole chicken breasts, halved, boned, and skinned		Salt and freshly ground pepper
½	cup dark rum	⅓	cup clarified butter
½	cup fresh bread crumbs	½	cup chutney
			Parsley
			Lemon wedges

*P*ound each boned breast thin between waxed paper with a rolling pin. Place in a shallow dish and marinate in the rum for an hour or more in the refrigerator.

To cook, drain the breasts, reserving the rum, and roll in bread crumbs seasoned with salt and pepper. Fry 2 to 3 minutes per side in clarified butter. Mix the chutney with 4 tablespoons of the rum marinade and top the breasts with it. Garnish with parsley and lemon wedges.

Serves 4.

These are well accompanied by Thomas Jefferson's Pilau (page 266), or simply buttered rice tossed with toasted pine nuts as I first had the dish. Any chutney will do, but homemade peach chutney is used in the South. And certainly it deserves a chilled, full-bodied white wine.

Domestic Game

A couple of centuries of wilderness behind us, there are many secrets of our savage larder that could have turned up here: venison hamburger, ragoûts of tiny quail and pies of prairie chicken, pheasant slumgullion, roast porcupine, possum grilled with sassafras twigs. Squirrel and turtle, canvasback and antelope—anything that moved (and could be shot or netted) was eaten. It is in this field our amateur cook really shines in inventiveness and native presumption. But I've had to content myself, like the most of us who do not hunt, with what we can catch in the market in the way of domesticated game: duck, goose, rabbit, a holiday turkey breast for a small family, and a few uses for the rest of that national favorite. Besides those listed here, other fine dishes that use leftover turkey are Ancestral Turkey Rice Soup (page 22), Turkey Oyster Gumbo (page 34), and Turkey Pilau with Walnuts (page 177).

ROAST LONG ISLAND DUCKLING

2 ducklings (4 to 5 pounds
  each)
2 carrots, scraped and sliced
2 onions, sliced
1 stalk celery, trimmed and
  sliced
1 sprig parsley
1 bay leaf

Pinch of dried thyme
Salt and freshly ground
  pepper
1 lemon, halved
Celery leaves
1 tablespoon cold butter
1 recipe Chestnut Purée (page
  229)

*P*reheat the oven to 450°F.

Remove the wing tips and cut the necks from the ducks. Add them to a kettle of water, along with the giblets (except the livers—use these for an appetizer). Add half the carrots and onions, the celery stalk, parsley, bay leaf, thyme, and salt and pepper to taste. Bring to a boil, skim, and simmer while the duck is cooking.

Rub the ducks inside and out with the lemon, salt them lightly, and place a few slices of onion and some celery leaves in the cavities. Prick the skin all around the thighs, backs, and lower breasts with a sharp fork. Put the ducks, breasts up, in a roasting pan, scatter the remaining onions and carrots around, and place in the oven.

Immediately turn the heat down to 350°F, and after 15 minutes turn the ducks on their sides. Half an hour later, turn on the other side. Fifteen minutes before done, put breast up and salt the ducks—they should roast about an hour and a half, or until the juice runs from a faint rose to pale yellow when you prick a thigh. Remove the fat from the pan as it accumulates with a bulb baster.

When done, remove the ducks and place on a serving platter; keep warm. Remove all the fat from the roasting pan and add 1½ cups strained duck stock. Boil this down, mashing the vegetables, until it has reduced by half. Remove from the heat and whisk in 1 tablespoon cold butter to finish the sauce.

To serve, carve the ducks and place on warm plates with a pile of Chestnut Purée (page 229) and perhaps fresh Cranberry-Orange Relish (page 311) in an orange cup.

Serves 4.

Domesticated ducks are an entirely different bird from the wild duck—they have been bred so they have an incredible amount of fat that must be drained off as they cook. However, they are more tender, so the legs can be eaten as well as the breasts, and when cooked properly so most of the fat is rendered from the skin, the skin itself is crisply succulent. Serving them with two contrasting purées makes a handsome preparation, and you will want to serve a vintage red wine.

NEW ORLEANS
ROAST DUCK WITH SAUCE PARADIS

1	duckling (4 to 5 pounds)		Cayenne
1	carrot, sliced	5	tablespoons butter
1	small onion, sliced	¼	cup flour
1	sprig parsley	½	cup dry Madeira
1	bay leaf	3	tablespoons red currant jelly
	Dried thyme	1	cup green seedless grapes
	Salt and freshly ground pepper		

*R*emove the wing tips and cut the neck from the duck. Place them, and all the giblets but the liver (reserve this for later), in a kettle with the carrot, onion, parsley, bay leaf, pinch of thyme, salt and pepper to taste, and water to cover. Simmer an hour or so, then strain. You will need 2 cups stock, so if necessary boil it down so the stock will be rich as possible.

Preheat the oven to 475°F.

Rub the duck inside and out with salt, pepper, cayenne, and dried thyme. Prick skin all around the thighs, back, and lower breast with a fork. Place, breast up, in a roasting pan and roast 20 minutes, then remove and sprinkle with more pepper, cayenne, and thyme. Lower the heat to 350°F and roast the duck 1½ hours, basting frequently with its own fat (use only a little for this, discarding fat as it accumulates.) During the last 20 minutes, turn the heat back up to 475°F. Dust the duck again with pepper and cayenne, baste, and return to the oven to crisp.

To make the sauce, melt 4 tablespoons of the butter in a saucepan, and when it bubbles add the flour. Cook, stirring, over medium heat, then lower the heat and cook until the flour becomes straw gold. Add 2 cups stock and stir until the mixture thickens and becomes silky. Add the Madeira, jelly, and cayenne to taste, then stir until the jelly melts.

Chop the reserved liver in tiny dice, and toss quickly over high heat in the remaining 1 tablespoon butter. Cook only about a minute or so—the flesh should still be slightly pink on the inside. Add to the sauce along with the grapes, turn off the heat, and let sit, covered, until needed.

To serve, cut the duck in half and ladle the sauce over.

Serves 2.

It has become fashionable to serve duckling pretty rare these days, and this recipe will seem terribly overcooked to such folk. However, this method results in extremely tender meat, and an exceptionally crisp skin. The sauce is also a fine one—the original calls for truffles, which is very elegant, but I think the duck liver does just as well, since canned truffles don't really have much flavor. You'll want an excellent red wine, and perhaps yeast rolls, to accompany the feast.

THOMAS JEFFERSON'S SALMI OF DUCK

1	duckling (4 to 5 pounds)		Salt and freshly ground
1	duck liver		pepper
3	tablespoons butter	½	pound mushrooms, sliced
½	cup Madeira		Lemon juice
			Minced parsley

*R*oast the duck as described in Roast Long Island Duckling (page 160), reserving all the giblets. When done, cool and strip off all meat from the carcass and reserve. If you wish, add the carcass (not the skin) to the kettle to cook along with the giblets (except the liver) at this time.

When the stock (make the stock using the same vegetables as in Roast Long Island Duckling) is flavorful, strain it and make the duck sauce ahead of time so the salmi can be put together at the last minute (in fact this is a splendid dish to be made in a chafing dish at table).

To put the dish together, sauté the duck liver in 2 tablespoons of the butter. When it is golden but still pink inside, mash it to a paste in the pan. Add the Madeira and salt and pepper to taste. In another pan, toss the mushrooms in the remaining 1 tablespoon butter till they start to give out juices, and add them as well. Add the duck stock, the duck meat, and a few drops of lemon juice and some minced parsley. Heat through and serve.

Serves 3 to 4.

A salmi was often prepared in the days when there was plenty of leftover game— wild duck, pheasant, quail, etc. Though few of us now have game at all, not to mention any left, it is still a carefree way to serve duck, since all the preparation is accomplished well before company arrives and no carving is involved. I like to serve it with tiny fresh peas or green beans, and Saratoga Chips (page 254).

STUFFED ROAST GOOSE WITH CRANBERRY ICE IN ORANGE SHELLS

1 goose (8 to 9 pounds)	1 apple, peeled, cored, and grated
1 small onion, sliced	
1 carrot, sliced	¾ cup chopped cooked prunes
1 stalk celery, sliced	½ cup peeled and chopped cooked chestnuts
1 sprig parsley	
1 bay leaf	¼ cup chopped celery leaves
Pinch of dried thyme	¼ cup minced parsley
Salt and freshly ground pepper	1 fresh sage leaf, minced
	Salt and freshly ground pepper
½ lemon	
2 onions, chopped	1 recipe Cranberry Ice in Orange Shells (page 389)
3 cups diced crustless bread	

*P*reheat the oven to 425°F.

Trim wing tips from goose, and put with the giblets (not the liver—sauté that in butter and chop for the stuffing), sliced onion, carrot, celery, parsley sprig, bay leaf, thyme, and salt and pepper to taste in a large kettle. Add water to cover, bring to a boil, skim, and simmer while you cook the goose.

Remove any loose fat from the cavity of the goose. Prick it around the thighs, back, and lower breast with a sharp fork. Rub the cavity with lemon. Put any extra goose fat you can pull off in a small saucepan, and cook it over low heat until you have rendered at least 2 tablespoons of fat. Use this to sauté the chopped onions until they are transparent.

Put the onions and bread cubes in a bowl, and add the rest of the ingredients up to the Cranberry Ice. Add enough stock to moisten the dressing lightly.

Stuff the goose and truss it. Cook exactly as you do duck (see Roast Long Island Duckling, page 160), but baste it every 15 minutes with some boiling water to help remove excess fat. Roast the goost at 425°F 20 minutes, then lower the heat to 375°F and cook 20 to 25 minutes per pound. It is done when the drumsticks move slightly and the juices run pale yellow when you prick the thigh with a sharp fork.

When done, remove the goose to a serving platter and keep warm while you prepare the sauce. Drain all fat from the roasting pan (being careful to save it—goose fat is excellent for cooking potatoes, and will keep for months in the refrigerator).

Strain the stock, add it to the roasting pan, and boil down, uncovered, to half. You may wish to cut up the giblets and add them, or to whisk in some cold butter off the heat to give the sauce extra body.

To serve, carve the goose and arrange on warm plates with some of the sauce over, a heap of dressing, and cranberry ice in orange shells beside each portion.

Serves 6.

As it becomes increasingly difficult to find a turkey that tastes at all real, and has never been frozen, I turn more and more to goose for holidays. The cranberry ice makes an attractive and refreshing contrast, rather than the usual cranberry relish. You need only hot rolls and a fine bottle of red wine to complete your feast.

RABBIT TARRAGON

1	rabbit (2 to 3 pounds), cut up	1	teaspoon Dijon mustard
	Salt	½	cup heavy cream
	Flour	¼	cup canned beef bouillon (or
½	cup butter		concentrated stock)
⅔	cup dry white wine		Sprig of fresh tarragon or
4	juniper berries (optional)		parsley
1	teaspoon dried tarragon (or 2		
	tablespoons chopped fresh)		

*R*eserving the liver, shake the rabbit in lightly salted flour. Sauté in the butter in a large frying pan, over medium heat. Be careful not to let the butter burn. Turn each piece till golden, then add the wine and juniper berries, and let it bubble up. Cover tightly, turn the heat to low, and simmer gently 40 minutes. While the rabbit cooks, mix the tarragon into the mustard, then slowly incorporate the cream. Let this sit to gather flavor. Take the liver, chop it into tiny dice, and sauté in a bit more butter for only a minute or two over high heat. This may sit, also, till needed.

To assemble the dish, add the tarragon cream to the rabbit, mix all around to flavor the meat, and let simmer, uncovered, 5 more minutes. Remove the rabbit pieces to a warm plate. Turn heat up high, add the beef bouillon, and boil the pan juices down, uncovered, till the sauce is silky. Strain it in a fine sieve to remove the tarragon and juniper.

Finally, scrape the liver pieces into the pan, add the strained sauce, and heat for several minutes. To serve, glaze the rabbit with the sauce and decorate with a sprig of fresh tarragon or parsley.

Serves 4.

Inspired by a simple rabbit dish with tarragon I dined on in France years ago, this dish has taken on new characteristics through many subsequent cookings. It is best, of course, with fresh tarragon, but quite tasty enough without. I like to serve it with the same white wine it has been cooked in rather than a red, but that is up to you. Either Zucchini-stuffed Baked Potatoes (page 258), or Portland Potatoes (page 259) make a fine partner.

CAJUN RABBIT WITH ORANGE RICE

1	rabbit (2 to 3 pounds), cut up	2	tablespoons butter
	Red wine	1	tablespoon vegetable oil
2	cloves garlic, flattened	1	tablespoon flour
	Pinch of dried thyme		Salt and freshly ground
1	bay leaf		pepper
	Sprinkle of ground allspice		Orange Rice (page 265)
1	slice orange peel		

*P*ut the rabbit to marinate in red wine to cover, the garlic, thyme, bay leaf, allspice, and orange peel. Leave it for 24 hours, turning once or twice during the time.

When ready to cook, remove the rabbit from the marinade (save 1 cup of it), and pat dry with absorbent paper towels. Let the butter and oil sputter in a frying pan, then add the rabbit pieces, and sauté till golden on each side over medium heat.

Remove the rabbit with a slotted spoon and add the flour to the pan. Whisk it into the fat till golden, then add the reserved 1 cup marinade. Stir until thickened and smooth, then put the rabbit back in the pan. Cover and simmer over low heat 45 minutes, or until tender. Turn once or twice during the cooking, and when a fork pierces the meat easily, remove and keep warm in the oven.

Rapidly boil the sauce down over high heat till it coats a spoon, and glaze the rabbit with it. Serve in a ring of orange rice.

Serves 4.

This recipe I would enter in The Great American Regional Cookery Sweepstakes, if we had one. Both rabbit and rice are adapted from Mary Land's epic Louisiana Cookery, published in 1954. It runs bristling clear through the higher flights of Brennans and other New Orleans watering holes, through humbler fare of Creole and Acadian at home, right down to campfire edibles from the backwater hunter: "banquette, byroad, and bayou" indeed. You will learn how best to handle a catch of possum or muskrat, how snipe (steeped in local orange wine) or octopus (she offers a tempting fricassee of its tentacles), how the lowliest gleanings from the field (my favorite being a pretty-sounding stew of marsh marigolds and early blue violets, with salt pork). Unfortunately, few attempts are made at measure, process, or progression, and not some few receipts are puzzling to the point of incomprehensibility. However, to the cook and cookbook reader alike she offers still more than most, in the way of pleasure and simple culinary profit—her recipe for Fowl à la Westerfield is almost worth the price of the book itself, if you can find it. She begins "Take one quail, dressed; one duck dressed; one goose, dressed; one turkey, dressed." Each are then sautéed in butter, the quail is stuffed with pecans and stuffed in the duck, apples are stuffed around that, then the duck is stuffed in the goose with orange segments, and lastly the goose is stuffed into the turkey with cornmeal dressing around it! No advice given as to carving all this, but as we will never cook it, that seems purest quibble.

LOUISIANA
BREAST OF TURKEY EN DAUBE

1	half breast of turkey	4	carrots, sliced
4	stalks celery with some leaves, chopped	½	cup minced parsley
2	onions, chopped	2	cloves garlic, minced
		¼	teaspoon dried thyme

2 bay leaves	1 cup fine dry white wine
⅓ cup diced (¼ inch) salt pork	2 tablespoons brandy
6 whole cloves	3 tablespoons butter
Salt and freshly ground pepper	3 tablespoons flour

*B*one the breast of turkey as you would a chicken breast. Simply cut along the breastbone separating the meat, then detach the flesh from the rest of the bones—they are large and this is easily done. Do not remove the skin from the breast, but locate the large white tendon on the underside and carefully pull it out with the assistance of a small sharp knife.

Put the bone with any meat clinging to it in a kettle, cover with water, and add half the celery, onions, carrots, parsley, garlic, thyme, and bay leaves, and some salt and pepper to taste. Simmer an hour or more, or until the stock is flavorful.

To cook the turkey make a bed of the salt pork, the rest of the vegetables, cloves, and salt and pepper in a Dutch oven or casserole. Place the turkey on top, pour the wine, brandy, and 2 cups of the stock over, and bring to a boil. Lower the heat and simmer gently, with the pot covered, for 1 hour, basting occasionally as it cooks.

After an hour, drain the liquid off into the stock kettle. Cover the pan and keep turkey warm while you prepare the sauce.

Stir the butter and flour together in a saucepan over low heat until it turns a delicate straw color—about 10 minutes. Strain 4 cups stock into the pan and simmer until it thickens, stirring as it cooks. Taste for seasoning and add more salt, pepper, or brandy as needed.

To serve, slice the meat and mask with the sauce. Garnish with either parsley or watercress.

Serves 6 to 8.

Turkeys around holidays tend to be so processed and packaged, and pumped with such adulterated oils, I can't recommend this most indigenous of fowls (Benjamin Franklin nominated it for Native Bird). The only thing is to look about in markets for signs advertising turkeys never frozen, and that still is a long shot. For even a small family a small turkey can be burdensome, after a few meals of leftovers. So this unusual Louisiana daube, adapted to the use of turkey "pieces" now so often found, is my choice for a Christmas or Thanksgiving that does not include all the aunts and uncles.

Good accompaniments would be, preceding the daube, Chilled Pumpkin Cream soup (page 5), with Parker House Rolls (page 331), then the daube with Rum and Orange Yams (page 261) and Colonial Green Beans with Mace (page 223) and perhaps a dab of Blueberry Rhubarb Relish (page 311). Then a course of Jerusalem Artichoke Salad (page 270), on to My Persimmon Pudding (page 380), and a dry native champagne throughout.

WYOMING TURKEY PUDDING

5	cups diced (½ inch) cooked turkey	1	onion, chopped
5	cups bread cubes	½	cup plus ⅓ cup butter
	Salt and freshly ground pepper	¼	cup flour
½	teaspoon celery seed	4	cups turkey or chicken stock, heated
½	teaspoon poultry seasoning	4	eggs

*P*reheat the oven to 350°F.

Put the bread in the oven—as it warms—to toast. When the bread cubes are golden, remove and mix with the seasonings.

Sauté the onion in the ½ cup butter till it is transparent, then toss with the bread till the cubes are coated with butter. Reserve 1 cup of the bread cubes for later.

Line a large shallow greased casserole with the bread dressing and arrange the turkey in the middle. Melt ⅓ cup butter in a saucepan, add the flour, and cook, stirring, for 10 minutes over low heat. Add the hot stock all at once and cook, stirring till it is smooth and thickened, for 10 minutes more.

Beat the eggs and pour the thickened stock bit by bit into them, beating constantly. Pour over the turkey and sprinkle with the reserved bread cubes. Bake 45 minutes, or until the custard is set.

Serves 6 to 8.

A church-supper delight to stretch leftover turkey.

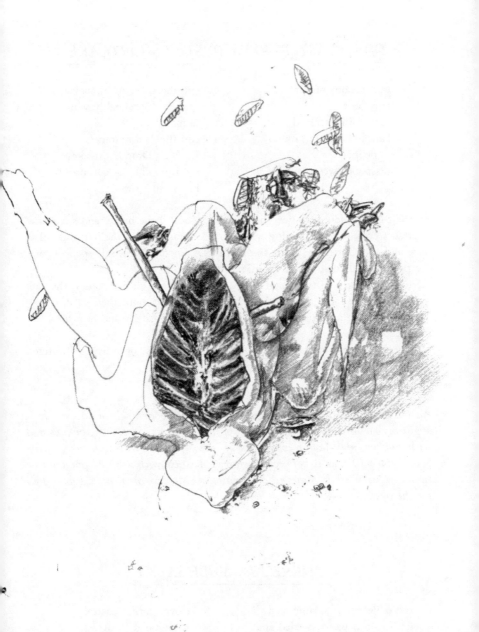

DOWNEAST TURKEY OYSTER SHORTCAKE

3 tablespoons butter	1 cup diced (½ inch) cooked
¼ cup flour	turkey, preferably white
2 cups milk, scalded	meat
Salt and freshly ground	1 cup shucked oysters
pepper	Helene's Drop Shortcakes
1 teaspoon sweet paprika	(page 324) (or cornbread)
	Pimiento strips

*I*n the top of a double boiler, melt 2 tablespoons of the butter and stir in the flour. Let cook over simmering water for 15 minutes. Add the hot milk all at once and cook, stirring, until the mixture is smooth. Add salt, pepper, and the paprika and cook gently 10 minutes.

Add the turkey to the cream sauce. Cut the oysters in half (unless they are quite small) and sauté in the other 1 tablespoon butter until their edges curl— only a couple of minutes or so. Add to the creamed turkey and heat for a few minutes.

Serve between and over any biscuit-type shortcakes, or split and buttered cornbread. Garnish with strips of pimiento.

Serves 4.

An old-fashioned dish that makes an unusually good lunch or supper. It is about my favorite among turkey leftover dishes. It may, certainly, be prepared with chicken, and though in the East it is always made with shortcake, in the South you will find it between cornbread flavored with a bit of poultry seasoning. Out West it comes to table on toast. Mushrooms may be substituted for the oysterless.

TURKEY IN MOLE SAUCE

6 tablespoons sesame seeds	5 cloves garlic, coarsely
2 green peppers, seeded and	chopped
cut up	¾ cup blanched almonds,
1 teaspoon anise seeds	coarsely chopped

2 cups canned tomatoes,
  drained
3 tortillas, chopped
1 teaspoon salt
½ teaspoon ground cinnamon
½ teaspoon ground coriander
2 ounces unsweetened·
  chocolate, grated
2 tablespoons chili powder

½ cup vegetable oil
2½ cups turkey or chicken
  stock, or as needed
6 cups diced (½ inch) cooked
  turkey (or chicken)
Hot cooked rice
Fresh coriander
Sliced limes

*T*oast 4 tablespoons of the sesame seeds and set aside.

In a blender or food processor, purée the peppers, anise seeds, 2 tablespoons untoasted sesame seeds, tortillas, garlic, almonds, and tomatoes. It should be a very fine purée. Add all the spices and chocolate and whirl until it makes a paste.

Heat the oil in a large saucepan and add the paste. Cook 5 minutes over medium heat, then add 2 cups stock. Cook over low heat 10 to 15 minutes, or until quite thick. Thin with extra stock until the consistency of heavy cream.

Add the turkey and let heat through. Serve on rice, sprinkled with the toasted sesame seeds and garnished with sprigs of coriander and slices of lime.

Serves 8.

The most surprising way to put a leftover turkey to account. It should be served either with a good full-bodied white wine or a fine beer, and perhaps Guacamole (page 190) on lettuce leaves. In the Southwest I have had it also superbly at an outdoor fiesta where guests spooned it into warm soft tortillas, topped it with guacamole, and rolled it up themselves to eat. Wonderful!

SPECIAL DISHES

In other words, the usual should be made unusual; extraordinariness should cloak the ordinary. So long after my decision to serve enchiladas on a Paris roof to Colette and the Prince, I still believe firmly in the attributes of the unexpected!

—M.F.K. Fisher, An Alphabet for Gourmets

Southern Beans and Rice

*T*he great rice and bean dishes tucked away in the South are to be found in homes, not restaurants. The restless recipe pioneer learns to sniff them out, if necessary by raising a pot lid on the back of a stove, to see what the cook eats. These days that cook is likely to be the hostess herself, who, like almost anyone in the South, will copy a recipe for the simple admiration of a dish. What secrets you uncover this way! You find how flexible the Jambalaya—all different as can be—and how full of sass and spice the pilaf (often termed "pilau" or even "perloo" along the byways). There are also even more secret dishes like red beans and rice, or Hopping John, only piping for family and friends, and not likely for any snooping Yankee. These are some of the best.

MISS EMILY'S PERLOO

1	cup rice	1	green apple, peeled and cored
2	tablespoons butter	½	cup raisins
½	teaspoon salt	1	cup diced (½ inch) cooked
⅛	teaspoon freshly ground		chicken
	pepper	1	cup diced (½ inch) cooked
⅛	teaspoon crushed saffron		ham
	threads	1	cup cooked shrimp, shelled
¾	cup chopped green pepper		and deveined
½	cup minced green onions		Slivered blanched almonds,
	with part of tops		toasted
3	cups chicken stock		Peach chutney

*I*n a heavy casserole, sauté the rice in the butter over a medium flame, stirring, for 6 to 7 minutes, or until the rice is opaque. Lower the heat and stir in the salt, pepper, saffron, green pepper, and green onions.

Add the chicken stock and bring to a boil. Lower the fire, cover, and simmer gently 15 to 20 minutes, or until the rice has absorbed most of the liquid and is nearly done.

Grate the apple over the rice, add the raisins and meats, stir up the rice, and cover again. Cook 15 more minutes, tossing occasionally.

To serve, place servings of the perloo on warm plates, sprinkle toasted almonds over, and place a dollop of chutney on top.

Serves 6.

Miss Emily—whoever you were—yours remains one of my favorite company dishes. I have even put up peach chutney for it, though of course any chutney will do. To prepare it for company, if need be, after you stir in the meats, etc., simply place the casserole in a 300°F oven for 30 minutes, then turn the heat off and let the pilaf sit till needed. It should be served with some such very fine chilled white wine, as a Chardonnay.

HAM AND EGGPLANT PILAU MADAME BÉGUÉ

1	small eggplant	2	cups water
	Salt		Freshly ground pepper
	Ham fat (or butter)	2	bay leaves
1	cup chopped onion	¼	teaspoon dried thyme
1	cup ham, diced (½ inch) cooked		Diced pimiento
			Minced parsley
1	cup rice		

*P*eel the eggplant and cut into 1-inch cubes. Salt lightly and let sit 30 minutes or more to sweat. Press as much juice as possible from the cubes, then refresh with water. Squeeze again.

Render some pieces of ham fat until there is about a tablespoon (or use butter). Sauté the onion and green pepper in the fat, then add the ham and eggplant. Toss all over a medium flame.

Add the rice and 2 cups water. Add pepper, bay leaves, and thyme—it will need no salt because of the salted eggplant and ham. Cover and cook 30 minutes, stirring occasionally. Serve sprinkled with diced pimiento and parsley.

Serves 4.

Sound, simple, and inexpensive to boot, this is New Orleans cooking at its homely best. Madame Bégué would have, in her restaurant, used this as a side dish, I suspect, but it makes a lovely main family dinner using up the rest of a baked ham. It even remains a sound one if you have no ham, and substitute a quarter pound of cut-up bacon (partly fried and all but a tablespoon of fat discarded).

TURKEY PILAU WITH WALNUTS

4	large onions, chopped	12	whole cloves
½	cup butter	1	stick cinnamon
2	cups rice	½	cup dried currants or raisins
2	cups diced (½ inch) cooked turkey		Salt and freshly ground pepper
3½	cups turkey or chicken stock	⅔	cup chopped walnuts

*S*auté the onions in the butter in a heavy casserole. When they are soft, add the rice and sauté, stirring, over low heat until it turns golden.

Add the turkey and stock, then all the ingredients except the walnuts. Cover the pan and simmer 20 to 30 minutes, or until all the liquid is absorbed.

Remove the cinnamon stick (the cloves are really not worth retrieving), and fold in the walnuts. Serve warm with chutney, or cranberry relish.

Serves 6.

Perhaps this is the most creative way of all to turn a leftover turkey to account. Like any of the pilafs, it may sit awhile if need be, for company.

CREOLE JAMBALAYA

4	medium onions, chopped	½	pound Chaurice (page 113) (or hot Louisiana sausage, smoked Polish or French sausages), sliced ¼" thick
2	tablespoons lard (or butter)		
1	green pepper, seeded chopped		
6	green onions, chopped with part of tops Minced parsley	2	cups rice
		3	cups beef stock (or ham cooking liquid) Salt and freshly ground pepper
1	pound lean pork, cut into small cubes		
1	cup chopped cooked ham (or ham hocks cooked in water)		Pinch of cayenne
		½	teaspoon chili powder
		2	bay leaves
		¼	teaspoon dried thyme Pinch of ground cloves

*I*n a heavy casserole, sauté the onions in lard till they are quite golden-brown. (Or, if using butter till they are transparent and limp.) Add the vegetables, 1 tablespoon parsley, and the pork and cook 15 minutes over medium heat, stirring occasionally.

Add the ham and sausage, then the rice, stirring until each rice grain is coated in oil. Add the stock and seasonings. Cover, then turn the heat down low and cook 30 minutes, uncovering now and again to stir.

Finally, remove the cover and cook 15 minutes more to allow any extra liquid to be absorbed. Sprinkle with chopped parsley and serve.

Serves 6.

Jambalayas are a native pilaf flexible as to ingredients, but always dark and spicy. Like gumbos, they come in many versions, but this recipe is probably best for inlanders for whom shellfish are rare and dear. To vary the recipe above, you can omit or reduce some of the meat ingredients and include shrimp or oysters. Or you could try a chicken, cut up and browned in oil—with water or chicken stock added rather than the beef. Anyway you prepare it, jambalaya makes a rich, satisfying meal easily put together. Some people even find it faintly addictive.

NATCHEZ SHRIMP JAMBALAYA

6	slices bacon, chopped	½	teaspoon Worcestershire
1	cup chopped onion		sauce
1	clove garlic, minced	3	tablespoons tomato paste
1	green pepper, seeded and chopped	3	cups fish stock (or 1 cup bottled clam juice and 2 cups water)
¼	teaspoon dried thyme	1½	cups rice
2	bay leaves	¼	cup minced parsley
	Pinch of ground cloves	1	pound small cooked shrimp, shelled and deveined
	Pinch of ground allspice		
	Tabasco		

Render the fat from the chopped bacon in a heavy casserole set over medium heat. When the bacon has begun to brown, add the onion, garlic, and green pepper. Sauté until the onion turns golden.

Stir in the seasonings, tomato paste, and stock. Stir until the mixture is smooth and begins to bubble, then add the rice and cover the pot. Turn the heat down low and cook 20 to 30 minutes, or until the liquid is absorbed.

Finally, stir in the parsley and shrimp and let heat through.

Serves 4 to 6.

An admirable and relatively inexpensive company dish—or at least it makes a pound of shrimp go a very long, tasty way. It can be held warm for some time, as can all the jambalayas, and served with a simple green salad, fresh bread or rolls, and an elegant dessert, it makes a complete repast.

RABBIT JAMBALAYA

1	rabbit (2 to 3 pounds)	4	cups vegetable oil
1	onion	4	tablespoons butter
1	carrot	2	cups chopped onion
1	stalk celery	1	green pepper, seeded and
1	bay leaf		chopped
¼	teaspoon dried thyme	2	tablespoons tomato paste
2	sprigs parsley	1	bay leaf
6	peppercorns		Pinch of ground cloves
	Cayenne		Pinch of ground ginger
	Salt	1	teaspoon Worcestershire
	Dried thyme		sauce
	Flour	1½	cups rice

Cut the rabbit meat off the bones. (Don't worry about some of the thinner pieces, but be careful to save the kidneys along with the meat.) Put the bones in a large kettle with the whole onion, carrot, celery, bay leaf, thyme, parsley, peppercorns, and salt to taste. Cover with water, bring to a boil, skim the pot, and cook about 2 hours. (This can be speeded up to an hour, in a pressure cooker).

Cut the meat into bite-sized pieces. Sprinkle with a generous dash of cayenne, and a little salt and thyme, then shake the pieces in a bag of flour. Heat the vegetable oil in a medium frying pan over medium-high heat. Sauté the rabbit pieces in batches till they are golden all over, and scoop out into a casserole. Discard the oil from the frying pan.

Add the butter to the pan and cook the chopped onion and green pepper over medium heat until the onion is limp. Add 4 tablespoons flour and stir until it starts to turn gold—about 10 minutes. Strain the rabbit stock and add 3 cups of it to the onions, stirring until a smooth sauce is achieved. Stir in the tomato paste, bay leaf, spices, and Worcestershire. Pour this over the rabbit.

Cover the casserole and simmer 20 minutes. Add the rice, cover again, and cook gently over low heat 30 more minutes, or until the rice is cooked and has absorbed all the liquid.

Serves 4 to 6.

Southerners treat all kinds of game to this kind of preparation. I even once had home-smoked wild duck made into a jambalaya, certainly a memorable experience. It's nice to serve this with a topping of homemade chutney, and either a red or white wine.

RED BEANS AND RICE

1 pound dried red beans	Pinch of dried thyme
1 cup chopped onion	Pinch of ground cloves
2 cloves garlic, minced	Cayenne (or Tabasco)
½ cup chopped celery tops	Salt
¼ cup chopped parsley	1 can beef bouillon (or ham
⅓ cup diced (¼ inch) salt pork	braising liquid)
2 ham hocks (or ham bone	1 pound hot sausage meat
with meat on it)	Hot cooked rice
2 bay leaves	

Wash the beans and discard any discolored ones. (Most beans these days are more carefully packaged than they used to be and you seldom find small stones among them, but it does no harm to check.) Cover with water in a large saucepan and bring to a boil. Turn the heat off, cover, and leave for an hour or more to soak and plump.

Bring the water again to a boil and add onion, garlic, celery, parsley, salt pork, ham hocks, bay leaves, thyme, cloves, and a dash of cayenne or Tabasco. (This dish can be hot as you like, but some of its subtlety is lost if the pepper takes over. I personally like to make the sausage a bit hot as a contrast, and then serve the dish with a bottle of Tabasco at table so guests may pick their own degrees.)

Lower the heat so the beans are just bubbling, and let cook until the beans are softened—about 1½ hours. Check now and again to make sure the beans have enough water. When the beans are soft, add salt to taste, and the bouillon—salt added to beans at the beginning of cooking tends to make them hard.

Preheat the oven to 350°F.

Remove the ham hocks or bone and separate the meat from them, then chop. Roll the sausage in nut-sized balls and add them, along with the ham. Cook slowly, uncovered, in the oven until a slight crust forms on the top (about 30 minutes). Stir and let crust form again. Do this several times—the beans at serving should have begun to break down so the dish is slightly mushy. (Like the French *cassoulet* this is best on second or third reheating, and it also freezes well.)

Serve the beans in a ring of fluffy rice.

Serves 6.

This is a quite overlooked dish outside the South, and even there it is considered "country" and thus never to be served guests. Actually it is probably the most inexpensive dish imaginable as company fare, and all but the most finicky will find it a splendid example of American regional cooking. I serve it with beer rather than wine (another economy) since it is a little hot and spicy for wine, and a salad and dessert.

PODRILLA À LA CRÉOLE

2	cups dried red kidney beans		Few drops of Tabasco
¼	pound salt pork, cut into ¼-inch dice		Freshly ground pepper
1	bay leaf	4	cups hot cooked rice
¼	teaspoon dried thyme	3	slices bacon, cooked and crumbled
¼	cup minced parsley		

Soak the beans overnight in water. Next day, bring the beans in the water to a boil and simmer gently 30 minutes. Fry the salt pork until golden, then add it with 3 tablespoons of the rendered fat to the beans. Add bay leaf, thyme, parsley, and Tabasco and pepper to taste to the bean pot and simmer 1 hour, or until the beans are tender.

Taste for seasoning—the beans should be slightly peppery, and there should be enough salt from the salt pork. To serve, fill a buttered ring mold with the cooked rice and press it gently. Turn it out onto a heated platter. Remove the bay leaf from the beans and fill the center of the rice ring. Sprinkle with crumbled bacon.

Serves 4 to 6.

A favorite side dish with Thomas Jefferson. To prepare it as a succulent main dish, another version adds a clove of garlic and a chopped onion along with the salt pork, then a chopped green pepper and a cup of chopped tomatoes near the end.

HOPPING JOHN

1 pound dried black-eyed peas	1 cup finely chopped red onion
1 onion, chopped	(or green onion chopped
1 meaty ham hock (or a ham	with part of tops)
bone)	¼ cup minced parsley
Freshly ground pepper	1 tablespoon vinegar
Salt	1 tablespoon olive oil
1 cup peeled, seeded, and diced	Freshly ground pepper
fresh ripe tomato	Hot cooked rice

Soak the peas overnight in water to cover. The next day bring to a boil in the water and add the onion, ham, and pepper. Lower the heat and simmer an hour, or until the peas are nearly soft.

Add salt to taste and continue cooking slowly until the peas are done. Water should be added at any time they tend to get dry—but the water should be boiling when you add it.

Combine the tomato (canned may be used if summer tomatoes are not available) with red onion, parsley, vinegar, olive oil, and salt and pepper to taste. Let sit for an hour or so in the refrigerator to mellow and gather flavor.

To serve, remove any meat from the ham and chop it fine. Place the peas on a bed of rice, sprinkle with ham, and top with the tomato-onion relish.

Serves 4 to 6.

In many Southern homes, Hopping John is served each New Year's Day with the toast that the more black-eyed peas one eats the more prosperous will be the coming year. I like to perpetuate this custom wherever in the world I find myself, and invite friends for Hopping John, hot cornbread, and pecan pie— welcome and simple after rich indulgences from the holidays. But I don't stop there—it's one of my favorite dishes anytime.

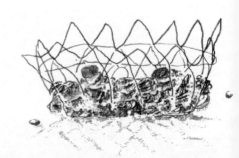

Southwestern Foods

*B*ased on harmonious combinations of corn, beans, and chilies, the fourth leg to the American table is a happily self-contained cuisine. Not only is it different from any of our other food, it is also served differently. It is possible (I know I do it sometimes) to serve Southwestern dishes in courses, but generally, after some appetizer, one is served a plate heaped and crammed full of different things: one enchilada, one taco, one quesadilla—all with differing fillings—and these nestled among refried beans and lettuce garnish and sliced radishes, etc., etc., etc. All this, of course, is highly influenced by foods south of the border, but Southwesterners have evolved a cuisine different from anything you will find in Mexico. It has acquired the rather derogatory name of "Tex-Mex" food, probably from the fact that there are (even in the Southwest itself) so few really fine restaurants that serve it, but as it is cooked in the home it is one of our glories—and best-kept secrets.

RED CHILI SAUCE

½ pound dried red chilies (New   2 cloves garlic, peeled
   Mexican, ancho, or pasilla)   2 teaspoons dried oregano
3 cups chicken stock   ½ teaspoon salt

Remove the stems and seeds from the chilies. (These are very hot, so some people use rubber gloves for the process—I don't, but I take care not to rub my eyes, etc.) You can also remove any vein ribs inside the chilies: these are where the seeds gather and are hotter than the flesh of the chilies.

Place the seeded chilies in a saucepan with the stock. Simmer, covered, 15 minutes. Place in a blender or a food processor with the garlic cloves, oregano, and salt. Blend until smooth. Place this mixture back in the saucepan and simmer for 15 minutes more.

This makes 3 cups chili paste, which can be thinned with water or stock if you need a sauce of lighter consistency. It freezes well.

In the Southwest, fresh red chilies are available in season, and later they are dried and hung in great fragrant strings, called Ristras, *to be picked during the long winters. In other parts of the country Hispanic markets carry not only these, but also the darker-flavored ancho and pasilla chilies. By all means, search out chilies if possible, for this basic sauce, so full of zip and freshness, is a far cry from the canned sauce found in every market.*

GREEN CHILI TOMATILLO SAUCE

1 cup chopped mild green   1 tablespoon minced parsley
   chilies (either fresh or   1 tablespoon minced fresh
   canned)   coriander
¾ cup peeled and chopped   1 tablespoon flour
   tomatillos (either fresh or   ½ cup chicken stock
   canned)   Salt
1 tablespoon butter   Pinch of sugar
1 clove garlic, minced

If you use fresh chilies, you will need 10 to 12 Anaheim chilies. Roast them in a 400°F oven on a cookie sheet for 10 minutes or so—or until the skins blister all over. Remove, sprinkle with cold water, cover with a moist towel, and let sweat for 10 minutes. Slip the skins off, remove the tops, and scrape out all the seeds. Tomatillos have a thin dry papery skin that must be peeled off before using.

Heat butter in a saucepan set over medium heat. Add the garlic and sauté a minute or two, then add the chilies and tomatillos. Sauté over medium heat for 5 minutes, then add parsley, coriander, and flour. Cook 3 to 4 minutes, then add the stock. Stir as it thickens, and add salt to taste and a pinch of sugar. Let cook, uncovered, 15 to 20 minutes. Don't overcook—if you use fresh tomatillos they should still be a mite crisp.

Makes 2 cups.

Prepared with fresh ingredients, this sauce from New Mexico chef Richard Freeby is one of the best Southwestern sauces of all, and even with canned ingredients it is better than any restaurant green chili sauce I've ever tasted. In New Mexico a sauce like this, or the preceding red sauce, is used in nearly every dish. When you order in a restaurant, the waiter will immediately say, "Red or green?" It is so instinctive that I sometimes expect this response when ordering a cup of coffee. My favorite use for this sauce is as a topping for cooked pinto beans, with a dollop of sour cream. Canned green chilies are to be found practically everywhere, but you will probably have to seek a Hispanic market for either fresh or canned tomatillos—they look, when peeled, somewhat like tiny green tomatoes, but they come from another family altogether, and have a much more acidic taste than green tomatoes.

ALDA'S CHILI MEAT SAUCE

1½   pounds ground beef
2   tablespoons bacon fat (or vegetable oil)
2   large onions, chopped
2   cloves garlic, minced
1½   cups canned tomatoes (or ½ cup tomato sauce, or 4 tablespoons tomato paste)
1   cup beef or chicken stock (or beer)
1   can (4 ounces) mild green chilies, chopped
¼   cup minced fresh coriander
¼   cup chili powder
1   teaspoon sugar
    Salt
    Pinch of ground cloves
½   teaspoon dried oregano

Sauté the ground beef in a casserole or Dutch oven until it starts to brown. Remove with a slotted spoon to absorbent paper in order to drain off the fat, and pour off any fat in the pan. Add the bacon fat, then sauté the onions and garlic over medium heat until the onion is limp. Add the beef and all the other ingredients.

Turn the heat low and simmer for 3 to 4 hours, or until the sauce is dark, dense, and tasty—adding stock or beer from time to time if it gets too dry. (If you have a pressure cooker, cook it for 1½ to 2 hours.)

Makes 5 cups.

This is a recipe from my Aunt in Gallup, New Mexico—though it has picked up many of my own (and my mother's) touches from having cooked it for so many years. Aside from its first use—on cheese and green onion enchiladas— it may garnish huevos rancheros, make a further foundation for a taco or tostada, and combined with beans it can become chile con carne or the filling for a tamale pie.

GREEN CHILI SALSA

½ cup chopped fresh or canned tomatoes
½ cup chopped green onions with part of tops
1 4 ounce can mild green chilies, chopped
1 clove garlic, minced
3 tablespoons minced parsley
3 tablespoons minced fresh coriander

2 jalapeño peppers (bottled en escabeche), seeded and minced
Salt and freshly ground pepper
Pinch of sugar
1 tablespoon lime or lemon juice

Combine everything and let sit in the refrigerator for at least an hour before serving.

Makes 1½ cups.

Bottled, salsas are pure fire and no taste, and most all recipes and restaurants use such commercial products. Homemade salsa is a must. This, the lesser of two hots, can be interchangeable with Frances Sommer's Jalapeño Salsa (recipe follows) in any dish. Salsa can go on anything but the dessert in Southwestern cooking. Its first use can be with homemade Tortilla Chips (below) as a dip for appetizers, then it can go on the beans, or any of the tortilla combinations.

FRANCES SOMMER'S JALAPEÑO SALSA

6	jalapeño peppers (bottled en escabeche)	1	tablespoon lime or lemon juice
½	cup chopped green onions with part of tops	½	teaspoon Worcestershire sauce
2	tablespoons minced parsley		Pinch of sugar
¼	cup minced fresh coriander	½	cup fresh or canned
	Salt		tomatoes, chopped
1	tablespoon olive oil		(optional)

Slice the jalapeños lengthwise first, and remove all the seeds under running water—otherwise this sauce will be too hot for ordinary human consumption. Combine all the ingredients (Mrs. Sommer sometimes adds a slosh of white wine, as well) and let chill for an hour or so before serving.

Makes 1 cup.

Frances Sommer is the wife of photographer Frederick Sommer, and I owe to her some of the best meals I've ever had in Arizona—or elsewhere. I had to watch her to get the recipe, and like her I cook it without measuring these days. It is, I suppose, my favorite all-around American sauce for hot or cold meats, fish and shellfish, as well as for every Southwestern feast.

TORTILLA CHIPS

Corn tortillas	Salt
Vegetable oil	

Cut tortillas in eighths, like a pie. Put about ½ inch of oil in a heavy cast-iron frying pan and set it over high heat. When the fat starts to shimmer (but not smoke), test one chip: when the oil stops bubbling around it, it should be golden and crisp. If it is still chewy the fat is not yet hot enough, and if it gets more brown than gold the fat is too hot.

Cook the rest in batches of one layer in the frying pan. Lift out with a slotted spoon, and drain on absorbent paper. Salt while they are warm.

No meal in the Southwest is complete without these. They can now, of course, be bought packaged like potato chips everywhere, but they are nothing like homemade (which usually disappear before your eyes as you cook them). They are used at the beginning of a meal as an appetizer to scoop up salsa or guacamole, and they look very pretty stuck in a pile of refried beans (where they are also used as a kind of spoon to eat the beans). A basket ought to be put on the table, in fact, to use for anything.

REFRIED BEANS

1	pound dried pinto beans (or half pinto and half black beans)	Salt
		Lard or bacon fat
		Sour cream
1	onion	Frances Sommer's Jalapeño Salsa
1	clove garlic	(page 188)
3	slices bacon	Tortilla Chips (see preceding
2	teaspoons chili powder	recipe)

Soak the beans in water overnight, or cover with water, bring to a boil, and let sit an hour covered. When ready to cook, bring to a boil, then lower the heat to a simmer and add the onion, garlic, bacon, and chili powder. Simmer several hours, adding hot water if the beans get too dry.

When the beans are tender, add salt to taste, and cook them till they start to almost fall apart. They should have about an inch of cooking liquid over them by the end, for you will need the bean liquid later. If they are too dry, simply add hot water and stir the pot.

Heat lard or bacon fat in a skillet, and add about 1 cup beans per serving to about 1 tablespoon fat. Toss the beans in the fat, then mash them with a potato masher and let fry over low heat until a crust forms on the bottom. If they get too dry, add some bean liquid, and let crust again.

Serve the beans, crust up, with sour cream on top, a little jalapeño salsa, and tortilla chips stuck point down in them.

Delicately crusted with creamy dark insides, I think none of our starches quite outdoes refried beans, for glorious sustenance. Though in the Southwest most all refried beans are made from pinto beans, I like to use half black beans with them for superior flavor—if you can get them, try it. Topped with sour cream, jalapeño salsa, and with three or four tortilla chips stuck in (with a handy basket of more to eat the beans with), they are as good as any dish in the whole cuisine.

LETTUCE GARNISH

This is the only time I ever use iceberg lettuce. In salads it is the most boring of all the lettuces, but it is the only lettuce that can stand up to being sliced like cole slaw, as is done in the Southwest. It is an indispensable garnish to any platter. The best way to slice the lettuce is to detach the leaves, pile them up, and cut with a long sharp knife in shreds. They should then be put in a bowl of water to crisp, and drained and dried before using. Usually the lettuce is completely unadorned, but it is nice sprinkled with just a hint of white wine tarragon vinegar and a little salt. Or I often shred radishes and let them soak with some salt and vinegar, then sprinkle them over the lettuce.

GUACAMOLE

2   large avocados, peeled and seeded
    Juice of lemon (or lime)
4   green onions, chopped with part of tops
1   tomato, peeled, seeded, and chopped (optional)

1   clove garlic, minced to a paste
    Tabasco
½   teaspoon chili powder
    Pinch of sugar
    Salt

Either mash the avocados fine or chop them up. (There are people who prefer their guacamole to be almost a purée and those who like it chunky—I like either). Sprinkle immediately with lemon or lime juice, then add all the rest of the ingredients. Taste for seasoning, place the avocado pit in the bowl, cover with plastic wrap, and refrigerate for at least 30 minutes to mellow. If kept too much longer the avocados will start to darken.
Serves 4.

Arguably our finest native salad, all by itself on a leaf of tender lettuce, with a basket of warm Tortilla Chips (page 188) to scoop it up. In the cuisine of the Southwest it is used also as a cocktail dip, or one of the toppings and/or fillings of enchiladas, tacos, tostadas, burritos—you name it. It is also lovely as a cold sauce for grilled meats or for cold or hot fish.

AVOCADO SLICES MARINATED IN RUM

2	large avocados, peeled, seeded, and sliced	2	tablespoons light rum
3	tablespoons lime juice	1	clove garlic, minced
½	cup olive oil		Salt and freshly ground pepper

Toss the avocado slices in the remaining ingredients, cover with plastic wrap, and refrigerate for an hour or so before serving. (The lime, rum, and oil combination keep the avocados from darkening.)
Serves 4.

A kind of superior guacamole. The avocado slices make, arranged in a fan on Boston lettuce leaves, a fine first course to any meal, or they can replace the lettuce garnish on a Southwestern platter.

PICKLED JALAPEÑOS
STUFFED WITH WALNUT CHEESE

5 to 6	jalapeños (bottled en escabeche)	¼	cup finely minced walnuts
1	package (3 ounces) cream cheese		Salt

Remove the stems from the jalapeños with a sharp knife, and take out their seeds with a small knife under the faucet. Drain. Mash the cream cheese with walnuts and salt to taste, and stuff the peppers with the mixture. Chill for an hour or more in the refrigerator. To serve, slice into rings.
Serves 4 to 6.

Stuffed, then chilled and sliced, these make for more than garnish to shredded lettuce, taco or tostada. In fact, they lift any Southwestern meal to notice down to the finest detail. They may also be used to top Tortilla Chips (page 188), for an appetizer.

CHORIZO

1	pound ground lean pork	1	bay leaf
1	teaspoon salt	4	cloves garlic, minced to a
2	tablespoons chili powder		paste
	A pinch each of ground	2	tablespoons vinegar
	cinnamon, ground cloves,		
	dried oregano, dried		
	thyme, ground cumin,		
	freshly ground pepper,		
	ground ginger, nutmeg,		
	coriander seeds		

*P*lace the pork in a bowl. Put all spices from the salt to the bay leaf in a blender, and whirl till the coriander seeds and bay leaf are powdered. Add to the pork along with the garlic and vinegar, mix well, and refrigerate for a day or more. (This can be made, divided in ¼–½ cup batches, and frozen for future uses.)

Chorizo is available in the stores, but none of it is as good as your own home-made variety. Its uses are legion in Southwestern cooking, from simple frying, crumbled as filling for a taco, etc., to adding spice and spark to many casseroles, meat loaves, and egg dishes.

CARNITAS

1	pork shoulder (4 to 5	½	teaspoon dried oregano
	pounds)	2	onions, chopped
	Salt	1	clove garlic, flattened with a
½	teaspoon ground cumin		knife
½	teaspoon coriander seeds	2	carrots, scraped and chopped

Place the pork in a large kettle with water to cover. Add salt to taste, and the remaining ingredients and bring to a boil. Lower the heat and simmer 2½ hours.

Preheat the oven to 350°F. Take the pork out of the kettle and place in a shallow baking pan. Bake 45 minutes to 1 hour, or until the meat is well browned all over.

Remove the meat from the oven, discard as much fat as possible, and shred the meat with knife and fork.

All this boiling and baking produces an incredibly soft-textured meat, yet with crispy edges. Simply with cooked pinto beans and salsa it makes one of the best fillings for tortillas in the whole cuisine.

TINGA

2	cups Carnitas (see preceding recipe) (or leftover baked pork, shredded)	1 cup chopped tomatoes
1	tablespoon bacon fat (or vegetable oil)	1 jalapeño pepper (bottled en escabeche), seeded and minced
½	cup chopped onion	½ cup stock (preferably from Carnitas)
1	clove garlic, minced	1 cup water
½	cup Chorizo (page 192)	Salt

Prepare the meat and measure it. Sauté the onion and garlic in the fat till soft, then add the chorizo to the pan and mash to crumble it. Cook slowly, uncovered, 10 minutes, stirring now and again to cook the sausage.

Add all the rest of the ingredients and cook, uncovered, over medium-high heat until the liquid has cooked away and the Tinga begins to brown. Remove from the heat.

Tinga may be served by itself, topped with onion rings that have been soaked in salted water, then sprinkled with vinegar, and avocado slices. Accompanied by warm fresh tortillas, it makes an excellent meal. It also makes a splendid filling for tacos, or tostadas, etc. (also topped with chopped onion and avocado).

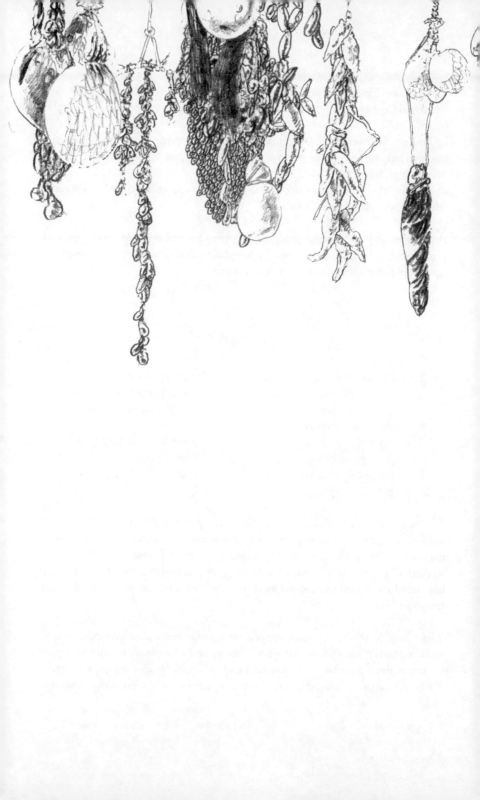

PICADILLO

1	pound ground beef	¼	teaspoon ground cumin
1	cup Chorizo (page 192)		Salt
1	onion, chopped	1	bay leaf
1	clove garlic, minced	½	cup raisins
1	cup chopped canned tomatoes	½	cup slivered blanched
1	tablespoon vinegar		almonds (optional)
	Pinch of sugar	½	cup chopped pitted black
1	teaspoon ground cinnamon		olives (optional)
	Pinch of ground cloves		

Put the beef and chorizo in a frying pan and cook, mashing down to crumble the meats, until the beef starts to brown. If too much fat is released, drain on absorbent paper and put back in the pan.

Add the onion and garlic and cook a few minutes, then add all the other ingredients except the raisins, almonds, and black olives. Let simmer, covered, 30 minutes, then add the raisins, etc., and cook, uncovered, 10 to 15 minutes.

This dish is sometimes served as is, with bowls of garnish such as grated cheese, shredded lettuce, guacamole, chopped tomatoes, little chunks of cream cheese, etc. But it is perhaps best as a filling for tortillas in the form of enchiladas, tacos, tostadas, etc. One seldom comes upon it, but one of the most spectacular ways to eat it is as a stuffing for green chilies, which are then fried in a light batter and served with a fresh tomato sauce.

CHEESE AND GREEN ONION ENCHILADAS

Corn tortillas	Sharp cheddar, grated (or
Vegetable oil	Monterey Jack)
Alda's Chili Meat Sauce (page	Green onions, chopped with part
186)	of tops

Heat ¼ inch oil in a small frying pan and fry tortillas in it only a second or so on each side—just until they soften. They should not get crisp. Do this

with a pair of tongs, and as they bubble up and soften, dip each one in a pot
of hot chili meat sauce, then lay on a plate.

Sprinkle each tortilla with cheese and green onion (about 3 heaping tablespoons cheese to 1 heaping tablespoon onion) and roll up. Place side by side
in a baking dish and sprinkle with any leftover cheese and onion. Cover with
foil and let sit until ready to serve.

To serve, heat the chili meat sauce, and warm the enchiladas in a 350°F
oven 5 to 10 minutes—or just until the cheese begins to melt. Serve with a
good spoonful of chili meat sauce on top.

Serves 1 to 2 per person, depending on other dishes.

*My favorite simple enchilada is definitely this one. In fact, I seldom serve a
Southwestern meal without it. Two of them, with Refried Beans (page 189)
and Lettuce Garnish (page 190), make a splendid meal anytime—but they are
also nice as one of a selection of tortilla dishes. They can also be made with
plain Red Chili Sauce (page 185) for a tasty meatless main dish.*

GREEN CHILI ENCHILADAS

	Vegetable oil	2	tablespoons minced fresh coriander
6 to 8	corn tortillas		Salt
½	cup chopped green onions with part of tops		Pinch of sugar
1	clove garlic, minced	1	tablespoon cornstarch
2	tablespoons minced parsley	1	cup milk
1	green pepper, seeded and grated (discarding the skin)	1	tablespoon lemon juice
1	tablespoon olive oil	1¾	cups grated natural Monterey Jack cheese
1	can (4 ounces) mild green chilies, chopped	¼	cup toasted pinon nuts, or pumpkin seeds

*H*eat oil—about ¼ inch—in a small frying pan, and with a pair of tongs
dip the tortillas in just until they bubble and soften. Place on a plate.

Sauté green onions, garlic, parsley, and green pepper in olive oil in a medium saucepan over medium heat. After 5 minutes, add the chilies, coriander,
salt to taste, and a bit of sugar. Cook 5 minutes.

Dissolve the cornstarch in the milk, then add it, with the lemon juice, to the saucepan and simmer 10 minutes. Stir now and again, as the sauce thickens to make sure it is smooth. Taste for seasoning, and reserve.

Preheat the oven to 350°F.

To assemble the dish, warm the sauce up and add 1 cup of the cheese. Place a tortilla in the bottom of a round casserole the size of a tortilla, like a soufflé dish. Top with some of the sauce, then continue layering tortillas and sauce. Finally, top with the rest of the sauce, a sprinkling of pinon or pumpkin seeds, and the rest of the cheese.

Place foil over the dish, and when ready to serve, heat in the oven 10 to 15 minutes, or until starting to bubble. Slice in pie-shaped wedges, and lift out onto plates.

Serves 4 to 6, depending on other dishes.

Enchiladas come in two forms—the rolled up and the pie stack. This is perhaps the best of the stacked, with a splendid sauce, only faintly hot, that contrasts well with more fiery dishes.

AZTEC PIE

5 corn tortillas	⅔ cup heavy cream (or milk)
6 ounces cream cheese	1 teaspoon salt
1 can (4 ounces) mild green chilies	

*P*reheat the oven to 350°F.

Divide the cheese in fourths, and spread it on 4 of the tortillas. Put the green chilies in a blender or food processor, and whirl till smooth. Spread a little of this on each cheese-coated tortilla.

Stack all the tortillas except for the plain one in a round casserole the size of a tortilla—a soufflé dish is perfect. Mix the cream and salt together and pour over the tortillas. Top with the last tortilla, and cover tightly with foil. Bake 20 to 30 minutes—or until all the liquid is absorbed. Serve cut into pie-shaped wedges.

Serves 4 to 6, depending on other dishes.

A splendid bland dish I serve often to balance all the hot spicy ones.

SIMPLE TACOS

Vegetable oil	Cooked pinto beans
Corn tortillas	Grated cheese
Alda's Chili Meat Sauce (page	Shredded lettuce
186) (or Carnitas [page 192] or	Sliced radishes
fried Chorizo [page 192])	Chopped green onions

*H*eat oil in a small frying pan—there should be at least ½ inch in the pan. When quite hot, take each tortilla with tongs and start to fry in the oil. As they cook, while they are still pliable form into a U shape by folding over with the tongs and frying first one side and then the other. Make sure, as they crisp, that you maintain at least a 2-inch opening at the top of the U. When they are crisp and golden all over, drain on absorbent paper.

These can be made well ahead during the day, and reheated in a warm oven. To serve, warm them, fill with a good spoonful of hot meat sauce, then some warm beans, cheese, lettuce, radishes, green onions, etc.

Tacos are one of the best simple balanced meals, all in one package, ever devised. To my taste, they beat almost any sandwich or hamburger anytime. In practice they can be filled with almost any spicy hot meat (or chicken) mixture, with perhaps beans as well, then garnished with any selection of cheese, lettuce, guacamole maybe, and hot salsa, chopped fresh tomato, what have you.

CHICKEN TACOS WITH GREEN CHILIES AND SOUR CREAM

8 to 10	corn tortillas	¼	cup minced fresh coriander
	Vegetable oil	1	cup sour cream
2	cups chopped onion		Salt
1	can (4 ounces) mild green chilies, chopped		Grated Monterey Jack cheese
			Sliced avocados
2	tablespoons butter		White wine vinegar
2	cups cooked chicken, diced (½ inch)		

*F*ry tortillas in the oil as in Simple Tacos (see preceding recipe). Sauté onion and chilies in the butter for 5 minutes, or until the onion is tender. Add the chicken and coriander and heat through. Add the sour cream and salt to taste, and warm through—do not let it boil.

Fill the tacos with a good bit of the chicken mixture, and top with cheese, avocados, and a sprinkle of vinegar and salt.

8 to 10 tacos.

A sensuous, mild combination, useful when other dishes are hot and spicy. It is also one of the best ways ever devised to use leftover chicken.

SIMPLE TOSTADAS

Corn tortillas
Vegetable oil
Alda's Chili Meat Sauce (page 186) (or Carnitas [page 192], or fried Chorizo [page 192])
Cooked pinto beans
Grated cheese

Shredded Lettuce Garnish (page 190)
Sliced radishes
Chopped green onions
Green Chili Salsa (page 187) or Frances Sommer's Jalapeño Salsa (page 188)

*F*ry tortillas in about ½ inch hot oil. As they cook, press down with tongs in the middle so they form a crisp cup as they fry. Drain on absorbent paper. (Like taco shells, they can be cooked well ahead during the day and reheated in a warm oven—they only get nicely crisper.)

Serve a basket of the tostadas with warm bowls of meat sauce (or other meats) and pinto beans, and an assortment of garnish for guests or family to pile up as they wish. (And plenty of napkins).

When I cook Southwestern food, and have scraps of this and that left, I always feast on tostadas for a meal of their own at the very end. With glasses of fine frosty beer, they make a wonderful simple party dish for guests, set on a buffet with the warm things in chafing dishes, and bowls and bowls of garnish— aside from those listed you can have two different cheeses, pumpkin seeds, Guacamole (page 190), two different kinds of salsa, chopped fresh tomatoes. On, and on. And scaled down a bit, they make a favorite family dinner— always pleasing.

BLACK BEAN TOSTADAS WITH SOUR CREAM

12 corn tortillas
    Vegetable oil
2   cups Refried Beans (page
    189) made with half pinto
    and half black beans (or
    with ½ can of undiluted
    black bean soup added to
    plain refried beans)

2   cups sour cream
1   can (4 ounces) mild green
    chilies, chopped
    Parmesan cheese (or dry
    Monterey Jack), grated

*F*ry the tortillas in the oil as in Simple Tostadas (see preceding recipe). Drain on absorbent paper and keep warm. Heat the beans and make sure they have enough liquid in them to spread well (but not be soupy). Mix the sour cream with the green chilies.

To assemble, spread the crisp tortillas with warm beans, then top with the chili sour cream and sprinkle with Parmesan, or aged dry Monterey Jack freshly grated.

Serves 6 to 12, depending on other dishes.

There is something about this combination which I find nigh irresistible. You would not want to serve them with a platter that includes refried beans, but they make themselves a fine meatless meal with a substantial lettuce garnish—including tomatoes, radishes, sliced avocados (or Guacamole—see page 190), etc. And of course cold, full-bodied beer.

PICADILLO TOSTADAS

12 corn tortillas
    Vegetable oil
1   recipe Picadillo (page 195)
    Sweet onion rings

Salt
Avocado slices
Lemon juice

*F*ry the tortillas in the oil as in Simple Tostadas (page 199). Drain and keep warm. Heat the picadillo, prepare onion rings and place them in a bowl of cold salted water, and dribble lemon juice and salt over the avocado slices.

To assemble, spread warm picadillo over the shells and top with onion rings and avocado slices.

Serves 6 to 12, depending on other dishes.

A very spicy tostada, but since it has no chilies it is not a hot one. The avocado and onion rings top it prettily and succulently, but if you serve these by themselves rather than as a platter of specialties, you might wish to have bowls of various garnish as in Simple Tostadas (page 199), for guests or family to top their own.

SIMPLE QUESADILLAS

Corn tortillas   Chili powder
Monterey Jack or sharp cheddar,   Vegetable oil
  grated

*P*lace about 3 tablespoons cheese on one half of each tortilla, then dust the whole with a bit of chili powder. Fold over in half moons, and fasten with toothpicks.

Fry a minute or so in about ½ inch hot oil, drain on absorbent paper, remove the toothpicks, and serve warm.

The Southwestern grilled cheese sandwich. If done with inferior cheese, they are rather tasteless and stringy—but with either natural Jack or the best aged cheddar they are beautiful crispy snacks. To make them even better, try coating each with Guacamole (page 190).

GORDON BALDWIN'S QUESADILLAS

4   wheat flour tortillas   1   sweet onion, sliced and
½   cup grated Monterey Jack   punched into rings
    cheese   1   can (4 ounces) green chilies,
½   cup grated cheddar cheese   chopped
    Grated Parmesan cheese   Melted butter

*L*ay out the tortillas and distribute the ingredients as listed (except for the melted butter) over half of each tortilla. Fold over so they make half moons and brush each side with melted butter.

Place under a broiler and broil each side about 2 minutes. Serve immediately.
Serves 4.

Quesadillas are usually prepared with corn tortillas, but these made with flour tortillas, simply broiled and not fried in deep fat, seem to outdo them all. They can, if you wish, be topped with a cold salsa at table.

SIMPLE BURRITOS

Large flour tortillas
Carnitas (page 192)
Cooked pinto beans

Green Chili Salsa (page 187) or
    Frances Sommer's Jalapeño
    Salsa (page 188)
Grated Monterey Jack cheese
    (optional)

Sprinkle large flour tortillas with a bit of water, wrap them in foil, and heat about 10 minutes in a 350°F oven to steam and soften.

Make sure the carnitas and beans are warm, then assemble the burritos by placing about ¼ cup each carnitas and beans on one edge of the tortilla, then top it with salsa (and cheese if you wish). Roll the tortilla once towards the middle, fold over the side edges to make an envelope, then finish rolling up. Serve at once.

These are a specialty of a tacqueria several blocks from where I live, and though I live in San Francisco with all its restaurants, I think this is my favorite lunch out—and all rolled before your eyes in minutes. Fast food can be good indeed. You can fuss with their filling, and slather them with guacamole, etc., but their simplicity is hard to improve on.

CHIMICHANGAS

Wheat flour tortillas
Alda's Chili Meat Sauce (page
    186)
Cooked pinto beans

Vegetable oil
Guacamole (page 190)

*R*oll up flour tortillas with meat sauce and pinto beans as in simple Burritos (see preceding recipe). You will not need to steam the tortillas, simply use them as they come from the package. Fasten each with a toothpick.

Heat at least 1 inch of oil in a heavy frying pan, and when it starts to shimmer fry the rolls until golden on all sides—this will take only 2 to 3 minutes. Drain them on absorbent paper and keep warm. To serve, slather generously with guacamole. (Or serve sprinkled with shredded lettuce, grated cheese, slices of radish, cubes of tomato, etc.)

Chimichangas are simply burritos deep fried, but like all changes of this sort— what a difference! Like any of the Southwestern tortilla dishes you can, of course, fill it with practically anything, but this version is so good I stick with it as a rule.

HUEVOS RANCHEROS

Alda's Chili Meat Sauce (page 186) (or Red Chili Sauce [page 185])
Corn tortillas
Vegetable oil

Eggs
Grated cheddar cheese
Green onions, chopped with part of tops (optional)

*H*eat the sauce in a saucepan. Meanwhile, fry tortillas in hot oil only a minute or so to soften, then dip each in the sauce and lay on a plate. Keep them warm in the oven. Fry 2 tortillas for each person.

Either fry or poach 2 eggs per person, and lay them, when done, on the tortillas. Pour the hot sauce around and over them (not covering the yolks). Sprinkle with cheese and let warm in a medium oven till the cheese just begins to melt. Sprinkle with green onions—if you use them—and serve at once.

May be adapted to any number.

I am frankly not as fond of eggs as many people seem to be, but these I can eat anytime. They are usually, of course, served for breakfast, but they also make a fine light supper.

NATILLAS

2	cups milk	⅛	teaspoon salt
3	eggs	1	teaspoon vanilla
½	cup sugar	2	sticks cinnamon
2	tablespoons cornstarch		

*P*ut the milk in a saucepan and bring it just to the boiling point. While it heats, separate the eggs in this manner: place three yolks and one white in one bowl, and reserve the other two whites in another bowl for later.

Beat the yolks and white until light and frothy. Combine sugar, cornstarch, and salt and beat into the egg mixture.

Pour a bit of the hot milk into the eggs, then a little more, beating with each addition Beat the whole thing into the milk. Cook in a double boiler set over simmering water until the mixture thickens—about 10 minutes. It should be stirred almost constantly.

When thick, remove from the fire and let cool to room temperature. Stir in now and again so a skin doesn't form on top. When cooled, stir in the vanilla.

Whip the reserved egg whites until they hold a soft peak. Fold them gently into the custard—this should be done carefully so that there are pockets of egg whites in the pudding here and there, and the whole thing is not completely smoothed out.

Divide the pudding into 4 serving cups and chill in the refrigerator. To serve, break the cinnamon sticks in half and stick one in each pudding.

Serves 4.

For sweets after a hearty Southwestern meal, even the best restaurants in the Southwest seldom go beyond the bounds of a plain flan or undigestible deep-fried sopapillas dribbled with honey. But after all the complexities of this hot and spicy cookery, one wants only the lighest clearest taste to end the meal: fresh sliced pineapple, melon balls with lime, a fresh fruit ice. My choice for a simpler family meal, however, would be this wonderful bland pudding.

Cupboard Meals

*E*veryone is caught sometime with a sturdy meal to put together from what at first looks like thin air. Rather than scramble a couple of eggs, there are main dishes you can serve with a flair, quickly produced from any cupboard or refrigerator. In a pinch, from the corner or country store. They are the secretest of meals, we eat on our own, or whip together for the kids, who hunger for such private festivities, humble abracadabra. The best of these would be a simple soufflé—the dish that really *is* thin air—but that would be to crop in ever Frencher fields.

JAMBALAYA AU VALOIS

4	smoked sausage links, sliced (about 1 cup)	2	tablespoons tomato paste
2	tablespoons butter, bacon fat, or olive oil		Salt and freshly ground pepper
2	cups chopped onion	3	cups hot water
1½	cups rice	½	cup minced parsley
		2	cloves garlic, minced

*U*se a roomy pan with a cover for this dish. Put it over medium heat, and sauté the sausage slices in the fat. Add the onion and stir till it turns limp.

Add the rice, and stir 5 to 8 minutes over low heat. The rice will turn opaque and be filmed with oil. Stir in the tomato paste and salt and pepper to taste (it should be fairly peppery), and add the hot water.

Turn the heat up, let it come to a boil, and cover closely, then turn the heat low. Let steam gently 20 minutes. To serve, stir in the minced parsley and garlic and place on warm plates.

Serves 4.

This, as well as the next recipe, comes from a rare Gourmet's Guide to New Orleans, put out in 1933. It seems to have been put together like any ordinary ladies' club cookbook, but most of the contributors are so fine, and knowledgeable about odd little recipes, that the book is a delight from cover to cover. I use ordinary smoked breakfast sausage for this dish—the smokiness is what gives it zip.

BOULETTE DE SAUCISSON

¾	pound sausage meat	2	tablespoons vegetable oil
2	cloves garlic, minced	1	cup chopped onion
	Pinch of cayenne	2	cans (14½ ounces each) hominy, drained
	Pinch of dried sage		Minced parsley
	Pinch of ground allspice		
	Flour		

Use ordinary mild sausage, and mix in the garlic and spices. Let sit at least an hour to assimilate the flavors.

Roll the sausage into marble-sized balls, and shake them in flour. Sauté in the oil in a frying pan over medium heat until they begin to brown slightly. Add the onion, and cook it till limp. Add the drained hominy and cook several minutes more, always stirring and tossing.

Sprinkle the parsley over and toss thoroughly. Serve on warm plates. Serves 4.

A lively dish that, in New Orleans, would likely be a breakfast dish, served with hot biscuits and coffee. But it also makes a fine quick supper, with beer, bread, and a salad.

BACON AND PARSLEY PUDDING

2	eggs	½	pound bacon, cut in ½-inch
½	teaspoon salt		slices
1	cup milk	2	tablespoons minced parsley
1	cup sifted flour		Grated Parmesan cheese

Preheat the oven to 450°F.

Break the eggs into a bowl and beat till frothy. Add the salt and half the milk, stirring. Sift in half the flour and stir till smooth, then add the rest of the milk and flour. Beat the batter till smooth.

Sauté the bacon in a frying pan until it is lightly brown, and remove to paper toweling. Pour ¼ cup of the bacon fat into a 10-inch oval gratin dish (or an 8 x 8-inch baking pan) and place it in the oven till it is very hot.

Stir the parsley into batter and pour into the hot gratin dish. Crumble the bacon and sprinkle it over the batter, along with some Parmesan cheese. Bake 15 minutes at 450°F, then reduce the heat to 375°F and cook 10 minutes more, or until the pudding is puffed high and golden. Serve at once. Serves 3 to 4.

A descendant of Yorkshire pudding that makes a good quick, light supper with a green salad and a glass of wine or beer. It is an equally good breakfast or brunch dish with fresh fruit and coffee. If you like, it can be prepared with ½ pound of sausage cooked in tiny balls rather than the bacon.

NEW ENGLAND CLAM HASH

4 slices bacon, cut in slivers	Salt and freshly ground
⅔ cup chopped onion	pepper
4 medium potatoes, cooked,	⅓ cup heavy cream
peeled, and diced	1⅓ cups fresh or canned whole
3 tablespoons butter	clams, drained
⅓ cup minced parsley	Paprika

*F*ry the bacon gently in a medium frying pan. When cooked but not yet crisp, add the onion to the pan and cook over medium heat until limp.

Add the potatoes and butter, tossing, then the parsley and salt and pepper to taste, then the cream. Toss the mixture over medium heat, then mash down and let cook until a brown crust starts to form on the bottom when you lift it over—about 10 minutes.

At this point add clams to the mixture, and mix well in. Cook another 5 to 8 minutes, lifting now and again to distribute the golden crust from the bottom. Serve on warm plates with a dusting of paprika.

Serves 3 to 4.

Of course this ought to be prepared from fresh clams, but I find it makes a quite good scratch meal with a tin from the shelf, for either breakfast or supper.

B. & O. RAILROAD CLAM POT PIE

4 cups peeled and thinly sliced	Heavy cream
potatoes	4 eggs
1 cup chopped onion	Salt and freshly ground
2 tablespoons butter	pepper
1 cup whole clams, with their	1 recipe biscuit dough
juice (fresh or canned)	

*P*reheat the oven to 375°F.

Parboil the potatoes in boiling salted water for 5 minutes. Drain in a colander and run cold water over. Sauté the onion in butter until it is limp.

Drain the clams, and measure the juices in a cup measure. Add enough cream to make 2 cups. Beat the eggs into the cream.

In 4 individual pot pie dishes, or in one soufflé dish, layer the potatoes, then add a sprinkle of onion and clams, some salt and pepper, then another layer of potatoes, etc. Pour the cream-egg mixture over.

Roll out the biscuit dough in 4 small rounds, or in one large one to fit your dish. Place over the filling mixture, tucking any extra under the edges. Place in the oven and bake 30 minutes, or until the crust is puffed and golden and the filling bubbly. Serve immediately.

Serves 4.

Such an easy and inexpensive dish makes one long for the lost days of railroad dining cars. For a hasty simple lunch or supper, I quite frankly prepare it from canned clams and packaged biscuit mix.

FARMHOUSE ONION PIE

2	large onions, thinly sliced		Freshly grated nutmeg
2	tablespoons butter	¼ to ½	cup grated sharp
2	eggs, lightly beaten		cheddar
¾	cup milk	1	cup fine cracker crumbs
	Salt and freshly ground	4	tablespoons butter,
	pepper		melted

*P*reheat the oven to 350°F.

Sauté the onions in 2 tablespoons butter until they are limp but not browned. Spoon into a pie plate. Mix the eggs with milk, spices and cheese, and pour over the onions. Mix the cracker crumbs with the melted butter and spread on top of the pie. Bake 30 minutes, or until the custard has set.

Serves 4.

A kind of country cousin to the quiche, and like the quiche it has possibilities of many variations. Any kind of cheese—good cheese—is pleasant, and a cup of shrimp in place of one of the onions is very good indeed. In fact it is one of those recipes which is useful on many occasions—a first course, a brunch, or supper—and best of all it is made from inexpensive ingredients usually found in any cupboard.

HUNT CLUB CREAMED CHIPPED BEEF

5	ounces chipped beef	1	tablespoon finely grated onion
2	cups heavy cream		Toast or waffles

Shred the chipped beef fine. Place in a bowl and pour boiling water over it, then drain immediately in a sieve (this will eliminate some of the saltiness of the beef).

Put the beef in a saucepan with cream and grated onion, and let boil over medium heat until the cream starts to thicken. This will take 15 to 20 minutes. Serve immediately over hot toast or waffles.

Serves 4.

Years ago I was invited to a private club by a gentleman who claimed it was Friday, and every Friday he made it a ritual to eat the creamed chipped beef at his country club. Now who honestly could refuse such a mystery, for who would drive twenty miles once a week for chipped beef on toast? At last it came, on good china, with mellow red wine, sprightly with parsley tufts, and it was inimitable. The only secret I could budge from the place was that it was cooked down in cream alone—there was no flour. This faintly approximates that far-off, unexpected feast.

McSORLEY'S TAVERN LUNCH

One of the tastiest native meals I've lucked upon comes from this famous New York watering hole. For many years women were not allowed inside, and among the regulars—from heavy laborers to smart businessmen—there have always been a smattering of artists and poets. All were there for good conversation and the best ale in the city.

When I first visited in the late 1950s, I saw a plate being delivered to a customer that consisted of a wrapped pack of fresh saltine crackers, a whole soft unwrapped Liederkranz cheese, and a Bermuda onion sliced thin as anyone could wish. We quickly caught on to this simple feast for the utterly fearless, and I continue eating it even though I don't have McSorley's around the corner.

Their famous ale cannot be reproduced, but you can come near with any fine local brew, or some dark and tasty imported beer. Liederkranz is our first native cheese and is available anywhere, as are the saltines. And though sweet onions have unaccountably disappeared from markets, by and large, any good-sized flat onion may be sliced thin and mellowed in salted ice water an hour or more, changing the water twice.

THING

Per person:

2 medium potatoes	⅔ cup cottage cheese
Vegetable oil	⅓ cup chopped green onions
Salt and freshly ground	with parts of tops
pepper	

*P*eel the potatoes and cut into ½-inch dice. Put in cold water to cover, then drain and pat dry with toweling. Fry in hot oil over high heat until they are crisp and brown.

Lift out onto paper towels to drain, and sprinkle with salt and pepper. Serve on plates, topped with a mound of cottage cheese and sprinkled with green onions.

This dish was given me in conversation (as most good recipes usually are) nearly twenty years ago, and as it was never named by the lady who passed it on, it acquired the name "Thing" from poet Jonathan Williams, who insisted it was his favorite breakfast dish. I have never grown tired of its pleasant contrasts, and served with hot coffee, or cold beer, its usefulness as a brunch or late supper dish is undeniable. It is perhaps the meal I most often sit down to when alone.

POTATO OMELET JOHN SHARPLESS

Per person:

2 medium potatoes	Parsley, minced
2 tablespoons butter	1 egg
Salt and freshly ground	1 tablespoon heavy cream
pepper	Grated cheese
Freshly grated nutmeg	

*P*eel and coarsely grate the potatoes. Put in cold water, and when you are ready to cook them, drain and press dry between paper toweling. Melt half the butter in an omelet pan (or larger frying pan if you are serving several). Add salt and pepper and nutmeg to the potatoes, and press them into the pan—shaking to make sure they don't stick.

Melt the rest of butter over the top, turn the heat down to medium, and cook till the potatoes start to turn golden on the underside. Cover the pan, turn the heat down to low, and cook slowly for 20 minutes or so, or until there is a good crust underneath and the potatoes on top taste done (but still al dente a bit).

Beat the egg and cream together with a little parsley and pour over the potatoes, stirring into the cake but not disturbing the bottom crust. Place under the broiler until the eggs are just set. Sprinkle lightly with any grated cheese, shake the pan, and flip crust up onto a hot plate, then sprinkle a little more cheese on top. Cut into wedges and serve.

With its combination of crustiness and soft creamy insides, this dish makes a satisfying meal anytime. It also lends itself to variations of all kinds—you could add onion, chives, herbs, black olives, salt pork or bacon, pimiento, green pepper, etc., etc., etc. Writer-chef Sharpless says this was the dish that gave him the special reputation of being able to prepare a gourmet meal from nothing.

PENNSYLVANIA
DUTCH NOODLES WITH EGGS

Per person:

1	cup loosely packed fine-cut egg noodles	Salt and freshly ground pepper
2	tablespoons butter	Minced parsley or chives, or paprika
1	egg	

*C*ook the noodles in boiling salted water 4 to 5 minutes, or till just tender. Drain, and pour cold water over them.

In a frying pan over medium heat, cook the butter until it turns golden brown, then add noodles and cook another 4 to 5 minutes, or until they begin to crisp slightly and turn golden.

Add the egg beaten with salt and pepper, and stir a minute or so until set. To serve, place on a warm plate and sprinkle with parsley, chives, or paprika.

A fine dish reminiscent of spaghetti carbonara, though the browned butter gives it a nuttier taste. I like it very much indeed served with sausages and applesauce, or Fried Apple Rings (page 220).

DENVER OMELET

½	cup chopped onion	1	pimiento, chopped
¼	cup chopped green pepper		Salt and freshly ground
3	tablespoons butter		pepper
⅓	cup diced (¼ inch) ham	6	eggs

*I*n a small saucepan over low heat, sauté the onion and green pepper in 1 tablespoon of the butter until tender. Add the ham and cook a few minutes longer, then add the pimiento and remove from the heat.

Beat the eggs lightly with salt and pepper to taste and add the ham mixture. Put an omelet pan over medium heat, and when it is hot enough to make a bit of water sizzle, add 1 tablespoon of the butter. When it stops bubbling, immediately pour half the egg mixture in.

Stir slightly and hold the edges of the egg up to let uncooked egg pour under, shaking the pan now and again to see it doesn't stick. When set, but still a bit undercooked on top, shake the pan a final time and slide it out onto a warm plate, flipping the pan over to fold the omelet onto itself. Repeat the process for a second omelet.

If you like, you can glaze the top with a bit more butter. Serve immediately.

Serves 2 (easily doubled).

This is one of the best, and best known, American omelets. If it is scrambled and placed between slices of toast it becomes a Denver sandwich, and that is equally good.

NEW YORK EGG AND ONION SANDWICH

1	medium onion, sliced into thin rings		A few drops Tabasco
2	tablespoons butter	4	slices rye bread
	Salt		Mayonnaise
3	eggs, beaten lightly		

Sauté the onion slices in the butter over low heat in a saucepan till they start to turn limp. Cover the pan and let them stew gently for 10 minutes, or until they are quite soft and have released some juices. (Peek and stir occasionally to see they are not burning on the bottom—if so, the heat is too high.)

After 10 minutes, take the cover off and turn the heat up to medium in order to boil any liquid down. This should only take a few minutes. Add the eggs and a few drops Tabasco, and stir until the eggs are set. Place on rye bread spread with mayonnaise, and slice the sandwiches in half.

Serves 2 (easily doubled).

This almost-omelet, served with perhaps a dill pickle and whatever else you fancy, makes a very satisfying quick meal. Beer is almost obligatory—though the most famous egg and onion sandwich, that from Mary Chase's play Harvey, was eaten simply on the run.

EGGS GOLDENROD

4	eggs, hard boiled	1½	cups milk, scalded
3	tablespoons butter		Salt
3	tablespoons flour		Toast

Shell the eggs and take out the yolks. Chop whites either coarsely or fine, as you wish. Melt the butter in a saucepan set over low heat, stir flour in, and cook 3 to 4 minutes, stirring. Add the milk all at once and stir till the sauce is thick and smooth. Cook the sauce slowly about 5 minutes.

Add the chopped whites to the sauce and cook another few minutes to heat them through. Season to taste with salt. Pour the sauce over toast, and over each serving rub egg yolk through a sieve.

Serves 2 to 4.

For no good reason I can see this dish is almost never cooked these days— perhaps because it was considered a dish from the nursery? At home we never thought it such—it was something like Welsh rabbit to warm the soul and tummy on winter evenings, and how suave the cream sauce, how pretty the dusting of bright yellow on top the color of meadow goldenrod. It is good with broiled tomato halves, for color contrast, and ham or bacon on the side, if you wish. Some like it spiked with Tabasco, or with curry in the sauce, or with a pinch of paprika to blush the top, but these I think only confuse its beautiful simplicity.

EGGS NEW ORLEANS

8	eggs		Tabasco
¼	cup tomato sauce	3	tablespoons butter
1½	tablespoons dry sherry	⅓	cup toasted slivered almonds
	Grated rind of 1 large		Buttered toast
	orange		Orange slices
	Salt		Watercress

*B*eat the eggs lightly with tomato sauce, sherry, orange rind, salt, and Tabasco to taste. In a frying pan, set over medium heat, melt the butter, and when it starts to foam add the eggs.

Scramble gently with a fork, and when the eggs are done (but still moist), place on buttered toast. Sprinkle almonds over the top and garnish with orange slices and sprigs of watercress.

Serves 4.

A dish of great subtlety in which no flavor is more pronounced than another. Cooked, the eggs assume an almost apricot color, which is as unusual as their taste. Use a very good, very dry sherry here.

SHAKER MAPLE TOAST

Bread
Maple syrup (or any syrup)
Butter

*T*ake as many slices of bread as you have persons, and spread maple syrup on both sides. Stack them up and let the syrup completely soak in. Let stand about 5 minutes, then check to see the bread is soaked through.

To cook, melt butter in a frying pan, and fry the bread slices over medium heat until crisp and golden brown on both sides—adding more butter as needed. Serve with sausage or bacon.

We Americans seem always fond of such sweet things as waffles, pancakes, French toast, etc. This, I think, outshines them all—crisp and sweet and sticky all at once, and beloved by children of all ages.

SIDE
DISHES

*Or that noble dish of green lima beans now already beautifully
congealed in their pervading film of melted butter; or that dish
of tender stewed young cucumbers; or those tomato slices, red
and thick and ripe, and heavy as a chop; or that dish of cold
asparagus, say; or that dish of corn . . .*

—*Thomas Wolfe,* Of Time and the River

Vegetables

*T*heir trick is simplicity. At the same time, any vegetable is expected to provide the unexpected, to assume the role of texture or taste contrast, and generally shine beyond the dutiful squirt of lemon, toss of shiny butter. This kind of recipe is hard to come by, and any cook can use more of them. The questing recipe hunter has all the more to prod and pry—for if he admires an obscure turnip concoction, or a new way of turning out the humble carrot, he at the same time runs the risk of offending the host or hostess's pride in their centerpiece *coq au vin* or angel cake. My solution is to admire whatever looks like much time expense and trouble was spent on, and then remark how fine the carrots were. It usually works.

FRIED APPLE RINGS

4	cooking apples (Greenings,	Salt
	Granny Smiths, Pippins,	Lemon juice
	Gravensteins)	Minced parsley
4	tablespoons butter	

*T*ake good, sharp-flavored cooking apples (if not available, Golden Delicious will do) and core and slice them in rings—leaving the skin on. Melt the butter in a frying pan, toss the apples till coated with butter, then fry gently over medium heat, turning every few minutes.

Cook 15–20 minutes, or until the rings start to brown slightly and have become almost translucent. Sprinkle with salt, a few drops of lemon juice, and minced parsley.

Serves 4.

Usually apples are fried with brown sugar, with perhaps a bit of rum or bourbon added toward the end. That is, of course, very nice, but with fine apples the method here is even nicer, with the only sweetness coming from the apples themselves. They are most often served with ham, pork, or sausages, but they are also excellent with many chicken dishes—and most certainly with Shaker Chicken in Cider Cream (page 150).

GRATIN OF APPLES, SWEET POTATOES, AND RUTABAGAS

2	pounds sweet potatoes, peeled and cut in ½-inch dice		Salt
1	pound rutabagas, peeled and cut in ½-inch dice	½	cup butter, melted
			Bread crumbs
1	pound cooking apples, peeled, cored, and cut in ½-inch dice		

*P*reheat the oven to 325°F.

Parboil the sweet potato dice 10 minutes, then drain and toss with the other vegetables, salt to taste, and melted butter.

Put in a baking dish with a good tight lid and bake at 325°F for an hour, tossing twice during the time. The different vegetable cubes should be tender but still hold their shapes.

Place them in a gratin dish, spreading so they are between 1½ to 2 inches deep. Sprinkle lightly with bread crumbs. Turn the oven up to 425°F, and when you are ready to serve them, place in the hot oven for several minutes, or until the vegetables are golden on top.

Serves 6.

A beautiful, festive dish to partner pork, ham, or best of all goose. They are good with some meat sauce poured over them, though you won't want to mask this colorful mélange completely with a heavy gravy.

STUFFED ARTICHOKES BIG SUR

4	artichokes		Salt and freshly ground
1	lemon		pepper
2	cups parsley leaves	2	tablespoons olive oil
1	clove garlic	3	tablespoons butter, melted

*R*emove the tough outer leaves on the artichokes. Slice off the stem and the top third of the leaves. Trim their bottoms with a vegetable peeler and drop them in a bowl of cold water with the juice of half the lemon. Remove them one at a time, spread the leaves, and scoop out the choke with a spoon.

To cook, mince the parsley with garlic and add salt and pepper to taste. Remove the artichokes to a saucepan in which they will all be able to stand upright. Stuff the center cavity with the parsley-garlic mixture and add an inch of water to the pan. Dribble olive oil over. Cut the remaining half lemon in eighths and place two of these, skin side up, over each artichoke.

Bring to a boil, turn down the heat to medium, cover the pan, and cook 30 to 40 minutes—or until a fork goes into the heart easily. When done, the artichokes may sit for up to 30 minutes kept warm. To serve, pour melted butter over the tops.

Serves 4.

A fine California (Italian-influenced) recipe for anyone's files. Most stuffed artichokes seem not to add anything to that subtle vegetable, but these have a wonderful savor that really doesn't seem to call for any extra dipping butter as you eat them. They should be served as a first course, with crusty fresh bread. A faint metallic taste is the consequence of drinking wine with artichokes, so it is best to hold wine for the following course.

ARTICHOKES À LA NEIGE

4	artichokes	1	recipe Sauce à la Neige (page
½	lemon		52)

*P*repare the artichokes as in the preceeding recipe, but also snip off the ends of the outside leaves with scissors all around so they appear in graduated scales to the top.

Boil over medium heat 20 minutes, or until a fork will pierce their bottoms easily. Remove and let drain upside down. Serve still warm, at room temperature, or chilled, with sauce à la neige dolloped over their tops.

Serves 4.

Sauce à la Neige, usually reserved for fish in its New Orleans habitat, is a perfect complement to artichokes I find. It is a very easy sauce, fortunately, to master, and it has the virtue of appearing here like snow capping an Oriental jade mountain.

ASPARAGUS SAN FRANCISCO

2	pounds asparagus		Salt
¼	cup ground pecans	1	tablespoon lemon juice
⅓	cup bread crumbs		Lemon quarters
4	tablespoons butter		

*R*emove the tough ends of the asparagus, tie in bundles of 12, and cook standing up in 2 inches of water so the stems boil and the tips steam. (If you don't have an asparagus steamer, use the bottom of a double boiler with the top inverted over as a lid.) Cook for about 12 minutes—or until just tender.

While the asparagus cooks, sauté the nuts and bread crumbs in 3 tablespoons of the butter until lightly browned. Salt the mixture to taste. Heat the lemon juice and remaining 1 tablespoon butter together.

When the asparagus is done, drain and untie it. Place on warm plates, pour the lemon butter over, then sprinkle with the nut-crumb mixture. Garnish with lemon quarters.

Serves 4.

A sumptuous variation on asparagus Polonaise that should be served as a course by itself, perhaps with a glass of wine, and certainly a crust of good bread. This preparation can be adapted for green beans, broccoli, or Brussels sprouts.

COLONIAL GREEN BEANS WITH MACE

1 pound green beans, trimmed and French sliced	Salt and freshly ground pepper
2 tablespoons butter	Pinch of ground mace
	A few drops lemon juice

Drop the beans in rapidly boiling salted water, a handful at a time, making sure the water never stops bubbling. Cook 6 to 8 minutes, or until just tender, then drain and run cold water over to make sure they stop cooking.

Melt the butter in a pan over medium heat, toss the beans in it, and season to taste with salt, pepper, mace, and lemon juice. Serve immediately. Serves 4.

Mace is a spice not now so widely used as in colonial time, but it makes a particularly happy marriage with green beans.

COUNTRY GREEN BEANS

1 pound green beans, trimmed	Chicken stock (or stock made
	     with a ham bone, onion, and
	     peppercorns, etc.)

Simmer the whole beans in stock to cover for 30 minutes. Drain and serve (the stock may be saved for soups). Serves 3 to 4.

These go against all we have been taught about green beans—that they should be bright green, slightly crisp still, and served with perhaps only a sprinkle of almonds browned in butter over them. But if you simply consider this another vegetable altogether, and attempt it, you might end by liking this method—I know I do. The stock gives the beans enough savor that butter seems redundant, here, for those who worry about calories, and they go well with all kinds of simple country dishes like meat loaf, spareribs, etc.

YALE BEETS

1	orange	2	teaspoons cornstarch
1	lemon	⅓	cup sugar
10 to 12	medium fresh beets,		Salt
	cooked and sliced	2	tablespoons butter
	(or canned beets)		

*P*eel the orange and lemon with a vegetable peeler, then cut the peels into tiny julienne slices. Save the fruit. Put in a small pan of boiling water and let cook over medium heat 5 minutes. Drain and reserve.

Reserve ¼ cup of the beet cooking water (or the juice from the can) and mix it with the cornstarch, juice from both the orange and the lemon, sugar, and salt to taste. Cook over a gentle heat until the mixture clears and thickens.

To serve, bring the sauce to a simmer and slip the beet slices in. Cook several minutes to warm through, then swirl in the butter. Place the beets in a serving bowl and sprinkle the orange and lemon peel over.

Serves 4 to 6.

It is said that Yale beets set out to rival that rather horrid preparation known as Harvard beets. If so they must be accounted a success. They are both attractive and pleasantly sweet-sour, and they make a tasty and colorful side dish (or even first course) for many simple meats.

BEETS WITH
THEIR GREENS IN SOUR CREAM

10	young beets with their leaves	Salt and freshly ground pepper
2	tablespoons butter	Sour cream
1	tablespoon finely grated	Lemon wedges
	onion	

*T*op the beets and put their greens in a large pan of water. Put beets in boiling salted water to cover, and simmer about 15 minutes, or until a fork pierces them easily. Place in cold water and slip off their skins. Cut into ½-inch dice.

Change the water on the greens, and make sure they are thoroughly clean. Strip the leaves off the stems and put in a large pot. Add the butter and grated onion, cover, and let cook down slowly, as you would spinach, in their own water. This will take no more than 5 minutes. Remove them with a slotted spoon, pressing down to remove as much liquid as possible.

Chop the greens coarsely, and boil down any of the liquid they released so you have only a couple of tablespoons of liquid. Put the greens back in the pot, add the diced beets, and toss with 2 tablespoons sour cream. Salt and pepper to taste.

To serve, place on warm plates, garnish with a dollop of sour cream and lemon wedges, and bring them quickly to table. If they must wait, toss with the 2 tablespoons sour cream just before serving.

Serves 4.

As a course by itself, with yeasty homemade rolls or The Duchess of Windsor's Cornpones (page 316), and a glass of either fine white or red wine, this dish can hold its own with a plate of spring asparagus or the lofty artichoke. One would not ordinarily think of serving beets to impress company, but that's exactly what I do with this dish.

COLONIAL FRICASSEE OF CABBAGE

4	tablespoons butter	1 tablespoon lemon juice
1	pound cabbage, cored and coarsely grated	Salt and freshly ground pepper
		Pinch of mace

Melt the butter in a saucepan over medium high heat. Toss the cabbage till it is coated with butter, and when it is heated through, add the lemon juice and seasonings.

Turn the heat low, cover the pan, and cook 8 to 10 minutes, tossing once during the cooking. The cabbage should still be slightly crisp. Taste for seasoning and serve immediately.

Serves 4.

A simple and good way to cook cabbage, and its simplicity is not harmed by the addition of a pinch of fresh herbs (say, summer savory, or a bit of thyme) if you have them. Cabbage has a bad name since it is so often overcooked to almost a mush, but treated with as much care for timing as you would any green bean, it is a delight—and inexpensive, too.

SHAKER CABBAGE IN CARAWAY CREAM

1	pound cabbage	1	teaspoon sugar
½	cup water	1	teaspoon curry powder
2	tablespoons butter	2	teaspoons caraway seeds
2	tablespoons flour	1½	tablespoons white wine
1	cup milk, scalded		vinegar
	Salt	½	cup sour cream

Core the cabbage and shred fine with a sharp knife. Put it with the water into a large saucepan, cover, and steam over medium heat 6 to 8 minutes, or until the cabbage has wilted. Remove from the heat and let sit.

In a saucepan, melt the butter, then stir in the flour and cook over medium heat for several minutes, stirring the while. Add the milk all at once and stir until a thick and smooth sauce is achieved. Add salt to taste, along with the sugar, curry powder, and caraway seeds. Stir this into the wilted cabbage.

Cover and let cook over very low heat 20 minutes, stirring now and again to make sure the cabbage doesn't stick to the pan. To serve, stir in the vinegar and sour cream and turn into a serving bowl.

Serves 4.

What an incredibly good vegetable the Shakers have come up with. In the final dish the flavors are balanced in a way that quite makes cabbage seem a luxury vegetable. Beauty and proportion to the Shakers were innocent delights, and they sought it all around them—from a table or chair, to a cabbage cooked for their fellows.

CARROTS DRAPER MORROW

1	pound carrots		Dash of mace
4	tablespoons butter	½	cup heavy cream
	Salt		

Scrape the carrots and either grate them very fine by hand, whirl in a food processor, or cut in 1-inch chunks and put in a blender with cold water to the top—blending until they are quite fine, then draining well. All these methods are equally good.

Heat the butter in a saucepan over medium flame, then add carrots, salt to taste, and mace. Cover, turn the heat down, and cook 10 to 15 minutes. Stir the carrots now and again to make sure they cook without sticking or burning—they should just slowly steam in the butter.

Finally, add the cream and cook 10 minutes more, uncovered, stirring now and again until the whole is a suave, creamy mass.

Serves 3 to 4.

Perhaps the finest way to show a humble vegetable to effect, these carrots will hold their own with almost any meat that does not have a cream sauce. Freshly grated nutmeg may be substituted for the mace, and if carrots are long from the field and need a bit of extra flavor, it makes the dish even richer to add a slog of good brandy, or sharper with a few drops of Tabasco or lemon juice.

ROOT PUDDING

1   cup coarsely grated carrot,
1   medium onion, coarsely
     grated
1   medium turnip, peeled and
     coarsely grated

2   cups coarsely grated potato
     Salt and freshly ground
     pepper
6   tablespoons butter, melted
3   tablespoons heavy cream

*P*reheat oven to 350°F.

This is, of course, a very simple dish to prepare with a food processor, but it doesn't take much effort to grate the vegetables by hand. Put them into a bowl, sprinkle with salt and pepper to taste, and toss with some of the butter.

Grease a pie plate or gratin dish with more of the butter, and lightly press the mixture in. Dribble cream over, then the rest of the butter. Bake uncovered for an hour, or until golden but still moist and rich.

Serves 4.

A fine old-fashioned way to treat winter vegetables. It is also a dish that can accompany most any meat or chicken, or even game. I like to sneak in a little grated nutmeg as well.

MY MOTHER'S
SOUR CREAM PEAKED CAULIFLOWER

1 head cauliflower, trimmed	Salt	
1 tablespoon white wine	1 cup sour cream	
tarragon vinegar	⅓ cup fresh bread crumbs	
5 tablespoons butter		

*P*reheat the oven to 350°F.

Steam the cauliflower in ½ inch water and the vinegar 10 to 15 minutes. When a sharp knife will just penetrate the heart of it, remove and place upside down in a bowl. Cut about 2 tablespoons of the butter into bits. Let the bits melt a good sprinkling of salt down the branches of the cauliflower as it sits.

Place the cauliflower right side up in a baking dish that is about its size— a soufflé dish is excellent. Sprinkle with more salt, and about 1 tablespoon more of the butter, in dots. In a frying pan, melt the remaining 2 tablespoons butter, add the crumbs, and stir over medium heat until golden.

To cook the dish, spread sour cream thickly over the cauliflower, sprinkle buttered crumbs over, and bake 30 minutes at 350°F. To serve, slice in pie-shaped wedges.

Serves 4.

All childhood longings aside, this is my favorite alternative to the usual cauliflower in a cheese sauce.

PURÉE OF CAULIFLOWER

1 head cauliflower	1 tablespoon butter
Salt	Dash of Tabasco
1 tablespoon dry sherry	Freshly grated nutmeg
1 tablespoon heavy cream	

*R*emove the green leaves from cauliflower, cut out the core, and break into individual florets. Put in a saucepan with about a cup of water, some salt, and the sherry.

Cook over low heat 20 minutes, or until a knife point just pierces the stems.

Drain the liquid into a bowl and place the cauliflower in a blender or food processor.

Add the cream, butter, and 3 tablespoons of the cooking liquid and whirl till smooth. Add seasonings to taste.

Serves 4.

This should not be kept too long before serving. It is a wonderfully delicate dish—actually a kind of essence of cauliflower. For a company dinner it makes a fine show of flavor and texture with equal portions of glazed carrots and fresh green beans.

CHESTNUT PURÉE

1	pound (plus) chestnuts	½	cup milk
1	stalk celery	2	tablespoons butter
1	sprig parsley		Heavy cream
½	bay leaf		Salt and freshly ground
	Pinch of dried thyme		pepper
2	cups beef or chicken stock		

With a sharp small knife cut a small strip off each chestnut. Discard any "off" ones—(depending on how good the crop is, you may need more than a pound).

Put the chestnuts in a pan with cold water to cover, bring to a boil, and cook 1 minute. Remove from the heat and peel. They will need to keep hot for peeling, so if they start to be difficult, return the pan to the fire again and bring to a boil. Use a cloth or paper towel to hold them while peeling.

Put the chestnuts in a pan with the celery and the herbs (tied in a cheesecloth bag). Cover with stock. Simmer 45 minutes to an hour. When the chestnuts are tender, discard the celery and herbs and drain the chestnuts.

Sieve or rice them, adding the hot milk, butter, and enough cream to bring them to a desirable consistency. Taste for salt and pepper. (This may be kept hot for an hour in a double boiler.)

Serves 4.

If I didn't have to peel the chestnuts, I'd have this on the table nearly all the time. As it is, I anticipate it two or three times over the holidays, and plan whole meals around it. An instance of this is Roast Long Island Duckling (page 160) with Chestnut Purée. It is also splendid alongside the stuffing, in equal portions, from a turkey or goose.

CORN ON THE COB

*T*he best way to prepare this most American of dishes is to put the kettle on to boil before picking the corn, then to run back to the kitchen. However fewer and fewer of us have gardens to run from, and must settle for the less than fresh corn in markets. It is never as sweet and flavorful, but even some of the frozen varieties are acceptable, and any ear of corn in the market still has the makings of a feast about it. To prepare corn, shuck the ears and rub to remove the silk. Trim the ends, put in a kettle, cover with cold water, add some salt and sugar, and turn on the heat to high. When the pot comes to a boil the corn is ready to serve, and should be, of course, eaten with the hands with slathers of butter, and a little salt and pepper.

COLONIAL CORN PUDDING

4 to 5	ears fresh corn	¼	cup buttermilk
3	eggs		Salt and freshly ground
1	cup heavy cream		pepper
¾	cup milk	2	tablespoons butter, melted

*P*reheat the oven to 350°F.

Scrape the corn from the cob first with the sharp edge of a knife to remove kernels, then with the back of the knife to make sure all the milky juice is extracted. You should have 2 cups.

Beat the eggs well, then beat in the cream, milk, and buttermilk. Add the corn and salt and pepper to taste. Grease a 1½-quart gratin dish, or an 8 × 8-inch baking pan, with part of the butter. Add the corn and dribble the rest of the butter on top.

Place in a larger pan with about 1 inch hot water in it and bake for an hour—or until the top of the pudding is golden, and a knife inserted comes out clean.

Serves 4 to 6.

Just writing about this dish makes me long for it again. Surely it is one of our best native dishes. In earlier times it was an ordinary breakfast dish—rather more sweetened than need be—and it is indeed pleasant to have some left over the next day, served at room temperature with crisp bacon. I like the extra flavor buttermilk yields here, but it can be prepared with any combination of cream and milk, or with milk alone.

SUCCOTASH

¼	cup diced (¼ inch) salt pork (or bacon)	1	pound fresh (or frozen) lima beans
5 to 6	ears of corn, scraped from the cob		Salt and freshly ground pepper
⅔	cup heavy cream	3	tablespoons butter

*T*ry out the salt pork in a heavy saucepan over low heat. When it has given out some of its fat and begins to brown, add the corn, tossing the mixture with a spoon. Add the cream, cover, and let simmer 20 minutes—occasionally peeking and stirring.

Meanwhile, cook the lima beans separately in salted water, and drain. Add to the corn, with salt and pepper to taste, and the butter. Cover and let simmer another 10 minutes—or until there is a good balance between the vegetable flavors.

Serves 4.

Succotash (a variation of the Narrangansett msickquatash) was the first dish the Pilgrims learned from the Indians. It seems to have originally been a dish made from corn and dried beans, and it still is prepared in parts of New England with cranberry beans. Nowadays, however, fresh limas are usually preferred. It is a stodgy kind of vegetable, to me, but many dote on the combination.

CORN, OKRA, AND TOMATOES

4	slices bacon	1	small green pepper, seeded and minced
1	onion, chopped	½	teaspoon sugar (optional)
2	cups okra, cut into ¼ inch rings		Salt and freshly ground pepper
4	ears corn, scraped from the cob (2 cups)		
1	cup peeled and chopped tomatoes (or canned tomatoes)		

*F*ry the bacon till it crisps, drain it on paper towels, and crumble. Sauté the onion and okra in the bacon fat until the onion softens.

Add the corn kernels and cook slowly 10 minutes, stirring to prevent sticking. Add tomatoes, green pepper, and seasonings, cover, and cook slowly 20 to 30 minutes, stirring now and again.

To serve, put into a serving dish and sprinkle with bacon.

Serves 6.

This is the Southern succotash, and it is my personal favorite among that far-flung family. But then I like okra. If one has only store produce, canned tomatoes do well, and frozen corn and okra still make a fine dish. Try it with fried chicken or pork chops.

SHAKER YELLOW VELVET

4 to 5 ears corn (2 cups)	1 pound yellow summer squash,
⅓ cup heavy cream	trimmed
Salt and freshly ground	Few drops Tabasco (optional)
pepper	4 tablespoons butter
½ teaspoon sugar (optional)	

*S*crape the corn of its kernels with the sharp side of a knife, then scrape the "milk" out with the back side. Put in a saucepan with the cream, salt and pepper to taste, and a little sugar if the corn isn't fresh from the garden. Simmer 15 to 20 minutes, or until the corn is almost done.

Meanwhile, cook the squash in salted water to cover 15 to 20 minutes—or until it can be pierced easily with a fork. Drain and mash it (a food processor is easiest for this, but it can either be put through a ricer or puréed with a potato masher).

Add to the corn, with the Tabasco, butter, and salt to taste. Simmer another 15 minutes, or until the mélange has acquired some character.

Serves 6.

Yellow velvet indeed!

CHARLESTON CUCUMBERS

3 medium cucumbers
4 tablespoons butter
1 medium onion, finely chopped
¼ cup white wine tarragon
    vinegar

Salt and freshly ground
    pepper
Minced parsley

*P*eel the cucumbers and slice in quarters lengthwise. Cut down the center of each slice with a knife to remove the seeds, then cut the slices in 1-inch lengths. Put in salted water to cover, and simmer 12 to 15 minutes, or until done but still slightly crisp. Drain and reserve.

Heat the butter in a saucepan, add the onion, and sauté over low heat until limp. Add cucumbers, vinegar, and salt and pepper to taste. Cook, uncovered, 5 minutes over medium-high heat, stirring occasionally and letting the vinegar cook mostly away. Toss with parsley and serve.

Serves 4.

Every time I prepare this dish I am delighted anew at both its flavor and the lovely pale jade color. It is certainly one of the best accompaniments to fish ever devised, but it is also splendid with chicken as a kind of combination relish and vegetable.

DEEP-FRIED EGGPLANT

1 eggplant
  Salt
  Milk

Flour
Freshly grated nutmeg
Vegetable oil

*P*eel the eggplant and slice as for French fries. Salt, then let drain 15 minutes or more on absorbent paper. Put in a bowl and cover with milk and let sit until you are ready to cook.

At that time, drain off the milk and shake the slices in a bag with flour and nutmeg. Fry in deep hot oil at about 375°F (or until a test slice enters the fat sputtering and becomes straw brown—not dark brown—by the time the sputters subside). Remove with a slotted spoon and drain on absorbent paper. Salt and serve quickly.

Serves 4 to 6, depending on the size of the eggplant.

Even people who say they do not like eggplant often admire these delicate puffy strips. They are crisp on the outside and almost creamy at the center, though they should be served as soon as possible after cooking or their lightness subsides. They make an excellent companion for lamb.

LOUISIANA RATATOUILLE

1 medium eggplant, peeled and cut into 1-inch cubes	Freshly ground pepper
Salt	Pinch of ground cloves
1 cup chopped onion	Pinch of dried thyme
4 tablespoons olive oil (or bacon fat)	4 garden-fresh beefsteak tomatoes (or 1 can [1 pound] Italian plum tomatoes)
1 pound okra, trimmed and sliced	2 tablespoons red wine vinegar

*P*ut the eggplant in boiling salted water and cook 10 minutes. Drain. Cook the onion in a frying pan with 2 tablespoons of the oil, for several minutes, or until limp. Add the okra and toss with salt, pepper, cloves, and thyme. Cover, and cook slowly 10 minutes.

Meanwhile, preheat the oven to 325°F.

Drop the tomatoes in boiling water for a minute, remove with a slotted spoon, and peel and slice. (Or, if you are using canned tomatoes, drain and chop coarsely.)

To assemble the dish, oil a shallow baking dish. Make a layer of the eggplant in the dish, cover with the onion-okra mixture, and finally arrange the sliced tomatoes on top. Sprinkle with the rest of the oil, cover with a lid or foil, and bake 1½ hours.

Remove from the oven, sprinkle with the vinegar, and return to the oven for another 10 to 15 minutes. Remove and let cool.

Serves 6 to 8.

A dish that should be served at room temperature, or cold the next day. I like it better than most ratatouilles I've tasted, and I also secretly like it better with bacon fat than with olive oil.

GREENS

2 bunches turnip, mustard, or collard greens	¼ cup chopped onion (optional)
2 cups water	2 to 3 turnips, peeled and cut into ½-inch dice (optional)
¼ pound salt pork (or bacon), finely diced	
Salt and freshly ground pepper	

*C*lean any mixture of greens in a large pan of water. Strip the leaves off the stems and place them in a large kettle with 2 cups water. Sprinkle salt pork over the top and add salt and pepper to taste (remember the salt pork will add almost enough salt to the completed dish).

Add the onion if you wish the extra savor, and if you've used turnip greens, add the turnips as well. Bring to a boil, then cover the pot, turn fire down low, and let simmer several hours. (In some places in the South they are cooked nearly all day—I find a pressure cooker ideal for greens, and they are just right in about an hour.)

Serve 4 to 6.

Most people not brought up in the South find the mention of this dish rather appalling. It goes against all rules for cooking delicate greens, certainly, but for rough, bitterish greens it is simply wonderful. And don't worry about loss of vitamins, for the juice left is not called "pot liquor" for nothing. It is a broth of minerals and vitamins that may be used to cook cornmeal dumplings (though I can never get them to hold together), or to sauce cornbread, etc. Greens should be served with equally forthright meat such as barbecued pork or fried chicken.

COTTAGE ROASTED JERUSALEM ARTICHOKES

1½ to 2 pounds Jerusalem artichokes	1 roast beef in progress (or leg of lamb, baked chicken)

*M*ost people peel Jerusalem artichokes, but it is not really necessary—so peel or not, as you wish. Slice them about ½ inch thick. An hour before your roast

is done (assuming it is cooking at 325° to 350°F), place the slices around the roast in its pan drippings. Baste and turn them occasionally, and remove them when they are golden brown. Serve around the meat.
Serves 4 to 6.

No relation to the "globe" artichoke, these are tubers from sunflower roots (and sometimes marketed as "sunchokes"). They have a lovely crispness rather like a water chestnut, and are delightful cooked around a roast rather than the usual potatoes. They are also good for those on diets, as the tubers have virtually no starch.

FRIED OKRA, KENTUCKY STYLE

1 pound okra	3 tablespoons bacon fat (or 2
Salt and freshly ground	tablespoons butter and 1
pepper	tablespoon vegetable oil)
½ cup white stone-ground	Lemon wedges
cornmeal	Tabasco

*T*rim the okra by cutting off the tops of the pod and the tip end. Place in a kettle of boiling water and cook till almost tender—about 5 minutes, depending on the size of the pods.

Drain, sprinkle with salt and pepper, and shake in a bag of cornmeal. Heat the bacon fat in a skillet large enough to hold all the okra and sauté them till they are golden, turning once during the cooking. Serve with wedges of lemon and Tabasco.
Serves 4.

For those who like okra, this is one of the very best ways to prepare it. (For those who do not like okra, there is no hope.) There are two other basic ways to cook it, as well. If you have small tender okra, simply boil it (whole and just trimmed on top) in salted water as little as possible until it is done to taste, then dress and toss with butter, lemon juice or white wine vinegar, salt, and pepper. Larger okra are prime for the final method in which you top the pods and slice them about ¼ inch thick. Drop them as you slice into a bowl of cornmeal. Salt and pepper, and toss to coat the slices. Fry these in hot fat until golden, then drain on paper toweling.

FRENCH-FRIED ONION RINGS

2 large mild onions, peeled and   Flour
    cut in ¼-inch slices   Salt and freshly ground pepper
1 cup water   Vegetable oil
1 cup milk

*P*ut the onions in a bowl and cover with water and milk. Let them sit for 30 minutes or more. To cook, drain the onions, then separate into rings and shake them in flour generously seasoned with salt and pepper. Fry in hot oil (350° to 370°F) until they are golden brown, remove to paper toweling, sprinkle with salt, and serve quickly.

Serves 3 to 4.

Twenty years ago these were served everywhere to great delight. Now they come frozen, constructed of reconstituted onion pulp and, oddly enough, breaded. They are so awful that I wonder who remembers the real right thing, so much better than any French fry with a steak or hamburger.

BRAISED ONIONS,
FRENCH QUARTER STYLE

6   Spanish or Bermuda onions   Salt
    (or any large flat white   ½ teaspoon dried thyme
    onion)   ½ cup Madeira
12 whole cloves   ¼ cup capers
1   cup water   1 teaspoon caper juice
½   cup beef stock

*T*rim the onions, but don't cut through the root end completely so they will hold together during cooking. Stick 2 cloves in each onion and place them in a saucepan or casserole large enough to hold all of them. Add water, stock, and thyme, and just a pinch of salt.

Bring to a boil, cover, and cook over low heat 30 minutes, or until the onions are tender. Remove the onions with a slotted spoon and keep warm.

Turn the heat on high and boil the liquid down, uncovered, to about ½ cup. Add the Madeira, capers, and caper juice, and taste for seasoning. To serve, pour the sauce over the onions.

Serves 6.

What an ideal way to begin a meal, in the French manner, with crusty bread and a glass of wine. The meal itself could only be a simple romantic one such as a tossed herb omelet, and fine fruit and cheese, then steaming thimbles of coffee.

SPOKANE SCALLOPED ONIONS

6	onions, sliced	Salt and freshly ground
3	tablespoons butter, melted	pepper
½	cup heavy cream	Freshly grated nutmeg (or
1	egg, beaten	mace)
2	tablespoons dry sherry (or Madeira)	

*P*reheat oven to 350°F.

Place the onions in a large kettle of boiling salted water and parboil 10 minutes. Drain thoroughly and put in a 1½-quart casserole greased with a bit of the melted butter.

Mix the cream with egg and pour over the onions, then add the sherry and seasonings. Toss lightly to make sure the flavorings are spread evenly. Dribble melted butter over the top and bake 45 minutes, or until the top is crusty gold.

Serves 6.

All savory simplicity, and right with many a meat. It may easily sit in a warm oven for a spell, and it makes an inexpensive side dish for company. You could halve it for family by using only an egg yolk, etc.

CAROLINA PARSNIP SOUFFLÉ

1	pound parsnips	1 cup milk, scalded
	Salt	3 eggs, separated
3	tablespoons butter	Freshly ground pepper
3	tablespoons flour	Freshly grated nutmeg

*P*reheat oven to 350°F.

Peel the parsnips, and if they are large, quarter them and cut out the inner tough core. Chop and place in a pot of boiling salted water. Boil 30 minutes, or until tender. Drain and put them through a ricer or sieve.

In a saucepan, melt the butter over medium heat. Add the flour and cook, stirring, several minutes. Add the milk all at once and stir until the sauce is thick and smooth. Take off the fire and beat in the egg yolks one by one, then add salt, pepper, and nutmeg to taste.

Whip egg whites stiff (but not dry) and fold them into the parsnip mixture. Put in a greased soufflé dish and bake at 350°F 40 minutes, or until puffed and set.

Serves 4.

The best parsnip dish I know of, from anywhere. It makes an unusual accompaniment to sturdy braised or sautéed meats of all kinds. It is especially good with pork, and I once served it with rabbit to great acclaim.

BRAISED PEAS WITH CUCUMBERS

1 cucumber	Pinch of sugar
2 tablespoons butter	¼ cup chicken stock
Salt and freshly ground pepper	1 package frozen tiny peas (or one pound fresh, shelled)
1 teaspoon minced chives (or some parsley)	

*P*eel the cucumber, cut it lengthwise in quarters, then scoop out the seeds. Cut the strips into ¼-inch dice and put in a saucepan with the butter. Cover the pan and cook the cucumber over medium heat for 4 to 5 minutes. Add salt and pepper to taste, the chives, and the sugar.

Add the stock and bring to a boil, then add the peas, and when they come again to a boil, cook another 2 minutes, covered.

Serves 4.

If I remember rightly, this comes from a handbound "book" mimeographed by homesick Korean army wives. Nothing of much interest turned up in it, but this recipe I use constantly. Though infinitely better with fresh garden peas, or course, the cucumbers here bring out frozen peas to distinction.

CREAMED SPRING
PEAS AND NEW POTATOES

Each season's creamed peas and potatoes was the very best vegetable I can remember eating through my childhood, and I have tried in vain to reconstruct the dish from current store produce. No peas seem fresh enough, though new potatoes are found now and again with much flavor. The closest you may come, if you yourself don't grow peas, is to use fresh Chinese snow peas (or even frozen in a pinch).

To do this, boil the potatoes in their skins in salted water, then drain and keep warm. Prepare a simple white sauce using the proportions of 1 tablespoon butter and 1 tablespoon flour to 1 cup hot rich milk or light cream. Trim the snow peas, put in water to cover, and cook only till they come to a boil. Drain, then stir into the sauce with potatoes and season to taste with salt and freshly ground pepper.

POMPION

4	cups pumpkin (or any winter squash), cut in ¼-inch dice		Salt and freshly ground pepper
1	shallot, minced	1	cup heavy cream
¼	cup minced parsley		Grated Parmesan cheese
¼	cup flour	3	tablespoons butter, melted

Preheat the oven to 350°F.

Cut off the hard peel of a pumpkin or any red-fleshed winter squash such as Hubbard or butternut. Dice and place in a bowl.

Toss the pumpkin with shallot (a scrap of garlic minced with some green onion may substitute for the shallot, if you wish), parsley, flour, and salt and pepper to taste.

Use some of the butter to grease a 12 x 8-inch gratin dish. Add the pumpkin, pour the cream over, sprinkle with Parmesan, and dribble the rest of the butter over. Bake at 350°F for 1 hour, or until the pumpkin is quite dark gold and the cream has been absorbed.

Serves 4 to 6.

This dish, named for the early explorer's word for pumpkin, will be a revelation for those who have only tasted squash and pumpkin sticky sweet and spiced. *This preparation is rich and handsomely flavored, and is at home with turkey, game, or pork.*

PENNSYLVANIA GRATED RUTABAGAS

6 tablespoons butter
2 pounds rutabagas, peeled and
    coarsely grated
    Salt and freshly ground
    pepper

6 slices bacon, fried and
    crumbled (optional)
    Minced parsley

Melt the butter in a large frying pan, and when it begins to sizzle add the rutabagas and salt and pepper to taste. Cover the pan and cook gently 15 minutes, tossing now and again as they cook.

Uncover and cook 15 minutes more, or until the rutabagas are soft and start to brown slightly. Serve sprinkled with bacon and parsley.

Serves 4 to 6.

Cooked so, these make a light unusual dish to partner pork, game, or even lamb. A hint of nutmeg or mace will not be out of place, and minced chives tossed in the end of cooking (rather than the bacon and parsley) make it more delicate. Rutabagas have a coarse, unlovely reputation, and it is true that cooked to a mush as usual they are almost as unsavory as a soggy Brussels sprout, but this is a dish apart.

SPINACH WITH
CREAM CHEESE AND CHIVES

2 pounds fresh spinach, washed
    and stripped of stems
1 package (3 ounces) cream
    cheese

    Milk
1 tablespoon minced chives
    Salt and freshly ground
    pepper

Place the spinach leaves in a large kettle with just the water that clings to the leaves. Cover the kettle, put over medium heat, and let the leaves wilt—this will take only about 5 minutes. Immediately dump them into a colander and run cold water over.

Squeeze out all the water with your hands and chop the spinach fine. Put the chopped spinach in a small saucepan with the cream cheese and stir over low heat until it forms a paste.

Add enough milk to make the mixture soft and creamy, then add the chives and salt and papper to taste. Cover, and let cook gently for 10 minutes.

Serves 4.

A beautiful and easy way to serve spinach. It has a slightly different quality than the usual French method of marrying cream, butter, and spinach—and chives make a welcome change from the traditional nutmeg. I suppose it would be possible to concoct this dish from frozen spinach and chive cream cheese, but with a good deal of loss in flavor.

GEORGIA SUMMER SQUASH SOUFFLÉ

2	pounds yellow summer squash (or patty pan or zucchini)	¼	cup minced parsley (optional)
		¼	cup bread crumbs
		1	egg
	Salt		Milk
4	tablespoons butter, melted		Freshly ground pepper
1	cup chopped onion		

*P*reheat the oven to 350°F.

Boil the squash in salted water till just tender. Drain, then mash coarsely with a potato masher.

Sauté the onion and parsley (if using) in 2 tablespoons of the butter until the onion is limp. Add this to the mashed squash along with the bread crumbs. Break the egg into a cup measure and add enough milk to make a full cup, then mix gently into the squash.

Add salt and pepper to taste (if the squash is not quite small and fresh, sometimes I also add a pinch of sugar or a drop of Tabasco).

Grease the bottom and sides of a gratin dish with some of the butter, then add the squash and dribble the butter that is left on top. Bake 45 minutes, or until puffy and golden on top.

Serves 4 to 6.

Of course not a soufflé in the French sense of the word, this is more a pudding. Nevertheless, homely as it sounds it is one of the very best ways to cook tender little squash there is, and I never tire of it.

ACORN SOUFFLÉS

2 matched acorn squash	Salt and freshly ground
2 tablespoons minced shallot	pepper
2 tablespoons butter	⅓ cup heavy cream
Pinch of ground mace	2 eggs, separated, plus 2 egg
Lemon juice	whites
	Parmesan cheese (optional)

*P*reheat the oven to 350°F.

Bake the squash whole for 1 hour, or until a toothpick enters the skins easily. Remove from the oven, then slice in half lengthwise so they form four equal cups. Spoon out the seeds and discard.

Sauté the shallot (or chopped green onions with a scrap of garlic) in the butter till soft, and place in a bowl. Scoop out the flesh of the baked squash and mash it into the shallot, or rice through a ricer into the bowl.

Add mace, a few drops of lemon juice, salt and pepper to taste, cream, and the 2 egg yolks. Taste for seasoning. Beat the 4 egg whites till they hold peaks but are not dry, then fold into the squash mixture carefully.

Place the squash shells in a buttered baking dish, heap the soufflé mixture in each shell, and sprinkle with parmesan cheese. Bake 20 to 30 minutes at 350°F, or until puffed up and golden. Serve immediately.

Serves 4.

These beautiful soufflés can make either a first course or a side dish to meats. They lend a simple roast pork distinction, or a grilled lamb chop substance. They are, I think, splendid enough for holiday goose or turkey, and at the same time they are comfortable as a small supper with some sausage and applesauce.

HERBED CHERRY TOMATOES

2 tablespoons butter	2 teaspoons minced fresh basil
1 shallot, minced	(or 1 teaspoon dried)
2 green onions, minced with	1½ cups cherry tomatoes,
part of tops	washed and stemmed
1 tablespoon minced parsley	Salt and freshly ground
	pepper

*M*elt the butter in a frying pan. Add the shallot, green onion, parsley, and basil and cook over low heat a few minutes, or until the shallot and onion are wilted.

Add the tomatoes, sprinkle with salt and pepper, and stir very gently as they cook over low heat. Cook 5 minutes or until they are heated through (too much cooking will cause their skins to burst).

Serves 4.

Even cherry tomatoes are in a decline these days, and come to market still greenish. But if you can find ripe tasty ones, this makes an attractive vegetable garnish to almost any plate.

CARAMELIZED GREEN TOMATOES

2	pounds small green tomatoes	4	tablespoons butter
	Flour	½	cup light brown sugar

*R*emove the stem ends of the tomatoes and cut them in half crosswise. Dip the cut ends into flour, and fry in hot butter in a large frying pan over medium heat until they are golden on the cut side. This will take 6 to 8 minutes.

Turn them over and sprinkle sugar on and around them. Cook gently for 5 minutes, then turn them cut side down again and cook until caramelized—about another 5 minutes. Serve cut side up to garnish meats, etc.

Serves 4 to 6.

Edible tomatoes have nearly disappeared in American markets, even in season. Among them, however, the diligent will often find nice tart green tomatoes that are quite good. This recipe may also be adapted to large green tomatoes cut in slices, but they take less time to cook. They are good with ham, or pork in almost any form, but they can be used anywhere a delicate sweet-sour flavor seems fit.

GRATIN OF CURRIED GREEN TOMATOES

6	medium green tomatoes, sliced		Salt and freshly ground pepper
2	medium onions, sliced	1	cup sour cream
2	tablespoons butter	½	cup buttered bread crumbs
1	teaspoon curry powder		

*P*reheat the oven to 350°F.

Sauté the tomatoes and onions in hot butter till the onions are limp and the tomatoes are cooked but not mushy.

Add the curry powder, salt and pepper to taste, and stir gently. Let cook a few more minutes, then stir in the sour cream. Pour into a buttered 10 × 6-inch gratin dish and top with buttered crumbs. Bake for 30 minutes, or until golden and bubbly.

Serves 4 to 6.

Another favorite vegetable. Somehow green tomatoes have an affinity for curry powder (and ginger as well) and this dish shows them at their finest. I like it particularly with roast lamb, or pork, but it is useful for many meals more.

JAMES BEARD'S
TURNIPS WITH MUSHROOMS

	Salt		Freshly ground pepper
6	turnips, peeled and sliced ¼ inch thick	½	pound mushrooms, cleaned and sliced ¼ inch thick
6	tablespoons butter		Minced parsley (or chives)

*C*over the sliced turnips with boiling salted water and cook over medium heat 8 to 10 minutes, or until tender but still crisp. Drain and toss with 2 tablespoons of the butter and some pepper.

While they are cooking, sauté the mushrooms in the remaining 4 tablespoons butter, seasoning with salt and pepper to taste. This will take only 3 to 4 minutes.

Scrape the mushrooms and their juices into the turnips and cook gently for 2 minutes more. Serve sprinkled with parsley or chives.

Serves 4 to 6.

A recipe picked up on the trail of the indefatigable James Beard, our most venerable and intelligent champion of native food—though I'm not sure how much it has changed during the years I've cooked it with pleasure. Typical of Mr. Beard's forthright gustatory sensibilities, here two earthy flavors play off and complement each other toward a new succulence. As partner to a lamb chop—or for that matter game—they are not to be beaten.

SHAKER ALABASTER

4	medium turnips, peeled and halved	Salt
4	medium potatoes, peeled and halved	Heavy cream Tabasco (or white pepper)

*P*lace the turnips and potatoes in a saucepan of boiling salted water to cover and boil 20 to 30 minutes—or till a knife pierces each easily. Drain, then put turnips in a blender or food processor. Return the potatoes to the saucepan.

Put paper toweling over the potatoes, and cover with a lid to sit till dry—about 5 minutes. Add ¼ cup cream to the turnips and whirl to a fine purée. Mash or rice the potatoes, add the turnips, and beat smooth.

Add as much more cream to the mixture as will make it slightly more liquid than regular mashed potatoes. Season to taste with salt and Tabasco. Put in the top of a double boiler over simmering water (or in a 300°F oven) till puffed slightly—about 20 to 30 minutes. They may stand for as long as an hour.

Serves 4.

A beautiful conceit of the Shakers, with nothing to yellow the whiteness, and a surprisingly good accompaniment to any duck dish, to braised meats with lots of sauce, or to a lamb chop for all that. Surprise is the word—they are always surprising.

ZUCCHINI FRITTERS

2	cups coarsely grated zucchini	½	teaspoon salt
1	teaspoon lemon juice		Freshly ground nutmeg
1	tablespoon grated onion	¼	cup flat beer
¼	cup minced parsley		Vegetable oil
½	cup flour		Grated Parmesan cheese
1	teaspoon baking powder		(optional)

*P*ut the zucchini in a bowl, sprinkle with lemon juice, and mix with the onion and parlsey. Sift the flour, baking powder, and salt over, grate some nutmeg in, and mix together lightly. Pour the beer in and mix again thoroughly.

Heat at least 1 inch oil in a pan, and fry walnut-sized spoonfuls of the zucchini mixture till crisp and golden. Drain on paper toweling, and sprinkle with Parmesan cheese if you wish before serving.

Serves 4.

Zucchini fritters make very good combination starch and vegetable to serve with all kinds of meats. In my house they tend to disappear before they can even get to table.

Starchy Dishes

*H*enry James (no noted gourmet) once asked his British cook if she could not do other than boil or mash a potato to accompany his chop, and suggested she might fry them. She, in turn, suggested that method might be French, and no, she didn't know of any other ways. Henry knew otherwise. His French visits bristled with ways of surprising a chop, and he suspected even his brash countrymen knew a trick or two, for he had tasted the newly invented "Saratoga chips"—that paper-thin crisp heaped beside the duck, prepared in a way that certainly couldn't be called French. In fact, the potato is a magical vegetable, quick to take on new character with every marginal change in shape, or twist in cooking. We have a host of ways (and nearly as many with the noodle and grain of rice) treasured up, out of the past, for one and all.

MISS DOROTHY'S MASHED POTATOES

Per person:

1 medium potato	1 to 2 tablespoons butter
Salt	Freshly ground pepper
About ¼ cup milk, scalded	

*B*oil the potatoes in salted water till they are tender, or a fork will pierce them easily. Drain well, return to the pot, and cover first with a double layer of paper toweling, then with the pot lid. Let sit 5 minutes, or until the potatoes are dry and mealy.

Peel, rice them into a bowl, and with a potato masher (or better yet with an electric mixer) work in milk, bit by bit, until you think there is too much, and then add a little more. It is better to add too much than too little.

Beat in the butter, and salt and pepper to taste. Put the potatoes in the top of a double boiler set over hot water (or covered in a 300°F oven) and let them sit over low heat for 20 to 30 minutes. They will puff up and have a very light consistency without being filmed with butter or cream as most recipes tell you. (They can be held up to an hour in this manner, and really only get better.) Serve with a little more butter in a pool on top if there is no sauce to the meat.

This, along with my mother's pie crust, are just about the only two things I have learned firsthand from great cooks. Anyone can make complex things, but to make the simplest ones fine is the mark of the truly expert.

MY MASHED POTATOES

*P*reheat the oven to 425°F.

For these you proceed exactly as for Miss Dorothy's Mashed Potatoes (see preceding recipe), except you take good strips of peel with a vegetable peeler from the potatoes before boiling.

When you have the mashed potatoes in a double boiler or warm oven, pile the strips of peel up in stacks and cut them in julienne strips (about ⅛ inch wide) with a sharp knife. Toss with a bit of melted butter—only about a tablespoon per cup of peel is necessary.

Place in a shallow pan and bake 15 minutes, or until the strips of peel are crisp as potato chips and golden brown. They should not get dark brown. They may be kept warm until you are ready to serve the potatoes, then sprinkle a pile of crisp strips over every serving. These are quite tasty enough without any salt.

Vitamins aside, this makes quite the most possible of an already good thing. It probably is a sin to waste anything as good as these peelings. In fact, even when you prepare other potato dishes remember they can be cooked as they come from the peeler in large strips to make an excellent appetizer. They can also be prepared from baked peel (about 5 minutes), or boiled peel (about 20 minutes). Warning: If you see a hint of green under the peel of any potato, don't use it. This means the potato has been stored improperly, and the green part is slightly poisonous.

OHIO BUTTERMILK MASHED POTATO SOUFFLÉ

4	medium potatoes	2	teaspoons sugar
	Salt	2	tablespoons butter
¼	teaspoon baking soda	½	cup (or more) milk
½	cup buttermilk	2	tablespoons butter, melted

*B*oil the potatoes in salted water till a fork goes through. (It is preferable to do this with the skins on, for flavor, but not necessary.) When done, drain and return to the pan. Place a double paper towel over the pan, then cover with the lid. Let set to dry 5 minutes or so.

Preheat the oven to 325°F.

While the potatoes sit, stir the soda into the buttermilk. Place 1 teaspoon salt, the sugar, and butter into a bowl. Peel the potatoes and place in a ricer. Rice them into the salt, sugar, and butter. Mash with the soda-buttermilk until smooth. Add enough milk to make the mixture thickly soupy rather than stiff. (2 cups liquid in all are just right for 1½ pounds potatoes, but in practice no two batches are quite alike. Don't worry, but don't make them too dry either.)

Use a bit of the melted butter to grease a soufflé dish. Put the potatoes in, smooth over with a spatula, and dribble the rest of the butter on top. These can sit awhile if you wish, for 30 minutes or so, and then be cooked at 325°F

for 30 minutes. They can cook in a slightly higher oven, even, but they should not brown. The final dish should just puff up slightly, and still be creamy.
    Serves 4.

More "mashed" than soufflé, these farmhouse potatoes are still about the best tasting in the world.

MY NESTED POTATOES

4 medium potatoes	4 tablespoons butter, melted
Salt	½ cup sour cream (optional)

*P*reheat the oven to 350°F.
    Boil the potatoes till tender in salted water, then drain and return to the pan. Place paper toweling over the pan then cover with the lid. Let sit to dry 5 minutes or more.
    While the potatoes sit, use some of the melted butter to grease the bottom and sides of a soufflé dish. Peel the potatoes and place in a ricer, then rice them carefully into the dish. (The reason for a soufflé dish is that the sides of it are high enough so the riced potatoes are not mashed down in any way.)
    Put directly in the oven and cook 30 minutes, or until the potatoes begin to get golden and a slight crust begins to form on top. Gently pour the remaining melted butter over the potatoes, and cook another 30 minutes.
    Properly made, the potatoes will be crisp and golden all over, and not stick to the sides or bottom. You will be able to tip them out and place on a warm plate without changing their shape. Shake the dish to see if they are loose, and if not cook some more.
    When done, unmold on a serving plate and fill the center of the nest with sour cream if desired. Bring to table and slice in pie-shaped wedges.
    Serves 4.

A ricer necessarily produces a ring mound with a center depression, and these potatoes are formed around this. I have given the smallest amount of butter here, but there is no use being stingy about it, and I use sometimes nearer ½ cup. After the potatoes are crisp extra butter on top will not harm the light puff inside. I don't think they need any salt or pepper, but you might.

AMERICAN FRIES

4   medium potatoes   Salt and freshly ground pepper
    Vegetable oil

Peel the potatoes and cut into ½-inch dice. Drop into a bowl of cold water to wash the starch off. Drain and dry on paper toweling.

Heat oil to the depth of about 1 inch in a large frying pan set over high heat. When the oil begins to shimmer, test a potato cube—and it should sizzle up immediately and cook in earnest.

Add all the potatoes and fry until golden brown (they should be turned now and again to ensure that they cook evenly). When done, lift out with a slotted spoon onto paper toweling, and sprinkle with salt and pepper.

Serves 4.

Essentially French fries in another form, these also form the basis of Brabant Potatoes (see following recipe) and all its variations—see Sirloin Clemenceau (page 80).

BRABANT POTATOES

4   medium potatoes   ¼   cup minced parsley
    Vegetable oil   Salt and freshly ground
¼   cup butter   pepper
2   cloves garlic, minced   Good wine vinegar (optional)

Cook the potatoes as in the preceeding American Fries.

Preheat the oven to 175°F.

When the potatoes are done, and drained, put the butter in a small saucepan and cook the garlic in it till the garlic starts to turn golden—be careful not to burn it. Remove from the heat.

Put potatoes in a baking dish, pour the garlic butter through a sieve over them, and discard the garlic. Sprinkle the parsley and salt and pepper to taste over the potatoes, and toss thoroughly.

Place in the oven and cook 15 to 20 minutes. If you wish, sprinkle a very little vinegar over them before serving.

Serves 4.

It is a mystery to me why this dish—widely cooked in both homes as well as restaurants in New Orleans—never seems to travel. These fries are certainly livelier than any French fry, and are easier to prepare, since they have to sit in the oven for a time rather than being rushed to the table.

BALTIMORE FRIES

| 1½ | pounds red potatoes, each 2 | Salt |
| | inches in diameter | Vegetable oil |

*S*crub the potatoes and cut them in quarters. Drop in boiling salted water and cook 15 minutes—they should be almost done but not soft. Drain and dry on taper toweling.

Heat at least 1 inch of oil in a large frying pan, and when it starts to shimmer (but not smoke) add one potato quarter to test. In 4 minutes it should be golden brown all over. Cook the rest of the potatoes, drain on paper toweling, and lightly salt them. Serve immediately.

Serves 4.

An example of how potatoes, by being a slightly different form, and by being cooked slightly differently, can take on magic newness and goodness. These are not widely known, and I like to surprise guests with them alongside steaks or chops or many another dish.

SARATOGA CHIPS

| 4 | baking potatoes | Salt |
| | Vegetable oil | |

*P*eel the potatoes (or not, if you like chips with skins on) and slice as thin as possible—a vegetable grater usually has a slicer on it that makes these well, but they are best carefully done with a regular vegetable peeler, one by one. Soak the slices 1 to 2 hours in cold water, changing the water once.

Drain and dry thoroughly before cooking. To do this, bring oil to heat in a deep-fat fryer. The fat should be 375°F, or at the point a test slice enters the fat sputtering and becomes straw-brown by the time its sputters subside. Fry the chips in batches, making sure they don't stick together. Drain on paper toweling, and sprinkle with salt while still hot.

Serves 4.

These homemade potato chips are the traditional partner to game, in this country, but they are perfect with steaks or grilled chops, even hamburgers. But be prepared—your family or guests will most likely eat all you can turn out. These were the invention of one George Crum, chef of Moon's Lake House at the fashionable nineteenth century spa, Saratoga Springs. It is said a finicky patron returned his French fries saying they were not thin enough, and Crum sliced some potatoes paper thin. A new dish was born—and as Brillat-Savarin says, "The discovery of a new dish does more for human happiness than the discovery of a star."

RUSSIAN HILL POTATOES

1½ cups coarsely grated potatoes	4 tablespoons butter, melted Salt and freshly ground pepper

*P*ut the grated potato in a bowl of water, then drain and rinse under the faucet in a sieve or colander. Squeeze the water out by hand and put the potatoes in a bowl. Use a bit of the butter to grease a 10-inch cast iron frying pan (or a nonstick pan) and toss the rest with the potatoes. Add salt and pepper to taste.

Put the frying pan over high heat and spread the potatoes in with a spatula. When they start to take a bit of color on the underside, lower the heat and cook 20 minutes, shaking now and again to make sure a crust forms evenly without burning. (It is better to cook it too slow, after it first forms a crust, than too fast.)

When the bottom is a gold-brown crust, flip the cake onto a plate, crust side up, then slide it back into the pan on the uncooked side. Cook another 15 to 20 minutes, adding more butter if needed, until the whole is a lacy golden brown throughout, and can be lifted with a spatula (or hand) onto a plate.

Cut in 4 pie-shape wedges and serve. (The potatoes can also be held in a warm oven, if need be, for 30 minutes or so.)

Serves 2 to 4.

My only complaint about this dish is that it's almost impossible to make enough unless you have a battery of skillets going. Once you get the hang of them, they are really quite easy, though, and they go well with everything but fried meats. They put hashed browns in the shade, at breakfast, as well. They are the invention of chef John Sharpless, who cooks them in a hot oven as restaurant cooks do everything, but I get better results on top of the stove.

FARMHOUSE
SKILLET CREAMED POTATOES

¾ cup heavy cream	Salt and freshly ground pepper
¾ cup milk	Freshly grated nutmeg
2 tablespoons butter	
4 to 5 medium potatoes, peeled and cut into ¼-inch slices	

*P*lace the cream, milk, and butter in a frying pan. Slice the potatoes into the pan and add salt, pepper, and nutmeg to taste. Turn up the heat and bring to a simmer.

Cover the pan, turn the heat way down, and cook gently 30 minutes. Uncover and turn the potatoes with a pancake turner. Check the seasonings and simmer another 30 minutes, uncovered, or until the potatoes are tender and their sauce is thick and creamy.

Serves 4.

These are purely wonderful. The sauce achieved is incomparably better than potatoes in a white sauce. They can accompany practically any meat that is not sauced itself.

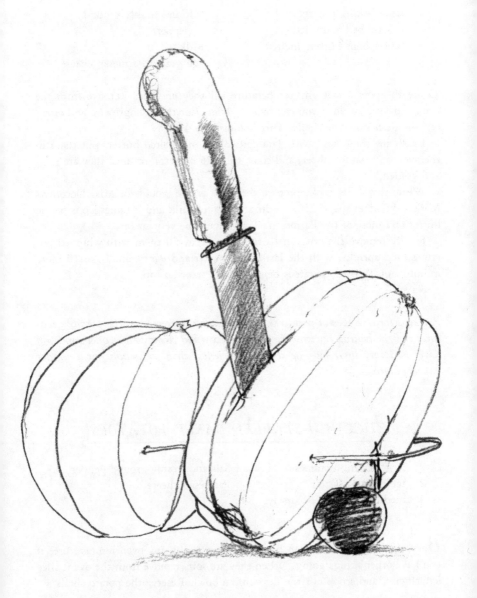

THRICE-BAKED POTATOES

2   large baking potatoes,
scrubbed and oiled
4   tablespoons butter, melted

Salt and freshly ground
pepper
Milk
⅓   cup grated Parmesan cheese

*B*ake the potatoes at any temperature till they are soft. Remove from the oven and let cool until you can handle them. Cut them lengthwise and scoop out the flesh from the shells. Turn the oven to 425°F.

Brush the shells well with 1 tablespoon of the melted butter, put them in the oven on a baking sheet, and cook 10 to 15 minutes, or until they are crisp and golden.

While the shells cook, prepare the flesh as you would for Miss Dorothy's Mashed Potatoes (page 250), adding plenty of milk and 2 tablespoons of the butter and most of the Parmesan. They should be very creamy.

Finally remove the crisp shells from the oven, fill them with whipped potatoes, and sprinkle with the last of the butter and Parmesan. Bake 10 more minutes, or until the potatoes begin to take color on top.

Serves 4.

A recipe for devotées of potato skins, and those interested in the possible evolution of the baking potato. They are crunchy and creamy all at once, and you have used very little fat—or at least much less than you would for a regular baked potato.

ZUCCHINI-STUFFED BAKED POTATOES

2   large baking potatoes
2   tablespoons butter
2   medium zucchini, coarsely
grated

Salt and freshly ground pepper
Parmesan cheese

*B*ake the potatoes—this can be done at practically any oven temperature, if you have other things going. When they are soft, remove from the oven, slice lengthwise, and scoop out the flesh into a bowl. Reserve the potato shells.

Either mash the potato or put it through a ricer. Melt the butter in a small pan, and when it sizzles, toss the grated zucchini in it over medium heat 3 to 4 minutes—or till cooked but still firm to the bite. Add salt and pepper to taste as it cooks.

Fold the zucchini lightly into the potatoes, then spoon back into the potato shells. Sprinkle with cheese. (These can be held, covered, for an hour or more before baking.)

About 20 minutes before your meal is to be ready, preheat the oven to 425°F.

Bake the potatoes 5 to 10 minutes—or until heated through, with the tops beginning to brown.

Serves 4.

These wonderful things seem to be the invention of Colorado chef Barbara Conwell, and they come from a splendid Junior League of Denver cookbook called Colorado Cache *that offers "a goldmine of recipes"—as indeed it does. Copies may be obtained from The Junior League of Denver, Writer's Center II, Suite 400, 1805 South Bellaire Street, Denver, CO 80222. They are a kind of spinoff of Julia Child's famous grated zucchini recipes, and everyone I've ever served them to goes into ecstasies and copies the recipe down. They can be prepared ahead, and in any amount, and couldn't be better, as a combination starch and vegetable, with any casual or stately meal. They are also much less calorific than a baked potato with all the trimmings.*

PORTLAND POTATOES

4	baking potatoes	8	slices thin bacon
	Salt		Paprika

Scrub the potatoes and drop them unpeeled in boiling salted water. Boil until just tender, then drain and put them back in the pan. Cover with paper toweling and the lid, and let sit 5 minutes.

Heat the oven to 350°F.

Peel the potatoes and place in a baking dish. Cut the bacon slices in half and wrap 4 slices around each potato, securing with toothpicks. Sprinkle with a dust of paprika.

Bake 20 to 30 minutes, or until the bacon crisps golden. Remove the toothpicks before serving. (These may be kept warm some time in the oven, if necessary.)

Serves 4.

Easy to prepare and delicious, these certainly look better on a plate than a boiled potato, and basted naturally they need neither sauce nor condiment.

DEEP-FRIED SWEET POTATOES

4 medium sweet potatoes	Salt
Vegetable oil	Freshly grated nutmeg

*P*eel the sweet potatoes, square off the ends and sides, and cut, like French fries, in ¼-inch strips. Heat oil in a deep-fat fryer until it is 375°F (or until a sample sputters when dropped in, and gets brown when the bubbles subside).

Drop the potatoes, in batches, into the hot fat. Remove with a slotted spoon, drain on absorbent paper, and sprinkle with salt and freshly grated nutmeg.

Serves 4.

If you appreciate French fries, you will find the nutty flavor of a mound of these a welcome surprise with many dishes—from plain lamb chops to Madame Bégué's Liver (page 134). Some recipes call for them to be cut thicker and parboiled before frying, but I think these are superior.

BAKED YAMS

*G*et yams all of a size so they bake evenly. They can bake at any temperature, and as there is little danger of cooking them too much, add along with meat in the oven as it cooks, or before.

At 350°F, medium-sized yams take a minimum of an hour to get done. Squeeze them to test, and when they are quite soft they are ready. They can be kept warm for an hour or more if need be. To serve, slice in half lengthwise, then cut slashes through the flesh and melt butter into them, as much as they will hold, and sprinkle with a bit of salt.

The yam is much better than the regular sweet potato. They can be distinguished in the market for their quite dark color, and on the tastebuds by a texture just this side of an avocado. They not only have more flavor than a sweet potato, they are also sweeter and so need no sugar. Baked, they outshine plain potatoes by far. Though they are usually served with pork or ham, I like to serve them, to the surprise of company, with any dish (and it doesn't have to be American, either) not overly delicate, or with which the sweetness of the yams would not be out of place.

RUM AND ORANGE YAMS

2 pounds yams, baked (page 260)	1 tablespoon rum (or brandy)
Juice and finely grated peel of 1 orange	Salt
	½ cup finely chopped black walnuts (optional)
2 tablespoons butter	

*H*alve the cooked yams and scoop the flesh into a ricer. Rice the yams into a bowl, then add the juice and grated peel of the orange and the rest of the ingredients except the nuts.

Mash and beat the ingredients into a light purée, then fold in the nuts. The yams can be kept in a double boiler for 30 minutes to an hour, and they will puff slightly. (Or you can cook them in a 300°F oven for the same time, perhaps with a dribble of butter over the top.)

Serves 4.

If anything, this is my version of dread candied sweet potatoes with marshmallow topping. These have only the fine natural sweetnesses of the yams and orange, and I think a better texture and depth of flavor. The black walnuts are my mother's addition, and they make the dish into a masterpiece. I have tried regular walnuts, but they do not so equally balance the orange and rum flavors, and seem there only as a pretext for texture.

GRITS PONTCHARTRAIN

1 cup grits	6 egg yolks (or 3 eggs)
Salt	1 cup diced (¼ inch) sharp cheddar cheese
4 cups water	
1 cup heavy cream	2 tablespoons butter, melted

*P*reheat the oven to 350°F.

Cook the grits in salted water according to package directions. When done, remove from the fire and let cool a bit.

Beat the cream with the egg yolks until frothy, then mix into the grits. Add the cheese and mix in as well. Butter an 8-inch casserole with a bit of the melted butter. Add the grits, then dribble the rest of the butter over the top.

Cover with a lid, or foil, and bake 30 minutes. To serve, cut in squares (or pie-shaped wedges if the pan is round) and place on warm plates to accompany sausage, bacon, or kidneys, etc.

Serves 4 to 6.

Good solid American fare, made so well as to please those who have never heard (and have never wanted to) of Southern grits. They are slightly more delicate when all egg yolks are used, but if you are not planning meringues the next day the difference becomes a matter of small note. The very best aged sharp cheddar should be used, however, for there is no substitute for good cheese.

GRITS SOUFFLÉ

1	cup grits		Tabasco
	Salt	4	tablespoons butter, melted
4	cups water		Grated Parmesan cheese
1	cup heavy cream		
3	eggs, separated, plus 1 egg white		

*P*reheat the oven to 350°F.

Cook the grits in salted water according to package directions. When done, remove from the fire and let cool a bit.

Beat the cream with the 3 egg yolks and mix well into the grits. Add a few drops of Tabasco and salt to taste. Mix in 2 tablespoons of the melted butter.

Beat the 4 egg whites till stiff but not dry, then fold them carefully into the grits. Butter a soufflé dish with some of the remaining butter and gently spoon the mixture into it. Sprinkle with some Parmesan and dribble the last of the butter on top.

Bake 30 minutes, or until the soufflé is puffed and golden on top.

Serves 4 to 6.

In effect another kind of spoonbread, this may be used as a starch dish to accompany nearly any meat, with butter if there is no sauce. In the south it would most often be served for breakfast, and it does make a special treat with eggs and sausage, etc.

PENNSYLVANIA NOODLE PANCAKE

1	pound wide egg noodles		Freshly ground pepper
	Salt		Paprika
4	tablespoons butter	¼	cup minced parsley

*C*ook the noodles in boiling salted water until just tender. Drain well and toss with half the butter. Season to taste with salt and pepper, then toss with paprika and the parsley.

Melt the rest of the butter in a large skillet. Add the noodles, press down, and cook slowly until a golden brown crust has formed on the underside.

Shake the pan occasionally as the noodles cook to make sure they do not stick. When the crust has formed, flip them out like a pancake onto a plate, with the crust on top. Sprinkle with extra paprika, and serve cut into pie-shaped wedges.

Serves 6.

An excellent change from plain buttered noodles, and also a good way to use leftover noodles—adjusting the recipe, of course, if there is a smaller amount of noodles. They may be topped with a dollop of sour cream, if you like.

MY GRANDMOTHER'S DROP NOODLES

3	eggs	1	cup (plus) flour
3	tablespoons water		Beef or chicken stock
½	teaspoon salt		

*B*eat the eggs, water, and salt to a froth. Add the flour slowly, beating with a fork till smooth after each addition. Add flour until the dough becomes a little stiff and begins to leave the side of the bowl as you mix it. (Three large eggs will take 1½ cups flour).

Have the stock simmering in a kettle. Drop the dough in by the ¼-teaspoon, dipping the spoon into the hot stock each time so the dough doesn't stick to the spoon. Cook about 6 minutes—or until they are no longer doughy at the center.

Remove with a slotted spoon and serve either lightly buttered or with sauce from a meat or chicken dish.

Serves 4.

This pioneer-style recipe makes a kind of spaetzle. *If cooked too long they become tough, but captured right they are light but chewy—a texture truly not to be found in any other noodle, and what could be simpler. My grandmother used these to stretch a budget over seven people at family table by boiling a meaty soup bone up—the meat and noodles were served in some broth in a soup plate. I still like them with things like fricassee.*

SOUTHERN DRY RICE

1 cup long-grain rice	Salt (optional)
1¼ cups water	Toasted sesame seeds (optional)

*P*ut the rice in a sieve and wash it in several waters as follows: dip the sieve in a bowl of water, then under running water, then back in a bowl of clean water, etc. This will wash off all the starch on the rice.

Bring 1¼ cups water to a boil. Add the rice and bring back to a simmer, then cover the pan and cook over as low a fire as possible for 15 minutes. Do not lift the lid until 15 minutes are up.

Test the rice—every grain should stand apart and they should be still a bit firm to the tooth. If you wish it less al dente, cook very slowly another 5 minutes. Sprinkle with sesame seeds, if you like, before serving.

Serves 4.

Dry rice is a radical departure from the way you usually cook rice, but it is well worth trying. Once you get the knack of it you might not want rice any other way. It somehow doesn't need salt if it's to be served with a sauce or gravy, but add it if you wish. I like it simply buttered and sprinkled with sesame seeds that have been toasted in a dry skillet, as they do in Charleston.

ORANGE RICE

1 cup long-grain rice	½ cup finely chopped pecans
1½ cups orange juice	2 tablespoons butter
1 tablespoon lemon juice	1 teaspoon grated grapefruit rind

Wash the rice through several waters, as in Southern Dry Rice (see preceding recipe), and drain. In a medium saucepan, bring the orange and lemon juice to a boil, add the rice, cover, and cook over as low a fire as possible for 15 to 20 minutes, or until the rice is slightly nutty still but the liquid is absorbed.

Sauté the pecans in the butter till they are toasted through, and toss them, with the grated grapefruit rind, into the cooked rice. Serve immediately.

Serves 4.

Adapted from Mary Land's Louisiana Cooking, *this is wonderfully paired with her recipe for Cajun Rabbit on page 165. It is also particularly good with simple fish, or barbecue, on a warm day as well. It tastes every bit as good as it sounds.*

KENTUCKY RED RICE

⅓ cup diced (¼ inch) salt pork (or bacon)	2 tablespoons tomato paste
1 tablespoon butter	2 cups water (or chicken stock)
½ cup minced green onions with part of tops	Salt and freshly ground pepper
1 heaping teaspoon sweet paprika	1 cup long-grain rice

Sauté the salt pork in the butter over medium-low heat until it is slightly golden. Add the green onions and cook them till limp, then add the paprika and stir the pot for a few minutes off the fire.

Stir in the tomato paste, add the water or stock, bring to a boil over high heat, add salt and pepper to taste, and finally add the rice.

When the pot returns to a boil, lower the heat, cover the pan tightly, and simmer 20 minutes, or until the rice is done but not too soft. Serve immediately.

Serves 4.

A sort of home grown risotto, and a very good one, too. The tiny cubes of salt pork give another savor altogether than is to be got from olive oil or butter. I first had it as a side dish to cold sliced meats, with homemade rolls and an assortment of chutneys, pickles, and relishes, but it makes a fine accompaniment to many a meat.

THOMAS JEFFERSON'S PILAU

1 cup rice	⅓ cup pistachios
2 cups water (or chicken stock)	⅓ cup pine nuts
4 tablespoons butter	Ground mace
½ teaspoon salt (if using water)	

Wash the rice thoroughly. In a large saucepan, bring water or stock to a boil, along with 1 tablespoon of the butter and the salt (if used). Add the rice, stir, and when the water comes to a boil, lower the heat well, and cover the pan. Let simmer gently 20 minutes.

Cover the pistachios with boiling water and let sit a minute. Drain and rub off their skins. Sauté the pine nuts and pistachios in the remaining 3 tablespoons butter over low heat, tossing until they are golden. Remove from the heat (the butter shouldn't burn, but if it has, drain the nuts and toss with new butter).

When the rice is done, toss it gently with the nuts, pile on a platter, and sprinkle with mace.

Serves 4.

A fantasy dish like something out of dear Alice Toklas. If pistachios and pine nuts seem too expensive, it is equally interesting with toasted almonds and pumpkin seeds, say, or what your cupboard affords. It works as well, with fish, if cooked with half clam juice and half water.

FEATHERED RICE

1 cup long-grain rice	3 tablespoons butter (optional),
2½ cups boiling water	cut into bits
1 teaspoon salt	

*P*reheat the oven to 400°F.

Spread the rice on a cookie sheet and bake, stirring occasionally, for 10 to 15 minutes, or until golden brown.

Turn the oven down to 350°F, and remove the rice to a casserole with a cover. Add the boiling water, and salt, cover the pot closely and bake for 30 minutes, or until the rice has absorbed all water and is light and puffy.

If you wish butter, fold the bits in lightly before serving (I don't think it needs any at all if the meat has sauce).

Serves 4.

This process completely changes ordinary rice into another consistency and flavor—the one light and feathery, the other rich and nutlike. I don't know why it is not served more often, for it makes an easy alternative to the usual starches. It is particularly happy with game dishes where you might wish to serve expensive wild rice—no one will miss that rather overpraised delicacy.

Salads and Slaws

The state of the American salad reminds me of this recipe, from an old-timer, for sheepherder's salad: "Well, you take some cold beans and some cold potatoes and cut the potatoes up and throw them in with the beans, and some cold meat if you got it, and cut up an onion or anything else that's around, and put the oil off some sardines on it and some vinegar and salt and pepper, and if you got some cold pancakes left, why, just cut them up, too, and shake the whole works together and you got something."

The first rule for a salad should be that you don't have to throw everything in the refrigerator in, but to find two that look likely as partners. See if there isn't some herb that will compliment both, then toss with the best vinegar and oils you can afford. The second rule should be (with the exception of Southwestern Lettuce Garnish and the Shaker bean salad listed here) never even buy iceberg lettuce, let alone use it in a salad. Look for tender Boston lettuce, for chicory and escarole, remember the spinach and watercress—and if necessary go out and pick dandelion leaves off the front lawn. *Then* you got something!

DRESSING A GREEN SALAD

Nothing could or should be simpler. Choose among the freshest greens of garden or market, then wash them carefully, shake out any excess water from the leaves, and dry thoroughly—one of the new spin dryers is best, or you can roll the salad up in paper towels and place in the refrigerator till ready to serve.

The chilled dry greens want only a toss, first lightly with oil (to coat the leaves), then with good vinegar, in the proportion Escoffier proposed: "Be a miser with vinegar and a spendthrift with oil." The salad needs then to be adequately salted and peppered, given a tang from some good mustard, and flavored as you wish with minced onion or garlic.

Years ago I learned a trick for all this from a fine French cook. She mixed the vinegar with a little grated onion or minced garlic, salt and pepper, Dijon mustard, minced parsley and fresh herbs, etc. in a salad bowl. This was let to steep for 30 minutes or so, then at serving time she placed the lettuce leaves in the bowl, poured olive oil over, first tossed the leaves to coat with oil lightly, and finally she tossed deeply and deftly from the bottom of the bowl to bring up the flavored vinegar.

A good cook has his habits, and knows the value of a drop of bitters, what dried herb or fresh will complement his whole meal, and how to secure the best available oils, vintage vinegars.

There are no other secrets.

SAN FRANCISCO GREEN SALAD
WITH WALNUTS AND ORANGE PEEL

1	head Boston lettuce	⅔ cup coarsely chopped walnuts
	Grated rind of 1 orange	½ cup oil and vinegar dressing

Wash the lettuce leaves, gently shake the water off them, and pat dry. Chill. At serving time, toss everything together till all the leaves are coated.
Serves 4 to 6.

Working with caterer Draper Morrow, in San Francisco, we always called this "Boring Salad," after a Nob Hill client who declared it so over the telephone, when described to her as a possible tossup. Of course it is anything but bor-

ing, and equal to any occasion great or small. Mr. Morrow's only secret was the quality of his oil and vinegar.

JERUSALEM ARTICHOKE SALAD

½ pound Jerusalem artichokes
⅓ cup oil and vinegar dressing

1 head Boston lettuce, washed, dried, and chilled

*T*he artichokes can be peeled or not, as you wish. If not scrub them first, then slice thin. Combine them with the dressing and let them marinate several hours.

To serve, toss with the lettuce leaves and place on chilled salad plates. Serves 4 to 6.

When these little sunflower tubers are available, they make a splendid salad in this manner. By all means try them if you've not before—they are crisp as water chestnuts and have as subtle a flavor as artichokes themselves.

CREAM DILLY BEAN SALAD

1 pound green beans
   Salt
¼ cup white wine vinegar
1 clove garlic, flattened and peeled

1 tablespoon chopped fresh dill (or 2 teaspoons dried)
   Freshly ground pepper
¼ cup olive oil
¼ cup heavy cream

*T*rim the beans and leave them whole if not too large—in that case, cut them lengthwise as for French-cut green beans. Drop into boiling salted water and cook 6 to 8 minutes—or until they are cooked but still a bit crisp.

Drain, run cold water over, and pat dry with paper toweling. Place in a bowl to marinate with the vinegar, garlic, dill, and salt and pepper to taste. Put in the refrigerator for several hours, tossing now and again to distribute flavors.

To serve, shake the oil and cream together until smooth. (Sometimes this will take some doing, so they won't separate. I use a small jar with a tight fitting lid and shake them until they hold in suspension.)

Drain the excess vinegar off the beans, pick out the garlic clove, and toss well with the oil and cream.

Serves 4.

This Midwestern salad is one of my favorites for all kinds of meals. It is even good enough to make a first course with fine bread to accompany it, and on hot days it can replace the vegetable that usually partners the meat.

SHAKER STRING BEAN SALAD

2 cups cooked green beans	6 nasturtium leaves
2 cups finely shredded iceberg lettuce	12 nasturtium flowers
2 cups minced green onions with parts of tops	1 tablespoon capers
	½ cup oil and vinegar dressing
2 teaspoons chopped fresh summer savory (or 1 teaspoon dried)	

*T*oss all together and be sure the nasturtium leaves and flowers show themselves off.

Serves 6.

I suspect this recipe may be good even with canned green beans, though I usually prepare too many Country Green Beans (page 223) for use the next day in this. It could be gussied up with romaine, but though I thought I'd never say I liked iceberg lettuce, it makes a fine lacy texture here if sliced thin as slaw. The green onions are a whiz in a food processor, and all in all it is an excellent dish to add to your files even if you haven't nasturtiums to harvest. The original recipe calls for pods of nasturtiums as well, whatever they are. But as nasturtium seeds were often put up in the past to substitute for capers, I throw some of those in to boot.

COACH INN FOUR BEAN SALAD

2	cups cut-up stringless green beans (1-inch lengths)	2	teaspoons chopped fresh summer savory (or 1 teaspoon dried)
2	cups baby lima beans		
2	cups cooked kidney beans (or canned)	¼	cup minced parsley
2	cups cooked chick-peas (or canned)	6	green onions, minced with part of tops
¼	cup good vinegar	2	stalks celery, minced
¾	cup olive oil	1	clove garlic, minced
1	tablespoon Dijon mustard		Lettuce leaves, washed, dried, chilled (optional)
	Salt and freshly ground pepper		Pimiento strips (optional)

Cook each of the beans separately, until tender but still a bit crispy. Drain all, and mix while warm with the other ingredients.

Let sit in the refrigerator, tossing now and again, for an hour or overnight. Serve as is, or on lettuce leaves, garnished with pimiento strips.

Serves 8 to 10.

This colorful and tasty American salad is as pleasant as many French "composed" salads. Served with a crusty bread, there is no reason it mayn't be served as a first course, take the place of a hot vegetable entirely for a light summer supper, or be one of the mainstays of a picnic.

GREAT NORTHERN BEAN SALAD

1	cup dried Great Northern beans (or other white beans)	½	cup chopped celery
		½	cup chopped onion
		½	cup chopped sweet pickles
3	cups water	½	cup sour cream
¼	cup oil and vinegar dressing	½	cup mayonnaise
1	clove garlic, minced		

Put the beans in a 2-quart pan with 3 cups water and bring to a boil. Cover the pan, turn the heat off, and let sit for an hour or so.

Then simmer gently for an hour or two, or until the beans are tender—but not falling apart. Drain the beans and toss in a bowl with the salad dressing and garlic while they are still warm.

Put the bowl in the refrigerator and let marinate for several hours. To serve, toss with the remaining ingredients.

Serves 4 to 6.

A Northwestern speciality that can stand with any potato salad, and it is simpler than most of those. I had it once in Seattle as the sole accompaniment to a barbecued butterflied leg of lamb, and thought it could not be improved upon.

COLE SLAW

*T*he whole country seems to have collective amnesia on the subject of cole slaw. First came the rage for sweetness (even unto the adding of such things as pineapple and marshmallow bits), then everyone started grating the cabbage rather than cutting it in slivers, and finally came the strange notion that it ought to sit in its dressing a long time so all fine crispness is lost. No wonder it has fallen in disrepute as an accompaniment to good meals. The dressing for any slaw should no more be sweet than any tossed green salad, surely, and the cabbage should be treated with as much respect as lettuce—tossing at the last moment before serving.

Cutting cabbage is really no great chore either. It *is* difficult, even with a sharp knife, to make delicate shreds if you quarter the cabbage and then cut. But if you detach the cabbage leaf by leaf, then place the leaves in stacks, it goes like a breeze. This done, it ought to be kept in cold water to crisp further, then redrained and dried either with paper toweling or by whirling in a salad spinner. Now you have a salad that can go hand in hand with fried brook trout, plump oysters fresh from their shells, barbecued ribs, steaming bowls of chili, the feasts of autumn.

GRISON'S STEAK HOUSE SLAW

1	pound cabbage, cored and thinly sliced	1 teaspoon finely grated onion
1	cup sour cream	Pinch of sugar
½	cup mayonnaise	Salt and freshly ground pepper
1	tablespoon prepared horseradish	

*P*lace the cabbage in a bowl of ice water in the refrigerator to crisp. Mix the sour cream, mayonnaise, horseradish, onion, sugar, and salt and pepper in a small bowl. This should sit at least 30 minutes to gather flavor.

To serve the slaw, drain the cabbage, pat dry with paper toweling, and toss with the dressing.

Serves 4 to 6.

The classic slaw is made with a boiled dressing—most usually sweet beyond belief. I've tested a boiled dressing decreasing the sugar in favor of tarragon, and it is good, but this dressing from an old San Francisco restaurant remains my favorite easily prepared slaw.

OLD-FASHIONED COLE SLAW

1	pound cabbage cored and thinly sliced	Tabasco
¼	cup olive oil	1 tablespoon sugar
1	tablespoon flour	¼ cup wine vinegar
½	teaspoon salt	½ cup heavy cream
2	teaspoons dry mustard	1 egg yolk
		Tarragon (optional)

*P*ut the cabbage in a bowl, cover it with cold water, and keep in the refrigerator until needed.

Put the oil in a saucepan over low heat, whisk in the flour until smooth, and cook several minutes. Add salt, mustard, a drop or so of Tabasco, and the sugar. Stir to blend, then add the vinegar.

Beat the cream with the egg yolk, then stir this into the sauce over low heat. Add some chopped fresh (or dried) tarragon, if you wish, and stir the sauce till it is thick and smooth.

Remove from the fire and taste for seasoning. You may wish to make it sweeter, or more tart, etc. (Also, if it is too thick, you may thin it with more cream.)

Let the dressing chill for a couple of hours before tossing with the cabbage. To serve, drain the cabbage and pat dry with paper toweling—it should be very crisp from sitting in the cold water. Toss with the dressing and serve. Serves 4 to 6.

The classic slaw with boiled dressing. Most usually, these days, this dressing is made sweet beyond reason, but it really only needs, to my taste, a hint of sugar to balance the vinegar. It is a slaw that might be served with simple fried fish, hamburgers or any barbecue, or fried chicken.

MY SLAW

1 pound cabbage, cored and thinly sliced	½ teaspoon (or to taste) prepared horseradish
⅔ cup mayonnaise	1 tablespoon lemon juice
Grated peel of 1 orange	Salt
	Capers

*P*lace the cabbage in a bowl of cold water, and keep in the refrigerator.

Mix the mayonnaise, orange peel, horseradish to taste (some is bland and some blazing—the dressing should not be overly hot), lemon juice, and salt to taste. Chill for an hour or so, to mellow.

To serve the salad, drain cabbage, pat dry with paper toweling or spin in a salad dryer, and toss lightly with the dressing. Garnish with capers. Serves 4 to 6.

The orange and horseradish give a zing to an otherwise bland dressing.

WILTED SOUR CREAM SLAW

1 pound cabbage, cored and coarsely grated	¼ cup wine vinegar
2 tablespoons minced onion	Salt and freshly ground pepper

3 tablespoons minced parsley	1 teaspoon caraway seeds
3 tablespoons olive oil	1 teaspoon Dijon mustard
Pinch of sugar	1 cup sour cream

*P*our boiling water over the grated cabbage and let sit 5 minutes. While it is sitting, mix all but the sour cream together. Test the cabbage—it should have cooked slightly, and still be a bit crisp. (If you think you'd like it more wilted, pour some more hot water over it and let it sit a bit more.)

Finally, drain the cabbage and mix with the dressing while still warm. Toss gently with sour cream and serve on salad plates.

Serves 4 to 6.

A fine addition to our slaws, and one particularly good with pork, or fat, garlicky steamed sausages.

CARROT SLAW

1 pound small carrots	Pinch of sugar (optional)
2 tablespoons olive oil	1 tablespoon minced fresh mint
Lemon juice	(or minced chives)
Salt and freshly ground	
pepper	

*S*crape the carrots and cut them in quarters lengthwise. Cut out the yellow cores unless they are very young and tiny. Grate the orange part very fine (they can be whirled in a food processor almost to a coarse paste, or put in a blender with a lot of water and whirled until fine then drained thoroughly, but the very best texture is achieved in the most tedious way—with a hand grater that has a side with holes for shredding very finely).

Mix the carrots with the oil and lemon juice, salt, and pepper to taste. Add a pinch of sugar if they don't seem tasty enough, or young enough, then mix in the mint or chives. Let sit in the refrigerator for 30 minutes to gather flavor.

Serves 4.

I suppose children are still being fed that particularly ugly combination of grated carrots, raisins, and mayonnaise—and all in the name of "health," too. I do not see anything healthy about them especially, and raisins can be eaten in many another way, but these delicate grated carrots are enough to wipe the far-off taste of those from our young mouths.

CELERY VICTOR

1 bunch celery	Pimiento strips
2 cups chicken or beef stock	2 eggs, hard boiled and
1 cup oil and vinegar dressing	chopped (optional)
(made with Dijon mustard)	Fresh-cracked crab claws
Anchovy fillets, washed in	(optional)
water	

Remove the outer stalks from the celery and cut off the top part with its leaves. Split the whole bunch lengthwise, first in half, then quarters. Save the tender inside leaves for garnish and the rest for other uses.

Simmer the celery quarters in stock 20 to 30 minutes, or until tender. Let cool in their broth. Drain, then marinate in dressing for several hours in the refrigerator, turning now and again.

To serve, drain the celery, place on salad plates, and garnish with crossed fillets of anchovy, strips of pimiento, some of the reserved celery leaves, and eggs if you wish. (The finest celery Victor I've had also included 2 cracked crab claws.)

Serves 4.

A justly famed California first course, with Italian antecedents. There it is served with crusty sourdough bread, but dinner rolls or other hot breads may accompany it as well. If the vinaigrette is light, I like also to drink with it whatever wine is to be served for the main dish.

JADE CUCUMBER STICKS

2 large cucumbers	2 tablespoons white wine (or dry
Salt	vermouth)
¼ cup tarragon white wine	Pinch of sugar
vinegar	Fresh tarragon sprigs (optional)

Pare the cucumbers and cut in eighths lengthwise. Cut out the seeds of each slice, then cut the slices in half. Drop in boiling salted water, let the pot return to a boil, and cook exactly 1 minute.

Immediately drain and run cold water over the cucumbers until they are

SALADS AND SLAWS   279

tepid. Pour the vinegar, wine, and sugar over them and toss. Chill, turning
now and again, for 30 minutes to an hour. Serve with tarragon sprigs if you
have them.
Serves 4.

*These are a jewel. They are lovely as a garnish for fish, on a warm day, or
they can make up a plate with stuffed eggs, green onion curls, and radish
roses—particularly nice for a picnic.*

CAROLINA OKRA SALAD

1	pound small okra		Tabasco
	Salt	¼	teaspoon grated lemon rind
1	tablespoon white wine	4	green onions, minced with
	tarragon vinegar		part of tops
3	tablespoons olive oil		Nasturtium flowers (optional)
	Freshly ground pepper		

*T*rim and wash the okra—if small and fresh enough, do not cut off the tops,
as this causes some of the insides to escape. Drop in boiling salted water and
cook barely 5 minutes. Drain, and while hot toss with the vinegar.

Add oil, salt and pepper to taste, a few drops of Tabasco, and the lemon
rind. Let marinate in the refrigerator an hour or more, tossing now and again.

Shortly before serving, toss again with the green onions. Serve garnished
with nasturtium flowers.
Serves 4.

*It is possible to substitute whole frozen okra for this, but it will never be as
crisp and flavorful. The best bread to serve with the dish would be Zephyrs
(page 317), because of the contrast between the two different crispnesses.*

LYLE'S BLACK-EYED PEA SALAD

3	cups cooked black-eyed peas	⅓	cup chopped green onions
2	tablespoons lemon juice		with part of tops
¼	cup olive oil	⅔	cup fresh or canned chopped
	Salt and freshly ground		tomatoes
	pepper		Sweet onion rings

*F*rozen black-eyed peas are perfect for this salad. They have a fresher taste than dried, and they cook to tender (with just a bit of snap) in 18 minutes. They should then be drained and tossed, while still hot, with the lemon juice, oil, and salt and pepper to taste.

Let sit 30 minutes, then toss in the green onions and tomatoes. Chill for at least 1 hour to bring out flavors. Cut rings from Bermuda, Spanish, or sweet red onions and chill in icy salted water for an hour, changing the water twice.

To serve, place the peas on salad plates and garnish with onion rings. Serves 4.

A recipe from Lyle Bongé, one of the country's best photographers (and cooks). In Texas such a dish is called "poor man's caviar" and is served as an appetizer, but I like it as part of the meal along with hot cornmeal Zephyrs (page 317) or The Duchess of Windsor's Cornpones (page 316).

NEW POTATO SALAD

2 pounds tiny new potatoes	½ cup olive oil
Grated rind of 1 lemon	Salt and cracked pepper

*B*oil the new potatoes in salted water until tender—they take a surprisingly long time to cook considering their size. When done, drain, then place them in a bowl.

While warm, toss with lemon rind, olive oil, salt to taste, and rather a lot of coarsely milled pepper. Poke holes with a fork several times in each potato, toss again, and chill.

Toss several times more as you open the refrigerator. They should sit several hours before serving. Serves 4 to 6.

The simplest and best of potato salads. It is superb tasting by itself, with all the sweet flavor of the new potatoes in evidence, and it makes a fine appetizer. Or, it makes a lovely salad plate nestled in shredded lettuce and garnished with deviled eggs and radish roses.

MY MASHED POTATO SALAD

4	large potatoes (2 pounds)	¼	cup tarragon white wine
	Salt		vinegar
4	green onions, with half their	1	tablespoon Dijon mustard
	tops		Freshly ground pepper
¼	cup parsley leaves	½	cup olive oil
½	cup celery leaves and/or heart		About ⅔ cup milk, scalded
	stalks	½	cup mayonnaise
2	tablespoons chopped green		Lettuce leaves, washed,
	pepper		dried, and chilled
1	teaspoon dried summer		Paprika
	savory (or 2 teaspoons		Radish slices (optional)
	fresh chopped)		Sliced hard-boiled eggs
1	clove garlic		(optional)

Boil the potatoes till tender in salted water, then drain and return to the pan. Place paper toweling over the pan, then the lid, and let the potatoes sit 5 minutes to get dry and flaky.

While the potatoes are cooking, mince very fine all the herbs and vegetables—a food processor is a boon for this. When chopped, place in a bowl with the vinegar, mustard, salt and pepper to taste, and the olive oil.

Put the cooked potatoes in a ricer, then rice directly onto the vegetable-oil mixture. Mash thoroughly with a potato masher, and add enough scalded milk to make them light and fluffy.

Fold in the mayonnaise and place, covered, in the refrigerator for an hour or more to mellow flavors. Serve on lettuce leaves, dusted with paprika, and garnished (if you wish) with radish slices and sliced hard boiled egg.

Serves 4 to 6.

Some years ago I heard rumors of a mashed potato salad consumed in Atlanta, Georgia, and set out to construct one if I could. The secret, if there is any, is not to use leftover mashed potatoes certainly, but to rice them hot onto the herbs and oil. The recipe here is for the most elaborate of versions, and I seldom prepare it the same way twice. At simplest best it folds in only mayonnaise, a little crumbled hard-boiled egg, and a speck of pickle or capers.

FRESH SPINACH AND MUSHROOM SALAD

1	pound young spinach	½	cup oil and vinegar dressing
¼	pound mushrooms		

Wash the spinach and tear the leaves from the stems. Drain and pat dry with paper toweling, then chill in the refrigerator.

Clean mushrooms, slice thin, and marinate in the dressing for 1 hour, or until you are ready to serve the salad. At that time, toss the two gently together in a salad bowl and serve on salad plates.

Serves 4.

When you find tender spinach in the market, it is one of the best salad greens of all. Mushrooms set it off perfectly without the need for a mess of other vegetables thrown in, or dressings overelaborated with blue cheese.

WILTED SPINACH AND WATERCRESS SALAD

1	pound tender spinach		Salt and freshly ground
1	bunch watercress		pepper
4	slices bacon	¼	teaspoon dry mustard
1	egg	¼	teaspoon dried tarragon
1	cup light cream	6	green onions, chopped with
¼	cup wine vinegar		part of tops
1	tablespoon sugar	8	radishes, sliced

Wash the spinach and watercress and remove tough stems. Tear into bite-sized pieces, then drain and dry thoroughly but gently.

Cut the bacon into small strips and fry slowly in a saucepan. When it is crisp, remove with a slotted spoon and drain on paper toweling. Pour out the hot bacon drippings and measure 2 tablespoons back into the pan.

Beat the egg in a bowl with the cream until it is frothy. Add the vinegar, sugar, salt and pepper to taste, the mustard, and tarragon. Add this to the bacon fat in the pan and stir over a low flame until the mixture thickens. Do not let it come to a boil.

When it has thickened, pour hot over the greens in a salad bowl. Toss thoroughly, and serve immediately garnished with bacon bits, green onions, and radishes.

Serves 4 to 6.

Maybe nothing in our gastronomic pantheon is purer than a summer wilted lettuce salad, its limestone lettuce cut hot from the garden to be tossed quickly in hot bacon fat, sprinkled with sugar and vinegar, thence to be put on plates topped with crumbled bacon, radish slices, and green onion. There is no way to repeat it, but this comes near as possible with grocery produce and subterfuge. It should always be served as a course alone, with a basket of rolls or bread to break.

COUNTRY TOMATO SALAD

Garden-ripe tomatoes
Fresh basil
Salt and freshly ground pepper
Pinch of sugar

Wine vinegar
Olive oil
Parsley sprigs
Onion rings (optional)

*P*ut tomatoes in boiling water for about 5 seconds, then remove with a slotted spoon and run cold water over them. Peel—the skins should almost slide off—and slice them carefully about ¼-inch thick into a shallow wide bowl.

Tear basil leaves and scatter over them, sprinkle with salt and pepper to taste, a bit of sugar, some good vinegar (not too much), and some olive oil. (They do not need even a great deal of oil, just enough to give the juices some body.)

Let marinate, either in or out of the refrigerator, for at least 30 minutes. Serve in an overlapping fan with some of the juices poured over, and a sprig of parsley for garnish. If you like, they may be combined with the mildest onions you can find, sliced and punched into rings, and sweetened in a bowl of iced salted water for 30 minutes or more.

When I come upon any real vine-ripened tomatoes—an all-too-rare occurrence without my own garden—this is the first dish I rush to the kitchen to prepare. It is one of the glories of American saladry, but it can do little for our store plastic "tomato."

CREAM TOMATO SALAD

4	ripe beefsteak tomatoes (or 1 large can Italian plum tomatoes)		Salt and freshly ground pepper
1	Bermuda, Spanish, or mild red onion, chopped	2	tablespoons wine vinegar
¼	cup minced parsley	¼	cup olive oil
		¼	cup heavy cream

*P*eel the tomatoes as in Country Tomato Salad (see preceding recipe), but rather than slicing them, cut into cubes. (If you are using canned tomatoes, drain, then cube.)

Add onion, parsley, salt and pepper to taste, and vinegar. Shake the oil and cream together in a small jar with a lid until they no longer separate, and toss the tomatoes gently with it.

Let sit 30 minutes at room temperature before serving.

Serves 4.

Though fresh tomatoes are best here, it is the one tomato salad I have found in which canned tomatoes (if they are good ones) can hold their own. The addition of cream gives the salad a particular suaveness that is very refreshing. It should be served with good homemade bread, or a crusty French bread to sop up the juices.

TURNIP SLAW WITH CAPERS

3	cups (loosely packed) coarsely grated turnips	¼	cup olive oil
2	teaspoons lemon juice		Salt and freshly ground pepper
		1	tablespoon capers

*T*oss the turnips with lemon juice, olive oil, and salt and pepper to taste. (They might need a little more lemon juice to your taste, but they should not be tart enough to obscure the fresh light turnip flavor.)

Let sit in the refrigerator 30 minutes, tossing now and again. Serve on salad plates with a scattering of capers.

Serves 4.

A preparation from the late great Edouard de Pomiane who was practicing nouvelle cuisine long before it had a name. Even though it has been a mainstay of my kitchen for years, and I call it slaw rather than navets râpées, it is only hopeful thinking on my part to claim it as American. My excuse is that much of this book was inspired by Pomiane's example, and I think more people ought to know of him. Two of his books are still in print in the country: French Cooking in Ten Minutes, from McGraw-Hill, and Cooking with Pomiane, from The Cookery Book Club. His recipes are all witty and simple and sizzle and bounce.

WATERCRESS SALAD À LA GERMAINE

1 bunch watercress	1 tablespoon white wine
4 ounces cream cheese	tarragon vinegar
1 tablespoon olive oil	Salt and freshly ground
	pepper

Wash the watercress, cutting off the larger stems as you go. Drain it in a colander and pat gently with paper toweling; reserve chilled.

Divide the cream cheese in half—put one in your refrigerator and the other in a warm bowl. When the cheese in the bowl has softened, mash it with olive oil, vinegar, salt to taste, and rather a lot of freshly ground pepper.

To serve the salad, put the chilled watercress into the bowl on top of the cream cheese dressing, and cut the chilled cream cheese into small pieces on top of the cress. Toss gently with a fork and spoon and lift onto chilled salad plates.

Serves 3 to 4.

A salad named after the daughter of Count Arnaud Cazenave who established Arnaud's Restaurant in New Orleans. She was renowned in that city for her elaborate hats, but she should be famed everywhere as one of our finest restaurateurs. The salad is perfectly balanced and may follow any superb main course.

ZUCCHINI SLAW

2	tablespoons Dijon mustard	½	teaspoon sugar
¼	cup olive oil	4	medium zucchini, trimmed
2	teaspoons red wine vinegar		

Shake the mustard, oil, vinegar, and sugar in a jar till smooth. Coarsely grate the zucchini into a bowl, and toss with the dressing. Cover and let sit in the refrigerator for 15 to 20 minutes. Taste for seasoning—I don't think it needs any salt, but you might.

Serves 4.

A zesty, easy invention. Scooped onto a tender lettuce leaf, garnished with sieved hard-boiled egg yolk over the top, surrounded by a small ring of chopped boiled egg white, with maybe a sprinkle of capers, it can easily stand with any salad.

SAUCES & CONDIMENTS

On a hot day in Virginia, I know of nothing more comforting than a fine spiced pickle, brought up troutlike from the sparkling depths of the aromatic jar below stairs in Aunt Sally's cellar.

—Thomas Jefferson, Letters

Sauces

*E*xcept in Southwestern cooking, where they take on great importance, and a deal of hot spiciness, the book of native sauces remains embarrassingly slim no matter who finds what to write about it. For some reason, home cooks even are impatient preparing an ordinary white sauce—so much so that when canned concentrated soups became commonplace, recipes using them instead of sauces cropped up like toadstools in every little cookbook and magazine. No matter that these were all too salty for that use, cooks went right ahead inventing new uses for all cream soups on the market. The one that swept the country, when I was a child, was a tunafish casserole that used canned mushroom soup plus salty tuna plus crumbled salty potato chips! It must have given a whole generation high blood pressure. Others creamed perfectly fine vegetables, like green beans, in celery soup sauce, and then sprinkled cheese and nuts on top. Fortunately this craze seems to have largely passed—though we still have few sauces. Consequently this will seem a very strange chapter indeed for cooks used to thumbing their Escoffier.

GOURMET CATSUP

1	can (28 ounces) tomato purée	1½	teaspoons dried thyme
1	medium onion, chopped	1½	teaspoons dried marjoram
1	clove garlic, chopped	2	tablespoons (or to taste)
¾	cup dry red wine		brown sugar
¾	cup red wine vinegar		Salt and freshly ground
2	tablespoons minced parsley		pepper
1	bay leaf		

Preheat the oven to 325°F.

Combine half the tomato purée with the onion and garlic and blend till smooth in a blender or food processor. Put in a casserole and bake in the oven for an hour or more, or until slightly thickened. Stir the sides down occasionally as it cooks.

While the purée is catsuping, put the wine, vinegar, and herbs in a saucepan and boil them down, uncovered, till you have barely ¼ cup liquid. When the catsup stirs thickly, take out of the oven, and strain the herb vinegar into it.

Add brown sugar and salt and pepper to taste. Store, covered, in the refrigerator.

This is the favored sauce of the land. Both commercial or homemade catsups, however, are more ordinarily prepared with spices such as cloves, mace, allspice, and even cinnamon. This easily got together recipe has a much fresher and more delicate aftertaste, I think—even more so if you are able to use fresh herbs (about a tablespoon each). The catsup will keep for months in your refrigerator.

CURRIED APRICOT CATSUP

1	cup dried apricots	1½	teaspoons curry powder
3	tablespoons honey	¾	teaspoon ground ginger
2	tablespoons dry mustard	2	tablespoons dry sherry

Simmer the dried apricots in water to cover for 20 minutes, or until quite soft. Drain, saving the juice in a bowl, and put the apricots through a ricer or sieve.

Beat in the rest of the ingredients, and as much of the apricot cooking juice as will make a fine paste. Store in a covered jar in the refrigerator.

Makes 1½ cups.

Old recipes offer many kinds of reductions made from cucumbers to goose-berries, rather than just tomatoes. I have tasted a few fine aged mushroom, and even one dark black walnut ketchup, but this strange ruse of a friend has become a distinguished inhabitant of my refrigerator. I always serve it as part of a range of picklings and chutney with any of our pilaf dishes (such as Miss Emily's Perloo, page 176), and many of our meats. It may also add the final touch to a barbecue sauce, or marry a bit of boiled-down cream in the sauté pan from pork chops, or chicken, with a couple of cooked dried apricots for garnish.

HOMEMADE FRENCH-STYLE MUSTARD

¼ cup dry mustard	½ teaspoon salt
¼ cup white wine tarragon vinegar	3 egg yolks
⅓ cup dry white wine	1 teaspoon dried tarragon (optional)
1 teaspoon sugar	

*I*n a bowl, whisk together the mustard, vinegar, wine, sugar, and salt, then let sit several hours.

To cook, beat the egg yolks and tarragon into the mustard, then stir in a double boiler set over hot water 5 to 6 minutes, or until it has definitely thickened.

Remove from the heat and spoon into a jar. Store, covered, in your refrigerator.

An easy creamy mustard, flavorful enough to enhance salad dressings, and to be used in all recipes that designate Dijon-style mustard in this book. If your children insist it must be bright yellow, add some turmeric in the first stirring. It is also a good base on which to experiment with other herbs, green peppercorns, grated rind of lime, cloves, horseradish, tomato paste, to put by your own specially spiced and pretty product.

BLENDER MAYONNAISE

1 egg	1 tablespoon lemon juice (or
½ teaspoon salt	white wine vinegar)
¼ teaspoon dry mustard	1 cup olive oil (or vegetable oil,
	or half of each)

*P*ut the egg into the blender jar (or into the food processor, which works equally well). Add the salt and mustard and whirl until the egg is foamy. Add the lemon juice and blend a bit more.

Pour the oil in droplets through the top hole, as you blend at top speed. As more and more oil is absorbed into the egg, it is possible to add it in a very thin stream, but don't push this too much or the sauce will separate. (If it does, mix 2 tablespoons of the turned sauce into a teaspoon of Dijon-style mustard, and start the whole process over, pouring the turned sauce drop by drop into the mixture.)

When all the oil is absorbed, taste for seasoning. If you wish a thinner sauce, add a little more lemon juice.

Makes 1¼ cups.

Hand-whipped mayonnaise is better, but not that much, and I like blender mayonnaise because it is the only way to make fresh green mayonnaise, when herbs are fresh in summer. A tarragon one is nice for fish, or one with basil on top of a tomato slice, or a judicious mixture (about ¼ cup) makes a delicious spread for sandwiches—or wherever one would use mayonnaise.

TARTAR SAUCE

1 cup homemade mayonnaise (see preceding recipe)	1 tablespoon finely chopped green olives
1 teaspoon Dijon mustard	1 tablespoon chopped capers (optional)
1 tablespoon minced parsley	
1 teaspoon minced green onions with part of tops	1 egg, hard-boiled and chopped (optional)
1 tablespoon finely chopped sweet pickles	Salt and freshly ground pepper

Mix all thoroughly and let chill in a covered jar or bowl for at least 30 minutes before serving.

Any cook worth his salt ought to be able to put together this sprightly accompaniment to fish, sandwich spread of note, and friend to all cold meats. It lasts a week at least in the refrigerator—where it gets even better, becoming a temptation to pan-roast oysters next day.

FRENCH QUARTER SAUCE

2 tablespoons good vinegar
6 tablespoons olive oil
3 tablespoons Dijon mustard
1 clove garlic, minced
6 anchovy fillets

1 tablespoon parsley leaves
1 tablespoon coarsely chopped
    green onion tops
1 hard-boiled egg yolk

Combine the ingredients one by one in a blender or food processor. Cap in a jar and store in the refrigerator.

I would admire always, as Southerners say, to be served this sauce with cold shrimp and crab, rather than the usual doleful hot tomato-ness known as "cocktail sauce." It is also excellent mixed with cream to the consistency of salad dressing, for tender lettuce leaves.

PIÑON AND PARSLEY SAUCE

½ cup minced parsley
½ cup chopped pine nuts
2 tablespoons lemon or lime
    juice
1 jalapeño pepper (pickled en
    escabeche), seeded and
    minced

¼ cup olive oil
Salt
Pinch of sugar

Combine all the ingredients and let sit, covered, in the refrigerator for at least 30 minutes before serving.

A pleasant—and not too fiery—Southwestern sauce with many uses. It is very good with cold shrimp, or over plainly sautéed fish fillets, or with cold roast beef. I even had it once tossed with hot steamed cauliflorets—a delicious experience.

GREEN GODDESS DRESSING

1   cup mayonnaise
4   anchovies, chopped
1   tablespoon minced parsley
1   tablespoon minced chives
2   teaspoons minced fresh
      tarragon (or 1 teaspoon
      dried)

1½   tablespoons white wine
        tarragon vinegar
Salt and freshly ground
   pepper

Combine all the ingredients and store covered, at least 30 minutes in the refrigerator to bring out flavor.

Green Goddess dressing was originated at the famed Palace Court, of the Palace Hotel in San Francisco, as a salad dressing. Since then it has gone into the native repertoire with additions of any number of greeneries, sour cream, etc. Prepared as above, however, I think the original makes a fine substitution for tartar sauce with fish, etc.

BARBECUE SAUCES

Probably to outsiders a native barbecue, of whatever stripe, would appear peculiarly typical of our New World ways. Things haven't changed much since the press brouhaha over Eleanor Roosevelt serving hot dogs to George VI on the lawn. Spanish explorers gave the name *barbacoa* to the Indians' practice of cooking meat on a stick over a fire—a method that was to prove necessary to many a settler as well. In the West and South, barbecue comes nowadays to mean more than chops grilled outdoors. Pits are dug and lined and brought to coals by professionals, and whole haunches are slowly fired all night for the neighborhood to flock to, dance and drink to.

Most of us make do with stoves in the winter, and an occasional hickory grill set up in our summer backyard. But whenever and whoever we are, no two barbecues are alike, and everyone has a secret ingredient. (Or a secret,

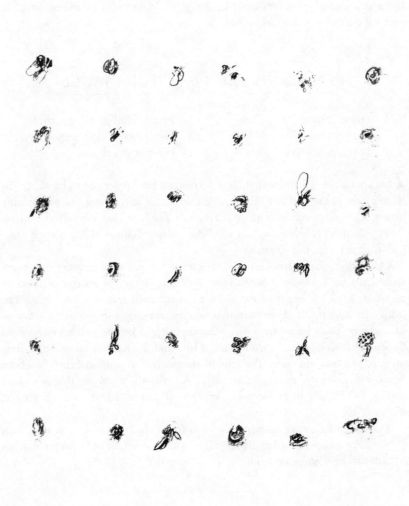

period.) This can be the use of a thyme sprig as the basting tool for a delicate orange-soy marinade, or a downright full-scale production. My favorite of the latter is a sauce I sometimes put up for gifts. It seems to be the result of an admirer's request to a Florida chef:

PENDENNIS CLUB BARBECUE SAUCE

1 bottle chili sauce	1 bottle Worcestershire sauce
1 bottle catsup	1 bottle Major Grey's chutney
1 bottle A-1 sauce	1 cup fine bourbon

*T*his should be whirled a little in a blender or food processor to break up the large pieces in the chutney. It keeps forever in the refrigerator, only becoming better. The recipe comes from Jean Hewitt's *The New York Times Heritage Cook Book,* which is probably the best available compendium of amateur cook's recipes from all over the country.

Other than that I have no secrets, except I never ever measure—so every sauce may be different. I work from a dollop of this to a drop of that. In between, I stick a finger in the sauce to taste, until it seems just right. The things to hold in mind here are that you are making a spicy, slightly sweet-sour sauce. The sweet can come from anything (like the peach preserves in Georgia Barbecue Spareribs on page 110), and a sour can range from lime juice to the best vinegars. The rule of thumb is if you use delicate flavors or fresh herbs, don't overpower needlessly. As suits the republic, this is a sauce fiercely individual, so go for your own spot of sherry or grate of fresh ginger, splash of soy.

The recipe following is only a skeleton from which to work, and also, as it only makes a cup and a half, you might want to prepare it in larger batches in order to have some on hand.

COMPOSITE BARBECUE SAUCE

1 onion, chopped	2 tablespoons wine vinegar
1 clove garlic, minced	2 tablespoons Worcestershire
4 tablespoons butter (or bacon fat)	sauce
	Juice of ½ lemon
1 cup beer	2 tablespoons brown sugar

1   can (6 ounces) tomato paste
1   teaspoon salt
1   teaspoon paprika
½   teaspoon dry mustard
1   teaspoon freshly ground
        pepper
     Tabasco (or cayenne)

½   teaspoon dried rosemary
1   tablespoon soy sauce
        (optional)
1   teaspoon chili powder
        (optional)
3   drops liquid smoke (optional)

*P*ut a saucepan over medium heat and sauté the onion and garlic in the fat till the onion is limp. Add the rest of the ingredients, stirring as you go. Cook over low heat 20 to 30 minutes, or until the sauce is balanced to taste. If it gets too thick, add some more beer.

Strain through a sieve, pressing down on the onion to release its essence, and keep in a covered jar in the refrigerator.

BOTTLED SAUCES

*C*ondiments, really—we have inherited from the British a taste for spiced dusky sauces. Of these descendants from home-bottled mushroom or walnut catsups, the most widely known and used being Worcestershire. Practically everyone uses it to some degree, and though it is possible to overdo a good thing, it builds a rich dark base in barbecue, or gives a proud shove to stews, meat loaves, hamburgers—what have you. "Wooster," as it is pronounced, needs no introduction.

With its bright and handsomely designed label, Tabasco was made first by the Avery family, who found in the wake of the Civil War some business was needed to bring in hard cash. An invention of a plantation cook (presumably black) was turned into a best seller, out of local vinegar and some tiny red peppers brought home by a soldier in the Mexican War. Their Louisiana product is quite quite hot, but used sparingly it has a hundred uses. As a rule of thumb I use it where the French suggest white pepper, though Tabasco is much livelier. It is a long true friend to any kitchen. When sauce or stew seems not up to par, drop in two shakes of the bottle, and taste a singing difference. Don't put in any more—the secret of Tabasco is to have the lightest of hands.

Angostura Bitters is in everybody's cupboard, disguised as a cocktail ingredient. But it is tonic brace to many foods: salads, soups, fruits, mincemeat, and as you use it now and again, you'll get the hang of its unidentifiable yet distinctive tone unlike quite anything else. (But all this information can be studied on its old-fashioned be-medaled label.)

Recently imported from Bermuda, and found only in fancy food sections, is a sauce that has some of the qualities both of bitters and Tabasco: Outerbridge's Original. If you find some, snap it up. Made from peppers and more than a dozen different unstated spices, it is steeped in casks of sherry for months before bottling—with a few of the pretty little peppers inside. Like Tabasco, hot, it gives more subtlety, complexity, aroma. A few drops will give you a reputation for champion salad dressings. It is the secretest of secrets, as yet.

Older, but hardly known outside the South, is Jamaica's Pickapeppa Sauce. It is closest to A-1 sauce, but very much more condensed and fragrant. It has a label of a red and green parrot contemplating a bough with a single red pepper, and is made from tomatoes, onions, sugar, vinegar, mangoes, raisins, tamarinds, salt, pepper, and unnamed spices. Dollop it in barbecue sauces, cheese dishes, meat loaf, bland gravies—a dab of it is even fine brushed on plain broiled fish. Some folks (in Texas) won't eat eggs without it.

Pickles and Relishes

*I*f we can't boast much about sauces, we certainly can about our chowchows and piccalillis. The Pennsylvania Dutch think no meal should be put on the table without seven sweet and seven sour condiments, and in the South even a simple repast may have a petaled plate with clove-stuck brandied peaches, translucent blades of pickled watermelon rind, dilled okra, and summery hot corn relish nestled in its sections. In parts of the country a cook is not to be considered unless she puts up her own chutney every fall. With the advent of the freezer, many gardeners started automatically freezing any surplus, but those who stuck to their kettles know the satisfaction of row on row of colorful jars waiting in the pantry, the year through.

PUTNEY CHUTNEY

6	green tomatoes, peeled and chopped	1	cup sugar
6	green apples, peeled, cored, and chopped	1	cup (packed) brown sugar
		2	cups vinegar
8	green peppers, seeded and chopped	1	cup raisins
3	large onions, chopped	1	cup chopped crystallized ginger
1	clove garlic, minced	1	tablespoon salt
4	lemons	1	tablespoon ground ginger

*P*reheat the oven to 325°F.

Put the tomatoes, apples, green peppers, onions, and garlic in a large kettle. Add the juice of two of the lemons, and chop the other two, being careful to remove the seeds. (A food processor is a good tool for all this, but be careful not to get everything too fine.)

Add all the other ingredients and bring to a boil over medium heat, stirring now and again. As soon as the mixture is heated through, put the kettle in the oven and cook, uncovered, for 1½ hours, stirring every 15 to 20 minutes.

The chutney will be done when the mixture becomes a bit thickened and starts to take on a darker color. Bottle immediately in sterilized jars.

Makes 9 to 10 half pints.

This chutney makes a particularly fine balance of flavors, and though it can be cooked on top of the stove, I like this method as there is little fear of burning, and only minimal stirring is required.

When you make chutney, remember any recipe can be played with, and there are no hard and fast rules. For instance, here are three other apple-green tomato chutneys I picked up from the files of a friend: (1) 4 cups apples, 4 cups green tomatoes, 2 onions, 1 cup brown sugar, 1 cup raisins, ½ cup shredded almonds, 1 small ginger root; (2) 8 green apples, 4 green tomatoes, 3 green peppers, 3 onions, 3 tablespoons salt, 1 tablespoon celery seed, 1½ cups sugar, 1½ cups vinegar; (3) 12 apples, 6 green tomatoes, 1 cup raisins, 2 tablespoons mustard seed, 4 green peppers, 2 cups sugar, 4 small onions, 1 quart vinegar, 2 tablespoons salt.

This, as you see, gives quite a lot of leeway—and also bear in mind that chutneys may be constructed around most any fruit—the most popular being apples, peaches, and pears, though the more exotic run to gooseberries, plums, or rhubarb.

MOCK MANGO CHUTNEY

9 cups unripe peaches, peeled
  and cut in dice (½ inch)
2 tablespoons plus 1 teaspoon
  salt
¾ cup peeled and minced fresh
  ginger
2½ cups sugar

2 cups white wine vinegar
4 cloves garlic, minced
¾ cup Worcestershire sauce
1 cup minced onion
¼ teaspoon cayenne
1½ cups lime juice

*P*ut the fruit in a crock with water to cover and 2 tablespoons salt. Let sit for a day or two in a cool place.

When ready to cook the chutney, put the ginger in a large saucepan with a good bit of water, bring to a boil, and simmer over a medium-low heat 45 minutes to an hour, or until the ginger is tender. Drain it and save the water.

Pour 1¼ cups of the ginger water back in the saucepan, mixing with sugar, vinegar, garlic and Worcestershire. Boil over medium heat until the sugar dissolves, stirring occasionally. Drain the peaches and add them to the syrup. Cook gently until the fruit is clear—15 to 20 minutes.

Remove the peaches with a slotted spoon to a bowl, and add the 1 teaspoon salt, onion, cayenne, and lime juice to the saucepan. Cook over low heat (or in a 325°F oven) until it is thick, making sure not to burn it. (If you cook on top of the stove, it will mean nearly constant stirring.)

When the mixture is thick, return the peaches and bring to a boil. Taste for seasoning and pour into sterilized jars.

Makes 6 half pints.

A fine chutney that produces at home something like the imported bottled chutneys at fancy prices in the store.

PICCALILLI

4	cups finely chopped cabbage	2	cups water
12	green tomatoes, cored and chopped	12	cups vinegar
12	cucumbers, chopped	3	cups sugar
6	onions, chopped	½	cup mustard seed
4	cups chopped celery	1	tablespoon dry mustard
3	green peppers, seeded and chopped	1½	teaspoons freshly ground pepper
2	red peppers, seeded and chopped	1½	teaspoons ground cloves
½	cup salt	3	teaspoons ground cinnamon
		½	teaspoon cayenne

*P*ut all the vegetables in a large bowl or crock with ½ cup salt. Mix thoroughly and let stand 2 hours. Drain thoroughly.

Combine 2 cups water with 4 cups of the vinegar in a large kettle and bring to a boil. Add the drained vegetables, bring to a boil, and simmer 10 minutes. Drain again thoroughly, discarding the liquid. Pack the vegetables in sterilized jars. Combine 3 cups sugar with the remaining 8 cups vinegar in the kettle and cook until the sugar is dissolved. Add the spices and bring again to a boil.

Pour the syrup over the vegetables and seal the jars.

Makes 12 pints.

Piccalilli is a fine crisp, slightly hot relish for any cold meat, or hamburgers and hot dogs. No one remembers where it got its name—but the Shakers, with their penchant for a lively name, used to put up huge crocks full of summer vegetables all spiced and chopped and vinegared that they called "pickled lilly."

CHOWCHOW

4	cups chopped green tomatoes	1	tablespoon mustard seed
4	cups chopped cabbage	1	tablespoon celery seed
4	cups chopped cucumbers		1-inch stick cinnamon
1	cup chopped onions	12	whole allspice
1	cup chopped green peppers	12	whole cloves
	Salt	6	cups vinegar

⅓ cup sugar   ½   teaspoon turmeric
2 tablespoons dry mustard

*C*over the vegetables with a brine made of ½ cup salt to 2 quarts water. Let stand in a crock overnight, then drain thoroughly. Taste for salt, and if too salty, rinse and drain again.

Put the whole spices in a muslin bag and tie securely. Add to the vinegar in a large kettle and simmer 15 minutes. Add sugar, dry mustard, turmeric, and drained vegetables and bring to a boil.

Simmer gently for 1 hour, then remove the spice bag and bottle in sterilized jars. Seal.

Makes 6 pints.

Chowchow seems to be originally a Chinese name for any mixture, but the British inherited it from India, where it designated any mustardy pickle. It comes in all varieties—some with little pieces of green bean, cauliflowerets, lima beans, scraped corn, red peppers—but this one is good because it is a quite sour chowchow, particularly good if served also with some sweet pickle such as watermelon rind.

STATE FAIR CORN RELISH

2   cups vinegar   3   cups peeled and chopped
1   cup sugar   fresh or canned tomatoes
1   tablespoon salt   1½ cups chopped green peppers
1   teaspoon celery seed   ¾   cup chopped red peppers
1   teaspoon mustard seed   1   cup chopped unpeeled (if
4   cups corn cut from the cob   unwaxed) cucumbers
                                                        1   cup chopped onion

*B*ring the vinegar, sugar, salt, celery seed, and mustard seed, to a boil in a large kettle.

Add all the vegetables, bring again to a boil, lower the heat, and simmer gently 1 hour. (Or put in a 325°F oven an hour or more, or until the whole is thick and melded in flavor.)

Seal immediately in hot sterile jars.

Makes 11 to 12 half pints.

The very best blue-ribbon relish, with all one taste of summer sealed in.

PHILADELPHIA PEPPER RELISH

3	cups finely chopped cabbage	⅓	cup cider vinegar
1	cup finely chopped green pepper	¼	cup (packed) light brown sugar
½	cup finely chopped red pepper	2	teaspoons mustard seed
1½	teaspoons salt	1	teaspoon celery seed

Salt the finely chopped vegetables and chill overnight in the refrigerator.

Next day, drain the mixture and squeeze out any excess moisture with your hands. Spoon into a quart jar.

Cook the remaining ingredients over moderate heat until the sugar is dissolved, then pour over the vegetables, shake to combine, and chill, covered, in the refrigerator for at least 3 days before serving.

Makes 1 quart.

Another "fresh" relish, and a very simple one too, to have on hand for hamburgers, hot dogs, and many other meats and sandwiches. It keeps well for several months, though mine is generally gone long before then. The fine chopping is most easily done in a food processor.

BEST BREAD AND BUTTER PICKLES

7	unwaxed cucumbers, sliced ¼ inch thick (with skins on)	¼	cup salt
5	medium onions, thinly sliced	2½	cups vinegar
1	green pepper, seeded and chopped	2½	cups sugar
1	red pepper, seeded and chopped	1	tablespoon mustard seed
		1	teaspoon celery seed
		12	whole cloves
		¾	teaspoon ground turmeric

Place the vegetables in a bowl or crock with the salt and ice cubes to cover. Let stand in a cool place (or the refrigerator) 3 to 4 hours, then drain thoroughly.

Put the rest of the ingredients in a large kettle, add the iced vegetables, and heat just to the boiling point, stirring now and again. Do not let the pickles boil.

Immediately pack them in pint jars and pour the pickling liquid over. Seal and store.

Makes 6 pints.

A very pretty pickle indeed. Bread and butter pickles are, I suppose, America's most typical home-canned product, and they are my favorite all-around cucumber pickle for simple munching.

ICICLE PICKLES

1　quart cucumbers (preferably small unwaxed ones 3 to 4 inches long), cut lengthwise in eighths	1　teaspoon celery seed
	1　cup vinegar
	¾　cup sugar
	1　tablespoon salt
1　small onion, sliced	½　teaspoon curry powder
1　tablespoon mustard seed	

*S*oak the cucumber spears in ice water 2 to 3 hours. Drain them, then pack in a hot sterilized jar (or jars) with the sliced onion, mustard seed, and celery seed.

Bring the vinegar, sugar, salt, and curry powder to a rolling boil, then pour over the cucumbers. Seal immediately.

Makes 1 quart.

A very easy pickle, and one that can easily be doubled and redoubled, etc. The unexpected curry powder gives them an unusual punch.

TRIPLE PICKLES

4　cups peeled and sliced thinly cucumbers	2　cups vinegar
	1　cup sugar
4　cups sliced (¼ inch) green tomatoes	1　tablespoon mustard seed
	½　teaspoon celery seed
2　cups sliced thinly onions	12　peppercorns
¼　cup salt	½　teaspoon turmeric

Layer the vegetables in a bowl or crock, with a sprinkling of salt over each layer. Cover and let stand in a cool place overnight.

In a large kettle, bring the rest of the ingredients to a boil. Drain the vegetables thoroughly. Add them to the kettle and boil 5 to 10 minutes, or until the cucumber and tomatoes become clear. Do not overcook, however.

Pack the pickles into sterile jars and seal.

Makes 7 half pints.

As I am quite frankly fond of green tomatoes, this pickle (not so sweet as bread and butter pickles) makes a handsome relish with meats, or particularly on hot dogs and hamburgers, but it takes about a double recipe to last me a whole year.

SPICED CRAB APPLES

4	pounds crab apples	2	sticks cinnamon
4½	cups sugar	1	tablespoon whole cloves
4	cups white vinegar	1	blade mace (optional)

Pick over the apples to make sure they have no spots, and are firm and ripe. Leave the stems on, but prick each with a fork.

Combine the sugar, vinegar, and spices in a large kettle and cook slowly 5 minutes. Add the fruit and bring to a boil, then turn down the heat and cook slowly until the apples are tender but not broken.

Pack into hot sterile jars, filling to within ¼ inch of the tops. Pour the syrup over and make sure that it covers the fruit. Seal immediately and store.

Makes 6 pints.

When crab apples are available, this is one of the most typical and pleasant of American garnishes for either hot or cold meats. Unfortunately, it is necessary to put up your own, as all commercial varieties are packed with a rather garish red coloring.

DILLED GREEN BEANS

4	pounds green beans (young and stringless)	Garlic cloves
		Fresh dill (or dill seeds)

Hot peppers (optional)	5	cups vinegar
Mustard seed (optional)	5	cups water
Bay leaves (optional)	½	cup salt

Wash the beans and pack vertically in hot sterilized jars. Into each jar put a split garlic clove, an umbel of dill, and any of the optional ingredients you might wish.

Heat the vinegar, water, and salt to a boiling point and pour over the beans. Seal.

Makes 7 pints.

These wonderful tidbits are ready to eat in a week or so. They will keep for a month or more, but for longer shelf life the sealed jars should be processed in a pot of boiling water for 5 minutes. Although they are oftenest served with meats as a relish, they also make excellent appetizers.

PICKLED OKRA

2 pounds young okra (about 3 inches long)		Onion slices
Celery leaves (or seed)		Mustard seed
Dill weed (or seed)	2	cups vinegar
Garlic cloves	1	cup water
Hot peppers	1	tablespoons sugar
	2	tablespoons salt

Wash the okra and trim the stems a bit (don't cut off too much though). Pack them in sterile jars, stem end down for one row, and stem end up for another.

Add whatever seasonings above you wish to each jar—for instance a split clove of garlic, an umbel of dill, and a small hot pepper.

Mix the vinegar, water, sugar, and salt together and boil for several minutes. Pour over the okra and seal. These should stand at least a month before serving.

Makes 4 pints.

My favorite pickle of all—wonderful as an appetizer, with a slice of French pâté (rather than a cornichon), beside a sandwich, or as part of any assortment of relishes for a grand meal.

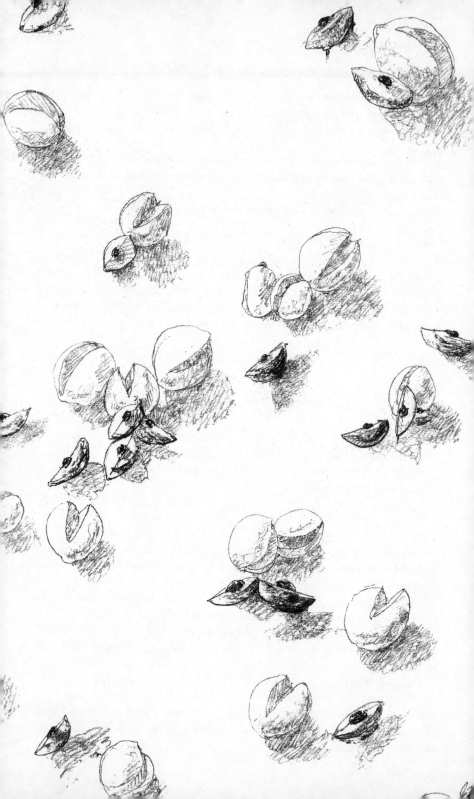

WATERMELON RIND PICKLES

1	rind of watermelon	1	tablespoon whole allspice
3	tablespoons salt	1	tablespoon broken-up
5	cups sugar		cinnamon stick
2	cups vinegar	1	lemon, sliced
1	tablespoon whole cloves		

*P*repare the rind by removing all green and pink, and cut into 1-inch cubes. Depending on the size of the melon this will make 8 to 12 cups. Place the cubes in a crock, cover with water, and add the salt. Let stand overnight.

Drain the cubes, cover with fresh water, and cook in a large kettle until the cubes are tender—45 minutes to an hour. Drain the cubes.

Mix the sugar and vinegar in the kettle and boil for 10 minutes. Tie the spices and lemon slices in a spice bag and drop into the pot, add the rind, and cook till it is transparent—another hour or so.

Remove the spice bag, pack the rind into sterile jars, and fill with syrup. Seal.

Makes 5 to 6 pints.

Our sweetest pickle by far, with a lovely look and crisp texture, one needs only a cube or two to be satisfied. They are particularly fine with thin slices of salty country-cured ham.

DIXIE PICKLED PEACHES

3	pounds peaches (about 12)	4½	cups sugar
12	whole cloves		4-inch piece of stick
3	cups vinegar		cinnamon, broken up

*D*rop the peaches in boiling water, remove with a slotted spoon, and slip the peels off. Stick a clove in each peach and place them in hot sterile jars.

Bring the vinegar, sugar, and cinnamon pieces to a boil and cook until the sugar dissolves. Ladle the syrup over the peaches, and add a few pieces of cinnamon to each jar.

Seal at once and refrigerate.

Makes 2 quarts.

The traditional accompaniment to baked ham in the South, where they are to be seen glimmering from a silver bowl beside the platter of hot steaming biscuits.

SHAKER APPLESAUCE

2 pounds green cooking apples (or any cooking apple such as Gravensteins)	Sugar (optional)
	Lemon juice (optional)
	Cinnamon (optional)
2 cups hard apple cider	

Cut the apples into quarters and core. Place them in a kettle with the cider, cover, and cook over medium heat about 10 to 15 minutes, or until they are soft.

Remove the apples with a slotted spoon and purée them through a ricer. Turn the heat to high under the cider and let it boil down till it becomes almost syrupy, then add to the apples and let cool.

If your apples are tasty, this is about all that is necessary for an excellent tart applesauce. But you may add sugar to taste, lemon juice to heighten flavor, or cinnamon for memory's sake.

If you are able to obtain good hard cider this makes an applesauce beyond belief, appley beyond appley, to accompany pork, ham, or even duckling.

FRESH TURNIP RELISH

1 cup grated turnip	2 tablespoons sugar
1 cup grated white onion	2 tablespoons prepared horseradish
⅓ cup white wine vinegar	

Combine all the ingredients and chill thoroughly in the refrigerator. This can be eaten as soon as it is chilled, but it is better after at least 24 hours, and it will keep a week or more.

An unusual "fresh" relish that makes a quite lively contrast to almost any cold or hot meat.

CRANBERRY ORANGE RELISH

1 pound cranberries
1 large seedless orange

1 to 2 cups sugar (depending on
your taste)
2 tablespoons brandy
(optional)

Wash the berries and pick out any bad ones. Either put the berries and orange through a grinder or chop them fine in a food processor.

Add the sugar and brandy, mix thoroughly, and store, covered, in the refrigerator for at least 2 days before serving.

Makes 3 cups.

Our best known and most widely served chutney is this "fresh" one meant to be kept in the refrigerator to age rather than be canned. As the flavor only gets better with age, you should make the relish several months before you first use it, though. My friend Dorothy Neal says she has tasted it a year later and found it still more delicious. I make it when cranberries first come on the market in the fall, and make enough to last through the holidays and on into the next year, for it is a graceful, bracing, colorful condiment to any meat you see fit—not just turkey.

BLUEBERRY RHUBARB RELISH

2 cups blueberries (fresh or
frozen)

4 cups rhubarb
½ cup sugar (or to taste)

In the past the blueberries for this recipe were ground in a meat grinder, and the rhubarb was finely diced. If you have a food processor, everything is much easier. Place the blueberries in the processor (thawed, if frozen) and run with the metal blade until they are ground fine. Slice the rhubarb fairly thin, put it in with the blueberries, and add the sugar. Process with an "on and off" motion until the rhubarb is cut in tiny pieces. Taste for sugar, and also check to see there are no large pieces of rhubarb—if so, process several twitches more.

This is a little-known relish from the Northwest, where blueberries abound. It is similar to the familiar cranberry-orange relish, and is used in the same manner, but the combination has an exotic—almost unearthly—flavor that no one is quite able to identify. Unlike cranberry-orange relish, it doesn't seem to keep more than several weeks in the refrigerator, but it needs at least a day to age before serving, and it freezes well if you make it in large batches. It compliments turkey, game, chicken, pork, and ham.

BREADS

God bless you for the Bread!
Now—can you spare it? Shall I
send it back? Will you have a
Loaf of mine—which is spread?

   —Emily Dickinson, Letters

Quick Breads

I know of no other cuisine that puts forth such a large range of breads. The tiniest village in Europe often has one proud loaf unlike their neighbors, but here a great variety may be turned out even from one home—biscuits of all kinds, cornbread in several different forms, flapjacks, waffles, loaves both wheat and white, plump rolls for holidays. A definitive cookbook such as *The Joy of Cooking* often lists over a hundred such breads. It is our tradition of quick breads, using baking powder rather than yeast, that accounts for much of this wide range. In most of the South they are made up for every meal, still. I don't go that far, but the breads put down here I cook, and cook often. Many of the best of these breads, though, need good cornmeal with the germ still in it—I have friends send it, stone ground, from the South, but most parts of the country never get a sniff of it. For those, look under cornmeal in the Methods and Ingredients section on page 399 for suggestions on how to handle tasteless market meal.

THE DUCHESS OF
WINDSOR'S CORNPONES

2   cups stone-ground white
       cornmeal (or 1½ cups
       ordinary meal and ½ cup
       masa harina—see page 401)
1   teaspoon baking powder
1   teaspoon salt

½   cup milk
1   cup boiling water
       (approximately)
3   tablespoons melted bacon fat
       (or butter)

*P*reheat the oven to 425°F.

Measure the cornmeal, baking powder, and salt into a bowl and mix well with a fork. Stir in the milk, then add ¾ cup of the boiling water. (There is no telling how much water to use with a particular meal, though it is safe to say it's better to use too little rather than too much. Let it sit 10 minutes, and see—its consistency should be that of wet sand, so that it holds a shape in the hand. If it looks too thick, add the other ¼ cup of water—or more. One cup is exactly right for good Southern meal.)

To cook the pones, put the fat in a heavy 12-inch frying pan and put it in the oven as it heats. (If you use butter, this will take only heating up so it bubbles, but with the preferable bacon fat it ought to heat almost to smoking.)

Pour the melted fat into the cornmeal mixture and stir it in. Form pones by scooping up a small handful of meal and shaping it with the other hand the length of your fingers—in the manner of prayer.

Drop these shapes in a radial pattern around the bottom of the sizzling hot skillet as you form them. If you don't have a large heavy pan, the alternative is to use cast-iron cornstick pans treated with fat in the same manner (In fact they make the best possible cornsticks, and as they are prettier I most often make them rather than pones for company—one recipe will fill 2 regular cornstick pans.)

Put the skillet or cornstick pan back into the hot oven and bake 20 minutes, or until the pones are golden on top with browned crisp bottoms and steamy insides. Serve immediately to be split and buttered.

Makes 12.

Published in 1943, all crisply upper Baltimore in the old sense, Some Favorite Southern Recipes *by the Duchess of Windsor is the very example of inherited local bride's cookery, each dish put down deft enough to program a new cook*

*(for one doubts The Duchess bothered herself much in the kitchen). As good
as these recipes all are, one hopes the Simpson cornpones survived the Riviera
and itinerary, for the Duchess goes on to "some foreign recipes" learned on
her travels—some handy haddock rules, a reckless Bahamian turtle pie, a sound
chicken curry, and a simply lovely dish of boned loin of lamb cut open, broiled
with mustard, then laid on sautéed eggplant slices with a garnish of watercress and pan juices, thence to a risotto of leftovers, and a glacé aux mangoes.
I would forego any of them for the cornpones of the Duchess anytime—indeed, they are one of my favorite breads.*

ZEPHYRS

2   cups boiling water
½   cup stone-ground cornmeal
      (or ⅓ cup regular
      cornmeal plus masa harina
      to measure ½ cup—see
      page 401)

1   tablespoon lard, bacon fat, or
      butter
½   teaspoon salt
2   egg whites

*P*our the boiling water over the cornmeal, fat, and salt in the top of a double
boiler. Cook over simmering water for 20 minutes, stirring now and again to
make sure it stays smooth.

Remove from the heat, film the top with butter, and let cool. (This can sit
covered a good while before you make the zephyrs, but it must be whisked
smooth before cooking.)

Preheat the oven to 375°F.

Whip the egg whites stiff but not dry and gently fold them into the cooled
mush. Drop by tablespoonfuls on a greased cookie sheet (one should hold them
all) and bake 30 minutes, or until still soft and mushy inside but crisp without.

Makes 24.

*These light crisp mouthfuls are one of the pleasantest treasures of all our hot
breads. Exactly what they sound, they are a cornmeal mush cooked crisp with
only egg white for leaven. Topped or not with a dab of soft butter, the amount
above is perfect for 6 at soup—though if served with a main course, as a starch,
the amount serves barely 2 they are so briefly delicious.*

BACON BUTTERMILK CORNBREAD

4	slices bacon (optional)	1	tablespoon sugar
¾	cup stone-ground cornmeal (or regular cornmeal)	1	teaspoon salt
		4	tablespoons cold butter
1	cup flour (or if using regular meal, ½ cup masa harina and ½ cup flour)	1	cup buttermilk
		2	eggs, separated
2	teaspoons baking powder	¼	teaspoon baking soda
		1	tablespoon water

*P*reheat the oven to 400°F.

This makes a superior cornbread without the bacon, but if you are using it, slice the strips into ⅛-inch slivers. Put them in an 8-inch square baking pan and put it into the oven as it heats.

Combine the dry ingredients and cut in the cold butter till it is reduced to the size of peas (this can be done with a couple of crisscross knives or with a twitch or two in a food processor).

Beat the buttermilk with the egg yolks. Dissolve the baking soda in the water. Stir these both into the dry ingredients till just moistened.

Beat the egg whites stiff but not dry. Remove the bacon from the hot pan—the strips should have begun to cook and release fat. Sprinkle the bacon over the cornmeal mixture and fold in along with the egg whites.

Spoon the batter into the hot greased pan and bake 20 to 25 minutes, or until gold and springy.

Serves 6 to 8.

Though bacon is optional in this recipe, I like the way the pieces render a bit of fat while cooking so there are spots and pockets of goodness throughout. If you wish to omit the bacon, grease your baking pan with butter and heat just before adding the cornmeal mixture—this assures a good crust. Be sure not to bake this bread too much, for it will dry out if left too long in the oven. Any leftover pieces are definitely to be split and spread with butter to broil the next morning (or for lunch or dinner).

TEXAS JALAPEÑO CHEESE CORNBREAD

*M*ake this exactly like Bacon Buttermilk Cornbread (see preceding recipe), except leave out the bacon and in its place fold in 1 cup grated sharp cheddar cheese, and ¼ cup jalapeño peppers (bottled en escabeche), seeded and minced.

This is a fine half-bread sired between Southern and Southwestern cuisines. Texans serve it with their large steaks and generous barbecues usually, though I had it once with simply a platter of well-seasoned beans, and a glass of beer, and felt well fed. It is also good the next day, split and toasted with butter— and when cut in small pieces it makes a very good appetizer.

SHAKER CORNBREAD (OR MUFFINS)

¾ cup stone-ground cornmeal (or regular cornmeal)
3 teaspoons baking powder
1 teaspoon sugar
1 teaspoon salt

½ cup flour (or masa harina if you use regular meal— see page 401)
2 eggs
1¼ cups milk
3 ears corn, scraped (1 cup)
3 tablespoons butter, melted

*P*reheat the oven to 350°F.

Sift the dry ingredients together in a bowl. In another bowl, beat the eggs with the milk, then mix them into the dry ingredients.

Fold in the corn kernels and melted butter. Pour into a buttered 8-inch square pan (or into muffin pans—the recipe will make eight 2-inch muffins).

Bake 40 to 45 minutes, or until the bread is set and beginning to brown. Serve hot with butter.

Serves 6 to 8.

Definitely one of the best of our cornbreads—this is moist, rich, and with the extra flavor of fresh corn. You might wish to substitute canned or frozen corn, but I wait and save it for the summer months when fresh corn is available.

GEORGIA SPOONBREAD

1 cup stone-ground cornmeal (or ¾ cup regular cornmeal and ¼ cup masa harina— see page 401)
3 cups milk, scalded

1 teaspoon salt
1 teaspoon sugar
1 tablespoon bacon fat (or butter)
3 eggs, separated

*P*reheat the oven to 375°F.

Sprinkle the cornmeal over the scalded milk and cook over low heat for 5 minutes, stirring to make sure there are no lumps and the "mush" doesn't stick to the bottom. (Cornmeals vary, and it takes less of some to make a good mush than others, so the first time you try this recipe use the above amount, and adjust next time if necessary—the mush should be thick, but not so thick that folding in the egg whites later is difficult.)

Stir in the salt, sugar, and half the fat. Remove from the fire and let cool a bit. Put the rest of the fat in a soufflé dish or casserole and place in the oven till it nearly smokes (or only to heat and sizzle, if using butter).

Beat the egg yolks into the mush. Beat the egg whites till stiff but not dry, then fold them lightly into the mush. Spoon into the hot dish and bake for 45 minutes, or until the bread is puffed and golden.

Serve immediately, to be spooned out at table and topped with butter or meat sauce.

Serves 4 to 6.

This cornmeal soufflé—for that is exactly what it is—makes one of the glorious triumphs of U.S. cookery. There is probably no other dish I would invariably serve a foreign visitor to impress and delight. Light and crusty, it can be served with almost any meal, simply buttered. But I also like to use it as the Italians would polenta, as a side dish to hearty braised meats with plenty of rich sauce. The next day, any left over can be sliced and sautéed lightly in butter for a side dish to eggs, bacon, or sausage.

HUSH PUPPIES

1 cup stone-ground cornmeal (or ¾ cup regular meal and ¼ cup masa harina—see page 401)	Freshly ground pepper
	2 green onions, minced with part of tops
½ teaspoon baking power	1 egg
½ teaspoon salt	¼ cup milk
	Fat for deep frying

*C*ombine the cornmeal, baking powder, and salt and pepper. Beat the green onions and egg into the milk. Let both sit until you are ready to fry the hush puppies.

After you have fried fish in the fat (heated to about 370°F), mix the egg-milk mixture into the dry ingredients. Drop by teaspoonfuls into the hot fat.

Let fry 3 to 4 minutes, or until they are golden brown on both sides. Place on absorbent paper as each batch is done, to drain. Serve with Tartar Sauce (page 292).

Serves 4 to 6.

Frankly a campfire dish for fishermen, long since tamed for the kitchen. Often they are flat and greasy, but done with care to proper temperature they are the perfect accompaniment to fresh-caught fish flipped over the fire in a lacy cornmeal crust. I like to serve three or four of them as a side to fresh sizzled trout, with a garnish of watercress, a cruet of fine vinegar, and good home-made tartar sauce.

WILD RICE
AND CORNMEAL GRIDDLE CAKES

2	tablespoons wild rice	¼	teaspoon baking soda
	Salt	¼	teaspoon salt
½	cup cornmeal (preferably stone-ground)	1	cup water
			Vegetable oil
¼	cup flour		

Cook the wild rice in plenty of salted water 45 minutes, then drain in a sieve. While the rice cooks, stir together the cornmeal, flour, soda, salt, and water in a bowl, and let sit. Stir the rice into the batter.

Drop the batter by the tablespoonful onto a well-greased griddle set over medium-high heat. Cook the cakes about a minute per side. Stir the batter each time you make a batch, and make sure the pan is well oiled.

Makes 20.

These delicious lacy cakes have a variety of uses. They can, of course, be served with maple syrup in the grand old tradition of native pancakes, but they are equally welcome as a side dish for meat dishes such as Thomas Jefferson's Salmi of Duck (page 162).

HAPPY VALLEY BISCUITS

1½	cups flour	¼	cup cornmeal (preferably
1	teaspoon salt		stone-ground)
2	teaspoons sugar	¼	cup lard (or butter)
1	teaspoon baking powder	1	cup buttermilk
½	teaspoon baking soda		

*P*reheat the oven to 450°F.

Sift the flour, salt, sugar, baking powder, and soda into the bowl of a food processor fitted with the steel blade. Twitch a few times to mix, then add the cornmeal and the lard or butter. Twitch several times more, until the mixture has the texture of cornmeal.

Add the buttermilk and turn on and off a time or two only until it seems well mixed. (This can also be done pretty quickly in a bowl as well, cutting in the fat first, then stirring the buttermilk in quickly with several strokes.)

Grease muffin tins, and sprinkle with a little cornmeal in each cup. Shake to coat the sides and bottoms of the pan. Drop the dough from a spoon, filling the cups about two-thirds full. Sprinkle a little more cornmeal over the tops and bake 12 to 15 minutes, or until golden and crusty.

Makes 12.

A few years ago I came on a recipe for biscuits, hid in a small farm magazine collection importing Gugelhupf and blintzes to Omaha, which called for a measure of cornmeal in a rich buttermilk mixture. I set to with their recipe during two dispiriting batches, until I went to Irma Rombauer for general guidance. In one try it became a favorite, still called "Happy Valley," pretty and of crusty character enough to become called for by family, worthy of any company when there's no time for yeast, toasted split with butter the next day. The next best thing about them is they take about as little time as a packaged mix.

SUMMER CLOUD BISCUITS

2	cups presifted flour	½	teaspoon salt
1	teaspoon sugar	4	teaspoons baking powder

¼   cup minced parsley and/or
    watercress, chives,
    tarragon, basil, etc.
½   cup cold butter (lard or
    vegetable shortening)

1   egg
⅔   cup milk

*P*reheat the oven to 450°F.

Sift the dry ingredients into a bowl, add the herbs, and cut in the fat with two knives or a pastry blender until it is the consistency of coarse meal. (This can also be done with a couple of twitches of a food processor.)

Whisk the egg till frothy, beat in the milk, then add them all at once to the flour mixture. Stir only until moistened.

Turn onto a lightly floured board, knead gently and quickly a few times, and roll out ¾ inch thick. Cut with a biscuit cutter dipped in flour, place in an ungreased baking pan (preferably glass), brush the tops with milk, and bake 12 to 15 minutes.

Makes 24.

These biscuits seem to rise sky-high for everyone. They are fine in winter, when only parsley or watercress is available, but they are a wonder when you have the summer herb patch to choose from—even without herbs they are superb.

WHIPPED CREAM BISCUITS

1   cup heavy cream
2   cups presifted cake flour
2¼   teaspoons baking powder

¾   teaspoon salt
Pinch of sugar

*P*reheat the oven to 450°F.

In a good-sized bowl, whip the cream till it just holds soft peaks—do not overbeat. Sift the dry ingredients over it, and quickly fold together until the dry ingredients are just moistened.

Turn onto a lightly floured board and knead gently and quickly a few times. Roll out ¼ inch thick, and cut straight down with a biscuit cutter dipped in flour.

Bake on an ungreased baking dish (preferably glass) 10 to 12 minutes.

Makes 24.

When you have the cream and cake flour on hand, these make the lightest, most delicate biscuit of all. Those who associate biscuits only with coarse country cooking might do well to try these rather than yeast rolls at their next dinner party.

HELENE'S DROP SHORTCAKES

1	cup buttermilk		Pinch of salt
½	teaspoon baking soda	1	teaspoon baking powder
1½	cups flour	6	tablespoons butter
3	tablespoons sugar		

*P*reheat the oven to 450°F.

Mix the buttermilk and soda in a small bowl (it will puff up like a yeast as you mix the other ingredients). Sift the flour, sugar, salt, and baking powder into a medium bowl. Cut the butter into this with a pastry cutter or two knives until the mixture resembles coarse cornmeal. Lightly stir in the buttermilk just until there are no floury lumps. (This is the traditional way, but if you have a food processor, just flick the dry ingredients a little without sifting them, cut in the butter in a few more flicks, and then pour in the buttermilk and mix very lightly.)

Drop about ¼ cup of the dough onto an ungreased baking sheet—do this with a fork, and smooth the dough out a bit to make a 3-inch circle. Repeat to make 6 cakes. On top of each of these drop a dollop of dough, dividing it evenly among the cakes. With the fork tines lightly prick up the tops of the cakes so there are little peaks. (This later will make crispy nuggets to hold the juices, and making the drop in two processes insures easily divided shortcakes.)

Bake 12 to 15 minutes, or until crusty and beginning to brown. Remove from the oven and let cool. To serve, split the cakes open, cover the bottoms with sweetened juicy fruit, place the top on, pour cream over and around the cakes, and place a few more pieces of fruit on top.

Serves 6.

These delights are a specialty of Helene Sharpless from Bloomington, Indiana. The buttermilk gives them a good delicate crumb, and dropping them with a fork makes for a much better cake than the usual rolled variety. (To make shortcakes for a savory filling rather than a sweet, put in 1 teaspoon of salt, rather than a pinch, and substitute a pinch of sugar for the 3 talbespoons.)

WHOLE-WHEAT BISCUITS

1	cup presifted all-purpose flour	4	teaspoons baking powder
1	cup presifted whole-wheat flour	½	cup cold butter (or lard or shortening)
½	teaspoon salt	1	egg
		⅔	cup milk

*P*reheat the oven to 450°F.

Sift the dry ingredients into a bowl and cut in the fat with two knives or a pastry blender until it is the consistency of coarse meal. (A food processor is fine here.)

Whisk the egg until frothy, beat with the milk, and pour all at once into the flour mixture, stirring only until moistened.

Turn onto a lightly floured board, knead gently and quickly several times, and roll out ¾ inch thick. Cut straight down with a biscuit cutter dipped in flour. Brush the tops with more milk and bake on an ungreased baking sheet 12 to 15 minutes.

Makes 24.

Biscuits with whole-wheat flour never rise as delicately as white flour biscuits, but these are light enough and much more savory than most plain biscuits. Since there is more flavor to the flour, I don't feel it necessary to add sugar here, but you may wish to—or brown sugar, or honey.

PARSLEY DUMPLINGS

1½	cups presifted flour	½	teaspoon minced fresh rosemary, thyme, or basil
2	teaspoons baking powder		
¾	teaspoon salt	3	tablespoons butter (or lard or shortening)
2	tablespoons minced parsley		
		¾	cup milk (approximately)

*S*ift the flour with baking powder and salt. Add the parsley and rosemary (or other herb). Chop the fat (with two forks, knives, or a pastry blender) into the flour until the mixture resembles coarse cornmeal.

Add enough milk, while tossing lightly with a fork, to make a batter that can be dropped from a spoon.

Cook the dumplings in a stew (or steamed in a colander), tightly covered, for 15 minutes—or until a toothpick inserted comes out clean.

Makes 12.

Because they happen at the last minute, I am usually mistrustful of dumpling recipes. Sure-fire cornmeal dumplings can fall to pieces over a pot of good greens, turning them into an unsavory mush as well as not, or you may have a succulent sauce suddenly pulled up by leaden cloudings. I have never had these fail, however, and they are splendid with any of the fricassees.

PENNSYLVANIA POTATO MUFFINS

2	eggs, separated, plus 1 egg white	½	cup flour
		¾	teaspoon baking powder
2½	cups finely grated potatoes	1	teaspoon salt
3	tablespoons finely grated onion	4	tablespoons butter, melted

*P*reheat the oven to 400°F.

Mix the egg yolks into the potatoes and onion in a medium-sized bowl. Sift the flour with baking powder and salt over the potatoes, and mix in lightly. Stir in the melted butter.

Beat the 3 egg whites in another bowl until stiff but not dry, then fold them into the mixture very gently. Grease muffin tins and spoon in the batter, filling no more than two-thirds full.

Bake for 20 to 25 minutes, or until the muffins puff up and are golden. Serve immediately with butter.

Makes 12.

My fellow countrymen have a great liking for sweet and even fruited muffins with their meat. In this I cannot share, though I can imagine they would be excellent with coffee for breakfast, or for an afternoon tea. These old-style potato muffins with a hint of onion, however, are to my taste a successful substitute for the starch in many a meal—try them.

BEATEN BISCUITS

2	cups flour	4	tablespoons butter
1	teaspoon salt	½	cup ice water
¼	cup lard		

Preheat the oven to 350°F.

Place the flour and salt in a food processor fitted with the steel blade. Turn on and off a few times, then add the lard and butter cut into small pieces. Process with a few more turns until the mixture resembles a coarse meal.

Turn the processor on. Pour ice water through the tube and process until the whole forms a ball. Continue for 2 to 3 minutes, or until the dough is quite smooth and elastic.

Roll out very thin on a lightly floured board, then fold the sheet of dough over on itself. Cut with a 1½-inch biscuit cutter dipped in flour and place on an ungreased cookie sheet.

Prick the tops of the biscuits three times with the tines of a fork. Bake 25 to 30 minutes, or until browned and puffed up.

Makes 48.

These distinctive unleavened biscuits have not been prepared for some years, even in the South, for their lightness depends on the cook (usually a black one) who had the wrist and time to hammer the dough with a mallet for 30 minutes or more, until it "blistered." With the advent of the food processor, however, these are brought within the range of the modern cook, for it takes only a few minutes to achieve this lovely crisp accompaniment to delicate soups.

CHARLESTON BENNE WAFERS

¼	cup sesame seeds	½	teaspoon salt
1	cup flour	¼	teaspoon cayenne (optional)
1	teaspoon baking powder	4	tablespoons butter (or lard)
¼	teaspoon baking soda	½	cup buttermilk

Preheat the oven to 400°F.

While the oven heats, toast the sesame seeds in a pie plate or cake pan, stirring now and again, until they turn pale amber. This will take about 10 minutes.

Sift the dry ingredients together, then cut in the fat till the mixture is the consistency of coarse meal. (This can also be done in a food processor.) Add the sesame seeds, then stir in buttermilk until the dough just holds together.

Turn out onto a lightly floured board and knead gently 5 or 6 times. Roll out about ¼ inch thick and cut in 1 inch rounds (if you don't have a cutter that small, some bottle caps are that size, and do nicely).

Place on an ungreased baking sheet and bake 10 to 15 minutes, or until the wafers are gold and crisp.

Makes 48.

Benne (or sesame) seeds are grown extensively in South Carolina, and are used in many of the local cookies and candies, as well as in this lovely biscuit. They are usually served as a cocktail tidbit, but as I like my cocktails unadorned, I make these to accompany soups for a dinner's first course. They can be made ahead, and last several days in a tin.

MY GRANDMOTHER'S GOOEY BUTTER ROLLS

1¾	cups presifted flour	1	cup sugar
2	teaspoons baking powder	5	tablespoons butter, at room temperature
½	teaspoon baking soda		
¼	teaspoon salt	⅓	cup milk
¼	cup lard (or butter)	½	teaspoon vanilla
¾	cup buttermilk		

*P*reheat the oven to 450°F.

Sift the flour, baking powder, soda, and salt into a bowl. Cut in the fat until the mixture resembles coarse meal, then add the buttermilk and stir to mix. (Both these steps can be adapted to a food processor.)

Knead lightly on a floured board just until you have a smooth dough. Shape it into a rectangle and roll out with a rolling pin to a rectangle approximately 13 × 9 inches.

Mix ½ cup of the sugar and 4 tablespoons of the butter together in a bowl—they don't have to be "creamed," but just to hold together. Spread this over the dough, then roll up into a long jelly roll. Grease an 8 × 8-inch square baking pan. Slice the roll into 16 sections and place the sections in the pan, cut side up.

Bake the biscuits for 10 to 12 minutes, or until they are lightly golden. As they bake, combine the milk, remaining ½ cup sugar, and remaining 1 tablespoon butter in a saucepan. Cook over high heat, stirring, for several minutes, until the mixture has thickened slightly. Let cool a bit, then stir in the vanilla.

When the biscuits look done, pour the sauce over them and put back into the oven for 2 more minutes. Remove and let cool.

Makes 16.

Everyone knows those glorious sticky buns made from yeast rolls, sprinkled with sugar, butter, and cinnamon, then cooked on a nutty caramel base. These are similar, take no time at all as yeast rolls must, and are, I think, every bit as good when you want to turn out a hasty sweet treat for the family. I like the simplicity of the basic vanilla version my grandmother made, though often as not I make one of the following variations I evolved: (1) Orange Butter Rolls: *Before rolling up the dough, sprinkle the butter-sugar mixture with grated rind of 1 orange and a little cinnamon. Substitute orange juice for milk in the final sauce, and omit the vanilla. (2)* Caramel Nut Butter Rolls: *Substitute brown sugar (either light or dark) for all the sugar in the recipe. Before rolling up the dough, sprinkle the butter-sugar mixture with chopped nuts and cinnamon. When you cook the final sauce, the milk will be likely to clot up, but don't worry—just keep stirring and it will smooth out as it cooks.*

Yeast Breads

*T*hese are everyone's memory of what a fragrance can be, whose mothers or grandmothers baked the daily loaf. Nothing is so sweet and cleanly in its smell, unless a meadow just cut for hay. Every cook who bakes bread will also remind you there is nothing near as liberating to the soul as kneading yeast dough, and anyone who has eaten bread just out of the oven will understand nothing else tastes quite as good. Economists point out how cheap it can be, and dieticians how wholesome—this "staff of life." So why do so few make bread? I can't answer this, but I know it's possible to put a batch together in the time it takes to watch one television program (addicted, you can manage both), and it can be set to rise in the refrigerator overnight. The next day it takes 10 minutes to punch down and form into loaves, and you can do anything else while it rises and bakes. Why not?

PARKER HOUSE ROLLS

1	tablespoon sugar	2	tablespoons warm water
3	tablespoons butter	1	egg
½	teaspoon salt	2 ⅔	cups flour, sifted
1	cup milk, scalded		Melted butter
½	cake yeast (or ½ package active dry)		

Add the sugar, 3 tablespoons butter, and the salt to the scalded milk, and stir off the fire till the sugar is dissolved. Cool till lukewarm. Dissolve the yeast in the warm water and let sit 10 minutes to "proof" and puff up.

Combine the milk mixture and yeast in a good-sized bowl. Beat in the egg, then the flour in batches. Add enough additional flour to make a dough that can be handled easily.

Turn the dough out onto a lightly floured board and knead until it is smooth and elastic. Put in a lightly buttered warm bowl and turn to coat the entire surface with butter. Cover with a towel and let rise in a warm place until doubled in bulk—about 2 hours.

Punch the dough down and form into rolls. This may be done by filling greased muffin tins with 3 small balls, and brushing with melted butter. (Or, by rolling out the dough, cutting it with a biscuit cutter, and creasing each across the middle with a knife. These are then brushed with butter, and folded over—pressing the edges tightly together—and placed on a baking sheet to rise. The latter method is the classic Parker House shape, but more often these days the "cloverleaf" roll is thought prettier.)

Whichever you prefer, let the formed rolls rise again until doubled, covered again with a towel. It will take about 30 minutes.

Preheat the oven to 400°F.

Bake for 15 to 20 minutes, or until golden on top.

Makes 24.

No native holiday feast is complete without these delicate yeasty rolls, and in many a home they still grace any company, at any formal or informal meal. Though there are many recipes, the one from the Parker House in Boston has circulated most widely, and it seems a sound base on which all other rolls might be compared.

SHAKER ROSE GERANIUM ROLLS

1   recipe Parker House Rolls (see   2   tablespoons sugar
     preceding recipe)   6   rose geranium leaves

Make the preceding recipe with an extra 2 tablespoons sugar, and when forming rolls make one ball the size of your muffin cups, with a small piece of geranium leaf in the center of each. Let rise and bake as for Parker House rolls.

Another Shaker delectable. Rose geraniums are grown for their sweet-scented leaves rather than their flowers, and if you chance to have a plant available you can be blessed (as were the Shakers) with the most fragrant bread imaginable.

LIGHT SESAME ROLLS

¼   cup warm water   2   tablespoons sugar
1   package active dry yeast   1   cup water (or milk)
4   tablespoons butter (or   1   egg
     vegetable shortening)   3   cups unbleached white flour
1¼ teaspoons salt   Sesame seeds

These are refrigerator rolls. Early in the day, or the night before, pour warm water over the yeast, stir, and let sit to "proof" and puff up. Heat the butter, salt, and sugar in a saucepan with a cup of water or milk until the butter melts. Let sit till lukewarm, then stir in yeast and egg well, then the flour. This will make a rather sticky batter, which need not be kneaded.

Plop the batter into a greased bowl, oil your hands, and pat the top smooth. Cover the bowl with plastic wrap or foil and refrigerate. This dough kneads itself, as it were, while it sits.

About 2 hours before baking the rolls, punch down the dough and grease muffin pans. Sprinkle the bottoms and edges of the pans with sesame seed, shaking out what doesn't cling. Take the dough up (with oiled hands, if necessary, for it is a very soft dough) and drop about 2 tablespoonfuls of it into each muffin cup. The rolls will be nicest looking if you stretch the dough smooth and tuck the rest under as you go.

Sprinkle the tops with more sesame seeds, and let rise about 2 hours covered with a damp towel or plastic wrap. The dough should really fill the muffin cups.

Preheat the oven to 425°F.

Bake the rolls about 15 minutes—or until roundly brown. Shake out into a basket or bowl immediately, and serve warm with butter.

Makes 18.

Light, North Carolina, no-nonsense, no-knead rolls prepared well ahead of any kitchen rush, with a superior hard crust. They are so easy to make anyone with about 10 minutes forethought in the morning can serve up magnificent evening breads equal to any occasion. To make them cover two evenings, use half the dough. Oil the top of the rest and wrap again, then refrigerate for the next night.

CHILD'S FAMOUS BUTTER CAKES

2	packages active dry yeast	2	tablespoons soft butter
1¼	cups lukewarm water	2	teaspoons salt
1	teaspoon sugar	3½	cups flour

*P*ut the yeast in a large mixing bowl, stir in ¼ cup of the warm water, and the sugar, and let "proof" for 10 minutes—or until quite bubbly.

Add the remaining 1 cup warm water, the soft butter, salt, and 1 cup of the flour. Beat until smooth, and continue adding flour in batches as you stir. By the time all the flour is added the dough will start to come away from the sides of the bowl and form a ball.

Put dough in a warm buttered bowl and turn to coat all sides well with butter. Let rise, covered with a towel, in a warm place for 1 hour, or until doubled in bulk.

Punch the dough down and roll out ¾ inch thick on a lightly floured board. Cover with a towel, and let rise 30 more minutes.

Cut the dough in rounds with a 3-inch cutter or glass, then cook the cakes in a greased large frying pan over medium-low heat, 3 to 5 minutes on each side, or until golden brown.

Serve hot, or the next day split and toasted with butter.

These cakes have been known to make a strong New Yorker come all over goosebumps with memory. Though not widely known outside that city, and no one else I know—even there—makes them at home, I make them often. Reminiscent of English muffins, they are at the same time yeastier, more delicate, and certainly less expensive (unless you make your own muffins). I also believe they make a superior roll for hamburgers—a use Child's never put them to. They last several days in the refrigerator, and need only to be split like an English muffin, spread with butter, and toasted under the broiler.

MY WHITE BUTTERMILK BREAD

1	package active dry yeast (or 1 cake)	1¼	cups buttermilk
¾	cup warm water	4½ to 5	cups unbleached white flour
2	tablespoons sugar	¼	cup lard, melted
		2	teaspoons salt

Dissolve the yeast with the warm water and sugar. Stir it, and let sit till puffy. Combine this with the buttermilk, 2½ cups of the flour, melted lard, and salt in a bowl—an electric mixer of some kind is best. Beat it for several minutes on medium speed in the mixer, or by hand. Then beat in by hand the rest of the white flour. Add only enough so the dough no longer clings to the sides of the bowl.

Dump the dough onto a floured board and knead about 5 minutes. Place in a greased bowl and roll to cover with grease all over. Place a damp towel or plastic wrap over the bowl, place in a warm spot, and let rise till doubled in bulk.

Punch the dough down, knead a few times, then roll out with a rolling pin to get out the bubbles.

Divide in 2 pieces and shape into 2 loaves. Place these in greased bread pans, grease the tops of the loaves, and cover again with a damp towel or plastic wrap. Let rise about an hour in a warm place—or until doubled and filling out the pans.

When risen, place in a cold oven, turn the heat to 400°F, and bake about 40 minutes, or until the tops are brown, the loaves have separated from the sides of the pans, and they ring out when tapped with a knuckle.

Makes 2 loaves.

It took me some time to fix on this as my favorite white bread recipe, but the looking and cooking was worth it. All the loaves piled up month by fragrant month, from the kitchens of Lady Bird Johnson and James Beard, and more anonymous ovens, but I like the moist crumb this bread is given from its buttermilk, and I seem to like lard better than butter for a reason I can't put a name to. The sugar and salt are, to my mind, perfectly balanced (even if Lady Bird did go up to ½ cup of sugar in hers—a bread the former President was said to trot from the ends of the ranch for by nose—and many of the regular farm recipes from the past contained up to ½ cup). I don't budge far as L.B.J. while making this bread, certainly, but its sweet smell would carry on those wide Texas winds.

HOMEMADE GARLIC BREAD

White-flour bread dough for 1 loaf
4 tablespoons butter, at room temperature
1 teaspoon minced garlic
1 egg yolk
2 tablespoons heavy cream

When you make a two-loaf recipe for white bread, it's nice to make one plain and one garlic. Let the dough rise in the usual manner, punch it down, and roll out on a lightly floured board to a rectangle about 15 x 9 inches.

Mix the butter and garlic well, then spread it on the dough. Roll the dough up (starting with the short side) and seal the ends by pinching. Place in a well-buttered loaf pan. Cover and let rise until doubled in a warm place.

Preheat the oven to 350°F.

Brush the top of the loaf with the egg yolk mixed with the cream, and bake 35 to 45 minutes, or until well browned. (If you use My White Buttermilk Bread, bake it as in that recipe, on page 334.) Remove from the oven and cool on a rack.

A bread ever so much more subtle than the usual French bread split and slathered with garlic butter, then warmed in the oven.

SHAKER DILL BREAD

1 package active dry yeast	1 tablespoon minced chives
¼ cup lukewarm water	(or green onions)
1 cup cottage cheese, at room	1 teaspoon salt
temperature	¼ teaspoon baking soda
1 teaspoon sugar	1 tablespoon butter, melted
1 egg	2½ cups (or more) flour
2 teaspoons dried dill (or dill	
seeds)	

Combine the yeast and warm water, and let sit to "proof" and bubble up. Put all the other ingredients, except the flour, in a large bowl. Stir well, then stir in the yeast.

Add the flour gradually, stirring all the while, until you have achieved a stiff dough. Knead on a floured board for 10 minutes at least, or until the dough is smooth and elastic. (This whole procedure will take no time in a food processor.)

Place the dough in a buttered bowl and turn to coat evenly with butter. Cover with a towel or plastic wrap, and let rise for an hour in a warm place— or until doubled in bulk.

Preheat the oven to 350°F.

Punch down and shape into a loaf. Place in a buttered loaf pan, cover, and let rise again until doubled—about 30 minutes. Bake 30 to 40 minutes in the oven, or until golden brown and the top is hard when you rap it. Remove from the oven and brush the top with butter. Cool on a rack.

A remarkably modern-sounding bread (because it seems to have been copied again and again) that is another fine creation of the Shakers. If any is left the next day, it makes excellent toast or sandwiches. I don't know why, but I always think of eating it outside, with an outdoor barbecue, or spread with butter and lettuce leaves to accompany cold fried chicken on picnics.

ANADAMA BREAD

2 cups water	1 teaspoon salt
½ cup cornmeal	1 package active dry yeast
2 tablespoons butter	½ cup lukewarm water
½ cup molasses	5 cups (approximately) flour

*I*n a saucepan bring the water to a boil, then turn off the flame. Add the cornmeal slowly, stirring with a whisk to make sure there are no lumps. Turn the fire back on, bring to a boil, and let simmer gently for 5 minutes. Add the butter, molasses, and salt and allow to cool to lukewarm.

Dissolve the yeast in warm water till it "proofs" and puffs up, then add it to the meal. Beat in enough flour to make a stiff dough. Turn out onto a lightly floured board and knead well till elastic and smooth.

Put in a well-buttered warm bowl and turn to coat completely with butter. Cover and let rise for 1½ hours, or until doubled in bulk.

Punch down, shape into 2 loaves, and place in buttered loaf pans. Cover and let rise again until double—about 30 minutes.

Preheat the oven to 400°F.

Bake the loaves for 1 hour, or until golden brown.

Despite the fact that it appears in all the books of U.S. cookery, I know only a handful of people who actually bake this bread besides me. I first tasted it over twenty years ago, and it has been ever a friend to my kitchen since.

MISS DOROTHY'S BROWN BREAD

1 tablespoon plus 1 teaspoon granulated sugar	2 cups boiling water
2 tablespoons brown sugar	2 packages active dry yeast
3 tablespoons lard	½ cup lukewarm water
2 teaspoons salt	2½ cups white flour
1 cup oatmeal	2½ cups (approximately) whole-wheat flour

*P*ut the 1 tablespoon granulated sugar, the brown sugar, lard, salt, and oatmeal in a bowl. Add the boiling water, stir until the sugar is dissolved, then let sit till lukewarm.

Add the ½ cup lukewarm water to the yeast, and stir in the 1 teaspoon granulated sugar. Let sit till it "proofs" and puffs up, about 5 minutes. Add to the oatmeal mixture, stir, then stir in the white flour. Add enough whole-wheat flour to make a stiff dough, then turn out onto a lightly floured board and knead 10 minutes, or until smooth and elastic.

Divide into 2 loaves, and place in buttered loaf pans. Cover and let rise until nearly doubled in bulk—about 30 minutes.

Preheat the oven to 350°F.

Bake the loaves for 50 minutes, or until slightly golden on top and springy. Cool on a wire rack.

Truly a daily loaf, with both a superior texture and taste—some wheat germ, also, can be added as part of the whole wheat flour.

EMILY DICKINSON'S
RYE AND INDIAN BREAD

½	cup cooked pumpkin or sweet potato	2	packages active dry yeast
⅓	cup molasses	⅓	cup lukewarm water
5	tablespoons butter	¼	teaspoon sugar
1	teaspoon salt	2	cups rye flour
1	cup cornmeal	1½ to 2	cups white flour
1	cup boiling water		

Combine the pumpkin, molasses, butter, salt, and cornmeal in a large bowl. Pour the boiling water over, stir, and let stand 10 minutes.

Mix the yeast with the warm water and sugar and let sit till it bubbles up. Add the yeast to the bowl, then stir in the rye flour and 1 cup of the white flour. Mix well, then add enough additional white flour to make a stiff dough.

Turn out onto a lightly floured board and knead 10 minutes, or until the dough is smooth and elastic. Put in a well-greased bowl, and turn a few times to coat completely with grease. Let rise, covered, in a warm place for 1½ hours, or until doubled in bulk.

Punch the dough down, halve, and form each half into a ball. Place each ball in a greased 8-inch pie plate or cake pan and let rise, covered, for another hour, or until doubled again.

Preheat the oven to 375°F.

Cut a cross with a razor blade on the top of each loaf and bake for 15 minutes. Reduce the heat to 325°F and bake 45 minutes to 1 hour longer, or until browned and the bottoms sound hollow when tapped. Cool in a wire rack.

Of homegrown poets, only Emily Dickinson seems to have taken an active pride in cooking. She constituted a whole family's active baker till infirm, and if her gingerbreads were more well known than her poems to the neighborhood, that seems to be the way of the world. I used to balk at being introduced as "This is Ronald Johnson—he writes cookbooks," but since there are more people who read cookbooks than poems, I now just shrug my shoulders.

SALT RISING BREAD

2	potatoes, peeled and thinly sliced	2	cups boiling water
2	tablespoons stone-ground cornmeal	2	cups milk
2	tablespoons sugar	9 to 10	cups flour
	Baking soda	1	tablespoon salt
		¼	cup shortening, melted
			Melted butter

*P*ut the sliced potatoes, cornmeal, 1 tablespoon sugar, 1 teaspoon salt, and a pinch of soda in a quart jar and add boiling water to cover. Screw on the top and shake several times, or until sugar and soda look dissolved. Unscrew the top of the jar and put it back on the jar loosely (it needs bacteria to get in). Let stand in a warm place, out of drafts, for 24 hours, or until there appears to be about an inch of foam on top and it has a yeasty smell.

Scald the milk, add another pinch of soda, and cool to lukewarm. Strain a cup of liquid from the potato jar and add it to the milk. Stir in, cup by cup, enough flour to make a stiff dough.

Place in a greased bowl and turn to coat all sides. Cover and let stand in a warm place about 2 hours, or until doubled in bulk. Punch down, and knead in salt, the remaining 1 tablespoon sugar, and the melted shortening, making an elastic ball but never letting the dough get cold.

Return to the greased bowl, turning until the entire surface is coated, cover again, and let rise again until doubled.

Punch down again and shape into 3 loaves. Place the loaves in greased loaf pans and brush with butter. Let rise again, covered, until doubled.

Preheat the oven to 350°F.

Bake the loaves for 1 hour.

Even after living in San Francisco for some years, with its truly famed sour-dough breads available, this settler's found-yeast bread is one of my favorite white breads. There may be other crusts and ingeniously shaped loaves, but the strong fragrance and subtle taste of this is my undoing. I eat the first loaf, and the rest I bake in small individual loaf pans and freeze in plastic bags. They can then be taken out, wrapped in foil, and heated in a hot oven for 15 to 20 minutes, for guests.

SOURDOUGH BREADS

*I*n the Old West, where what we know as yeast was hard come by, most breads were either made from baking powder or from natural yeasts floating through the air. This was a tricky process, since the "starter" didn't always work, or its taste wasn't quite right, so that starters were often traded, jour-neyed for, handed down—as the ones for the famous San Francisco sourdoughs (these guarded closely as pots of gold). In fact, even with a good sourdough starter, it is impossible to reproduce these famed breads made in special ovens with hard-wheat flour. I know, I've tried, using all the methods Julia Child can summon up, and with pans of steaming water, hot tiles, etc. It's good, but just not good enough when you can get the real thing. However, there are other ways to use this unique leaven with a tangy savor.

If you wish to try your hand at making your own starter, stir a package of active dry yeast together with 2 cups hot water from the top and 2 cups white flour. Put the mixture in a warmed bowl, cover with plastic wrap, and let it sit at room temperature for 2 days or more. When and if ready, it will be bubbly and have some yellowish liquid on top. Store in the refrigerator in a covered container when it has "taken." It improves with age, but you will need to use it about once every 2 weeks or it gets very sour indeed.

To use your starter, remove from the refrigerator early in the day and place in a warm spot for an hour, or until it starts to bubble again. A cup of starter will approximate a package of yeast, though it will rise more slowly than yeast. For this reason many users, and most bakeries, often add a package of yeast as well as the starter—the sourdough being more for flavor than leaven.

Every time you use part of the starter for a bread, it will need to be re-plenished with a cup of flour and a cup of warm water for every cup used. Simply stir it in well, let bubble up again in a warm place, cover, and refrig-erate once more till needed.

The first time I tried this process I got a pretty good starter, but then I tasted a friend's sourdough that had been originally begun from commercial sourdough starter. It was so superior I went out and bought a packet. I recommend you do the same, if you want to make daily breads. Anyway, next to a good backrub, the process of rising, punching down, kneading, rising, and baking finally is probably the most soothing thing possible. The rest, Mae West could only comment gracefully on.

SOURDOUGH WHITE BREAD

½	cup milk	1	cup sourdough starter
1	teaspoon sugar	3¼	cups (approximately)
1	teaspoon salt		unbleached white flour
2	tablespoons butter (or lard or vegetable shortening)		

Scald the milk with the sugar, salt, and butter. Let cool to lukewarm. Place in a warm mixing bowl with the sourdough starter, then stir in the flour. Turn out onto a floured board and knead 5 to 6 minutes, adding any extra flour needed to achieve a nonsticky, elastic dough.

Place in a lightly greased bowl and turn to coat the surface all over with the fat. Cover with a towel or plastic wrap and let rise in a warm spot till doubled in bulk—this will take about 3 hours.

Punch the dough down, turn it out onto the board, cover with a towel, and let rest for 15 to 20 minutes. Then shape into a loaf and place in a greased bread pan. Cover and let rise until doubled again in bulk.

Preheat the oven to 375°F.

Bake for about 50 minutes, or until the crust is brown, the loaf is shrunk away from the pan, and it sounds hollow when tapped. Remove from the pan and cool on a wire rack. (Note: This can also be prepared as any basic white bread recipe for the food processor. I like to knead it, but you may not.)

The best easy first loaf to make with sourdough starter. You get all the flavor undiluted at once. You can speed up the process by cutting the milk down by 2 tablespoons, and adding half a package of active dry yeast dissolved in 2 tablespoons of warm water. Made alternately with the following Cracked Wheat Bread, and frozen, you will always have the soundest white and brown breads available.

SOURDOUGH CRACKED-WHEAT BREAD

1	cup milk	1	package active dry yeast
2	tablespoons shortening	2	cups sourdough starter
2	teaspoons salt	1	cup rye flour
2	tablespoons molasses	1	cup cracked wheat
½	cup warm water	5 to 6	cups unbleached white flour

Scald the milk with the shortening, salt, and molasses and let cool to luke-warm. Dissolve the yeast in the warm water till it bubbles up. Place both, with the sourdough starter, in a warm bowl. Add the rye flour, cracked wheat, and enough white flour to make a smooth, nonsticky, elastic dough as you knead it. (About 10 minutes of kneading will do the trick.)

Place in a lightly greased bowl, turning to coat the entire surface of the dough with grease. Cover with a towel or plastic wrap and let rise in a warm place until doubled in bulk.

Punch down and let rise till doubled again. Punch down once more, and let rest, covered, for 10 minutes.

Divide the dough in half, shape into loaves, and place in 2 greased bread pans. Cover and let rise till doubled again. Preheat the oven to 375°F.

Bake the loaves for 40 to 45 minutes, or until crusty brown on top and shrinking away from the sides of the pans. Turn onto wire racks to cool.

Makes 2 loaves (one can be frozen for freshness).

My alltime favorite for everyday eating, and I make it on schedule every 2 weeks to keep my sourdough starter alive.

OLD-TIME SOURDOUGH BISCUITS

1½	cups sifted flour	½	teaspoon salt
2	teaspoons baking powder	4	tablespoons butter (or lard)
¼	teaspoon baking soda	1	cup sourdough starter (page 341)

Sift the dry ingredients together, then cut in butter or lard with two knives or a pastry cutter until the mixture resembles coarse meal. Stir in the starter. Turn the dough out on a lightly floured board and knead—have a deft hand, and only knead until the dough seems smooth. Roll out ½ inch thick and cut with a glass or biscuit cutter about 2 to 2½ inches round.

Grease a baking pan and place the biscuits in it. Brush with melted butter and let rise for about an hour in a warm spot.

Preheat the oven to 425°F.

Bake the biscuits for 20 minutes. Serve piping hot, with plenty of butter. Makes 10 to 12.

Truly a biscuit like no other, light but rich and tangy—they become rather a habit, I find.

DESSERTS

The dessert reminded me of a postcard Virgil Thompson once sent us from the Côte d'Azur, delightfully situated within sight of the sea, pine woods, nightingales, all cooked in butter.

—*Alice B. Toklas,* The Alice B. Toklas Cook Book

Summer and Winter Pies

Pies were my mother's great specialty. When she sailed in to church suppers, every eye was nailed on that pie, and each succulent bit would be scooped up before we got to it. Fortunately, she always made one for us to eat later at home, or she would have had a bunch of savages on her hands. I think pies, out of all possible dishes, are our national glory. No one makes such delicate pastry, made to crumble at the poke of a fork: the French consider it a container, while we expect it to be as good as the filling itself. And an English woman I attempted once to talk pie crust with could not even conceive of what I meant by "flaky." Everyone knows the apple and berry and fruit pies of summer, but now that we get fruit the year long, many have forgotten the "winter pies" that used to be turned out—since most homes were never found pieless. These are some of the very best of all.

MY MOTHER'S PIE CRUST

2¼ cups flour	¾ cup cold lard (or vegetable
¾ teaspoon salt	shortening)
	6 tablespoons ice water

*P*ut the flour and salt in a medium bowl and cut lard into it with two knives or a pastry blender until no piece is larger than a small pea.

Sprinkle ice water over—preferably from a sprinkle top bottle (my mother uses a commercial sprinkler top used to cork pop bottles for wetting laundry, while I use an ordinary glass kitchen salt shaker that holds just 6 tablespoons ice water and needs only to be put in the freezer before crust-making).

As you sprinkle, turn with a fork until the meal is evenly covered and starts to compose a mass. If it looks too dry, don't worry, and don't add any more water because that will make it tough.

Dump the dough on a sheet of waxed paper and twist into a ball with the corners. Place in the refrigerator several hours, or overnight. (It needs this time for the particles of flour to absorb the water.)

To roll out, divide the mixture in two and make a ball of each. On a lightly floured board, or pastry cloth, flatten each and roll out to a 12-inch round (as the books say). In practice, you have to be pretty deft, and the dough is liable not to hold together, but if you pinch and patch, a round that can be attained the first roll is best. If not, fold the dough and start a second time.

Making sure the dough is loose from the floured board beneath, fold over in half and lift into a pie plate. Unfold. When the pie is filled, repeat the process for your top half.

Trim the crust—the bottom for a single-crust pie and top and bottom for a double-crust—to about a ½-inch overhang around. Fold under, and crimp the edges in scallops with the forefinger of one hand and the forefinger and thumb of the other meeting in an arrow—or by simply pressing all around with the tines of a fork to seal the pie.

The top crust should be pierced in some way for steam to escape, and each cook used to have a distinctive pattern. My favorite pattern among many is the old-fashioned "moon and stars": a crescent knifed out with fork pricks all over for the stars.

A lattice top is made with ½-inch-wide strips cut from the second crust, and it is sealed in the same way. Any top crust may be brushed with milk before cooking, or sprinkled with sugar after.

All easier done than said.
Makes 2 individual crusts, or top and bottom crust for 1 pie.

Of course, this can all be done in a whisk or three of a food processor, and rolled out in a trice, but the result is never so flakily tender. There are several good tools to make it go easier, however: a pastry blender to knife the flour and fat, and a pastry cloth kept floured to roll out on, along with a pastry sock or "sleeve" for the rolling pin. These make for assurance and speed in any pastry work. In the general alchemy of it all, one ought to remember the rule that everything ought to be kept as cold as possible.

This recipe makes a little more than is actually necessary for two crusts—most recipes call only for 2 cups flour. But actually this makes it easier for a beginner, as there is more leeway in rolling out your circle. The scraps that are left over may also be used. My mother gathered them all together, then rolled them out again. This she sprinkled with sugar, cinnamon, and dribbled a bit of butter over. It was then baked along with the pies for us kids. (It was a kind of sop thrown us so we wouldn't stick our fingers in the pie, I imagine.) Another thing to do is to cut out tiny rounds with a cutter, and spread them with anchovy paste, or as they do in the Carolinas, with sesame seeds and a little cayenne. These make fine cocktail nibbles.

If you are going to use a recipe which calls for only half the dough, you have two choices: you can either make two pies, or you can make half a recipe. The flour is easy to divide, as you will need 1 cup plus 2 tablespoons. The lard has to be played by eye. Since you measure lard by putting it in a cup measure with ¼ cup cold water, just put enough lard in to make the water level come up to between the ½- and ⅔-cup mark—don't worry, if it's a little more or a little less, it will still be fine.

UPSIDE-DOWN APPLE PIE

⅔ cup plus ½ cup (packed)
   brown sugar
⅔ cup whole pecans
4 tablespoons butter, melted
   Pastry for a 2-crust pie (page
   348)
2 pounds tart apples (about 5
   or 6)

   Pinch of salt
1 tablespoon flour
½ teaspoon ground cinnamon
   Freshly grated nutmeg (or ¼
   teaspoon ground cloves)
3 tablespoons butter
   Juice of ½ lemon (or a whole
   one if apples are sweet)

*P*reheat the oven to 450°F.

Press the ⅔ cup brown sugar over the bottom and sides of a pie plate, and arrange the pecans over it in a decorative manner. Press the pecans into the sugar, and dribble melted butter over. Roll out the bottom crust and lay it in over the pecans.

Peel, core, and slice the apples into a bowl. Toss them with the ½ cup brown sugar, the salt, flour, and spices. Arrange them in the crust, dot with the butter, and squeeze the lemon juice over. Roll out and place the top crust over, but instead of folding the crust edge under, fold it up from the bottom before you crimp the edges.

Prick the top of the pie several times with a fork, place in oven and bake at 450°F 10 minutes, then turn the heat down to 350°F and bake 45 minutes to 1 hour longer, or until the crust is golden and the insides bubbly.

Remove the pie from the oven and cool 15 minutes, then loosen the edges with a knife all around, place a plate over the top of the pie, and invert so the pie falls upside down on the plate.

Serves 6 to 8.

Reminiscent of the famous tarte Tatin, *this is perhaps even more luscious. It makes a beautiful presentation to be shown to your guests before slicing at table.*

PARADISE PIE

1 cup cranberries	3 large cooking apples (1½
¾ cup plus 2 tablespoons sugar	pounds), peeled, cored, and
Pastry for a 2-crust pie (page	sliced
348)	2 tablespoons flour
1 large quince (about ¾	Juice of ½ lemon
pound), peeled and cored	6 tablespoons butter
3 tablespoons honey	

*P*lace the cranberries in a blender or food processor with some of the ¾ cup sugar, and whirl until as fine as possible. Add the rest of the ¾ cup sugar, stir well, cover, and let sit in the refrigerator for an hour or more. (This can be done at the time you make the pie crust, and they can be put to chill together.)

Preheat the oven to 450°F.

Roll out the bottom crust and fit it into the pie plate. Refrigerate while you prepare the fruit. Grate the quince into a bowl (making sure all the hard core is well removed) and toss it with the honey. Toss the apple slices in another bowl with the flour and lemon juice, then toss fruits both together. Mix in half the cranberry mixture and put the fruit in the pie shell.

Pour the rest of the cranberry mixture over the fruit and dot with 4 tablespoons of the butter. Melt the other 2 tablespoons butter and set aside while you roll out the top crust and place it on the pie. Brush with the melted butter and sprinkle with the 2 tablespoons sugar. Bake at 450°F 10 minutes, then reduce the heat and bake at 350°F for 45 to 50 minutes longer—or until crisp and golden on top. Remove from the oven and cool.

Paradise Pie is named after that ineffable combination of apple, quince, and cranberry known as "Paradise jelly." Both live up to the name—from color to taste, all Paradisaical. Quinces somehow need other fruit to bring out their best perfume, and then they become a kind of catalyst flavor, sparking and perking and expanding their partner (usually apple). Quince trees are less common than they used to be, and they seldom come to market, and when they do it is usually not at cranberry time. For this reason I usually put up batches of sugared cranberry purée in season, freeze them, then keep an eagle eye out for the first golden, fragrant quinces.

SHAKER RHUBARB CUSTARD PIE

1½ cups granulated sugar	3 cups rhubarb, cut in 1-inch pieces
3 tablespoons flour	Pastry for a 2-crust pie (page 348)
½ teaspoon freshly grated nutmeg	Confectioners sugar
2 tablespoons butter, melted	
2 eggs	

*P*reheat the oven to 450°F.

Put sugar, flour, nutmeg, butter, and eggs in a bowl, and beat till smooth.

Roll out the pastry for the bottom crust; line a pie plate. Arrange the rhubarb evenly over the pastry lined plate, then pour the sugar-egg mixture over. Make a lattice topping with the rest of the pastry.

Crimp the edges of the pie and bake at 450°F for 10 minutes, then reduce the heat to 350°F and bake 30 minutes longer, or till golden brown and bubbly.

Remove from the oven and sprinkle confectioners sugar through a flour sifter over the top of the pie. Let cool.

Serves 6 to 8.

"Pie plant" is the old-fashioned name for rhubarb, and though these tart, tonic red stalks can be used in many ways, they shine in a pie. The Shaker method rather than gilding the lily seems simply better than the standard recipe in which all too often the sugar remains granular on the bottom rather than making juice. The nutmeg custard gives just the proper balance to the sour rhubarb, the balance and proportion the Shakers are famed for. After discovering this recipe, I seldom cook rhubarb any other way, and I find it is also a fine rule to follow for many a fruit—with a bit less sugar and nutmeg, and lemon juice and grated peel to make up for the sourness of the rhubarb. Particularly fine are sour cherries, green apples, and blueberries.

FRESH PEACH PIE

	Pastry for a 2-crust pie (page 348)		Pinch of salt
		2	tablespoons butter, melted
4	ripe peaches	2	eggs
1	cup sugar	⅛	teaspoon almond extract

*P*reheat the oven to 450°F.

Drop the peaches in a pot of boiling water for a minute or so, take out with a slotted spoon, and slip the skins off. Cut in half and remove the pits.

Roll out the pastry for the bottom crust; fit into a pie plate.

Place the peach halves, cut side up, decoratively in the pastry-lined plate (if they are large you will most likely only be able to use seven halves, so you can eat the other as you bake the pie).

Beat the sugar, salt, butter, eggs, and almond extract together, and pour over the peach halves. Make a lattice crust with the remaining pastry, place over the top, and crimp the edges.

Bake at 450°F for 10 minutes, or until beginning to brown, then turn the heat down to 350°F and bake 30 minutes more, or until brown and bubbly. Remove from the oven and cool.

Serves 6 to 8.

The almond-flavored custard in this recipe perfectly complements fresh peaches— and it is an extremely pretty pie to contemplate, or eat. If you like, it can also be sprinkled with slivered toasted almonds.

PLANTATION LEMON MERINGUE PIE

4	eggs, at room temperature	2	teaspoons grated lemon rind
½	teaspoon cream of tartar	3	tablespoons lemon juice
1½	cups sugar	2	cups heavy cream

*P*reheat the oven to 300°F.

Separate the eggs, and beat the whites until they foam up, then add the cream of tartar and beat until they hold stiff peaks. Add 1 cup of the sugar gradually, a tablespoon at a time, beating after each addition. The meringue should be thick, stiff, and glossy.

Spread it in a lightly greased pie plate so that the rim comes up higher than the center, and so will make a "crust" for the filling. Bake for 40 minutes. Remove and set on a wire rack to cool.

Beat the egg yolks until they are thick and light colored, then beat in the lemon rind and juice and remaining ½ cup sugar. Cook this in the top of a double boiler over simmering water 15 to 20 minutes, or until the mixture thickens. Cool.

Whip 1 cup of the cream and fold it into the cooled lemon mixture. Fill the center of the meringue with it and place in the refrigerator overnight—it should sit at least 12 hours before serving.

To serve, whip the other cup of cream and frost the top of the pie with it. Serves 6 to 8.

The most ethereal of lemon pies. It will last in the refrigerator for several days, getting even better, if possible.

SHAKER LEMON PIE

	Pastry for a 1-crust pie (page 348)	5	eggs
3	lemons	½	cup butter, melted
2	cups sugar		Pinch of salt
			Whipped cream

*P*eel 2 of the lemons thinly with a vegetable peeler, and cut the strips of peel with a sharp knife into very small slivers, the size of toothpicks. Simmer in water 10 minutes, then drain and run cold water over. Place on paper toweling to dry.

Squeeze the lemons—there should be ⅔ cup of juice—and put in a saucepan with the sugar. Bring to a boil, add the peel, and cook slowly 5 minutes, or until the peel is transparent. Remove from the heat and let stand 30 minutes.

Preheat the oven to 450°F.

Roll out the pastry and fit into a pie plate; crimp the edges. Beat the eggs, then add the sugared peel, melted butter, and salt. Pour into the pastry lined plate and bake at 450°F for 10 minutes, then turn the heat down to 350°F and bake 30 minutes longer. Cool, then serve with dollops of plain whipped cream.

Serves 6 to 8.

The other side of the coin to Plantation Lemon Meringue Pie (see preceding recipe)—this is dense, rich, and about as delicious as any pie could hope to be. This pie was served at the Pleasant Hill, Kentucky, Shaker community, open to the public now as a museum, the first time I went there. It became an instant favorite that I have continued to serve over the years. The Shakers made it a little differently. They sliced lemons thin, and let them sit for several hours in sugar, before beating in the eggs and butter. But I was attempting this pie at someone's home one day, only to find out there wasn't a knife sharp enough to cut them. So I tried this method, which I think is even better.

TALLAHASSEE LIME PIE WITH PECAN CRUST

1 cup flour	2 eggs
Confectioners sugar	5 tablespoons lime juice
¼ teaspoon salt	1 teaspoon grated lime peel
½ cup cold butter	½ teaspoon baking powder
⅓ cup finely chopped pecans	Whipped cream flavored with
1 cup granulated sugar	rum

*P*reheat the oven to 350°F.

Sift the flour, ¼ cup confectioners sugar, and salt into a bowl. Cut in the butter with a pastry blender (or with a whirl or two in a food processor) until the mixture resembles coarse meal. Add the pecans (they do not have to be ground, but a food processor is excellent for chopping them very fine).

Press the mixture into the bottom and sides of a pie plate and bake for 25 minutes, or until the crust is pale gold. Remove from the oven (keep it at 350°F) and let cool while you prepare the filling.

To do this, beat the granulated sugar, eggs, lime juice and peel, baking powder, and a pinch of salt until smooth. Pour the mixture into the pie shell and bake another 25 minutes. Remove from the oven and let cool. When cool, sprinkle the top with powdered sugar put through a flour sifter, and serve with dollops of rum-flavored whipped cream.

Serves 8.

Another rich confection with a dense consistency, lovely crunchy crust, and the unexpected tartness of lime. A little goes a long fine way.

GREAT AUNT HESTER'S ORANGE PIE

	Recipe for a 1-crust pie (page 348)		Pinch of salt
			Grated rind of 1 orange
2	tablespoons butter		Juice of two oranges (½ cup)
¾	cup sugar	1	cup heavy cream
4	eggs		Confectioners sugar

*P*reheat the oven to 450°F.

Roll out the crust and fit it in a pie plate; crimp the edges. Prick the bottom of the crust with a fork at about 1-inch intervals and bake for 10 minutes. Remove to a rack to cool while you make the filling, and turn the oven down to 350°F.

Beat the butter until it softens, then beat in the granulated sugar bit by bit (it won't really "cream," as there's not enough butter). Beat in the eggs, one by one, then the salt and orange rind and juice. Whip the cream till it holds a peak, then fold into the orange mixture. Do this delicately and carefully.

Pour the mixture into the pie shell—you'll have a bit left over, as a 9-inch shell can't quite hold it all. Bake for 30 minutes—or until a toothpick inserted in the middle comes out clean. Let cool on a rack, then dust lightly with confectioners sugar before cutting.

Serves 6 to 8.

A delicately flavored heirloom pie from Bob, Rose, and Cora Brown's 1940 America Cooks—an enormous treasury of regional cooking long out of print. It was submitted by a great-niece who found the pie in a diary dated 1801, and she says of it: "I have no idea how old this family recipe is, but my great-grandmother sold copies of it to help raise money for her Dutch Reformed Church in Manhattan."

I knew Bob Brown (his wife and mother were by then both dead) when I went to college in New York City. He was one of the legendary writers who attended the Gertrude Stein circle in Paris in the twenties, and had delightful tales to tell of everyone who was anyone, and some who were not. His own books from the period have been forgotten, except for a lovely book of picture poems reprinted by Jonathan Williams' Jargon Press. But you could go to his apartment in the Village and find the likes of Marcel Duchamp or Djuna Barnes leaning on a shelf, still talking of Alice, and Gertrude, and Pablo, and Ernest—no one, to my joy, ever had a last name.

My secretest joy, though, were the bookshelves that went up to every ceiling in the place. There were thousands of cookbooks crammed everywhere! How I would have liked to take a semester off from Columbia, and simply read and read them, but of course it was impossible, and an imposition, so the chance was lost. I often wonder where they all ended up, and if they are all together still. . . .

MY ORANGE PECAN PIE

2	small oranges	¼	cup butter, melted
1½	cups sugar		Pinch of salt
	Pastry for a 1-crust pie (page 348)	1	cup pecan halves
			Whipped cream
3	eggs		

Peel the oranges thinly with a vegetable peeler, and cut the strips of peel with a sharp knife into very small slivers, the size of toothpicks. Simmer in water 10 minutes, then drain and run cold water over. Place on paper toweling to dry.

Squeeze the oranges (there should be ½ cup juice), and add with the sugar to a saucepan. Bring to a boil, add the peel, and cook slowly 5 minutes, or until the peel is transparent. Remove from the heat and let stand 30 minutes to cool.

Preheat the oven to 450°F.

Roll out the pastry and fit into a pie plate; crimp the edges. Beat the eggs, then add the sugared peel, melted butter, and salt. Place the pecans in the bottom of the pastry-lined plate and pour the egg-orange mixture over. Bake at 450°F for 10 minutes, then turn the heat down to 325°F and bake 30 minutes longer. Serve topped with plain whipped cream.

Serves 8.

Anyone who likes sweets at all admires that most enduring of our winter pies— the Southern pecan pie. My version uses a homemade fresh orange syrup rather than the usual bottled dark "Karo," and has a lively zing not often found in this dark rich confection.

BURNT SUGAR WALNUT PIE

2	cups sugar	½	teaspoon vanilla
¼	cup hot water		Pinch of salt
¾	cup heavy cream	4	tablespoons butter, melted
	Pastry for a 1 crust pie (page 348)	1	cup walnut halves
3	eggs		Whipped cream flavored with vanilla (optional)

*P*ut the sugar in a heavy saucepan, and stir over a medium flame until it melts to a golden syrup. The flame should not be so hot that the sugar becomes dark brown.

When there are no more undissolved bits of sugar, carefully pour in, drop by drop, the hot water. (The sugar will boil up violently, so be careful not to add too much water at a time.) Let this syrup cool slightly and then stir in the cream.

Preheat the oven to 450°F.

Roll out the pastry and fit into a pie plate; crimp the edges.

Beat the eggs till frothy with the salt and vanilla, then beat in the melted butter and lastly the burnt sugar syrup. Arrange the nuts in the bottom of the pastry-lined plate, then pour over the sugar-egg mixture.

Bake at 450°F for 10 minutes, then turn the oven down to 325°F and bake 30 minutes longer. Serve, if you wish, with whipped cream flavored with vanilla.

Serves 8.

A jewel of a pie—darker than the darkest pecan pie, and less sweet, since a lot of the sugar is lost in the burning process.

BUTTERMILK CHESS PIE

Pastry for a 1-crust pie (page
348)
3   eggs
1   cup buttermilk
1   cup sugar
1   tablespoon flour
6   tablespoons sweet butter,
melted

½   teaspoon vanilla
Pinch of salt
2 to 3   tablespoons rum
Whipped cream flavored
with rum (optional)

*P*reheat the oven to 425°F.

In a mixing bowl, beat the eggs till frothy, then add the buttermilk and mix completely. Add the sugar, flour, melted butter, vanilla, and salt. Mix well and stir in the rum.

Roll out the pastry and fit into a pie plate, crimp the edges. Pour the filling into the pastry-lined plate and bake at 425°F 10 minutes, then turn the heat down to 350°F and bake 20 to 25 minutes longer. A knife should come out clean in the center when it is done.

Remove from the oven and cool. Serve, if you wish, with unsweetened whipped cream flavored with a hint of rum.

Serves 6 to 8.

There are a wide variety of "chess" pies in our past. All were true winter pies, baked up when there was no fruit, and usually consisting of eggs, sugar, and butter, with some flavoring such as nutmeg, etc. They were called "chess" pies because they were kept in pie chests—a screened box to keep the flies out before the days of refrigeration. This is an unearthly version, with a complex subtle flavor I find irresistible. I use sweet butter for its extra flavor here, but if you have only regular butter, use it and omit the pinch of salt.

MY MOTHER'S
TRIPLE LAYER CHEESE PIE

1¼   cups vanilla wafer crumbs
2   tablespoons unsweetened
cocoa powder

5   tablespoons butter, melted
8   ounces cream cheese, at
room temperature

2	eggs	¼	teaspoon vanilla
¼	cup plus 3 tablespoons sugar	1	cup heavy cream
3	tablespoons light rum		Chocolate curls
1	cup sour cream		

*P*reheat the oven to 350°F.

Combine the vanilla wafer crumbs with the cocoa and melted butter, then press onto the bottom and sides of a pie plate. Bake 10 minutes, then remove and cool. Keep the oven heat at 350°F.

Cream the softened cheese with the eggs, the ¼ cup sugar, and 2 tablespoons of the rum. (This can be done by hand, or in a blender or food processor.) When smooth, pour into the pie shell and bake another 15 minutes. Remove from the oven, keeping the oven heat at 350°F, and cool 10 minutes, or until the top is firm.

Mix the sour cream with the 3 tablespoons sugar and the vanilla, then spread on top of the cream cheese mixture. Bake another 10 minutes. Remove, and chill in the refrigerator.

Before serving, whip the cream and mix with the remaining 1 tablespoon rum, then spread lightly over the pie. Top with chocolate curls made by paring slightly warm semisweet baking chocolate with a vegetable peeler (or sharp knife).

Serves 8.

An incredible pie, better I think than any cheesecake—and like cheesecake, rich but not too sweet. It is also a tour de force dessert for those who feel shaky about preparing pie crust.

MY SOUR CREAM RUM-RAISIN PIE

	Pastry for a 1-crust pie (page 348)	¾	cup sugar
			Salt
½	cup raisins	1½	cups milk, scalded
⅓	cup plus 1 to 2 tablespoons rum (dark, if possible)	1	cup sour cream
		1	tablespoon lemon juice
4	eggs, separated		

*P*reheat the oven to 450°F.

Roll out the pastry and fit into a pie plate; crimp the edges. Prick the pie shell with a fork, cover the bottom with aluminum foil weighted with a few dry beans, and bake 10 minutes. Remove the foil and bake another 2 to 3 minutes, or until the bottom has browned. Remove and let cool. Keep the oven heat at 450°F.

Cook the raisins a few minutes with the ⅓ cup rum in a covered pan, then remove from the fire and let sit, covered, to plump up and absorb the rum.

In the top of a double boiler, beat the egg yolks with ¼ cup of the sugar and a pinch of salt, then pour in the hot milk and stir over simmering water till the sauce thickens slightly and coats the spoon. Let this cool, then add 1 to 2 tablespoons of rum to taste, cover, and refrigerate.

To make the filling, beat the egg whites till stiff, then add the remaining ½ cup sugar, bit by bit, as you continue beating—as you would for a meringue. When all the sugar is added and the whites are silken and glossy, fold in the sour cream, lemon juice, a pinch of salt, and the raisins. (If the raisins haven't absorbed all the rum, drain them first.)

Mound the egg white–sour cream mixture into the cooked pie shell and swirl it decoratively on top with a knife. Bake 10 minutes, or until the top is golden brown and the meringue has set. Cool the pie and serve sliced in sections, with the rum custard poured over.

Serves 6 to 8.

Fond as I have always been of the regular sour cream raisin pie—an old-fashioned winter pie served from New England through the Midwest—I think this recipe improves an already fine thing. I came upon a strange pie, in an old flimsy "Alumnae" spiral-bound cookbook given me by friends, that consisted of simply egg whites beaten with a cup of sugar and then with sour cream folded in. I tried it, and though it seemed much too sugary and had not much flavor, it seemed a fine process. So the next try I added rum raisins, toned the sugar way down, and made a custard sauce with the leftover egg yolks. I've been cooking my sour cream raisin pies this way since, and they are always a delight for family or guests.

KENTUCKY PIE

	Pastry for a 1-crust pie (page 348)	1½	tablespoons cornstarch
		1½	cups milk
1	envelope gelatin	1½	squares unsweetened
¼	cup plus ⅓ cup bourbon		chocolate, coarsely grated
4	eggs, separated	½	teaspoon vanilla
½	cup (packed) brown sugar	¼	teaspoon cream of tartar

½   cup granulated sugar   Finely grated semisweet
½   cup heavy cream (optional)   chocolate

*P*reheat the oven to 450°F.

Roll out the pastry and fit into a pie plate; crimp the edges. Prick the bottom with a fork all around, then bake for 12 to 15 minutes, or until golden. Remove and let cool.

Sprinkle the gelatin into the ¼ cup bourbon to soften. In the top of a double boiler, over hot but not boiling water, beat the egg yolks with the brown sugar and cornstarch. Gradually stir in the milk and the ⅓ cup bourbon, then cook, stirring constantly, until the custard is thickened and smooth. Remove from the heat and pour half the mixture into a bowl. Stir the dissolved gelatin into the mixture in the bowl and reserve.

Add the grated unsweetened chocolate to the custard remaining in the pan and place back over the heat. Stir till the chocolate has melted. Pour this into the pie shell and let cool.

Beat the egg whites with the cream of tartar until they hold a soft peak. Gradually add the granulated sugar until the mixture becomes a satiny meringue. Fold this into the gelatin custard, and spoon over the chocolate custard in the pie shell.

Chill in the refrigerator until firm. Whip the cream, if you use it, and pipe through a pastry bag around the rim of the pie. Sprinkle with finely grated chocolate.

Serves 8.

This Kentucky pie, served up during Derby time, is not only beautiful to look at, it is a gastronomical treasure in its combination of flavors and textures.

Cakes, Tortes, and a Cookie

I am frankly a pie man rather than a cake man, but there are some cakes I like in the way I like pie—in the old Yankee mode, at breakfast, with coffee. Midwesterners share this yen with them, and hanker after last night's pie for starters. So any cake I put out has to be one that gets only better for sitting awhile, promising moist slices from the refrigerator. And what gems turn up out of our sources: Raw Apple Cake (page 363) for an instant picnic, Shaker Carolina Cake (page 366) for breakfast or tea, Texas Long Cake (page 367) better than brownies for a crowd, Tennessee Jam Cake (page 372) for holidays. All enjoyable to the last crumb. I've also put in a few glorious tortes in lieu of Boston cream pie, and recovered a lost cookie.

RAW APPLE CAKE

1	cup butter, at room temperature	½	teaspoon salt
2	cups sugar	2	cups flour
2	eggs	1	teaspoon vanilla
2	teaspoons baking soda	4	cups peeled, cored, and chopped apples
2	teaspoons ground cinnamon	1	cup chopped pecans

*P*reheat the oven to 350°F.

Cream the butter and sugar together till light and fluffy. Beat in the eggs, one at time. Sift the flour with soda, cinnamon, and salt, and add it gradually to the butter mixture as you beat.

Stir in the vanilla, chopped apples, and nuts, then spoon the batter into a greased tube or Bundt pan. Bake 1 hour, or until the sides of the cake begin to come away from the pan. Cool in the pan.

This simple recipe makes a rich, moist cake, dense with apples. Apples, in fact, supply the only liquid in it. Like old-fashioned applesauce cakes, it slowly grows better covered with foil in the refrigerator. It is better the second week than the first (in fact it probably should age at least a week before cutting), so it is the perfect cake for a small family—or one person. I squirrel some away after the first serving and eat a slice with my morning coffee.

MY MOTHER'S ORANGE PEEL CAKE

2	oranges	1	teaspoon baking soda
1	cup golden raisins	¾	cup buttermilk
1½	cups sugar	2	cups flour, sifted
½	cup butter, at room temperature	½	cup finely chopped walnuts (optional)
2	eggs		

*P*reheat the oven to 350°F.

Halve the oranges and juice them. Save the juice. Take the peels and remove the white inside pith with a spoon. Cut the peel up and chop it fine with the raisins by whirling it a few times in a food processor (or by putting through a food grinder).

In a bowl, cream 1 cup of the sugar and the butter till light and fluffy. Add the eggs, beating in one by one. Dissolve the soda in the buttermilk. Add the flour and buttermilk alternately, beating well after each addition. Add the nuts (if used), and the chopped peel and raisins.

Pour into a buttered tube or Bundt pan, and bake 45 to 50 minutes, or until the cake shrinks from the sides of the pan and a toothpick inserted comes out clean. Remove and cool on a wire rack.

While the cake is baking, dissolve the remaining ½ cup sugar in the reserved orange juice. Pour this over the cake while it is still hot, over and down the edges.

To serve, flip out onto a plate, and sprinkle granulated sugar over it evenly with a flour sifter or sieve.

Another cake that grows better over the days. It is at its peak always at the time the last slice is served.

MISSISSIPPI MUD CAKE

1¾	cups strong brewed coffee		Pinch of salt
¼	cup bourbon	2	cups sugar
5	ounce unsweetened	2	eggs
	chocolate	1	teaspoon vanilla
1	cup butter		Unsweetened cocoa powder
2	cups flour		Sweetened whipped cream
1	teaspoon baking soda		flavored with rosewater

*P*reheat the oven to 275°F.

Put the coffee, bourbon, chocolate, and butter in a double boiler set over simmering water. Let the chocolate melt, stirring now and then to keep smooth. Meanwhile, sift the flour with the soda and salt into a bowl.

When the chocolate mixture is melded, pour into the bowl of an electric mixer. At low speed, add the sugar, bit by bit. Beat until the sugar is dissolved. Add the sifted flour, bit by bit, to make a batter. Beat in the eggs and vanilla until smooth.

Butter a tube or Bundt pan, and sift unsweetened cocoa in to completely dust the pan. Pour in the batter. Bake for 1½ hours, or until the cake shrinks away from the sides of the pan and a toothpick inserted in the middle comes out clean.

Let the cake cool completely on a rack before turning it out onto a serving plate. Dust with more cocoa, so that the cake is an even velvety brown all over.

Serve with whipped cream, flavored if possible with a few drops of rosewater. If you cook the cake in a Bundt pan, it is attractive to completely fill the middle hole with the fragrant cream.

I don't remember where I picked this recipe up, but I can certainly remember the times I've eaten it. It is rich enough to keep well, wrapped in foil in the refrigerator, for any chocoholic in the family.

OMAHA FEATHER RUM CAKE

1	cup vegetable shortening	1	teaspoon baking powder
2¼	cups granulated sugar	½	teaspoon baking soda
2	teaspoons vanilla	1	teaspoon salt
1	tablespoon lemon juice	¾	cup buttermilk
1	teaspoon grated lemon rind	¼	cup dark rum
6	eggs, separated		Confectioners sugar
3	cups cake flour, sifted before measuring		

*P*reheat the oven to 350°F.

Beat the shortening until creamy in a large bowl. Beat in 1½ cups of the granulated sugar until the mixture turns almost fluffy. Add the vanilla and lemon juice and peel, then beat in the egg yolks, one by one.

Sift the flour with the other dry ingredients, then add it, alternately with the buttermilk, to the shortening mixture, beating soundly after each addition. Finally beat the egg whites in a clean bowl with clean beaters until they hold a peak. Gradually beat in the remaining ¾ cup granulated sugar until the whites take on a satiny, meringuelike sheen. Stir some of this into the batter, then lightly fold the rest in.

Pour into a greased and floured Bundt or tube pan and bake for 1¼ hours. The cake is done when it is lightly springy on top and a toothpick inserted comes out clean.

Let the cake cool 15 minutes, then pour the rum over it in the pan. Cover with foil and let rest for several hours before unmolding. Sprinkle with a little sifted confectioners sugar before slicing.

An enormous, light, simply flavored cake perfect to serve large company or family gatherings—perhaps with sliced strawberries or a scoop of ice cream. If you wish, you could make a rum glaze with powdered sugar and dark rum to dribble over the cake. That might make it look prettier, but nothing is needed to improve the flavor of this lovely cake with a texture just this side of angel food. Also, kept well covered, it lasts for several days, and if it starts to dry a bit, some more rum may be sprinkled on as you go.

SHAKER CAROLINA CAKE

1 cup finely chopped nuts	2 eggs
Grated rind of 1 small orange	1 teaspoon vanilla
⅓ cup (packed) brown sugar	2 cups flour, presifted
1½ cups granulated sugar	1 teaspoon baking powder
1 teaspoon ground cinnamon	1 teaspoon baking soda
1 teaspoon ground ginger	½ teaspoon salt
1 cup butter, at room temperature	1 cup sour cream

*P*reheat the oven to 350°F.

Grease a 12 × 9-inch baking pan.

Combine the nuts, orange rind, brown sugar, ½ cup of the granulated sugar, and spices in a bowl, and mix thoroughly. (Or whirl briefly in a food processor.)

Beat the butter and remaining 1 cup granulated sugar in a large bowl until light and fluffy. Beat in the eggs, one by one, then the vanilla. Sift the flour with the baking powder, soda, and salt. Add it, alternately with the sour cream, to the butter mixture, beating well and soundly after each addition.

Spread half the batter in the greased baking pan, then sprinkle half the nut mixture over. Spread on the rest of the batter, and sprinkle the top with the rest of the nuts. Bake for 35 minutes, or until the cake is springy and a test toothpick comes out clean in the center.

Carolina cake, though constructed like a coffee cake, is as rich and light as any good butter cake. It can be served to company with a bit of whipped cream for dessert, and be even better the next morning with coffee. It keeps

*moist for several days, though with a family of cake eaters in and out of the
kitchen it will not last them—or even one.*

TEXAS LONG CAKE

1½ cups butter	2 eggs
1 cup water	1 cup sour cream
¼ cup plus 6 tablespoons unsweetened cocoa powder	6 tablespoons milk
	4 tablespoons unsweetened cocoa
2 cups flour	1 pound confectioners sugar, sifted
2 cups granulated sugar	
½ teaspoon salt	1 teaspoon vanilla
1 teaspoon baking soda	1 cup chopped nuts

*P*reheat oven to 350°F.

In a saucepan, melt 1 cup of the butter, then add the water and the 6
tablespoons unsweetened cocoa, stir until smooth. Bring just to a boil, then
remove from the heat. Pour into a bowl.

Sift together the flour, granulated sugar, salt, and soda. Add, alternately
with eggs and sour cream, to the butter mixture, beating after each addition.
Grease and flour a jelly-roll pan or rimmed cookie sheet (17 × 12 inches), pour
the batter in, and bake for 20 to 22 minutes, or until the cake is springy and
starts to leave the edges of the pan. Let cool.

To make the icing, melt the remaining ½ cup butter in a saucepan. Add
the milk and the ¼ cup cocoa and stir until the mixture comes to a boil.
Remove from the heat and beat in the confectioners sugar. Stir in the vanilla
and nuts, then spread with a spatula over the cake while it is still warm. Cool
to cut.

Makes 24 squares.

*Everything about this ample cake smacks of Texas. It can serve a party of 12
at least, and it is particularly good with plain vanilla ice cream.*

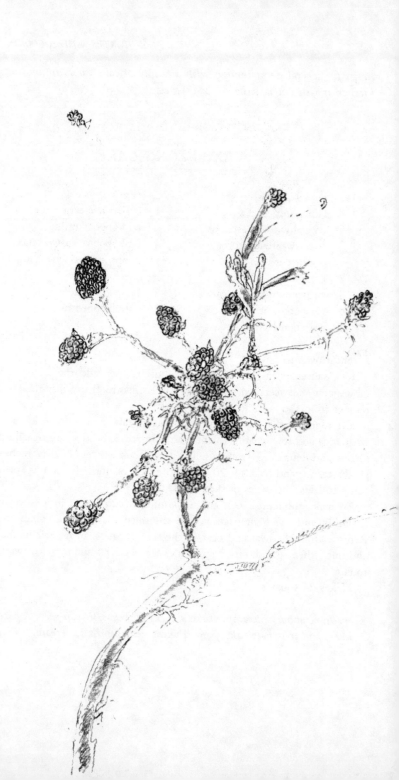

PENNSYLVANIA DUTCH PLUM CAKE

1 cup flour	¼ cup milk
1½ teaspoons baking powder	15 fresh ripe Italian plums
½ teaspoon salt	1 teaspoon ground cinnamon
6 tablespoons sugar	¼ teaspoon greshly grated
¼ cup vegetable shortening (or	nutmeg
butter)	3 tablespoons butter, melted
1 egg	⅓ cup current jelly
	1 tablespoon water (or brandy)

*P*reheat the oven to 450°F.

Sift the flour, baking powder, salt, and 3 tablespoons of the sugar into a bowl. Cut the fat in with two knives or a pastry blender until the mixture resembles coarse meal. Beat the egg and milk together, then stir into the flour mixture.

Spread this batter evenly in a greased 12 × 8-inch pan. (It will have to spread very thinly, and a spatula will help.) Cut the plums in half and remove the seeds, and place them, cut side up, in rows over the batter. Sprinkle with the cinnamon, nutmeg, and remaining 3 tablespoons sugar, then dribble the melted butter over the top.

Bake 35 minutes, or until the cake is puffed up slightly between the plums and it begins to brown. Remove from the oven to cool. Heat the jelly with water or brandy until it is smooth, and glaze the top of the cake with it.

A particularly fine cake when Italian prunes come on the market. If you like it cakier it may be baked in a square pan, but I like it spread out thin so there is little cake and lots of prunes.

NANTUCKET GLAZED LEMON CAKES

1½ cups sugar	1 teaspoon baking powder
5 tablespoons butter	⅓ cup sour cream
2 eggs	2½ tablespoons milk
1½ cups flour, sifted	⅓ cup chopped walnuts
½ teaspoon salt	Juice and pulp of 1 lemon

*P*reheat the oven to 350°F.

In a bowl, beat 1 cup of the sugar, the butter, and eggs till thoroughly mixed. Sift the flour, salt, and baking powder into a second bowl. Add it, alternately with sour cream and milk, to the batter mixture, beating the batter till smooth between. Fold in the nuts.

Pour into buttered cupcake pans, filling each about ⅓ full. Bake 25 to 30 minutes, or until the cakes are gold and springy.

While the cakes are baking, mix the lemon juice and pulp with the remaining ½ cup sugar. When the cakes are done, remove them from oven and spoon the lemon sugar over them until they are glazed. Let them cool in their pans.

Makes 30.

These are very good little glazed cakes, not too sweet and with a tart lemon glaze that makes them even better next day. A treat both for adults and children, and particularly good for picnics.

GINGERBREAD

½	cup vegetable shortening (or butter)	1	teaspoon ground ginger
½	cup (packed) brown sugar	½	teaspoon ground cinnamon
1	cup molasses	¼	teaspoon ground cloves
1	egg	½	teaspoon salt
1½	cups flour, sifted	1	teaspoon baking soda
		1	cup hot water

*P*reheat the oven to 350°F.

Grease and flour an 8-inch square baking pan.

Cream the shortening and brown sugar in a bowl. When they are light and fluffy, beat in the molasses and egg.

Sift the flour and spices over the mixture, then beat in. Dissolve the baking soda in hot water, then gradually stir it into the batter—the mixture will be very thin.

Pour into the baking pan and bake for 40 to 45 minutes, or until a toothpick inserted in the center comes out clean and the cake is light and springy.

Gingerbread remains our most characteristic simple cake, synonymous with our scarlet autumns, but shared through all the tucked-up long winters. Like any staple, it reaches from the gingery glazed cakes Emily Dickinson was famous in her neighborhood for, through New Hampshire Election Day cake—a rather dour bread—to the above very soft and richly spiced cake. Often it is eaten still warm with some whipped cream or homemade applesauce, but it really needs no accompaniment, fresh from the pan.

WASHINGTON PIE

1	gingerbread, fresh from the oven	2	tablespoons cornstarch
2	teaspoons unflavored gelatin	¼	cup milk
¼	cup plus 2 tablespoons water	¾	cup heavy cream, scalded
1	grapefruit	1	egg
½	cup granulated sugar	1	tablespoon rum
			Confectioners sugar

While gingerbread cools, soak the gelatin in the 2 tablespoons water. Set aside. Peel a grapefruit thinly with a vegetable peeler or sharp knife. Chop the peel very fine (this is easiest accomplished in a food processor).

In a saucepan set over medium heat, combine the granulated sugar, the ¼ cup water, and the grapefruit peel. Cook slowly for 15 minutes, or until the peel is candied. Pour the mixture into a sieve set over a glass measure. Measure the syrup and place ⅓ cup of it in the top of a double boiler. Set the candied peel aside.

Dissolve the cornstarch in the milk and stir into the syrup. Add the scalded cream and mix. Cook over hot water for 10 minutes, stirring until the mixture begins to thicken.

Beat the egg with the rum, then add it to the cream mixture along with the grapefruit peel. Cook a few minutes longer, still stirring, then remove from the heat. Stir in the softened gelatin and cool till firm in the refrigerator (or in a bowl of ice water). Stir now and again to ensure smoothness.

To assemble, split the gingerbread into two even layers. Spread the grapefruit cream between the layers, and sift powdered sugar over the top.

This recipe appears to be chef-writer Louis De Gouy's answer to Boston cream pie, and a very fine answer it is, too. His version reads for assorted candied fruit, but I like the simplicity of this candied grapefruit cream with the spicy ginger.

TENNESSEE JAM CAKE

1	cup sugar	1	tablespoon ground cinnamon
1	cup butter, at room	1	teaspoon ground allspice
	temperature	½	teaspoon ground cloves
5	eggs, separated	1	teaspoon baking soda
1	cup seedless blackberry jam	1	cup buttermilk
1	cup strawberry preserves	1	cup chopped nuts (preferably
1	cup apricot preserves		black walnuts, or hickory)
3	cups flour		

*P*reheat the oven to 350°F.

Butter three 9-inch round cake pans, then line with buttered waxed paper.

In a large bowl, cream the sugar and butter till light and fluffy. Add the egg yolks, then the jams, stirring well after each addition.

Sift the flour with the spices. Add the soda to the buttermilk and stir to dissolve. Beat the flour and buttermilk alternately into the batter, making sure it is always light. Stir in the nuts. In another bowl beat the whites till they hold a peak, then fold them lightly into the batter.

Divide the batter among the prepared cake pans. Bake for 50 to 60 minutes, or until a toothpick inserted in their centers comes out clean and the sides have begun to shrink from the pans.

This great purply cake is my candidate for all the mincemeat and fruitcake you can trundle out for holidays. In the South it is customary to frost it needlessly with a caramel cream frosting. I simply fill the layers with two different kinds of jam between, and top it with a glaze spooned over the top and dribbled down the sides. For a glaze, I stir together 1 cup confectioners sugar, 1 tablespoon hot milk, and ½ teaspoon vanilla (or kirsch). Kept covered and chilled, this cake will outlast most anything but the traditional aged fruitcake. I keep one in the back of the refrigerator from Thanksgiving to Christmas, to slice thin for any visitor.

FUDGE CREAM TORTE

¾	cup butter	1	cup flour, sifted
6	ounces unsweetened chocolate	½	cup chopped nuts
5	eggs	1	tablespoon hot water
¼	teaspoon salt	½	cup plus 2 tablespoons confectioners sugar
2	cups granulated sugar	1	cup heavy cream
1¼	teaspoons vanilla		

Melt ½ cup of the butter and 4 ounces of the chocolate in the top of a double boiler over simmering water and let cool to room temperature. At the same time, remove the eggs from the refrigerator to come to room temperature.

Butter two 8-inch round cake pans, then line with buttered waxed paper. Preheat the oven to 350°F.

Separate 4 of the eggs; beat the egg yolks in a bowl with salt until they are foamy. Add the granulated sugar bit by bit, as you beat. When well creamed, add 1 teaspoon of the vanilla. Fold in the chocolate butter, then the flour, nuts, and lastly the egg whites, beaten stiff.

Divide the mixture between the prepared cake pans. Bake for 25 minutes, or until a toothpick inserted in the centers comes out clean. Let the layers cool on a rack.

Melt the remaining 2 ounces chocolate in the top of a double boiler over simmering water, add the hot water, and stir off the heat with the remaining egg, beaten, and the ½ cup confectioners sugar. When smooth, add the remaining ¼ cup butter, bit by bit, beating until it is very smooth. Cool till slightly thick, in the refrigerator.

To assemble the cake, whip the cream till it holds peaks, and flavor with the 2 tablespoons confectioners sugar and the remaining ¼ teaspoon vanilla. Turn the fudge layers out onto a board. Frost each equally with the whipped cream. Place one layer on a cake server, and dribble some of the chocolate glaze over it. Place the other layer on top (if it wobbles a bit you can secure it with toothpicks till it chills). Dribble the rest of the glaze over the whole cake. Refrigerate till firm.

The ultimate American brownie. Also an example of what can be learned from Irma Rombauer's Joy of Cooking. *She tells of a cake there made by simply whipping egg whites into brownies, and adds it might be garnished with whipped cream. This is what I came up with. It is only for chocoholics, and should be consumed in small portions. I must confess it is the birthday cake I'd like most.*

PLANTATION NUT TORTE

3	cups pecans, walnuts, or black walnuts	6	eggs, at room temperature, separated
2	tablespoons cake flour	1½	cups granulated sugar
2	teaspoons baking powder	2	cups heavy cream
	Pinch of salt	¼	cup confectioners sugar
		1	teaspoon vanilla

*P*reheat the oven to 350°F.

Grease two 8-inch round cake pans, and lay in rounds of greased waxed paper to fit.

Chop the nuts very fine in a food processor (or you might be able to manage it slowly in a blender. The result should be like coarse meal.) Add the flour, baking powder, and salt to the ground nuts.

Separate the eggs. Beat the whites till stiff, and fold into the nuts. Beat the yolks with the granulated sugar until light and foaming. Fold this into the nut mixture.

Pour into the prepared cake pans and bake for 20 to 25 minutes, or until the tops of the layers are slightly golden and the edges are beginning to shrink from the pan. Remove from the oven and let cool on a rack for 30 minutes.

To assemble the torte, loosen the edges of the layers from the pan and flip the first layer onto a cake server. Whip the cream till it holds a peak, and add the confectioners sugar and vanilla. Spread half this on the first layer, top with the other layer and spread the rest of the cream on top of that. The torte should sit for at least an hour, in the refrigerator, before serving.

Whenever I come upon a bargain in fresh crop nuts, I think of this—worth throwing a party for. It is of a lightness that only grows better for being kept a few days in the refrigerator, so it can also be made a day in advance if need be. The original recipe called for Southern pecans, of course, but it is fine with walnuts, and ineffable with black walnuts if you can find any.

SNICKERDOODLES

1	cup vegetable shortening	2	teaspoons cream of tartar
1¾	cups sugar	1½	teaspoons baking soda
2	eggs	½	teaspoon salt
2½	cups flour	½	teaspoon ground cinnamon

*P*reheat the oven to 400°F.

Cream the shortening and 1½ cups of the sugar till light and fluffy. Beat in the eggs till creamy. Sift the flour with cream of tartar, soda, and salt, then beat into the shortening mixture till smooth. The dough will be quite stiff.

Roll into balls the size of a thumb tip. Roll them in the remaining ¼ cup sugar mixed with the cinnamon, and place on greased baking sheets. Bake for only 5 to 6 minutes, or until the cookies flatten and start to crinkle on top.

Makes 100.

We are great ones for cookies, and I have a file full of recipes for them. Snickerdoodles are, however, a lost classic that could stand beside the greats like chocolate chip, peanut butter, and oatmeal cookies. If you can keep your fingers out of it, they last in a tin for several weeks. A simple cookie, they well accompany ice creams and fruits as crisp chewy complement.

Puddings, Ice Creams, and Fruits

*E*arly on, most cookbooks spread a good bulk of their space over desserts. I resolved not to do this, from the beginning, but good sweets accumulate even when you only serve them to company. My apologies to all the family of grunts, slumps, crumbs, bettys, and cobblers—baked down here to only one state fair prize winner. Two other prize winners are included, never near a state fair: Mrs. Truman's Pudding (page 377), and Roanoke Rum Cream (page 382), both of which can be put together out of nothing, in no time, to general applause. Homemade ice cream used to be a national summer pastime, and should be again, so these could not be avoided, and besides we now have electric machines that do all of the work and spare us none of the wonders. And then certainly everyone needs a few delightful ways to vary fruit. But to each good thing there comes, even so, an end.

MRS. TRUMAN'S PUDDING

1	egg	½	cup peeled, cored, and grated
¾	cup sugar		apple
2	tablespoons flour	½	cup chopped walnuts (or
⅛	teaspoon salt		pecans)
1¼	teaspoons baking powder	1	teaspoon vanilla
			Whipped cream

*P*reheat the oven to 325°F.

Beat the egg and sugar well together until light and satiny. Sift the flour, salt, and baking powder over, then fold in. Mix in the apples, nuts, and vanilla.

Spread in a greased pie plate and bake for 30 minutes, or until puffed up and browned. Serve slightly warm, scooped out into dessert plates, with whipped cream (slightly sweetened and flavored with vanilla, if you wish).

Serves 4.

The former first lady's dessert is so simple that at first it is not credible how it could taste so sumptuous. I have served it for years, and neither I nor my guests tire of its levels of texture—from rather gelatinous to crispy light—and its honest flavors. On research, it seems to be an Arkansas pudding loosely modeled on something called a "Huguenot torte," but to me it will always be Mrs. Truman's Pudding.

BLUE RIBBON PEACH COBBLER

½	cup butter	⅛	teaspoon freshly grated
¾	cup flour		nutmeg
2	teaspoons baking powder	¾	cup milk
	Pinch of salt	2	cups peeled and sliced fresh
2	cups sugar		peaches

*P*reheat the oven to 350°F.

Put the butter in an 8-inch square baking pan, and place in the oven to melt as it heats. Mix the flour, baking powder, salt, 1 cup of the sugar, the nutmeg, and milk to a batter. Mix the fruit with the remaining 1 cup sugar.

Pour batter over the melted butter, then drop the peaches evenly over the surface. Bake for 1 hour. Serve warm, with a pitcher of cream.

Serves 6 to 8.

You were right if you looked twice at this state fair—winning recipe—it has more sugar and butter than anyone would expect, and cobbler tradition has been thrown to the winds. It is also better than any cobbler you've ever eaten, as all that butter and sugar combine to make a great beautiful crusty exterior with the fruit lusciously syrupy within. I've tried cutting the total of sugar down to 1½ cups, and it was good, but not as good. Any tart fruit or berry may be substituted for (or added to) the peaches, I've found. Some of the best of these are peach with boysenberries, apples with rhubarb, or rhubarb alone (really the best!)

COTTAGE CARAMEL PUDDING

2 cups (packed) light brown sugar	2 tablespoons butter, melted
1½ cups milk	1 cup flour
3 tablespoons cold butter	1 teaspoon baking powder
1 egg	1 teaspoon vanilla
3 tablespoons granulated sugar	½ cup chopped nuts (optional)

*P*reheat the oven to 350°F.

In a soufflé dish, or a 1½-quart baking dish, mix the brown sugar and 1 cup of the milk together. Cut the cold butter into bits over the top of the mixture.

In a mixing bowl, whisk the egg lightly, then beat in the remaining ½ cup milk, the granulated sugar, and melted butter. Sift the flour and baking powder over, beat well, and stir in the vanilla and nuts. Pour this batter over the brown sugar—milk mixture—it will float on top. Smooth it out with a large spoon or spatula.

Bake for 45 to 50 minutes, or until the top is puffed and golden. Serve still warm, spooning out portions onto dessert plates with caramel sauce from the bottom poured over each serving. If you wish, heavy cream in a pitcher, or even sour cream, may accompany it.

Serves 6.

Children dote on this golden pudding, and even adults who sniff they don't care for sweets I notice never leave a scrap on their plates. Perhaps we are all reduced to childhood before its generosity. As it is very simply prepared, it might well become a family favorite on chill autumn evenings.

DENVER PUDDING

1	cup granulated sugar	2	tablespoons butter, melted
1	cup flour	2	ounces unsweetened chocolate
½	teaspoon salt	½	cup (packed) dark brown sugar
2	teaspoons baking powder		
½	cup milk	1	teaspoon cornstarch
½	cup chopped black walnuts (or walnuts)	1½	cups boiling water
1	teaspoon vanilla	2	tablespoons bourbon or rum (optional)

*P*reheat the oven to 350°F.

Butter a soufflé dish.

Put 1 cup of the sugar in a bowl. Sift the flour, salt, and baking powder over it. Mix in the milk, nuts, vanilla, and melted butter.

Melt the chocolate in the top of a double boiler over simmering water. Add about three fourths of it to the above batter, and stir in. Into the remaining chocolate stir the remaining ½ cup granulated sugar, the brown sugar and cornstarch; stir in boiling water until the mixture is smoothly thickened. Add bourbon or rum, if you wish.

Pour the chocolate sauce in the bottom of the soufflé dish and spread the nut batter over it. Bake at 350°F for 45 minutes, or until a good puffed cake has formed on top of a bubbly sauce. To serve, spoon out and dribble some of the sauce over each serving. Pass cream, or serve with whipped cream.

Serves 6.

Another splendid pudding which makes its own ample sauce. It is similar to Cottage Caramel Pudding, but not so sweet.

MY PERSIMMON PUDDING

4	tablespoons butter	¾	cup milk
¾	cup granulatd sugar	1½	cups ripe persimmon pulp
1	egg		(either American or
1	cup flour		Japanese)
1	teaspoon baking powder	½	cup chopped walnuts
1	teaspoon baking soda		Confectioners sugar
½	teaspoon ground ginger	1½	cups heavy cream
¼	teaspoon salt	1	teaspoon lemon juice
		⅛	teaspoon ground ginger

*P*reheat the oven to 325°F.

Grease and flour a 9-inch round cake pan.

Cream the butter and granulated sugar until light and fluffy. Beat in the egg. Sift the flour with the baking powder, soda, ginger, and salt and add it, alternately with milk, to the butter mixture, stirring after each addition. Sieve 1 cup of the persimmon, or whirl it in a blender or food processor. Fold it into the batter, along with the walnuts.

Pour the persimmon mixture into the cake pan. Sift confectioners sugar over the top. Bake for 1 hour. Remove from the oven and let cool.

To serve, whip the cream until it holds a peak. Fold in the remaining ½ cup persimmon pulp, 2 tablespoons confectioners sugar, the lemon juice, and ginger. Place a dollop on each serving of pudding.

Serves 8.

This is my holiday pudding. Japanese persimmons are now very common in the markets, but this kind of pudding used to be made from the native persimmon, which is only edible after frost, the settlers found. They can pucker the tastebuds for hours, if eaten before then, but ripe they are the very tropics.

NEW ORLEANS BREAD PUDDING WITH BOURBON SAUCE

3	cups sliced leftover French bread	5	eggs
3	cups milk	2	cups sugar
		¾	cup raisins (optional)

2	teaspoons vanilla	¼	cup heavy cream
	Salt	¼	cup bourbon
½	cup butter		

*T*rim the bread of crusts or not as you wish. Cover with the milk, and let sit several hours or overnight.

Preheat the oven to 350°F.

Crumble the soaked bread with your hands. Beat 4 of the eggs with 1 cup of the sugar, then stir, along with the raisins, vanilla, and a pinch of salt, into the bread.

Pour into a buttered 8-inch square baking dish. Place in a larger pan containing about 1 inch hot water. Bake for 35 to 45 minutes, or until the top is slightly crusty. Remove and cool.

While the pudding cooks, make the sauce. Melt the butter in the top of a double boiler over simmering water. Stir in the remaining 1 cup sugar and a pinch of salt, and cook until the sugar dissolves. Beat the cream with the remaining egg, and whisk into the sauce until it thickens slightly. Remove from the fire and cool. Add the bourbon.

To serve, cut portions of the pudding and ladle bourbon sauce over each generously.

Serves 9.

Bread puddings are synonymous with thrift, and though everyone likes them, most cooks hesitate to serve one to company. I go right ahead, and use the best aged bourbon in this spectacular sauce. The recipe solves the problem of what, besides making bread crumbs, one does with a leftover French loaf from a small dinner party—you transform it into the simplest of puddings topped by a spiked sauce.

SHAKER LEMON
MERINGUE BREAD PUDDING

1	cup very fine fresh bread crumbs	½	cup plus 1 tablespoon sugar
2	cups milk	2	eggs, separated, plus 1 egg white
2	tablespoons butter		Juice and grated rind of 1 lemon

*T*he best way to prepare this fine pudding is to take 6 or 7 slices of decent white bread and put them in a low oven early in the day, then turn the heat off and forget about them. By dinner you have perfect fodder for a blender or food processor, and also the delicate beginning of your pudding.

Preheat the oven to 350°F.

Warm the milk, remove from fire, add the crumbs, cover, and let sit while you assemble the pudding.

Melt the butter, and use some of it to grease a soufflé dish. Beat the rest with the ½ cup sugar, the egg yolks, and grated lemon rind. Stir into the bread crumbs, and scoop into the soufflé dish.

Set in a larger pan containing 1 inch of hot water and bake for 30 minutes, then remove from the oven. Beat the 3 egg whites stiff, add the 1 tablespoon sugar, and beat until silky. Dribble the lemon juice in as you beat. Spread this meringue over the pudding and bake another 10 minutes, or until slightly golden on top.

Serves 6.

This dish is all balance and proportion—there is Shaker about it everywhere. It is, as the sisters report, of excellence either hot or cold, and needs no cream. They do not tell you that with very little time and money you have achieved a pudding to delight anyone, anywhere, anytime. Its base is the purest possible pudding, with a topping of nigh unbelievable sour meringue.

ROANOKE RUM CREAM

3	egg yolks	3	tablespoons rum
¼	cup sugar	1	cup cream, stiffly whipped
1	tablespoon lemon juice		

*B*eat the egg yolks with the sugar until they are thick and light colored. Add the lemon juice and rum in a stream while continuing to beat. Fold in the stiffly whipped cream and ladle into stemmed glasses. Chill. If you wish, these may be topped with extra plain whipped cream.

Serves 4.

What a friend this pudding is! With a good electric mixer or food processor you have a suave light dessert in minutes—one you could proffer Julia Child. Everyone needs at least one recipe like this as the perfect simple end to a complex meal.

BIG MOMMA'S FLOATING ISLAND

3	eggs, separated			Pinch of salt
½	cup sugar		1	teaspoon vanilla
3 to 4	cups milk		2	tablespoons aged bourbon

Whip the egg whites till stiff, then beat in ¼ cup of the sugar a tablespoon at a time. Scald 3 cups milk in a large frying pan. When it starts making little bubbles around the edges, turn the heat low and drop the meringue from a large spoon to make 4 to 6 large mounds on the milk. Poach, without letting the milk boil, 2 minutes on each side, turning with a skimmer or slotted spoon. Lift out onto a dry towel to cool.

The meringues will have absorbed about a cup of the milk. Measure to make sure, and add enough if necessary to make 2 cups milk. Place in the top of a double boiler set over simmering water. Beat the egg yolks. Add some of the hot milk to the yolks and beat in, then stir the mixture into the remaining milk. Add the remaining ¼ cup sugar and salt, and stir constantly over very low heat until the custard coats your spoon. Immediately remove from heat and add the vanilla and bourbon.

To serve, place the custard in a serving dish and place the meringues on top. Chill thoroughly.

Serves 4 to 6.

Big Momma was not named for her girth, but, in Atlanta gentility style, for her grandmotherhood. Indeed, I remember her, straight as a cameo profile, and as transparent and delicate, serving this pudding some twenty years ago now. On being complimented, she showed me her secret stash of Jack Daniels in the cupboard, used only for this company dish, as she "didn't touch a drop!" herself.

FLORIDA ORANGE FLAN

¾	cup sugar		3	eggs
1	tablespoon orange juice		1½	cups heavy cream, scalded
3	tablespoons bitter orange marmalade		1	teaspoon grated orange rind
				Orange slices

*P*reheat the oven to 350°F.

Combine ½ cup of the sugar, the orange juice, and marmalade (use the best dark marmalade you can find, or add a few drops of Angostura bitters). Boil over a medium flame until the mixture is slightly reduced and coats a spoon—about 5 minutes.

Pour two thirds of the mixture into the bottom of a baking dish—a soufflé dish is about the right size for this. Turn the dish to coat the bottom and sides, and place in the refrigerator to harden the glaze.

Beat the eggs with the remaining ¼ cup sugar. Add the scalded cream, bit by bit, whisking. Pour through a fine sieve and add the orange rind. Pour into the baking dish. Place it in a larger dish with about 1 inch of hot water in it.

Bake for 1 hour, or until a knife inserted in the center comes out clean. Remove, let cool, and refrigerate, covered, several hours or overnight.

Unmold on a platter. Heat up the reserved glaze till it is liquid. Slip thin peeled orange slices in the glaze and decorate the top of the flan with them.

Serves 6 to 8.

The bittersweet sauce from this richest of flans makes the most beautiful glaze. The result is a tour-de-force presentation to apex a company dinner.

WHITE WINE SNOW

1 tablespoon unflavored gelatin	3 tablespoons lemon juice
¼ cup water	3 egg whites
1 cup dry white wine (or champagne)	Pinch of cream of tartar
	Green grapes
⅔ cup sugar	

*S*prinkle the gelatin on the water and allow to soften for 10 minutes. Mix the wine, sugar, and lemon juice in a stainless-steel or enameled saucepan. Bring to a boil, then lower the heat and stir till the sugar is dissolved. Put in a bowl, stir in gelatin, and refrigerate until the mixture begins to set.

Beat the mixture with an egg beater or electric mixer until light and frothy. In another bowl, beat the egg whites with the cream of tartar until they hold stiff peaks. Fold the two mixtures gently together. Mound into 6 individual dessert cups, decorate with halves of seedless green grapes, and chill for an hour or more.

Serves 6.

In summer, or after any rich meal, often only a very light end is possible. The usual answer is to serve a refreshing ice or sherbet, but this delicate desert is an unusual answer. The better the wine used, of course, the more exquisite the final product. If you have the end of a fine bottle of champagne gone flat, that is best.

PHILADELPHIA VANILLA ICE CREAM

6	cups light cream	1½ vanilla beans, split
1½	cups sugar	lengthwise

*P*lace 2 cups of the cream, the sugar, and split vanilla beans in the top of a double boiler over boiling water. Stir 10 minutes, or until the cream is scalded. Remove from the heat.

Take the beans out and scrape the inner pulp and seeds back into the cream. Cool, add the rest of the cream, and freeze in an ice-cream freezer according to the manufacturer's directions.

Serves 6 to 8.

If ice cream did not originate here, it is certain that in this country it reached its widest appeal. As many of our foods, ice cream has suffered a decline till that bought in stores, nowadays, is little more than pig fat, sugar, and air. The bowls of our childhood, on a summer's dusk, seem to have vanished along with back porches, fireflies, and extra elbows to turn the crank. There are new small electric freezers on the market, however, that are the boon of small families with an appetite for the real thing again.

GEORGIA GINGER PEACH ICE CREAM

4	cups heavy cream	1½ teaspoons vanilla
1	cup sugar	6 ripe peaches
	Pinch of salt	½ cup chopped crystallized ginger

*H*eat 1 cup of the cream, with ½ cup of the sugar and a pinch of salt, in the top of a double boiler over simmering water. Stir until the sugar is dissolved and the cream is scalded—about 10 minutes. Pour into a bowl, add the vanilla and the rest of the cream, and chill in the refrigerator.

Drop the peaches in boiling water, then remove and slip off the skins. Take out the peach stones and chop the peaches coarsely. Put in a bowl, add the remaining ½ cup sugar and the ginger, and stir well. Let sit in the refrigerator to accumulate juices.

Freeze the cream mixture in an ice-cream freezer according to the manufacturer's directions. When the cream is nearly done, add the peaches and ginger and freeze for 10 to 15 minutes more.

Serves 6 to 8.

No ice cream to me is quite as good as pure vanilla, but this comes a shave close.

MY FROZEN DARK CHOCOLATE MOUSSE

1½	cups sugar	1	cup water
2	cups water	4	ounces unsweetened chocolate
1	vanilla bean, split lengthwise	¼	teaspoon salt
1	envelope unflavored gelatin	2	tablespoons brandy

Combine the sugar, water, and vanilla bean in a saucepan and cook over a medium flame 10 minutes, stirring to dissolve the sugar. Remove the bean, and when cool enough to handle scrape all the seeds out and return them to the sugar mixture.

Soften the gelatin in a cup of water for 5 minutes. Melt the chocolate in the top of a double boiler over simmering water. When melted, combine all the ingredients (except the brandy) and place in the refrigerator to cool. Freeze in an ice-cream freezer according to the manufacturer's directions, and when nearly done add the brandy.

Serves 6.

This has no cream or milk, so it is technically an ice, I suppose—but whatever you call it it is rich, and dark, and very smooth. I first made it as an attempt to duplicate a very dark chocolate ice sold by one of the better ice cream chains, and which I admired over all their flavors. Mine turned out smoother and subtler, so there seemed to be no reason to attempt exactitude.

CHARLESTON BUTTERMILK
RUM-RAISIN ICE CREAM

½	cup raisins		Pinch of salt
⅓	cup dark rum	2	cups buttermilk
2	egg yolks	1	cup heavy cream
½	cup sugar	2	teaspoons vanilla

*P*lace the raisins with the rum in a small saucepan. Bring to a boil and simmer gently 5 minutes. Turn off the heat, cover, and let sit for 1 hour.

Beat the egg yolks, sugar, and salt together. Bring the buttermilk and cream to a boil in a saucepan, then turn the heat down low and add the egg-sugar mixture bit by bit while whisking the cream. Cook over low heat, stirring constantly, until slightly thickened—about 5 to 6 minutes. Stir in the vanilla and cool in the refrigerator.

Freeze in an ice-cream freezer according to the manufacturer's directions. When the mixture begins to thicken, add the raisins, and any rum they have not absorbed, and freeze until firm.

Serves 6.

Sometimes it is necessary to wonder why one likes a thing that strikes all minor notes, as in this ice cream in which three things are an "off" flavor— buttermilk, rum, and raisins. Not in the eating, however.

PINK GRAPEFRUIT ICE

2	teaspoons unflavored gelatin	2	cups pink grapefruit juice
1½	cups water	¼	cup lemon juice
1	cup sugar	⅓	cup orange juice
	Rind from 1 grapefruit,	¼	teaspoon salt
	peeled with a vegetable	2	egg whites, beaten stiff
	peeler and cut into tiny		
	julienne strips		

*D*issolve the gelatin in ½ cup of the water. Combine the sugar and remaining 1 cup water in a saucepan and bring to a boil. Add the grapefruit peel and simmer 10 minutes. Add the gelatin and stir until dissolved. Chill in the refrigerator.

PUDDINGS, ICE CREAMS, AND FRUITS389

When cool, add the fruit juices and salt, and fold in the egg whites. Freeze
in an ice-cream freezer according to the manufacturer's directions.
Serves 6.

*The fine slivers of candied grapefruit peel lift this ice into another category
altogether.*

CRANBERRY ICE IN ORANGE SHELLS

1	quart cranberries	2	teaspoons gelatin
2	cups water	2	egg whites
1¾	cups sugar	12	large half orange shells
1	cup orange juice		

*P*ick over the berries, discarding any that are spoiled. Cook them in 1¾ cups
of the water till they pop. Sieve them (or whirl in a blender or food processor).
Put the sugar and orange juice in a saucepan, add the cranberry pulp, and
cook over low heat 5 minutes. Remove from the fire.

Soak the gelatine in ¼ cup of the water, then beat into the cranberries.
Chill in the refrigerator until the mixture begins to thicken. Beat the egg
whites stiff and fold them in.

Pour the mixture into ice-cube trays and freeze until mushy. Beat till smooth
in a blender or food processor, then scoop into the orange shells. Freeze until
just hardened—2 to 3 hours.
Serves 6 (or 12 as a side dish).

*These are wonderful as a relish to holiday goose, but they also make an at-
tractive, tart dessert any time.*

SHAKER ROSEWATER ICE CREAM

4	egg yolks	3	cups heavy cream, scalded
1	cup sugar	1	tablespoon rosewater
	Pinch of salt	1	cup milk

*B*eat the egg yolks with sugar and salt until frothy. Mix a little of the scalded
cream into them, then whisk all back into the cream. Reduce the heat to low,

then cook, stirring constantly, until the custard is slightly thickened—about 6 minutes.

Remove from the heat and add the rosewater and milk. Set in the refrigerator to cool, then freeze in an ice-cream freezer according to the manufacturer's directions.

Serves 6.

The Shakers put even their roses to work.

STRAWBERRY SHORTCAKE

Nothing could be a more typical, totally American, dessert than strawberry shortcake. It consists simply of a slightly sweetened biscuit—sometimes with a bit more fat cut in to insure richness (see Helene's Drop Shortcakes, page 324)—strawberries sliced and set to macerate in sugar to assure plenty of juice, and slightly sweetened whipped cream. What could be simpler—yet nowadays it has become lazily usual to use commercially packaged "Mary Ann" cakes, both overly sweet and artificially flavored. And perfectly awful. With only a biscuit standing between you and the pure real thing, then learn how easy it is to pop biscuits from the oven. Your family and friends deserve it.

STRAWBERRIES WITH STRAWBERRY SAUCE

1 pint strawberries   1 tablespoon brandy (or kirsch)
   Sugar

Wash and stem the berries. Take about two thirds of the best ones and slice in half into a bowl. Sprinkle with a tablespoon of sugar and reserve in the refrigerator.

Sieve the remaining berries. Measure the pulp and add equal parts of sugar. Cook this over low heat, stirring now and again, till it thickens slightly—10 to 15 minutes. Add the brandy or kirsch off the fire, and put to chill in the refrigerator.

To serve, ladle the strawberries into cups or dessert plates and pour the sauce over them.

Serves 2 to 3.

Every strawberry has just so much taste, from tiniest, wild scarlet-tucked zests, to pretty (but tasteless) giants. This, and the following recipe, put back some of the essence lost to size.

WHITE STRAWBERRIES

1	egg yolk	½	cup heavy cream, whipped
2	tablespoons butter, melted	1	pint strawberries, stemmed
1	tablespoon brandy (or kirsch)		and washed
½	cup confectioners sugar		

*B*eat the egg with butter and brandy, then the sugar. Fold this into the whipped cream and chill in the refrigerator for several hours, or until the butter has firmed it so that a spoon placed in the mixture will come out completely coated.

Toss the whole berries in the sauce, place in a large bowl or individual dessert cups, and chill until serving time.

Serves 4.

Not only would the superb sauce described here make nearly anything taste better, it completely coats the berries so no red shows through—a culinary conceit almost worthy of the Shakers. The berries look particularly lovely in a cut-glass bowl on a candlelit buffet table.

BANANAS IN RUM

4	bananas	⅓	cup sugar
2	tablespoons butter	⅓	cup rum (preferably dark)

*B*ananas for this dish should be ripe, but not so ripe they have started getting a speckle on their skins. Peel them, cut in half, then cut each half lengthwise, making 16 finger-shaped slices.

Heat the butter in a large frying pan set over low heat. When it begins to sizzle, put the bananas in, cut side down. Cook 3 minutes, then turn and cook another 3 minutes. Lift out into a shallow casserole large enough to hold them in one layer.

Add the sugar and rum to the pan and cook, stirring, until the sugar dissolves. Pour over the bananas, then cover and refrigerate several hours.

At serving time, lift the bananas out and arrange in a fan on plates. Put the sauce in a saucepan and cook over high heat until it bubbles brightly, then pour over the cold bananas.

Serves 4.

A recipe from my book Southwestern Cooking, *evolved over the years to suit any meal at all—from a fine touch for a simple supper, to a French repast with all the trimmings. To serve the bananas cold in a hot sauce is their real surprise, but in a push they can come straight out of the pan, so long as the sauce is reduced slightly. I used to serve them always with a dollop of whipped cream at the base of the fan, but fine as they are they don't really need it.*

ICED PINEAPPLE MADAME BÉGUÉ

At the turn of the century all New Orleans and Yankee beyond were lining up for Madame Bégué's "second breakfasts," long leisurely eleven o'clock repasts of six or so courses, from turtle or crayfish soups, light savory omelets (she was known to wield her long-handled skillet like a scepter, as her deft husband settled guests in the plain low-ceilinged room), such ducks and daubes, such artichokes and peppery snails, gumbos pungent with plump oysters, such rare beefsteak brightened on the plain linen by the stuffed tomatoes of Provence and local watercress, on to mostly simple heightened fruits, brandy, coffee, and cigars—all originally presented to please the hardy butchers and stall keepers of the French Market, after morning bustle with only a dawn cup of milky chicory coffee to last the stretch.

Long ago, in a high flat off London's Hampstead Heath, I first sat up to read Elizabeth David describing, as an elasticity of French cuisine, a Creole daube cooked with local home rum rather than the usual wine, all studded with olives, and culled from what my new-found author tantalizingly called "a little book of New Orleans cookery . . ." Later I was lucky to find a copy of a rare, browned *Mme. Bégué's Recipes of Old New Orleans Creole Cookery,* marked 50 cents on the cover. Though now her rules may seem too fuzzy and general, through the passing of time and modern temperament for quick exactitude, simple honesty in every mouthwatering example is undenied. Take her "recipe" for pineapple with white wine . . .

"Pare and slice a nice ripe pineapple. Place in a crystal dish a layer of pineapple and a layer of white sugar until all is used. Pour over this half a quart of white wine and let it stand two hours before sending to the table. When ready to serve stir well; pound a large piece of ice and spread thickly over the whole."

The recipe writer can tell at once that will be a very pretty dish in that crystal bowl, glittering with a topping of ice, but at once he is beseiged with a whole string of "buts" and "what-ifs" and "how muches" and "what kinds," not to mention that he must have enough savvy with pineapples to have it ripe enough, and to know it must be cut with a stainless knife. Even such a simple recipe can sometimes make for choices all down the road.

I go about this by choosing at the market a beautiful fruit going mostly from green to gold in the globe, with an arched powdery blue top. It is then put to look at as a centerpiece of fierce beauty in the kitchen or dining room. The day it has turned all gold, I go look for a suitable dish, and a suitable wine.

The wine poses the most choices of all, but since sweetness is not a question here, one can be a bit more reckless than usual about choosing a label, and so chance on a new bouquet fit to sip while relaxing before dinner. Slicing the thing is simple (remembering always the stainless knife)—it only has to be done well and roundly, cutting out any of the brown tucks, then sliced into ½-inch slabs.

At this point, another question turns up. Should the cook leave the woody centers in, for a diner to deal with, or should they be made less pretty by coring and quartering? Let's leave them whole, as this is to be a pretty dish by hook or crook. Now comes the sugar, left quite up in the air by La Bégué, but pineapple is a sweet fruit, so better too little than too much—more can be added later. Let us add ½ cup. When the fruit is sugared in our bowl (not cut crystal, but yet nicely glass) only 1½ cups of wine is needed to brim it— leaving just enough for two glasses for the cook.

After the dinner the final question looms: How to make the ice shine and glitter for this chilly tropic of a dish? Cubes from the tray, certainly not, and the clattering of a Cuisinart breaking ice is nerve-racking enough, even if there were not guests. So the cook remembers ice being chipped from a block on a back porch years ago, to feed the hand-cranked ice cream machine, and dumps a tray of cubes into a clean dish cloth, twists it into a compact ball to be hit lightly but well with a rolling pin, and brings the dish with good show to table.

Such are the trials and delights of the questing recipe hunter.

FOURTH OF JULY
WATERMELON WITH SNICKERDOODLES

1 watermelon	Snickerdoodles (page 375)
Light rum	

*C*ut a plug in a watermelon and add as much rum as the melon will absorb over the period of half an hour or so (a small melon should absorb at least ½ cup). Replug the melon and let it chill overnight, turning it once or twice to make sure the rum permeates the whole.

To serve, slice the melon in rounds, and accompany with Snickerdoodles.

Rum seems here to produce simply a more melony melon, without leaving much more than a ghost of itself. Snickerdoodles compliment it so well that I give a feast of both on our national Day of Independence.

AMBROSIA

6 seedless oranges	Juice of ½ lemon
3 cups shredded fresh coconut	⅓ cup sugar
Grated peel of 1 orange	

*P*eel the oranges, making sure to remove all the white pith. Slice into a bowl, then add the coconut, orange peel, lemon juice, and sugar and toss lightly. Refrigerate at least 2 hours before serving. Toss now and again as it sits to distribute flavors.

Serves 6 to 8.

Traditional Christmas fare in many Southern homes, where the dessert is served in the best cut-glass bowl from the sideboard. It makes sense to have a light end to all the rich heavy foods of the day, but it is a dessert anytime, anywhere, a delight.

METHODS & INGREDIENTS

With cooking on our own home ground there are fortunately few esoteric ingredients, and almost all methods are self-explanatory. There are a few fine points, however, that would clutter the recipes if repeated every time.

Almonds
The general use for these in the recipes is "slivered and toasted." This process is simple enough. To remove the brown husk and blanch the nuts, simply drop them in boiling water about half a minute. Slip the husks off by hand, and dry on paper toweling. Cut lengthwise into ⅛-inch slivers. Heat a mixture of half vegetable oil and half butter in a saucepan—about 1 tablespoon each for ½ cup nuts. Sauté over medium heat, stirring, until they are an even deep gold. This will take 4 to 5 minutes. Drain them on paper toweling to absorb the grease.

Baking Powder
Any baking powder has limited shelf life, particularly if any moisture gets to it. If you seldom bake, always test it before using, to see if it still has zip. Put a teaspoon in ⅓ cup hot water, and make sure it bubbles with some enthusiasm.

Beans (dried)
I've usually indicated the overnight soaking method for beans, but there is nothing wrong with the quick-soak method. This involves bringing beans to a boil in plenty of water, letting them cook 5 minutes or so, then they should sit covered off the fire for an hour or more—or until they plump up. These can then be cooked as any recipe indicates.

Bread crumbs

Not being an admirer of store-bought bread crumbs, I always make them myself. I use every scrap of leftover white bread, first cutting it and letting it dry out in a slow oven, then whirling it in a food processor—though a rolling pin does just as well. These crumbs can then be kept in a refrigerator jar, for any use.

Butter

For convenience I've just listed butter in recipes, but unsalted butter is always of a higher quality and superior flavor. It is particularly good in a buttery sauce, and in delicate baking. Of course the best thing would be to have churned butter as it was made with unpasturized cream, where bacteria could actually be tasted swimming on the tastebuds, but that would be the best of all possible worlds.

Buttermilk

I'm always surprised when people claim they don't like to drink buttermilk, and so never have it on hand. Drinking it aside (and I like it every bit as much as yogurt) buttermilk gives a certain tang to many dishes that used to be made with unpasteurized cream or milk, and it urges baked breads or cakes to a lighter, fluffier texture. I always keep it on hand. A bottle keeps a couple of weeks or more in the refrigerator, and tempts to new uses.

Cheese

Long gone are the days when only processed cheese foods were available, with maybe a slab cut off a green "longhorn." Not only cheese shops, but most large markets sell natural cheeses, aged and sharp or creamy and mild, of a wide variety. Always try to avoid large packagers in favor of local, and if possible buy from a store that cuts their own. Cheese should be brought to room temperature before serving.

Chicken

It's always cheaper to make a habit of buying a whole chicken and cutting it up yourself. I like to use breasts for one meal, then the legs and thighs for another, since the two cook at slightly different times for maximum succulence anyway. It also provides some variety. Cutting up a chicken is relatively simple, and doesn't require anything but a good knife. You can bend the leg back so the hip joint is easily seen. Cut there. The same applies for the joint between leg and thigh, if you want them in two pieces. Wings can be cut off by the same process of bending at the joint and cutting. Then you cut out the back in one fell swoop, or by cutting the first half off and cracking it back, then cutting the part out around the breast. The whole breast should be flattened with your fist, then cut up the middle bone from the back. The back and wings and giblets (minus the liver, which should be reserved for another meal) can be used to make stock (see *Stocks*).

Corn

It is a cliché that corn should have its pot put on the fire before picking, but it is true. Market corn is never as sweet or tender or flavorful—however, what ears you find in your market are preferable to frozen or canned any day. Choose ones with tiniest kernels, and that have their husk still on. Husk them, slip off the silk by rubbing your hand up and down the ear, knife the kernels into a bowl, then drag the dull edge of the knife down the ears to extract any juices.

Cornmeal

For those who have never tasted it, real stone-ground cornmeal with the germ still in it will be a revelation. Unfortunately, since it has a briefer shelf life, this is seldom found outside the South. There it is treasured, and constantly used. As I've never found any reliable mail-order source, I have friends send it to me. Even "gourmet" stores haven't caught on to this delicacy yet, though it can be found in some enlightened health food shops. But even there beware if it's not labeled from a Southern source. If you do find it, buy in bulk and keep in the refrigerator. A way to put some of the lost savor back is indicated in any recipe that depends on this meal to be completely successful. (See also *Masa harina*.)

Cream

Where cream is mentioned in a recipe, what I used was ordinary whipping cream. Except where the cream is actually whipped, however, a lighter cream may be used for a less rich dish.

Eggs

For convenience, I've used the size called "large eggs" in all the recipes. Whatever you have on hand is fine, though, except in the case of cakes— where the difference between small and jumbo eggs can seriously affect the outcome.

Egg whites

These ought to be at room temperature to whip to highest volume. They should not have any hint of yolk in them, and should be beaten in a grease-free bowl (neither plastic nor aluminum). By hand, you need a wire whisk and a steady rhythmic stroke, and in an electric mixer you must watch carefully. They should rise 3 to 4 times the volume, be firm, airy, glossy, and stand as a peak with a curl on top when you lift the beater from them. Folding these into a batter should be done quickly but gently as bathing a baby.

Fats

Everywhere I've indicated which fat is to my taste in a recipe. Often this runs to lard, butter, or bacon fat, but if for dietary reasons you must use vegetable "shortening," go right ahead, though do not expect flavor to accompany it. Lard especially has fallen out of favor, though it makes a shorter pastry than butter, and is excellent for baking and frying. My theory is that if you don't overdo fats, you should use the real right one when you do.

Fish

Almost all frozen foods are less tasty than fresh, but fish is a special case. When it thaws, delicate cells rupture and flavor runs out. This can be minimized by thawing slowly in the refrigerator, but never eliminated. I try to steer clear of frozen, in favor of the fresh catch with a shiny eye.

Frying

Frying technically means in some depth of fat, though I've been guilty of sometimes using it in its American sense of "pan-frying" or sauté. Any recipe that depends on deep frying either includes a thermometer reading, or tells you how the process should look and act. A thermometer is advised. 375°F is satisfactory for frying most foods. A way to test for this without a thermometer is a bread cube dropped in the fat: it should brown in 60 seconds. Never let the oil start to smoke, for it begins to break down at that temperature. Unless you are cooking some strongly flavored food, such as onions, oil can be cooled and strained and stored in the refrigerator for re-use. New oil should be added when this is done, and the oil should be thrown away if it becomes dark.

Garlic

Never ever use garlic powder or garlic salt. They have a flavor detectable as cheap scent across the room. Also, a garlic press is a useless instrument that tends to draw out unpleasant oils. Just go ahead and chop it. Smash the cloves slightly with the side of your knife, and slip the skins off. Mincing it with a little salt helps the garlic not to cling to the knife, if you like. Never let garlic cook to more than golden in a recipe, or it will lend a bitter taste to the dish. Finally—who knows what size a garlic clove is? They come in different sizes even from the same head, so use your own taste as judge, when it comes to measure.

Green peppers

Here and there are recipes that indicate green peppers grated without their skins. To do this, cut the pepper in quarters, remove the seed sections, then grate flesh forward on the coarse side of a grater. The skin will be too tough to grate, so just discard it.

Ham
Most these days are pumped with water and have little flavor but salt. They are never bargains. One good ham available everywhere is Hormel's Cure 81, of a fine flavor, boneless, ready to eat, and though more expensive, worth every penny.

Herbs
Except where fresh herbs seemed essential to a dish, I've indicated dried herbs. But if you grow your own, substitute at the rate of 1 tablespoon fresh for every teaspoon dried.

Knives
Any good cook knows that a knife is his closest friend. A whole battery is not needed, either. One fine small paring knife with a sharp point, a fairly large chef's knife, and perhaps a boning knife (all made of carbon steel) and you're in business. A serrated knife for slicing is also fine to have, but it needn't be carbon steel. Good knives last a lifetime, so don't be cheap, and while you're at it buy a sharpening steel to keep them razor edged.

Masa harina
This is found in any Hispanic market, for it is the flour tortillas are made with. (Don't ever attempt that, though—even so-called "tortilla presses" make a mess. Tortillas take years to learn to make.) Masa is useful, however, for making batters for the top of tamale pies, and since it has so much flavor I advise it as a help (if not a true substitute) in putting some back into ordinary cornmeal. When you can't get stone-ground meal, masa can take the place of regular flour in any cornbread recipe, and if only cornmeal is used let some of the meal be masa. Not only is flavor provided, but some of the smooth flouriness natural to stone-ground meal is put back.

Nuts
Why buy small expensive packages of nuts in the market, when you can look around and find fresh crop nuts sold in bulk? Most health food stores stock them, if you haven't a grove near. These can be kept frozen for long periods, and not only have a fresh taste but are inexpensive enough to use lavishly.

Oils
I use olive oil a lot in these recipes, but then I also buy it in a Greek store around the corner that sells it for less than corn oil at the supermarket. Vegetable oils can always be substituted if that is what you have, though they contribute no flavor.

Onions
I generally just go ahead and use the common yellow onion for cooking. But

402   METHODS AND INGREDIENTS

remember the white onions are milder and a bit more tasty, if more expensive. Any time you come on the really sweet varieties like Walla Walla or Maui, snap them up for eating raw—they are wonderful. Green onions are also called scallions (and, confusingly, in the South, shallots). The green tops are as tasty as the bulbs, so I always use at least an inch or two of the green when cooking a dish.

Paprika

Most Americans have a dried-out can or jar of this on the spice shelf, used to give a bit of color to a dull dish. But it ought to be a genial, living part of the kitchen, and definitely Hungarian. The Hungarians produce a range of paprikas from hot to sweet, but the sweet is the one to have for general purposes. Not only will color blush, but so will savor.

Pepper (black)

Everywhere this has been left up to taste, along with the personal choice in salt. Dishes that should be rather peppery are indicated in the text as such—these are almost always from New Orleans, or thereabouts. I always use a pepper grinder to get the liveliest flavor.

Portions

Where practicable, I've adjusted recipes to serve around four. However, almost any—except for pies and cakes and breads—can be halved or doubled at need. The exception is halving an egg, a process which the novice may find a boggle. It's possible, though. Beat the whole egg, then measure it—2 tablespoons is about right for half.

Potatoes

"Mealy" and "waxy" are about the only things to say about potatoes. Mealy are best for baking, while the waxy hold together better for sauté or salads. Except for the recipes that call explicitly for baking potatoes, I've used the ordinary market bag known simply as "potatoes." They work, but they're not the best—after all, something makes them cheaper. Spots have to be cut out, and sometimes they have not been stored properly, so have a layer of green under the skin. If so, they must be peeled before using, since the green part is slightly poisonous. Always make a test poke to see, unless you are using the absolutely top-notch spud.

Rice

I know some good cooks who swear by processed rice, but I see no reason for it (and certainly not for instant). With the fine texture and flavor of regular long-grain rice, what's a minute or so, when the difference is so evident?

Rum

Unless a recipe calls for light rum, dark is always preferable for deep flavor.

Get a good brand (these are of course more expensive) and keep it stored for cooking. Jamaica produces the best, and it will say so on the label.

Salt
Except where it must be measured to some exactness, I've left this also up to the cook. Everyone has a different taste for it. I've been told by those on a salt-free diet for a time, that the tastebud is assaulted by even a little, for sugar and salt are the most overpowering seasonings of all. A taste for more and more of it can amount to an addiction, so that some diners salt even before tasting. With this in mind, I usually undersalt rather than oversalt—it can always be added later. Kosher salt is preferable to ordinary salt, both for cooking and at the table, and it contains no additives.

Sauté
In English we seem only to have the term "pan-fry" for this process, and that is a little ambiguous, since frying usually means a certain depth of fat. Sauté is a process where something is cooked with a small amount of fat, preferably in a heavy-bottomed pan, over heat just high enough so you can cook quickly without burning the fat.

Spices
These have a limited shelf life. If possible, they should be stored in the cool and dark, rather than perched on a fancy shelf above the stove. I know, I keep mine there as you probably do, but I also go through them pretty quickly. Don't let any label get yellow, certainly, and when possible buy them whole, and grind in a coffee grinder kept for the purpose. Nutmeg is the perfect one to buy whole, for they are easy to grate, and have ten times the flavor.

Stock (beef)
Most home cooks find this stock too much of a chore to bother with. In a restaurant, not only are there lots of meat scraps and ends of vegetables, the stocks are a kind of by-product of everything that goes on. Certainly this kind of stock is the secret of the best sauces and soups, and the very best cook will not be deterred by the expense and fuss of keeping a stock pot on, now and again, and clarifying, and boiling down the result to a delectable brown essence for easy storage, but if you don't you don't. Rather than use bouillon cubes, however, I think canned beef bouillon has a better taste.

Stock (chicken)
This is easy for anyone to make. It's always cheaper to buy a whole chicken, anyway, and so one is provided with the back, wings, and giblets (not the liver, save that for another purpose) to make stock. The easiest is to put all these in a pressure cooker with an onion, a carrot, a stalk of celery, some parsley, a bay leaf, some thyme, a few peppercorns, and cook about an hour. This

can then be strained and cooked down to an essence which keeps well in the freezer.

Stock (fish)

Many recipes say you can use bottled clam juice for this, but if you do remember it is very salty. I have used it when in a hurry, but I prefer to dilute it half with water. It is easy to pick up fish scraps now and again, and cook them with the same things as the chicken stock above, and have some on hand in the freezer.

Temperature

All ovens vary. The only way to be exact is to purchase an oven thermometer. I've tried to indicate how things should look and feel in any recipe, but when in doubt pay attention to sizzle, sputter, and—above all—smell. Any dish about done will also start to smell good, except for bread, which smells good all the way through. The stovetop is another matter. I prefer the flexible heats that gas offers, and have always cooked with it, except in other people's homes. So with an electric stove, do not always take my instructions of things like "medium high" as gospel for a dial setting—use your knowledge of the instrument, and how it responds for you alone.

Tomatoes

Grow your own, is my advice. They no longer exist in an edible form in markets. There, they are picked green and sprayed with a gas to make them turn reddish: I boycott these out of principle, for what is better than a vine-ripened tomato? For this reason I've recommended canned tomatoes everywhere possible—these are at least picked ripe. The best of these are Italian plum tomatoes, and the best of the best are ones with an Italian label. By all means, if you garden, use fresh peeled tomatoes. I envy you.

Tomato Paste

When a recipe calls for only a little tomato paste, there's no sense wasting the rest of the can. Measure what is left by the tablespoon onto waxed paper, and freeze the sheet. When hard, remove from the paper and put in a container. That way you'll always have them, already measured, on hand.

Vanilla

Always use pure vanilla extract. Artificial vanilla has smell but not taste. Better yet, buy the beans and put one split in a canister of sugar. This can then be used in any sweet recipe calling for vanilla (the British use this for sprinkling on melon, a lovely idea). You can also split an inch of bean, and scrape out the tiny seeds, for a glorious substitute for vanilla extract in any recipe.

Vinegar

Vinegars are not expensive when you consider that even the fanciest are used so sparingly they last a long while. So when you come on any fine one, buy it, and keep a shelf in proud array. They pay for themselves again and again on the daily salad alone.

Wine

There are no hard and set rules about what wine should be eaten with any American dish. So many varieties come out of California these days, it's hard to sort them all out anyway. Follow your own nose, tastes, and pocketbook. If a novice, remember that, for drinking with food, any dry is better than a sweetish wine, and a decliate dish needs a delicate wine. Sherry and Madeira, even in cooking, need be the best you can afford, and always dry. There is no such thing as a "cooking sherry."

Yeast

A package of active yeast is equivalent to 6 ounces fresh yeast, and the only difference is that fresh yeast should be dissolved in lukewarm water, while the dry can take water up to 115°F. There is always a date on the package telling when the yeast might deteriorate, but any recipe also indicates the process of putting it in some liquid to puff up and "proof." This is "proof" it works.

Zests

The zest of oranges, lemons, limes, and even grapefruits—which I refer to as "rind" or "peel" in these recipes—are marvelous flavoring agents, but remember to use only the colored part of the skin, since the white beneath is bitter. It's also best to have a light touch with them, so in a recipe that calls for them you might want to decrease the amount I have given—which tends toward the maximum rather than the minimum.

Index

ground
   picadillo, 195, 200–201
   smoked oyster burgers, 92–93
Joe's special, 91
liver
   with herbs, 135
   Maryland, 136
meat loaf, Alfred Lunt's, 92
New England boiled dinner, 83–84
oxtail
   braised, with mushrooms, 90
   soup, 22–23
pot roast
   Madeira, 81–82
   Savoy Plaza, 82
ragoût of, 86
roast, with Yorkshire pudding and horseradish ice
   cream, 78–79
short ribs, braised, with celery, 89
sirloin Clemenceau, 80–81
steak pudding, 88
stock, 403
winter soup, 85
Beets
   with their greens in sour cream, 224–225
   "vichyssoise" of beet greens, 4–5
   Yale, 224
Benne wafers, 327–328
Beverly Hills Rangoon Racquet Club championship
   chili, 26–28
Big Momma's floating island, 383
Biscuits
   beaten, 327
   fried, fried chicken with milk gravy and, 147–
      148
   Happy Valley, 322
   sourdough, 343–344
   summer cloud, 322–323
   whipped cream, 323–324
   whole-wheat, 325
Bisque
   salmon, chilled, 8
   summer squash, 10
Black bean(s)
   soup, 21
   tostadas, with sour cream, 200
Black-eyed pea(s)
   hopping John, 183
   salad, 279–280
   soup, 23–25
Blueberry rhubarb relish, 311–312
Blue ribbon peach cobbler, 378–379
Bottled sauces, 297–298
Bouillon, court-, Creole, 36–37
Boulette de saucisson, 207–208
Bourbon
   Derby pie, 360–361
   sauce, bread pudding with, 380–381
Brabant potatoes, 253–254

Bread and butter pickles, 304–305
Bread crumb(s)
   -caper sauce, lamb chops with, 127
   general data about, 398
Bread pudding
   with bourbon sauce, 380–381
   lemon meringue, 381–382
Breads, 315–344
   anadama, 338
   benne wafers, 327–328
   biscuits
      beaten, 327
      fried, 147–148
      Happy Valley, 322
      sourdough, 343–344
      summer cloud, 322–323
      whipped cream, 323–324
      whole-wheat, 325
   brown, 338–339
   butter cakes, 333–334
   cornbread
      bacon buttermilk, 318
      jalapeño cheese, 318–319
      Shaker, 319
   cornpones, 316–317
   dill, 337
   dumplings, parsley, 325–326
   garlic, 335
   griddle cakes, wild rice and cornmeal, 321
   hush puppies, 36, 320–321
   maple toast, 216
   muffins, potato, 326
   rolls
      butter, 328–329
      Parker House, 331
      rose geranium, 332
      sesame, 332–333
   rye and Indian, 339–340
   salt rising, 340–341
   shortcakes, drop, 324
   sourdough, 341–344
      biscuits, 343–344
      cracked-wheat, 343
      white, 342
   spoonbread, 319–320
   white buttermilk, 334–335
   zephyrs, 317
Brown bread, 338–339
Burritos, simple, 202
Butter, 398
   cucumber, 42
   shad roe poached in, 51–52
Butter cakes, 333–334
Buttermilk
   bacon cornbread, 318
   chess pie, 358
   fried chicken and, 146–147
   general data about, 398
   mashed potato soufflé with, 251–252

ABOUT THE AUTHOR

Ronald Johnson was born in Kansas and received his bachelor's degree from Columbia University. An accomplished poet, he won the National Endowment for the Arts Award in 1970 and 1975. Cooking has been his hobby for over twenty years, and while teaching all over the country he amassed a huge number of regional recipes which became the backbone of this book. His book *Southwestern Cooking New & Old* is in its seventh printing. He lives in San Francisco.